THE GREAT NORTHERN RAILWAY

Volume I · Origins & Development

Other books by the author

The Midland and Great Northern Joint Railway
Famous Underground Railways of the World

THE GREAT NORTHERN RAILWAY

VOLUME I · ORIGINS & DEVELOPMENT

John Wrottesley, M.A. (Oxon.)
President, Railway Club

Partly based on research by the late J. R. Whittle
of Wood Green Railway and Canal Historical Society

B. T. BATSFORD LIMITED · *LONDON*

TO MY WIFE

While this book is partly based on research carried out by the late J. R. Whittle, the text of both Volumes I and II are entirely the copyright of the author.

First published 1979

ISBN 0 7134 1590 8

Filmset by Elliott Bros. & Yeoman Ltd.,
Speke, Liverpool L24 9JL
Printed and bound by Redwood-Burn Ltd.,
Trowbridge & Esher
for the Publishers B. T. Batsford Limited
4 Fitzhardinge Street London W1H 0AH

CONTENTS

LIST OF PLATES

Maps

INTRODUCTION

My interest in the Great Northern Railway goes back almost further than I can remember. I have been told that I first travelled on it when I was a few weeks old, and my personal recollections go back to 1913. So I have long wanted to tell its story. When I was at school, I was presented with a first edition of Grinling's famous book, *The History of the Great Northern Railway*, (which only told the tale to 1895), and Bird's book on the engines, so I began writing a few chapters then. In 1937, I considered the subject with a friend, the Rev. W. N. R. J. Back, of Doncaster, collected much material, and met Mr P. J. Dowsett, the former Assistant Secretary (then LNER Assistant Secretary), who gave me valuable information and some useful documents.

In 1939 I went into the army, and some years after the war Mr O. S. Nock's delightful study appeared, then later, Mr Borley and Mr Hamilton Ellis produced a new edition of Grinling, bringing it up to the 1920s. Commitments in other directions caused me to postpone my writing and research, but ten years later, I decided that the right time had come to complete the work, and again thought of a collaborator. Mr C. R. Clinker (whose advice and assistance have been of great value) suggested Mr J. R. Whittle, who, he knew, had been considering a similar work, but shortly afterwards I learnt that Mr Whittle had died suddenly. He had lived at Wood Green, where he had been a friend of the late Mr R. A. H. Weight, author of an excellent book on locomotives, and of the book on the Great Northern Railway in the *Railways Before the Grouping* series. Mr Whittle's grandfather was an old GN man, so he had had access to many personal memories, and, like myself, had examined many original records. His father was in the Railway Clearing House, often associated with GN affairs, and he himself was a member of the Stephenson Locomotive Society, and later of the Railway and Canal Historical Society. Mrs Whittle kindly allowed me to see the notes and manuscript which he had compiled, and much of the information which he had researched has formed the basis of several chapters.

During my army service, when I was stationed in Nottingham and in Yorkshire, and later, when I was in British Railways legal department, I met many old GN men, whose recollections often went back a long way. I should mention Lt. Col. Crampton (descendant of the famous locomotive designer) who was an apprentice at Doncaster in 1914. I eventually travelled over most of the line, including some sections confined to goods traffic.

There are so many friends and organizations who have helped in the compilation of this work. I should particularly like to mention Mr Borley (now Librarian, Railway Club) who has lent photographs and notices, Mr T. J. Edgington of the National Railway Museum, York, Mr A. C. Casserley, Mr T. G. Hepburn, Mr R. S. McNought, Mr J. E. Kite and Mr D. L. Franks, who have all provided illustrations; Superintendent Hinchley (LNER, and later British Transport, Police) who has supplied original documents; Mr J. P. Youell (Leeds University and Middleton Railway) whom I thank for research on early documents, and Acts; and Mr G. H. P. Beames (my former senior colleague in British Railways Legal Service) who gave me useful Airey maps. Mr G. Body (born at Sandy), formerly on the LNER, and now with Avon Anglia Publications has greatly encouraged me.

I should like to thank the staff of the British Railways Legal Library, Marylebone, of the former British Railways Record Office, Porchester Road, of the Record Office, and of the Inner Temple Library, for their unfailing courtesy in producing old records and statutes, and those of Doncaster Museum for showing me their remarkable treasures, and Mr Chapman and Mr Howarth, of Doncaster Library, for supplying illustrations.

Lord Grimthorpe, Lord Allerton and Lord Banbury, all descendants of former Chairmen, have kindly written to me.

Some, no longer with us, to whom I am grateful for their assistance are the late Kenneth Brown (a predecessor of mine as President of the Railway Club), who gave me valuable information, and with whom I walked over some disused lines (including the Edenham and Little Bytham) and visited the old Eastern and Midlands office at King's Lynn; the later Lt. Col. Rixon Bucknall, who gave me copies of his books; and the late H. P. Le Mesurier (some time engineer of the Bengal–Nagpur Railway in India) who was resident engineer of part of the Midland and Great Northern Joint, and Lancashire Derbyshire and East Coast.

Mr J. Ransome has supplied an unusual sketch, drawn in 1854, by an ancestor of his. Mr C. Woodroffe Peacock has supplied a copy of the *Night Mail*, which he received from Lt. Col. Bucknall.

Finally, I am particularly grateful to my younger son, Michael Wrottesley, who prepared the maps.

1

THE LONDON & YORK

The railways extending northwards from London in 1844 were few. The Eastern Counties had reached Colchester and the Northern & Eastern, with an authorised line to Cambridge, had paused for lack of money at Bishops Stortford. The London & Birmingham, the Grand Junction and the North Union formed a continuous line of rails from Euston Square to Preston where there was a connection to the recently opened harbour at Fleetwood. A steamer service operated from Fleetwood to Ardrossan whence the traveller could make his way to Glasgow by rail and to Edinburgh by coach.

The Midland was formed this year with George Hudson as its first chairman. It consisted of a fusion of the Birmingham & Derby Junction, the Midland Counties and the North Midland, amalgamated by an Act of 10 May. The Midland Counties had a main line from Rugby through Leicester to Derby, and a branch to Nottingham, while the North Midland extended from Derby to Leeds.

Hudson's 'pet' line, the York & North Midland, joined the latter a little north of Normanton at Altofts junction. Thus in 1844 the route from London to York was from Euston Square via Rugby and Altofts junction. From York, there extended the Great North of England as far as Darlington, where it connected with the Stockton & Darlington. On 19 June, Hudson got his Newcastle & Darlington Junction opened, and public services commenced between Darlington and Gateshead. On the previous day a special train conveying many of the leading railwaymen of the day, including George Stephenson, had made history. Leaving Euston Square at 5.03 a.m. the train covered the 303 miles to Gateshead in 9 hr 21 m., inclusive of stops taking 70 minutes.

This then was the picture of the railway map in that part of England which would concern the future Great Northern Railway. The counties of Cambridge, Huntingdon and Lincoln were still devoid of railways. The L & B was building its branch from Blisworth to Peterborough, and the EC had an authorised line to the same town.

A brief sketch of George Hudson, 'King Hudson' as he was already known, would not be out of place. The son of a Yorkshire farmer, he became a prosperous linen draper in the city of York. Quite early in life he was left a substantial fortune, which enabled him to exercise his undoubted talents in other fields. He was connected with the first project for a railway from York to Leeds. A chance meeting with George Stephenson when they both happened to be visiting Whitby led to a life-long friendship. The York to Leeds project was modified into the line from York to Altofts junction with the North Midland, which (laid out by Stephenson) became the York & North Midland. Hudson was chairman, and from now on he projected new lines of railway in rapid succession. The phenomenal speed with which he built his railways, and the early and substantial profits which became available for distribution to gratified shareholders overshadowed his dubious financial methods, which directors and proprietors mostly chose to overlook. He engineered the amalgamation which brought about the Midland, and by the time our story begins he could look forward to controlling a co-ordinated series of railways from Rugby to York and Berwick and perhaps even to Edinburgh. He was the most influential and outstanding personality in the railway world, and was on his way to becoming a millionaire.

For some years money had been tight, but the market was now easier. Most of the established lines were paying good dividends, and railways attracted the attention of speculators who were prepared to invest their money in building them.

In this year of 'Railway Mania' new railways were projected in every direction, including several to run south to north and west to east in the area just described. The schemes included the Direct Northern, surveyed by Sir John Rennie and William Gravatt, who proposed a line from King's Cross to York via Peterborough, Lincoln, Gainsborough, Thorne and Selby, and the Cambridge & York, surveyed by James Walker who had previously made plans for a line from London to York in 1835. Walker was later requested to survey a route right through to London. Then the EC, with Robert Stephenson as its engineer, proposed an extension first to Lincoln, and then to Gainsborough and Doncaster. Finally there was a Great Northern with a line surveyed by Joseph Gibbs from London via Huntingdon, Stamford, Grantham, Newark, Gainsborough and Doncaster to South Milford where it would make connections with the Y & N M, and the Leeds & Selby. The name, Great Northern Railway, so important to our story, had been that of an earlier scheme, surveyed by Gibbs, but with a different route; Whitechapel, London, to York via Cambridge, Sleaford and Lincoln. But the Bill for this was rejected by the Commons in 1836. In 1844, the Cambridge & York scheme developed into the London & York with plans to start from King's Cross and join the original line after passing through Peterborough.

The import of all these schemes was not lost upon Hudson, who could see plainly that if a direct railway was built between London and York his Y & N M, and Midland would lose their London traffic to a shorter route. He therefore made plans to occupy the empty counties, and provide a route to the south over which he would have control. The Y & N M was to make a branch to Doncaster, Gainsborough and Lincoln to March, where it would join the EC's projected line. Yet another was to be made by the Midland from Syston, near Leicester, to Peterborough via Stamford, which would also connect with the EC. The 'Railway King' must have had the EC in his sights even then and aimed to bring it within his growing empire.

The east to west schemes were first the Wakefield & Lincoln, later to become the Wakefield, Lincoln & Boston. Next there was the Sheffield & Lincolnshire Junction, associated with the existing Sheffield, Ashton-under-Lyne & Manchester. Finally the Midland proposed a further branch, entitled the Nottingham, Newark & Lincoln.

The objects of the Great Northern and London & York committees were very similar and a fusion of their interests took place. A committee was set up on 17 May. In one sense the GN may be fairly said to have been born on this day, although the title chosen at the time was London & York. William Astell, M.P., was chairman and Edmund Denison, M.P., and Francis Mowatt were vice-chairmen of a Committee of Direction. Almost immediately they were faced with the task of selecting a new engineer, for Walker retired from the project, having decided that his previous commitments precluded him from taking on the additional duties of surveying and constructing so vast an undertaking. The eminent engineer Joseph Locke was approached, and accepted the invitation to become engineer to the London & York. With a deputation of directors, Locke went inspecting the country to decide which was the best of the several routes surveyed.

Shortly afterwards negotiations were opened with the Wakefield, Lincoln & Boston committee. A Wakefield & Lincoln scheme had been brought forward early in the year by Sir Isaac Morley, and Captain Laws, manager of the Manchester & Leeds. Later it was decided to extend the line to Peterborough and, as this would conflict with the interests of the established navigations, opposition was bought off with the offer of permanent guarantees of 6%. The railway was to be built largely along the banks of the canals on land provided by the two concerns, the

Witham Navigation linking Boston and the Wash, and the Fossdyke (or Fossedyke) which connected Lincoln with the Trent at Gainsborough. Edmund Denison met Captain Laws at Normanton on 30 August, and an arrangement was made whereby the two committees were fused into one concern. The Wakefield, Lincoln & Boston committee was dissolved, and five of its members became directors of the London & York, which took over its scrip, thus adding £500,000 capital to the combined undertaking. The directors of the M&L were in agreement with the merger, and Captain Laws was one of the five who became directors of the London & York. Locke was instructed to continue his surveys to include the Wakefield line, and the Doncaster and York Section, on which there was not yet a firm decision. He was engineer to the Grand Junction, which, when he joined the London & York, had not been on good terms with the L&B. But these two companies settled their differences, and it is probable that they brought pressure to bear on Locke, for he resigned his position with the London & York, giving as his reason that he had not been properly consulted about alterations in the route which the new alliance involved.

No time was lost in engaging a fresh engineer. William Cubitt, who had laid out the South Eastern, and recently acted for the Wakefield, Lincoln & Boston, was just the man. Denison was fortunate in securing his services, going to his house in Clapham late one night. Little time remained for the plans to be prepared and deposited for the 1845 Parliamentary Session. Cubitt was soon making fresh surveys, to incorporate the plans of the London & York with those of the Wakefield, Lincoln & Boston. In the meantime another small committee had thrown in its lot with the London & York, the Sheffield, Chesterfield & Gainsborough, so a branch from Bawtry to Sheffield had to be proposed too. A further rival to the London & York had appeared late in the day, the Cambridge & Lincoln. The revised plan had put Lincoln at the end of a branch, or on a loop, so some dissatisfied people had decided on a fresh project which never came to anything.

The extent of the London & York undertaking, as submitted to Parliament, dwarfed that of any railway project in this country either before or since. The deposited plans consisted of:

A.	The main line to York	186	miles
B.	A loop line from Peterborough to Bawtry via Boston and Lincoln	86	miles
C.	A branch from Bawtry to Sheffield	20¾	miles
D.	A branch from Doncaster to Wakefield	20¼	miles

Branches to Bedford and Stamford and sundry other short lines brought the total to 328 miles. Cubitt estimated that the complete system could be built for £6½ million.

No fewer than 224 railway Bills were due to be considered in the 1845 Session. With a view to relieving the work of the Private Bill Committees the Board of Trade set up a committee of five members to inquire into the merits of the competing projects. These gentlemen, soon nicknamed 'The Five Kings', were the President of the Board of Trade (Lord Dalhousie), General Pasley, Captain O'Brien, Mr Porter and Mr Laing.

The London & York was placed in the same group for consideration as the other projects competing for a north to south route, while the Syston & Peterborough, Nottingham, Newark & Lincoln, Great Grimsby & Sheffield Junction and Wakefield, Pontefract & Goole were all placed in different groups. Thus the London & York had no opportunity of opposing these cross-country lines, although all of them could affect its position. They all received their Acts in 1845, as did the Caledonian.

Meanwhile the London & York successfully passed 'Standing Orders' stage, and 'second reading' in the Commons when the report of the Board of Trade was made known. Rumours had already been circulating that this would be against the London & York, as indeed it was. The 'Five Kings' had been influenced by the utterances of 'King Hudson', who found several opportunities to make wild prophecies with regard to engineering difficulties, estimated cost, and so on. Fortunately the London & York Committee was able through its solicitor, Robert Baxter, to provide a complete answer to the report, and had the support of all the towns through which its line was to pass. Joseph Pease, of the well-known north country Quaker family, supported the Bill, and created a most favourable impression when giving evidence about the London & York's promised through rate for coal traffic of only three farthings a ton per mile. He went so far as to say that he himself would be willing to guarantee the £300,000 which the promoters had credited themselves for coal traffic. Whilst it had been anticipated that a project of such magnitude would encounter strong and lengthy opposition, the London & York supporters could scarcely have expected that the Hudsonian tactics of obstruction and delay would result in the longest Parliamentary contest on record. Thus, although the London & York Bill emerged from the Commons shorn of its Sheffield and Wakefield branches, there was now no chance of getting it through the Lords in the current Session.

Hudson had to admit failure with regard to the north to south Bills of the railways over which he had control or influence. He did, however, obtain powers for his Newcastle & Berwick. His next move in the game was to 'arrange' to be invited to occupy the chair of the impecunious EC, a position which he held from 13 October 1845. Shortly afterwards it was announced that the EC, (which had leased the Northern & Eastern in 1844) would submit a Bill for an extension from Cambridge through Lincoln and Doncaster to South Milford, there to join the Y&NM and Leeds & Selby. At the same time the London & York sought powers for the Wakefield branch again, this year extended to Leeds. It also promoted branches to Dunstable via St Albans and Luton, and Hertford, and a line from Stamford to Spalding.

The 'Railway King' now made a fresh effort to eliminate his rival, proposing a conference between the London & York and the EC with a view to amalgamation. Particularly did he endeavour to undermine by one means or another the confidence of London & York scrip-holders. However the directors, and the great majority of the supporters stood firm in their determination to proceed with their undertaking.

The L&B opened its Peterborough branch on 2 June 1845, with its rails ending ⅜ mile short of the EC's authorised terminus, for the L&B had been unable to obtain possession of some intervening land. Strangely enough the EC was able to overcome the difficulty, and obligingly constructed its station and the necessary section of line for the use of the L&B, considerably in advance of its own branch reaching Peterborough, which did not happen until 10 December 1846, for goods, and for passengers, 14 January 1847.

Throughout the early months of 1846 Hudson continued to employ all the tactics at his command in an all-out effort to force the London & York to combine with the EC. Next the London & York was strengthened by the Direct Northern deciding to amalgamate with it, on 5 May. Eight days later the London & York Bill came before the Lords. A Wharncliffe meeting was called for 30 May. William Astell was in the chair. It was announced that the directors held proxies representing nearly two-thirds of the capital, which was more than sufficient to enable the Bill to be carried forward. At this meeting, the title of 'the Great Northern Railway' was adopted.

On 8 June a decision was announced that the Lords committee was 'unanimous in favour of the London & York'. Thus the main Bill of the company, now the Great Northern, was in the bag. The fate of the branches had yet to be settled, and the Bills, submitted for them at the close of 1845 were all rejected by the Lords. Twelve years later, Edmund

Denison, speaking on railway legislation, revealed that his company had spent £590,355 before the Bill became an Act which had been 82 days in the Commons and three to four weeks in the Lords.

The Great Northern Railway Act received Royal Assent on 26 June 1846, with capital of £5,600,000 and borrowing powers of £1,868,000; 36 directors were named in the Act. Other railways, in which the GN would have a vital interest, and which were incorporated in the same session were the Boston, Stamford & Birmingham, and the East Lincolnshire, on 26 June, and the Ambergate, Nottingham Boston & Eastern Junction, and Royston & Hitchin on 16 July.

Further railways in which we shall be interested and which received their Acts in 1846 were the Sheffield & Lincolnshire Junction and its associated Sheffield & Lincolnshire Extension. The Wakefield, Pontefract & Goole obtained powers for two branches; one from Knottingley to Askern (or Askerne) where it would connect with the GN, and the other from Pontefract to Methley, a junction with the Midland. The Wakefield company was then absorbed by the Manchester & Leeds. The West Riding Union was incorporated on 18 August, a network of lines totalling 45½ miles. There was a line from Sowerby Bridge on the M & L to Bradford via Halifax and Low Moor, another link with the M&L at Mirfield to Low Moor, a line from Leeds to the Bradford line at Bowling, and several small branches, with provision that the company should be amalgamated with the M&L within three months.

There were three important amalgamations among the GN's neighbours. The GJ, L&B, and Manchester & Birmingham combined to form the London & North Western. To the north the GN of E and the N&DJ united under the title of the York & Newcastle. Finally, the Sheffield, Ashton-under-Lyne & Manchester combined with the authorised Great Grimsby & Sheffield Junction and Sheffield & Lincolnshire Junction (and its extension) as the Manchester, Sheffield & Lincolnshire from 1 January 1847.

The North British was formally opened between Berwick and Edinburgh on 18 June 1846, the public being conveyed four days later. The Leeds & Bradford, leased to the Midland, was brought into use on 1 July. The Midland branch from Nottingham to Lincoln, completed in remarkably quick time, was opened on 4 August. The first section of the Midland Syston and Peterborough branch was brought into use as far as Melton Mowbray on 2 September. Another section from Stamford to a junction with the EC at Peterborough followed on 2 October. The branch was opened throughout in 1848, on 20 March for goods, and 1

May for passengers. Over in the north-west the Lancaster & Carlisle, and Kendal & Windermere had reached Kendal on 22 September 1846, the L&C being opened throughout on 17 December.

A house at 36 Great George Street, Westminster, had been leased by the London & York Committee. Here, the first meeting of GN directors took place on 1 July 1846. William Astell was chosen as chairman, With Edmund Denison and Samuel James Capper (lately chairman of the Direct Northern Committee) as deputy chairmen. The first business was to order a common seal from Taylor, the medallist, the design chosen combining the arms of England and Scotland. It was resolved that William Cubitt be confirmed in his appointment as Consulting Engineer to the company, that John Miller be Engineer to the northern part of the line, and Joseph Cubitt (son of William) to the southern part. A committee was set up to manage the Foss and Witham Navigations, with Thomas Michael Keyworth as canal manager.

Offices were acquired at 7 Lothbury, where the next directors' meeting was held on 7 July. The principal business was appointment of officers, James Ryder Mowatt becoming Secretary with Thomas Reynolds as his assistant. William Henry Clark was appointed Registrar of Shares and Andrew Mylne the Accountant. A fortnight later, the firms of Baxter, Rose & Norton and Johnson, Farquhar & Leech were appointed Joint Solicitors.

The first meeting of the shareholders was held on Saturday 25 July at the Hall of Commerce, Threadneedle Street, with Robert Baxter and Joseph Leech, (joint solicitors) in attendance. The chairman and deputy chairmen were duly elected, and appointments so far made by the directors were confirmed. Mowatt's salary was approved at £800 per annum, and the number of directors was reduced to 30. At this meeting it was resolved to appoint 'a gentlemen of known ability to construct and manage the railway at a salary of £2,000 per annum', a curious resolution, since the engineers were already engaged. However, three days later Captain Laws was requested to accept the office which was in no way to interfere with the duties or functions of the engineers. Next day, he accepted, and was appointed Managing Director. Soon afterwards the directors fixed the salaries of the assistant secretary, the registrar and the accountant at £500, £600 and £400 respectively.

By the middle of August decisions were taken about construction of the line. The most expensive section would be that from London to Peterborough, while the easiest would be that from Peterborough through Boston and Lincoln, invariably referred to as the 'Loop', as opposed to the main line through Grantham, Newark and Retford,

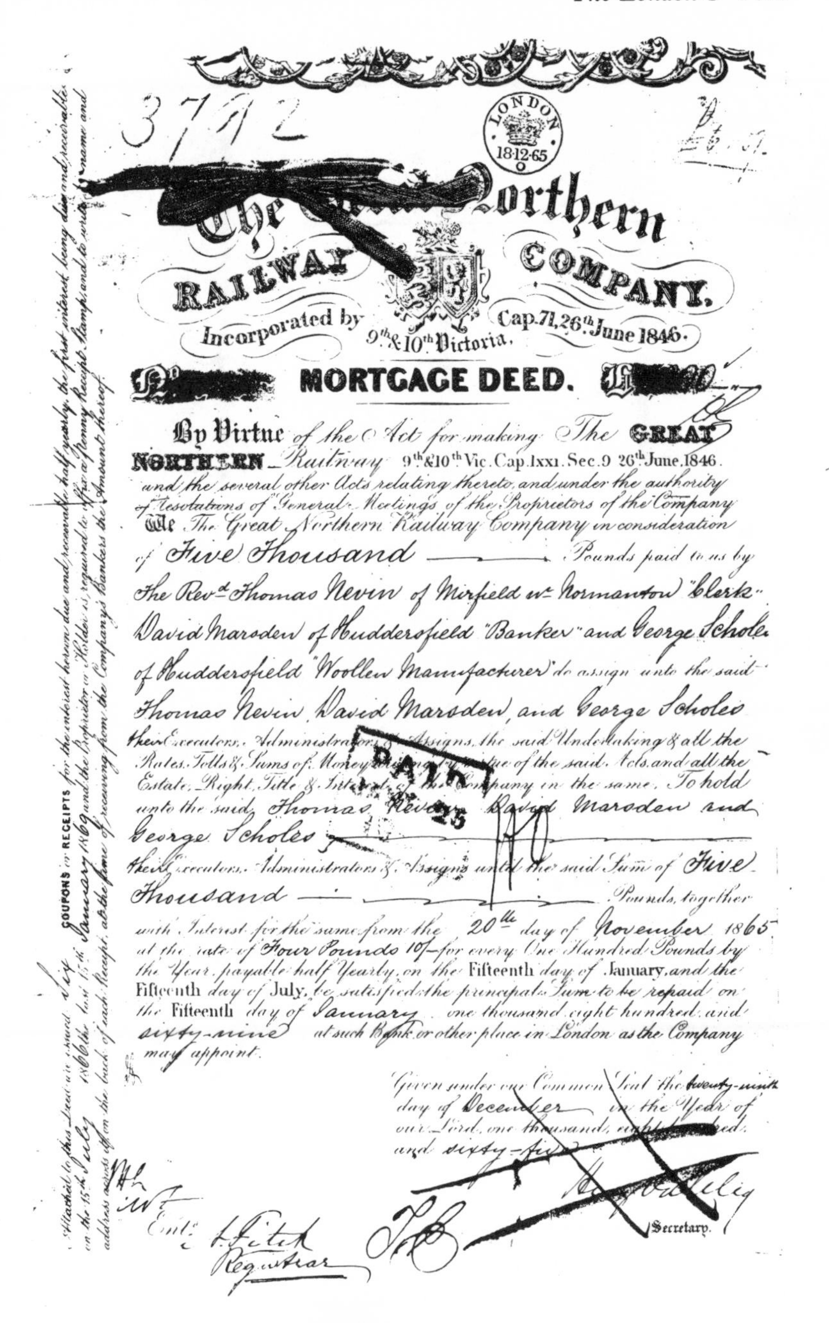
3782

LONDON 18·12·65

The Great Northern
RAILWAY COMPANY.
Incorporated by 9th & 10th Victoria, Cap. 71, 26th June 1846.

No. MORTGAGE DEED. £

By Virtue of the Act for making The GREAT NORTHERN Railway 9th & 10th Vic. Cap. lxxi. Sec. 9 26th June, 1846. and the several other Acts relating thereto, and under the authority of Resolutions of General Meetings of the Proprietors of the Company We The Great Northern Railway Company in consideration of Five Thousand Pounds paid to us by The Revd Thomas Nevin of Mirfield nr Normanton "Clerk" David Marsden of Huddersfield "Banker" and George Scholes of Huddersfield "Woollen Manufacturer" do assign unto the said Thomas Nevin, David Marsden, and George Scholes their Executors, Administrators & Assigns, the said Undertaking & all the Rates, Tolls & Sums of Money arising by virtue of the said Acts, and all the Estate, Right, Title & Interest of the Company in the same, To hold unto the said Thomas Nevin David Marsden and George Scholes their Executors, Administrators & Assigns until the said Sum of Five Thousand Pounds, together with Interest for the same from the 20th day of November 1865 at the rate of Four Pounds 10/- for every One Hundred Pounds by the Year, payable half Yearly, on the Fifteenth day of January, and the Fifteenth day of July, be satisfied: the principal Sum to be repaid on the Fifteenth day of January one thousand eight hundred and sixty-nine at such Bank or other place in London as the Company may appoint.

PAID 25

Given under our Common Seal the twenty-ninth day of December in the Year of our Lord, one thousand, eight hundred and sixty-five

Secretary.

Entd. Registrar

Attached to this Deed are issued Six COUPONS or RECEIPTS for the interest herein due and receivable half yearly, the first interest being due and receivable on the 15th July 1866 the last 15th January 1869 and the Proprietor or Holder is required to affix a Penny Receipt Stamp and to write his name and address across the face of each Receipt, at the time of receiving from the Company's Bankers the Amount thereof.

The Great Northern Railway
MORTGAGE DEED
INTEREST COUPON
PAYABLE
at Messrs SMITH, PAYNE & SMITHS, Bankers, Lombard St. London.
PAID
DEC 16 1857

which was christened the 'Towns Line'. It was considered that the Loop could be completed in about 14 months, and should be put in hand, as it would be the first to carry traffic, and bring in some revenue. At the same time it was recognised that a start must be made in the south, for it was estimated that the work would take at least two and a half years. The site chosen for the London terminus was occupied by smallpox and fever hospitals, which, as well as several streets of small houses, would have to be demolished, and the site excavated.

Bawtry might have become an important railway junction if the 1845 plans had succeeded in full. Since Parliament had decided in favour of the Sheffield & Lincolnshire Junction, and thrown out the Bawtry to Sheffield branch, the Loop need not rejoin the Towns line at Bawtry. The decision was therefore taken that a deviation north of Gainsborough, for the Loop to join further north, at Rossington, would be advantageous.

Joseph Cubitt's 'southern section' was London to Peterborough and on to Lincoln. John Miller's 'northern section' was Lincoln to Gainsborough and Doncaster to York. In October, it was resolved that each should receive £2,000 per annum plus expenses while travelling.

At Barnet the line of route passed through the extensive Lionsdown estate owned by John Catley, who was not disposed to sell only part of his land to the company. In October it was decided to purchase the whole estate, which cost £38,000. The company considered converting it into a good housing estate and had plans for this drawn up by an architect. Eventually however it was resolved to sell all the surplus land. Catley, who had remained as a GN tenant had to leave.

Negotiations with the hospital authorities at King's Cross broke down in October. The London & York valued the property in 1844. There was such a wide difference between the sum demanded and the amount offered that the matter had to go before a jury. To this the hospital authorities raised objection until the expiration of six months after the passing of the Act. Since the old hospital buildings could not be demolished before new ones were ready for the patients, it was obvious that the GN would have to make temporary arrangements. It was decided to erect a temporary terminus at Maiden Lane on the north bank of Regent's Canal adjacent to the goods yard.

So far the company had not appointed a locomotive engineer. William Cubitt recommended his brother Benjamin, and proposed that a committee of directors should visit the Wolverton works of the L & B as affording an example of the establishment he recommended. The committee visited Wolverton on Thursday 22 October and were received by Edward Bury. On Saturday 14 November, a party of directors visited the engine works at Crewe and then proceeded to Manchester where they inspected the M&L's works, and Sharp Brothers' Atlas works. Benjamin Cubitt was engaged as Locomotive Engineer on 3 November 1846 with a salary of £750 per annum.

By this time William Cubitt had completed his final surveys of the route. A few deviations were recommended. A further Act was necessary for a deviation of some 3 miles north of Peterborough, to run contiguous to the Midland in accordance with an undertaking given in the Lords. This would result in economy in construction of bridges, culverts, etc. The original levels of the GN here were considerably higher than those of the Midland.

Steps were now taken to prepare contracts for obtaining in due time supplies of rails and sleepers, and locomotives and rolling stock in time for opening any portion of the line. Advertisements were issued inviting tenders for wrought iron reversible rails and Memel fir sleepers. The rails were to weigh 72 lb to the yard, while the sleepers were to be triangular, four to be cut out of balks 13 in square and about 8 ft 6 in long with a minimum of 8 ft 4 in. The price of these materials was to include delivery at the ports of Goole, Gainsborough, Boston, Spalding, Wisbech, Lynn and London. Contracts for rails were let on 16 December, Bailey Brothers & Co of Liverpool agreeing to supply 35,000 tons at £9 18s 6d a ton and the Ebbw Vale Co a similar quantity at £10 14s 0d (£10.70). The offer of 500,000 sleepers at 4s 3¼d each by J. Dowson & Co was accepted on the same day.

A foundry, acquired at Lincoln when land was bought, was utilised for casting iron chairs, starting in December with Benjamin Cubitt in charge. These were made under the patents of Ransomes & May who lent a man to supervise manufacture. Soon sufficient chairs were turned out every week for a mile of railway.

A notable day in the history of the GN, was 11 December, for the first engines and carriages were ordered, and the first contract for construction of the line was placed. Three firms each received an order for six engines; Sharp Bros, William Fairbairn, and Bury, Curtis & Kennedy. Benjamin Cubitt was ordered to instruct Walter Williams of Glasshouse Yard, Goswell Street, London, to prepare six different pattern carriages. When completed these were to be displayed for inspection by directors and other carriage builders. It was agreed that the price of these should be the average of the cost of subsequent carriages which the company would have to purchase. (Locomotives and carriages will be discussed in more detail in the last chapter of this volume.)

Thomas Brassey, probably the foremost railway contractor of his time, undertook to construct the whole of the works from 1 mile north of the smallpox hospital, to Peterborough. He was confident in his ability to complete the 59 miles to Huntingdon by 1 July 1849 and to Peterborough by the following 1 November. A penalty clause of £15,000 per month was inserted in the contract, which was based on a schedule of prices, and according to Joseph Cubitt was worth £1,611,000. Brassey was not daunted by the magnitude of his task, which included construction of two large viaducts, seven tunnels and numerous bridges, and involved moving 9,750,000 cubic yards of earth. Soon afterwards, on 13 January 1847, the contract for the Loop line from Peterborough to Gainsborough was let to Samuel Morton Peto and Edward Ladd Betts. They undertook to complete the line by 28 February 1848 and agreed to a penalty clause of £1,000 a week. This contract was also based on a schedule of prices and later included construction of stations and other buildings.

Joseph Cubitt advised the directors to purchase a large quantity of sleepers in advance of requirements. Thus on 5 February 550,000 at 4s 3d (21p) each were ordered from Richard & Jonathan Harrison of Hull and on 17 February a further 500,000 from J. Dowson & Co at 4s 2d (21p). Switches and crossings were subsequently ordered from Ransomes & May of Ipswich, Fox & Henderson of Birmingham, and Lloyds & Foster of Wednesbury.

It is now necessary to return to the events of 1846. An extra-ordinary meeting of GN shareholders was held on 6 October to sanction purchase of the Stamford & Spalding, as provided for in its Act of 7 August 1846. This line, despite its title was only authorised from a point on the main line 6 miles north of Peterborough to the Loop line in Crowland parish. It would have been useful, but was not built. About this time there were arrangements with three other cross-country lines, the Royston & Hitchin, East Lincolnshire, and Boston, Stamford & Birmingham. The first had an authorised line only from Hitchin to Royston. Projected as the Cambridge & Oxford, it was cut down in the Lords. The GN hoped to use it to reach Cambridge. The East Lincolnshire was to run from Boston to Great Grimsby, while the Boston, Stamford & Birmingham, (never made), was authorised to construct a line from Helpstone (north of Peterborough) to Wisbech. All three companies were (somewhat improvidently) leased, their proprietors being guaranteed a permanent 6%. The agreements were dated 9 October, 2 December and 14 December respectively, all confirmed by an Act of 9 July 1847. The East Lincolnshire preserved its identity until 1 January 1923.

An offer of a guarantee was also made to 'the Ambergate', but it preferred to remain independent, no doubt expecting that its strategic line would command a better offer when complete. Negotiations continued sporadically over the next few years, and eventually it became part of the GN, as will be seen. Due to its unwieldy title the Ambergate, Nottingham, Boston & Eastern Junction was usually referred to as 'the Ambergate'. The little Ely & Huntingdon was another company to be offered 6%, but as it was already negotiating with two other railways it declined. Captain Laws thought that an extensive corn traffic would originate at Ely.

The proposed Leicester & Bedford attracted the directors' attention in August 1846. They were prepared to take any amount of stock, not exceeding one half, in that concern. Hudson was also interested in it, and called a meeting at Derby in October. The GN chairman and Captain Laws attended the meeting and took care to impress on Robert Lindsell, deputy chairman of the Bedford Committee, the importance of so treating with Hudson as not to compromise the interests of the GN. He was informed that the GN would not consent to any arrangements to which the EC was a party. The outcome of the meeting was that the Midland took over the Leicester & Bedford and agreed to deposit plans for a line to join the GN at Arlesey or Hitchin—there to terminate. The GN consented to this on the understanding that the new line would form an alternative route for traffic from the Midlands to London to that already established via Rugby to Euston Square. Denison and Hudson had a row on Derby platform afterwards.

The GN was particularly interested in the promotion of the South Yorkshire Railway which would join the GN at Doncaster and tap the South Yorkshire coalfield. It purchased about 17,000 shares of £20 each. One of the leading spirits in this venture was Robert Baxter. The project was warmly supported by Edmund Denison and a number of important and influential coalowners, including Lord Wharncliffe, Lord Fitzwilliam and Wentworth Vernon. A somewhat similar Bill had failed in the previous Session.

In October the GN, in conjunction with the Leeds & Thirsk, Leeds & Dewsbury, and M&L, arranged to deposit a Bill for a joint Leeds Central station to be built on the north side of the Aire. Shortly afterwards negotiations commenced with the M&L for use of each other's lines. An agreement was made on 1 May 1847 which gave the GN running powers from Askern to Wakefield, and Methley, and the M&L powers from Doncaster to Askern. William Cubitt was instructed to survey a line from Methley by Rothwell and Beeston to Leeds, and also, another from King's Lyn (sic) to Sutterton.

Bills for the 1847 Session included the Rossington deviation, an Isle of Axholme Extension, branches from Tattershall to Horncastle, and Sleaford to Hougham Mill, and an extension from Royston to Cambridge. Bills for the Hatfield–Hertford and Hatfield to St Albans, Luton and Dunstable lines were also to be re-deposited, but the L&B (by now the L&NW) applied for a line from Dunstable by Luton to St Albans and Watford, giving provision for GN trains over it and use of St Albans station. The GN was to be 'allowed' to make the line from St Albans via Hatfield to Hertford. William Cubitt was thereupon instructed to suspend re-deposit of the plans and extend the Hertford–Hatfield scheme to St Albans. But nothing came of these proposed branches, Dunstable, St Albans and Hertford all being connected to the GN by independent companies more than a decade later.

In the autumn Hudson deposited the Bill for the Midland Leicester-Hitchin line, and on behalf of the EC submitted projects for extensions from Hertford to Hitchin, (there to join the Midland from Leicester), Cambridge to Bedford, Wisbech* to the Midland at Newark, and Peterborough to Folkingham on the Ambergate's authorised line. Thus the GN was committed to another expensive Parliamentary contest, for all these Hudsonian projects were designed to abstract traffic from it.

Captain Laws was designated Superintendent of the GN at £2,000 per annum in January 1847, and William Cubitt's salary was fixed at £4,000 a year. The first half-yearly meeting of shareholders was on Saturday 27 February, at the Hall of Commerce. In the absence of William Astell, who was seriously ill, Edmund Denison took the chair. The number of directors was reduced to 22, and their allowances cut from £3,500 to £3,000. But the secretary's salary was increased to £1,200. Most of the directors ballotted off the board had been connected with the Direct Northern, and fallen into disrepute by the evaporation of that project's funds. £230,000 had been transferred to the GN on 1 July 1846, considerably less than the London & York men had been led to expect. The proprietors were informed that the company had bought sufficient land between London and Peterborough for four tracks but only two would be constructed for the time being. A few days later the company's offices were removed to 14 Moorgate, and remained there until 15 August 1850 when they were transferred to the temporary Maiden Lane station. The move to the permanent station took place in 1852.

*Wisbech was spelt Wisbeach prior to 1839, according to the local Cambridgeshire directories, and was given the official spelling of Wisbech in 1851. The Ordnance Surveys also used the spelling Wisbeach up until 1824, but had changed to the official version by 1886.

William Astell died on 7 March, and John Henry Astell was appointed a director in place of his father. Edmund Denison was chosen chairman and George Hussey Packe deputy chairman. Denison, who was reputed to be the wealthiest citizen of Doncaster, was a native of Leeds and M.P. for the West Riding. His eldest son, E. B. Denison, had been called to the Bar, and acquired the railway part of his work from the able Robert Baxter. In due course he was appointed Queen's Counsel, and as such he represented the GN in many a Parliamentary tussle.

The question of a site for the station at Gainsborough arose. Joseph Cubitt submitted three separate plans, the first two of which, while convenient to the town, were on high embankments, and the third, on a level formation, was ¾ mile out of the town. As a fourth alternative he suggested arrangements with the MS&L for use of its station, thus saving considerable expense. This last plan was adopted, so the GN did not have its own station at Gainsborough for another 20 years.

In May 1847 40 acres of land for the London goods yards were acquired from St Bartholomew's Hospital. The land was paid for in four annual instalments of £10,000 commencing in July 1848. In June, Joseph Cubitt reported on the state of the works. Brassey had made a good start. Shafts had been sunk at the longest tunnels, and brickworks established for making millions of bricks from excavated clay at the tunnels. Work has been commenced on the extensive cuttings, while rails and sleepers were arriving at the ports and being stacked upon the line. Cubitt stated that the men would be withdrawn from the London clay district in the autumn and put to work in the Hitchin area.

Also in June 1847 the M&L commenced its line to Askern. It was resolved to build about 4½ miles from Doncaster to Askern, and to instruct Miller to act in concert with the M&L engineers. So far, Miller had little to do, only planning the Doncaster–York route, and a GN station at York. He offered to take a reduced salary but, although thanking him for his handsome gesture, the directors were not disposed to accept the offer until the results of the current Parliamentary Session were known. Petos were awarded the contract for construction of the Askern line on 6 August.

Results of the 1847 Session were reasonably favourable to the GN, as Hudson's threats of aggression were beaten off. The EC was defeated in its attempt to join the Midland at Hitchin as, although the Leicester & Hitchin was sanctioned, it was not allowed to cross the GN. Having been shorn of its crafty purpose, Hudson did not proceed with construction.

The EC was authorised to make the Cambridge–Bedford, but was only partially successful with its extension from Wisbech to Newark which was reduced to a line from Wisbech to a junction with the GN at Spalding, over which the GN was given running powers. The latter was never made and the former eventually became a short connecting line to the R&H at Shepreth, as will be seen. Yet another Hudson project rejected was for a Y&NM branch from Selby to Gainsborough. The EC failed with its Bills for lines from Peterborough to Folkingham and Somersham to Ramsey.

The GN itself failed to gain independent access to Leeds only because of an error in the levels, as the Committee felt the GN should have its line, and rejected competing schemes of the Midland and the Leeds & Dewsbury. This disappointment was somewhat offset by the assured success of the Leeds Central station Bill, which passed the Commons but did not become an Act until 22 July 1848, to which was scheduled the running power agreement between the GN and M&L. The capital was £320,000, equally provided by the four companies, each represented by two directors, Edmund Denison and John Barff representing the GN. The M&L had just changed its name to the Lancashire & Yorkshire.

The GN Bill for the Axholme Extension was suspended until the next Session, but the remainder, the Tattershall to Horncastle, Sleaford to Hougham Mill, Royston to Cambridge, and Rossington deviation all failed. Of the Lynn line only 2½ miles from Sutterton to Sutton Bridge were sanctioned, and did not proceed. Rejection of the Rossington deviation was unexpected. The board had been so confident that it had made plans to let the contract for it, and an extension to York, to Peto & Betts. Miller resigned on 11 September, and Joseph Cubitt was given charge of the whole line but with no increase in salary.

Minor GN Acts which passed in 1847 were for deviations between Grantham and York on 9 July, and at Peterborough and Grantham on 22 July, which also provided that Grantham station should be joint between the GN and 'Ambergate'.

Amongst friends and rivals the following events must be recorded. The South Yorkshire, Doncaster & Goole Railway got its Act on 22 July 1847, for a main line from a junction with the GN at Doncaster to Barnsley, and one or two short branches. This concern, usually referred to as the South Yorkshire, was given running powers over the GN for 1¼ miles through Doncaster while the GN received running powers to Barnsley.

The Newcastle & Berwick was opened throughout on 1 July 1847 and a few weeks later amalgamated with the York & Newcastle as the York,

Newcastle & Berwick. The Caledonian, on 10 September, was opened from Carlisle as far as Beattock. The west coast now held a decided advantage, for it had a continuous line of rails from Euston Square to Beattock where coaches connected with Glasgow and Edinburgh, while the east coast route between Euston Square and Edinburgh had two highly inconvenient breaks in through services pending completion of the bridges over the Tyne and Tweed.

Reaction to the Railway Mania set in. There was a dearth of ready cash, shareholders having difficulties in meeting their calls. Under these circumstances, the directors had some trouble with a section of the proprietors who were anxious to abandon parts of the line. The purely speculative type of shareholder undoubtedly came under the influence of Hudson who was quick to take advantage of the situation. These people were loud in their demands that the London line should be given up in favour of using the EC south of Peterborough. Such a course was unthinkable, as the directors were by now fully committed to the London line and had laid out a great deal of money on its construction. No further contracts were to be let for the time being and, in view of the depressed state of the money market, Brassey was requested to slow down his works which were limited to about £10,000 a month. Work on the earthworks came to a standstill. Construction was also slowed down at the Gainsborough end of the Loop, deserted during the harvest period.

As a result of negotiations begun by Captain Laws, a conference was held at Normanton on 16 October, when the GN obtained running powers over the Midland from Methley junction to Leeds. Having Hudson's signature in its pocket the company did not lodge its intended Leeds Bill this year, but did re-deposit the Bill for the Rossington deviation.

S. J. Capper, for a short period a deputy chairman, died on 12 October and his death was followed on 12 January 1848 by that of Benjamin Cubitt. William Cubitt was prepared to recommend a successor to his brother and introduced Edward Bury to the directors on 1 February. Bury was a man with considerable experience, having been locomotive engineer to the L & B, and retiring soon after it had become part of the L & N W. He was also about to retire from the position of senior partner in the engine-building firm of Bury, Curtis & Kennedy. On the following day Bury was engaged as GN Locomotive Engineer at £2,000 per annum, it being stipulated that he should give full time to the company's business and have no other source of profit. He took up his duties on 22 February and took charge of all the engines, rolling stock, machinery, stores and buildings.

Keyworth, navigations manager, resigned on 4 January 1848. He was succeeded by George Thompson who was appointed Superintendent at Lincoln at £300 a year from 1 January. John Denniston, who had been secretary to the EL, was appointed Auditor of Traffic on 22 February. The opening of the EL was now imminent and Captain Laws had been busy making necessary arrangements. Fares were fixed at 2d a mile first class, 1½d a mile second, and 1d a mile third, and for express trains, 2½d a mile first, and 2d a mile second. Staff were appointed to the stations. The uniform to be supplied to them was dark green corduroy with metal buttons, embossed with the company's intials. Preparations were also made for opening the first portions of the GN proper. At a meeting on 25 February, William Cubitt, Bury and Laws were requested to estimate the number of engines and carriages required for opening the Loop. The two Cubitts were instructed to proceed with construction of workshops at Boston and to remove the engine and tools from the Lincoln foundry which was to be demolished. They also had to provide engine sheds at either Lincoln or Peterborough, as they judged best, for the reception of new engines when received from the makers. The latter place was selected and by 2 May Bury was able to report that seven engines and tenders were at the temporary shed. By 29 August, 10 passengers and 5 goods engines were on hand at Peterborough, with a further goods engine on loan to Peto & Betts.

Until such time as a GN station at Peterborough would be ready, it was decided to use the EC's as a temporary terminus for the trains on the Loop. Access to this would be over the Midland by a connection at Walton (or Werrington) junction. Early in May negotiations were opened with the EC, the Midland and the all-powerful L&NW for use of the station and lines. Final agreement with the Midland was arranged at Derby on 6 September, the GN agreeing to pay 66% of the receipts as maximum toll. Cost of the use of the EC station was ultimately settled by arbitration. When the GN commenced running, it was one of the first cosmopolitan examples with trains of four different major companies using it.

In April the GN and MS&L agreed to work together in the acquisition of land at Retford, Saxilby (or Saxelby) and Gainsborough. They arranged to provide accomodation for each other with all services, except booking clerks, at Lincoln and Sheffield. The passenger station at Grimsby was to be appropriated equally to the traffic of both companies and facilities were given to the EL at Grimsby Docks.

About this time it was discovered that Joseph Cubitt had been taking a nice little profit out of the company. In future he was to be provided with an office and his assistant engineers and others in his employ were to be paid by the company. Cubitt now expected to receive a salary of £2,500 with a fee of 7 guineas a day plus hotel and travelling expenses when engaged out of town on the company's business. His salary was fixed at £2,000 with ten guineas a day plus hotel and travelling expenses when out of town, and it was stipulated that he should devote the whole of his time to the GN. In July his report indicated that progress had been speeded up on Brassey's contract, but that the London tunnels were still in abeyance and the section from Hitchin to Huntingdon was still untouched. On the Loop the permanent way had been laid for 50 miles, 42½ miles being double. There was still two months' work in Warren House Wood cutting near Gainsborough, where there would be a junction with the M S & L. Near Doncaster the line from Askern junction to Bentley Bank was nearly completed. The directors now resolved to spend another £3,000 a month on the tunnels and a like sum on the Hitchin–Huntingdon section. In March, Brassey and Peto & Betts had declined to accept debentures as part payment owing 'to the sudden great change in the money market'.

Land at Maiden Lane was purchased in April, in connection with Copenhagen tunnel. It cost about £15,000 of which £3,000 was paid immediately. The company agreed to pay 5% interest on the balance and in the meantime would receive rents from the houses. At the end of July the contract for the southernmost section of the line from the south end of Copenhagen tunnel to Old St Pancras Road was let to John Jay. His schedule of prices was so low that both William and Joseph Cubitt were convinced that he would not be able to undertake the works satisfactorily. However Jay produced excellent references, and the directors were satisfied in awarding him the contract. Owing to difficulties in obtaining possession of land some time elapsed before he could commence operations.

Some of the workshop buildings at Boston were approaching completion in June, and Bury was authorised to have machinery and fittings erected. This commercially minded gentleman made the most of the opportunity, for he persuaded the directors that the machinery he required was not easy to obtain and was given a free hand in its purchase. In consequence most of it was supplied by his own firm, Bury Curtis & Kennedy. Early in June, Laws, Bury and the Cubitts, plus Baxter, were instructed to prepare a draft of 'By-Laws' to be exhibited at stations for guidance of the public. The same four officers (but not Baxter) were to devise a system of signals. It was Bury and not Laws who had to report the number and description of the various officers and servants required to work the line, and the rates of salary. He was to distinguish those who were to be clothed, and lodged by the company. He had to prepare a draft of instructions to be issued to officers employed in the locomotive and carriage departments. He had further to prepare a list of stores required for opening the line and also suggest the best course for obtaining them.

A couple of months later Bury recommended the appointment of a foreman to take charge of Boston Works, and in November, selected Frederick Parker who had spent 15 years with the L&B and its successor. He was engaged at £350 a year and soon afterwards was instructed that he was to take full charge in the event of Bury's absence. Bury also proposed the appointment of men to take charge of the locomotives at Peterborough, New Holland, Lincoln and Boston at salaries of £120–£180 per annum. At first they were graded as foremen but about a decade later those at the principal sheds were classed as district locomotive superintendents. James Johnson had already been appointed as foreman at Louth by Benjamin Cubitt and he had lately been busy supervising the delivery of the first few engines required to work the EL. Another appointment was William Pulford, engaged as Deputy Store Keeper on 1 November 1848 at £300 a year.

The Rossington deviation Bill was again rejected. This placed the directors in a quandry, for they had decided they would not revert to the original Bawtry line. As a way out of their difficulty they requested the MS&L to commence construction of its 'Leverton Branch' by means of which they could reach Retford. This 8 mile line had been authorised in 1846 as the Sheffield & Lincolnshire Extension, to commence at Clarborough junction east of Retford, with a long descent of 1 in 120 to the floor of the Trent valley with an extensive bridge over the river at Torksey, and to join the GN at Sykes junction near Saxilby. Although the MS&L had shelved the project, it proved very co-operative and gave the necessary instructions to John Fowler who was engineer to its eastern lines as well as to the EL. The GN let a contract to Peto & Betts on 5 July for construction of the portion of the Towns line between Retford and Doncaster. For this the schedule of prices agreed was about 10% less than that fixed for the Loop line.

The Axholme Extension Bill became an Act on 14 August 1848, empowering the company to construct a line from a junction with the Loop at Saundby (Nottinghamshire), passing through Misterton, Haxey and Epworth to a junction with the L&Y at Askern. There was also to be a branch through Thorne to link up with the authorised York line at

Heck. It was never built, but it will be necessary to refer to it several times before it was finally abandoned. On the same day the R&H obtained an Act to extend its line from Royston to Shepreth where it would form a junction with the EC's authorised Cambridge to Bedford branch.

WHEELS BEGIN TO TURN

On 1 March 1848 wheels began to turn and a meagre stream of coins commenced to tinkle into GN tills, for on this day the initial portion, 14 miles, of the East Lincolnshire was opened between Great Grimsby and Louth. The Manchester, Sheffield & Lincolnshire also opened its line from Grimsby to New Holland on this day. The MS&L and GN arranged to run over each other's lines, and the original passenger service was five trains each way on weekdays over the 30 miles between Louth and New Holland, with two trains each way on Sundays. The railway was almost straight and the earthworks were slight. There were two timber viaducts with three spans, 20 ft for one, and 25 ft for the other, and a masonry viaduct with two arches of 12 ft span. Of the other two bridges, one was of brick over the rails and the other was an underbridge with brick abutments and cast iron girders. The original stations, all roofed in, were Waltham & Humberstone, Holton-le-Clay & Tetney, North Thoresby, Ludborough and Louth. The station at Grimsby was the property of the MS&L. Turntables were available at New Holland and Louth, where there was a small engine shed. Reporting the opening of the line to the Board of Trade, Laws stated that all stations were unfinished, and there were no facilities for goods. At this date the GN had not taken delivery of a single goods vehicle. A junction with the MS&L's dock line, sanctioned by an Act of 2 July 1847, would have entailed an inconvenient reversal in order to enter Grimsby station. Shortly before the opening it was decided to construct a sharp 20 chain curve to allow trains to run direct into the station via Garden Street junction. Parliamentary sanction for the purchase of the land was obtained, in retrospect by an Act of 22 July 1848, which also gave power to abandon the branch to the dock line at Pasture Street junction. But the track was not taken up, as the line was available for passage of the royal train in 1854.

A further 19 miles 36 chains opened on 3 September, to reach Firsby (originally known as Firstby) with stations at Legbourne, Authorpe,

Claythorpe, Alford, Willoughby and Burgh. Again the earthworks were slight. One overbridge and three underbridges were of brick and a fourth underbridge had brick abutments and cast iron girders. Claythorpe viaduct was of brick with two openings of 20 ft and two of 10 ft, while the brick viaduct over the river Ludd had one span of 20 ft. There were no fewer than 49 level crossings, most of which were occupational.

The remaining portion of the line to Boston was ready at the same time, but it was not considered worthwhile having a temporary station on the EL at Boston. The GN was experiencing much difficulty in obtaining possession of land at Boston and built a temporary station itself, ready on Monday 2 October, so the final 13 miles 54 chains of the EL began to carry traffic on this day. The original stations were Little Steeping, East Ville & New Leake, and Hob Hole, which was soon renamed Leake & Wrangle, became Old Leake & Wrangle in 1849 and finally Old Leake in 1852, according to the October Bradshaw, which also showed East Ville & New Leake altered to East Ville. From Burgh to the sharp curve at the junction at Boston the line was dead straight, forming one of the longest straight stretches of railway in the country. There were 46 level crossings and no road bridges. Of seven viaducts, one was wooden with seven openings of 30 ft, three were built with cast iron girders and the other three were constructed with tubular wrought iron girders by Fairbairns of Manchester.

The EL provided one-man gasworks at Louth, Firsby and Alford. The permanent way was laid with rails weighing 71 lbs to the yard in 15 ft lengths, resting in joint chairs weighing 31 lbs and intermediate chairs weighing 21 lbs, the chairs being secured to the sleepers by two wooden trenails. The line was double except for 20 chains of single over a temporary curve at Boston. The engineer was John Fowler who received £4,694 8s 4d (£4694.42) for his services. His brother Henry was assistant engineer. Waring Brothers were originally engaged to build the line, but after it had been completed to Louth, Peto & Betts did the remainder. Signals with posts and lamps were by Stevens & Son. The company's offices were at Louth.

As soon as the line was opened one member of a railwayman's family was allowed once a week to travel free to the nearest market town. From February 1853 one up and one down train called at Fotherby Gate House between Louth and Ludborough on two markets days each week (later, on Fridays only) until Friday 28 June 1872. Many years later there was a halt there called Fotherby & Utterby (see vol. III).

By an Act of 2 July 1847 the EL purchased the lease of the Louth Navigation, which connected the Humber to the Ludd at Alvingham,

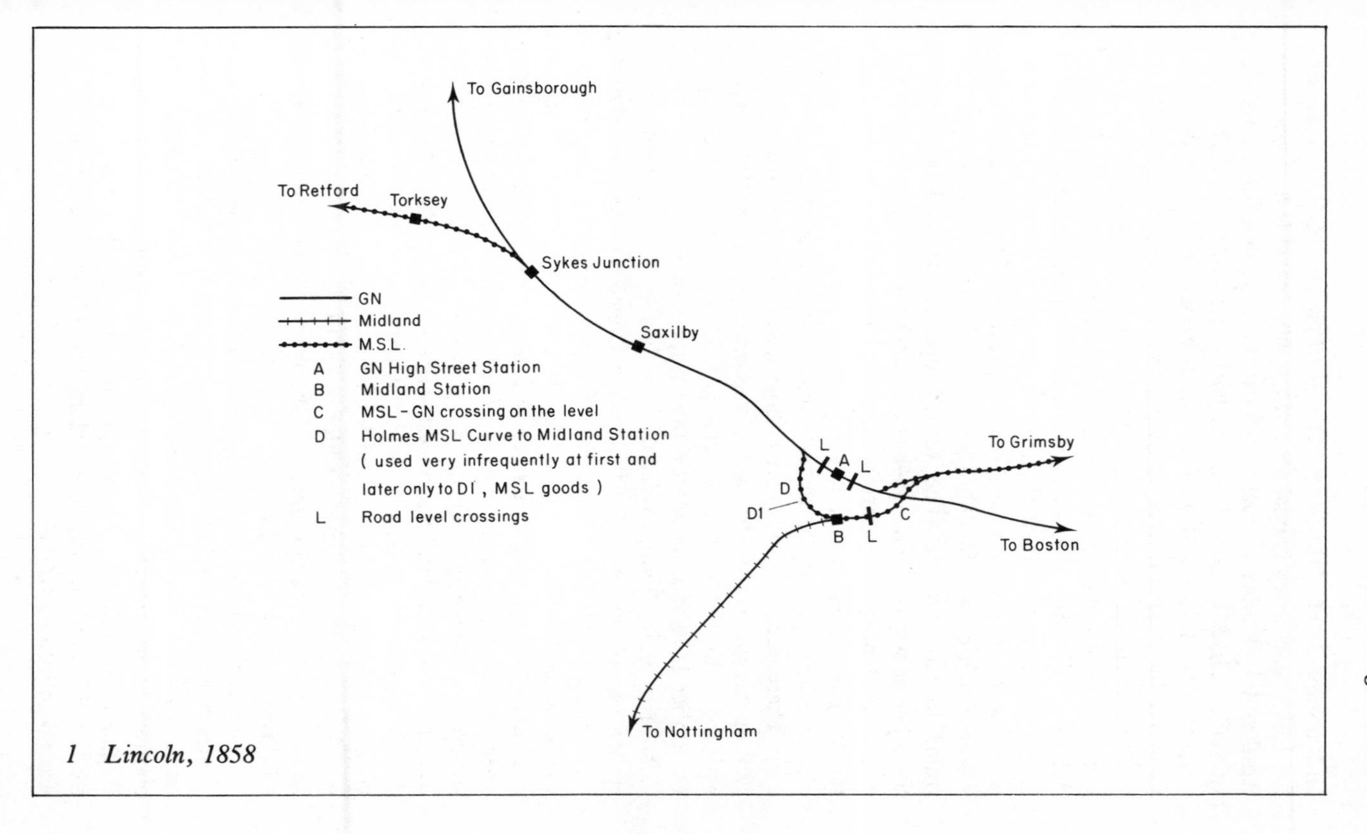

1 *Lincoln, 1858*

and continued to Louth. From 1 October 1848 the EL lease became one for 1,000 years at an annual rent of £36,000 (payable half-yearly on 1 April and 1 October), equal to 6% on the EL £600,000 capital. The subscribers had included Denison, Packe and other GN directors.

In May 1848 Bury and William Cubitt were instructed to draw plans for an engine shed and workshops at Doncaster, which were built to the west of the site of the future second station. In the same month orders were given for a station building at the level crossing on the Bentley to Arksey road, which was at first called Stockbridge. Early in June the L&Y, which opened its Wakefield–Goole line on 1 April, was ready to open the Knottingley–Askern junction section. The GN line between Askern junction and Stockbridge was sufficiently advanced for L&Y trains to run over it. The formal opening from Knottingley to Stockbridge was on 5 June 1848 amid minor celebrations; public traffic commenced next day between Knottingley and Askern, and on the following day, over the GN between Askern and Stockbridge, 2 miles 45 chains. There were no earthworks and the gradients and curves were easy. There were two brick underbridges, and a wooden viaduct with 14 12 ft openings. Stockbridge station was renamed Arksey & Stockbridge and then altered to Arksey, changes first shown in Bradshaw in December 1850 and September 1854 respectively.

The remainder, 2 miles 4 chains, from the Bentley road to a temporary station east of the Great North Road at Doncaster was opened on the following 5 August in time for the St Leger race meeting. The formation was all on embankment with an extreme height of 11½ ft. There were five underbridges, one of timber over a river and a road with three openings of 11 ft 6 in and two of 17 ft 6 in, and a temporary wooden structure with five openings of 18 ft 6 in and one of 26 ft. The viaduct over the Don, also of timber, consisted of five spans of 20 ft. The line was double except for 30 chains over the temporary viaduct. Later this viaduct was replaced and the line doubled. The permanent way was laid with 72 lb rails in 18 ft lengths which rested in joint chairs weighing 37 lb and intermediate chairs weighing 21 lb, secured to the triangular sleepers with two wooden trenails.

The L&Y provided a service, five trains each way on weekdays and two each way on Sundays. Pickfords undertook to handle such goods traffic as there was at Doncaster on behalf of the GN, which they continued until December 1849, when, under strong pressure from the Midland, they reluctantly gave notice to terminate their connection with the GN. Pickford's clerk, Thomas Hibbert, offered to serve the GN, and was taken into its employ.

The directors travelled over the line from Peterborough to Lincoln on 28 September and resolved that it should be opened on Tuesday 17 October 1848. Accordingly, 58 miles of the Loop from Walton junction to Lincoln were opened on that day. The event was celebrated by a holiday in the district, the festivities being rounded off a few days later by a banquet given by the Mayor and Corporation of Boston to the GN directors and others. The board spent nothing on celebrations, a pattern which was to be followed throughout its history with one minor exception.

Intermediate stations to Boston were Peakirk, Littleworth, Spalding, and Algarkirk, and beyond, Langrick, Tattershall, Kirkstead, Stixwould, Southrey, Bardney, Five Mile House, Washingborough, and Lincoln, nearly all adjacent to ferries. Besides the temporary shed at Walton junction, new engine sheds were provided at Boston and Lincoln, although the former was not then completed. The foreman there, Charles Reboul Sacré, was later to be MSL locomotive superintendent. Thomas Owen was in charge at Walton.

The line ran through flat country so gradients were slight, apart from a hump near Peakirk. From Walton junction to Boston it was almost straight, but between Boston and Lincoln there were many curves as the railway followed the course of the navigations. There were 42 level crossings, and only six road bridges, one over the line and the others under. The numerous waterways involved construction of 32 viaducts, seven with cast iron girders, but the rest of timber. The most notable was that near Bardney where the railway crossed the Witham at Horsley Deeps, which was 729 yd long and consisted of 58 land openings and three over the river. Some £30,000 worth of timber went into its construction. The line was double except for ¼ mile at the junction at Boston, laid to the same standards as the Askern line. The GN obtained an Act on 1 August 1849 for a deviation at Boston which sanctioned enlargement of the stations there and at Lincoln. Charles Ward of Lincoln undertook construction of the Boston deviation, 52 chains of line including 13 chains on the EL. The work was completed and connected up to the old lines on Sunday 11 May 1850, making the Loop and EL double throughout.

The company built the Great Northern Hotel at Lincoln, designed by Henry Goddard and erected by Charles Ward for £12,685. The furniture and fittings accounted for another £2,353. When it was completed in November it was let to J. Moyes, but he was an unsatisfactory tenant. When he vacated the premises in December 1853 he owed the GN nearly £900 of which about £750 was eventually written off as a bad debt.

The GN profited from the experience of earlier railways, and from the start provided semaphore signals. Fixed signals at stations were usually mounted on the opposite sides of the same post. They showed three positions. At horizontal they indicated 'danger', when lowered to 45° 'caution', and for 'clear' the arms dropped to vertical inside the slotted posts. Signals at junctions only indicated 'danger' and 'caution'. Auxiliary or 'distance' (as they were called at first) signals were set up 400 or 600 yd in advance of the fixed signals and repeated their indications. They were intended to be treated as stop signals, but drivers, once they had brought trains to a stand, were allowed to proceed cautiously to the fixed signal. The signals were usually operated by levers at the foot of the posts, but were in some cases connected by wires to a group of levers, which gradually led to erection of signal huts and then to raised signal boxes. In darkness a white light indicated 'clear', red 'danger', and green 'caution'. The signal lamps were illuminated with candles.

Signalling was supplied and installed by Stevens & Son of Darlington Works, Southwark Bridge Road, who continued to be the contractors for signalling for many years, until its prices were often substantially undercut by Saxby & Farmer, and McKenzie & Holland. Stevens made a contract in December 1851 to maintain all signals, lamps, wires, etc., for 8d per signal per week.

Traffic was worked under the time interval system, signals being put back to 'danger' after a train had passed, then released to 'caution', and then to 'clear' after the prescribed intervals had elapsed. Thus, except at junctions, the normal position of signals was at clear (the reverse of more modern signalling), a practice which continued for 30 years. In the event of a train breaking down, or even failing to keep time in a section, the guard was required to protect it from a rear-end collision by hand signals and/or placing detonators on the line.

On 3 April 1849 Denniston was instructed to open the stations at Kirton and Surfleet, both constructed with the line, but not opened. A month later it was resolved that a siding and a wharf should be erected at Dogdyke, also a passenger platform, which were built by Stephen Dawson and opened in September. Boston Works charged 5s for fixing the nameboards there, and debited the traffic department with 8s for painting, writing and fixing two nameboards for 'Crowland', opened on 1 August 1849. The name of this station varied frequently early in its existence, but settled down as St James Deeping. The station at Five Mile House soon closed. The directors decided on this when Clarke reported that the weekly receipts averaged 9s 4d (47p), so it went on 2 December 1850. Then in 1865 a large farmer in the district requested siding facilities, duly put in. The station re-appeared in the October Bradshaw, but it seems possible that it was in use earlier, perhaps in August.

With the opening of the Loop, South Lincolnshire was put in direct communication with London. By the EC, or the L&NW, from Peterborough, more than an hour was saved on a journey from Lincoln to London compared with the Midland's roundabout route via Nottingham and Rugby. By the New Holland ferry route, the journey from Hull to the metropolis was reduced by about 40 miles compared with that via Milford. From 1 January Her Majesty's mails to Hull were conveyed from Peterborough to Grimsby by the GN, for which the company was paid £17 a day, and also by connecting trains between Boston and Lincoln.

In December 1848 the board considered the report of its Lincolnshire Committee which severely criticised the work of the Cubitts, and Petos. At Lincoln the layout of the station, carriage shed and gatekeepers' lodges was considered unsatisfactory. At Boston the only permanent building completed was the carriage shed, as the workshops and engine shed were in course of erection. Water cranes at Boston, Lincoln and elsewhere were so situated that engines had to be detached from trains to take water. Petos paid three men 2s 6d (12½p) a day to pump water at Boston and then charged the company 3s 6d (17½p). The committee came to the conclusion that Petos' prices were exorbitant.

Lincoln station was roofed in. A refreshment room was improvised by Bury in the existing buildings at Boston and a temporary waiting room was also put up on the platform. In January 1849 Joseph Cubitt was instructed to visit all stations, and report on what windows could be dispensed with, to reduce Window Tax. A plan for permanent buildings at Boston was approved in April 1850.

Up to the end of June 1848 the receipts from the East Lincolnshire line had amounted to £2,500 and the total expenditure incurred by the GN up to the same date had exceeded £2,500,000. At the fourth half-yearly meeting on 12 August 1848 a policy of retrenchment of directors' allowances and officers' salaries was agreed. At a directors' meeting on 2 November, Edmund Denison arrived armed with proposals for cuts in salary, including that of Laws reduced to £1,500, Mowatt's to £800, Clark's to £300 with six months notice from 1 January, and William Cubitt's to £1,000. Denison had an intense dislike of Mowatt and called for his resignation, but this proposal was not even seconded. His fellow directors were not in accord with his proposals, which were defeated. On 25 November Denison wrote resigning the chair, giving as his reason that his proposals for cutting salaries were not carried, and he did not like the anxieties and responsibilities of the chair. He assured his colleagues that the possibility of again being an M.P. had no influence on his decision. Packe took over the chair only for a short time, for on the following 23 February it was minuted that Denison 'accepted the chair unconditionally'. It appears that he had resigned in a fit of pique, for he was accustomed to carrying the board with him. On the other hand, direction was apt to go wrong without him.

In February the number of directors had been reduced to 20 and now in December their allowances were cut to £2,000. Laws, realising that the company was unwilling to retain him at his old salary, intimated that he was determined to resign as managing director at the end of the month. He had been offered the position of general manager to the L & Y at £1,500. He did, however, consent to remain on the GN board.

On Packe's authority, the secretary instructed Denniston and George Thompson to take charge of the traffic from 1 January 1849. By 1 February Packe had decided that this arrangement for traffic was not working well, as he suggested only one superior officer, and proposed that Bury should be appointed general manager. There the matter rested until early in May when the Board resolved that it was disposed to make Bury General Superintendent of the line and required him to send proposals as to how he would prescribe other officers' duties, and which he would himself undertake. On 11 May he recommended that Denniston should be in charge of coaching traffic and Thompson of goods, and on the following day he described the duties he would undertake. A month later he laid down duties for Denniston and Thompson, who were appointed Superintendent of the Line, and Goods Manager, on 28 June. Bury took up his duties as General Superintendent, besides Locomotive Engineer that day. In November Denniston's salary was fixed at £500 per annum with a £250 bonus for extra services prior to the opening of the line. Thompson's salary was increased to £400. New rates of pay were back-dated to 1 January.

In his additional capacity Bury advised the board on systems of audit and accountancy, and on various aspects of railway working. He produced a plan for new works at Doncaster with repair shops for engines, carriages and wagons, a sawmill, and an area for timber storage. He disclosed that he had had an engine built to his own specification and at his own expense, and now requested permission for the engine to be sent forward. There is no record as to how the directors reacted to this startling revelation, but they ultimately consented to pay £2,200 to Bury, Curtis & Kennedy, who had built it.

At the fifth half-yearly meeting on 23 February 1849, with Denison in the chair, the number of directors was reduced to 16, the minimum allowed under the Act. The salary of Mowatt was cut to £800 'for the present'. A month or two later the reduction of Clark's salary was reviewed, and eventually he agreed to accept £500 a year, and undertake additional duties.

An agreement was concluded in February with Thomas Edmondson of Salford for use of his patent ticket apparatus, adopted ever since the EL's first opening. The licence cost 10s (50p) per mile per annum. Edmondson printed and supplied the tickets at 3s (15p) per 1,000 plain-backed and 3s 3d (16p) per 1,000 initial-backed until the price was cut to 2s (10p) per 1,000 in August 1861 by Waterlows who were the company's contractors for printing. He also supplied dating presses and ticket cases, and provided and fixed the counters.

Forty tenders were received for construction of Copenhagen tunnel, Pearce & Smith of Manchester securing the contract on 27 March 1849 with their price of £47,000. They made a spirited start in June and at the same time John Jay commenced excavations at the south end of the tunnel. Walter Marr Brydone, resident engineer of the Spalding district, offered his services as such of the Loop and East Lincolnshire lines, at £400 a year. Henry Fowler made a similar offer, except that he valued his services at another £100, was successful, and on 15 March was so appointed to the lines from Peterborough to Gainsborough, and Boston to Grimsby at £500 with the proviso that he gave his entire time and attention to the GN

The Gainsborough extension was inspected by Captain Wynne on 29 March 1849 at the same time as the MS&L line from Brigg to Gainsborough, which continued through Gainsborough to the east bank of the Trent at Bole. It had been anticipated that these would open simultaneously on Monday 2 April. However Captain Wynne refused sanction for the GN line until signals were erected at the swing bridge at Brayford Mere. He expressed great surprise on finding the junction with the MS&L's near Gainsborough since it was not authorised. Mowatt stated that the Acts of the GN and MS&L allowed their lines to cross on the level, continued that the junction was a mere curve allowable under General Powers, and it would be inconvenient not to have the junction. The GN line opened one week later, on Easter Monday 9 April 1849. Leaving Lincoln the line crossed High Street on the level, proceeded over the Witham by a drawbridge and then along the south side of the Fossdyke Navigation as far as Saxilby, where it was crossed. Up to this point the formation was level but thence to Gainsborough there were some moderate earthworks, sharp gradients and bridges. Stations were at Saxilby and Marton. Work had been commenced on a station at Lea, but on the board's instructions it was brought to a standstill. This station was not opened until 1 August. The engine shed at Lincoln was closed, and moved to a new position as a carriage shed, a new engine shed being erected at Gainsborough.

Gainsborough junction, 15 miles 66 chains from Lincoln was near the Trent. It faced Retford and necessitated reversal of GN trains in order to use the MS&L's station. By an agreement on 1 June 1848, use of the station was to be paid for on all classes of traffic equal to two miles of the maximum MS&L charges. The original passenger service consisted of four trains each way on weekdays. Two trains each way were provided on Sundays, but were discontinued in July 1863 after receipts had dropped to 7d (3p) a mile. Traffic was disappointing, and towards the end of 1858 the engineer recommended singling the line between Sykes junction and Gainsborough. The directors were inclined to adopt this suggestion but their solicitors doubted the legality of so doing. The MS&L line from Bole to Woodhouse junction was opened on 17 July 1849, the line thence to Sheffield having been in use since the previous 12 February.

Complaints were soon being received from the MS&L of unpunctuality of GN trains, due to the defective state of the engines. Bury was called upon to take immediate steps to remedy this. He reported particularly on engines numbered 23 and 54, that the former had leaky tubes and he had been in contact with the makers, and the latter's bad behaviour was due to bad water at Gainsborough. It turned out that the MS&L would not use this water and the GN quickly found alternative supplies.

In the May timetables Denniston provided that ordinary trains should run at 30 mph with 2½ minute stops and express trains at 36 mph. He reported that he had been able to fit in with the time of EC and L&NW trains at Peterborough, and did not have to ask those companies to change the times of their trains. As the trains were worked on time intervals, the actual times had frequently been in dispute when inquiries were made into irregularities. A master clock was provided at Boston in July. Guards of the first trains each day were required to set their watches by this clock, and communicate 'railway time' to all other stations. Bury built a clock tower at Boston by the end of the year.

In January, Joseph Cubitt had been instructed to confer with Fowler about forming a junction with the MS&L's line just east of Lincoln, opened from Market Rasen to the Midland station on 18 December 1848, and crossing the GN line on the level at Pelham Street. On 3 April it was resolved to have the junction formed forthwith, but the precise date on which it was brought into use is not known. The Midland began to charge for piloting GN wagons through the junction from 1 October. The Act sanctioning construction of this Durham Ox junction at Lincoln was not passed until 1851. C. W. Eborall, traffic manager of the MS&L, wrote proposing that his company should work all traffic at Gainsborough in return for the GN working all traffic at Lincoln, but this suggestion was not accepted.

On 15 July David Wells, a platelayer employed by Petos, discovered that the wooden bridge over the South Drive Drain near Deeping Fen was on fire. Although he swam the drain in order to raise the alarm the bridge was destroyed. Traffic was interrupted for four or five days, until the workmen from Boston Works improvised a temporary bridge. Fox, Henderson & Co secured the contract for a cast iron replacement with their price of £1,845 and undertook completion by 1 December. Wells was rewarded with a present of £3 and taken into the company's employ. The directors were now apprehensive about the other timber bridges, and resolved to build a cottage for the bridge-keeper at Brayford Mere swivel bridge and provide a fire engine to be kept at Bardney bridge.

The first portion of the Towns line, opened on Tuesday 4 September 1849, commenced with a junction at Retford with the MS&L, and ran for 17 miles 45 chains to Doncaster where it joined the Askern line. The double line was laid with similar materials to those on the Loop. Apart from a hump involving gradients of 1 in 198 on each side between Scrooby and Rossington most of the line was level or easily graded. The viaduct at Bawtry, constructed of timber, consisted of 58 bays of 19 ft, and one span of 29 ft, skewed over the river Idle. A viaduct over the Chesterfield Canal was built with brick abutments and cast iron girders having a span of 46 ft. Three other viaducts were of brick and three more of timber. The road bridges were of brick or brick and cast iron girders, and three were over and seven under the line. Of 35 level crossings 15 were over public roads. Stations were Sutton, Ranskill, Scrooby, Bawtry, and Rossington.

In May 1850 Charles Ward was instructed to proceed with building a new station at Doncaster 'for the use of the GN and South Yorkshire', which was about ¼ mile north of the original one, and was in use by the middle of 1851. Records at Boston indicate that the engines and shed at Doncaster had been in use prior to the opening of the new line, and it might well be that the company had commenced to work some traffic over the Askern line, for it had given notice on 31 July 1849 to the L&Y of its intention to do so.

The GN could now expect to commence its service between Peterborough and Leeds by using its running powers, over the MS&L between Gainsborough and Retford, the L&Y between Askern junction and Methley junction, and thence over the Midland, and a short section of the L&T on which reversal was necessary at Geldard Road junction, to reach Central station. Despite the October 1847 agreement, signed by Hudson and Denison, the Midland now demanded insertion of a clause abandoning for ever GN rights to apply for an independent line to Leeds, failing which it would stop the trains and take the maximum toll of every passenger. Bury wrote that the Midland had closed the junction at Methley and that he had arranged to run the trains to Leeds over the L&Y and Leeds and Dewsbury (by now part of the L&NW), via Wakefield and Dewsbury, although it does not appear that this plan was put into operation except for the Doncaster race trains for the St Leger meeting on 11–14 September. Actually the points at Methley were removed on the evening of 3 September, and almost a month elapsed before Baxter was able to announce that the Midland had consented to the GN using Methley junction upon the terms of the original agreement as from 1 October. This date was confirmed by Denniston when he reported that his trains had commenced to use Leeds Central.

By that time this dispute arose with the Midland, George Hudson had ceased to be its chairman, for he had resigned on 17 April, following disclosures of his misconduct (to put it mildly) at a meeting of the YN&B proprietors. Within a month, thoroughly discredited, he had resigned from the boards of all the railways with which he had been connected.

For financial reasons, the GN withdrew from the other three companies at Leeds Central, reserving only the right to the proportion of land belonging to it. As far back as February 1849 there had been a proposal to construct a joint L&T and GN low level station on half the land. In October Joseph Cubitt was instructed to prepare plans for a low level station for GN passengers and goods. On 7 March 1850 the contract for building the station was let to Wilks, Winn & Pawson for £759. An engine shed was also required. A turntable was supplied by James Lister of Darlington. Notice was given to the Central Station board that the GN did not intend to use the high level station after 1 May 1850, but it was not until Tuesday 14 May that the low level station opened. In giving his report Denniston stated that 20 yd of the railway at 300 yd from the station was single line. The GN paid the L&T £10,000 for perpetual rights to run over the short piece of line at Leeds.

The L&Y enquired whether the GN was prepared to carry its own goods traffic between Doncaster and Leeds after 30 June 1850, as it had received notice from the Midland to relinquish occupation of two bays of the goods warehouse at Hunslet Lane on that date. A reply was sent requesting the L & Y to make arrangements with the Midland for use of the two bays until Christmas, as the GN was not prepared to dispense with them, and stating that it would work its own goods traffic into Leeds as from 1 July. In the following month arrangements were made to cart merchandise from Leeds to Bradford at 7s (35p) a ton or send it by canal at 3s (15p) a ton. At a cost of £27 a week a contract was made with Joseph Baxter of Bradford to run omnibuses to Leeds in connection with GN trains.

The SY opened its line between Doncaster and a junction with the Midland at Swinton on Saturday 10 November 1849. It formed two junctions with the GN, one facing northwards at St James's junction where it joined a spur from the GN at South Yorkshire junction, with a second spur from the GN at Balby Bridge to the other SY fork at Balby junction, sanctioned by the SY Act of 22 July 1848. The SY started with little plant, only a few engines and no rolling stock. The Midland operated the passenger service between Sheffield (Wicker) and Doncaster, four trains each way on weekdays, the SY board not consenting to Sunday trains until later on. The GN supplied coal wagons, and, next year, the SY constructed sidings at Doncaster for their standage.

On 1 September 1849 there was an agreement securing to the SY, for £10,000 paid to the GN, use of ¾ mile of line out of Doncaster. The GN agreed to sell half the Axholme Extension line from Askern to Crowle, the SY to construct the line, pay 5% of the Parliamentary expenses, and give the GN perpetual running powers over it. The Midland arranged to pay £450 per annum for use of Doncaster station by an agreement of 3 November. There was a further agreement with the SY in June 1850 which provided that the GN should work the SY with its own engines and wagons and pay it a fixed sum of 10d per ton (of 20 cwt) from the collieries to Doncaster whatever the distance, the collieries being Moorend near Silkstone, Barnsley, Worsborough and Elsecar. Charles Bartholomew, engineer to the SY, was to act as GN agent. The agreement was to last for a year, then terminable by six months' notice.

With the opening of the SY to Barnsley on 1 January 1851 the GN commenced a passenger service between Doncaster and Barnsley, four trains each way on weekdays only. An arrangement was made with the L & Y whereby the GN worked coal trains from Horbury to Barnsley and thence over the SY to Doncaster.

Two proposals were made in 1849 for economising in the cost of the main line. In January a committee for diminishing costs suggested that the terminus should be built north of the Regent's Canal and thus save between £300,000 and £400,000. Joseph Cubitt was instructed to prepare plans, but it appears that the Cubitts, in collusion with some directors who were determined on all the glories of King's Cross on its original site, conveniently neglected to draw the plans. When the subject next came up it was deftly turned into a discussion upon the site of a temporary station. William Cubitt recommended that it should be as near King's Cross as possible without impeding the works for the permanent site. The site chosen was immediately over the intended Maiden Lane tunnel, and Jay was instructed in September to proceed with 250 yd of the tunnel. The method selected by Jay was 'cut and cover', construction of the aqueduct to carry the Regent's Canal over the tunnel not being commenced until April 1851.

In the autumn there was a proposal to purchase the EC station at Peterborough and utilise 6½ miles of the Midland's Syston to Peterborough branch. Officers were sent to inspect the station and report as to how it could be adapted to suit GN purposes, but the EC declined to transfer it although it was willing to afford accommodation. By December the board resolved to proceed with its own line and station at Peterborough. Petos were awarded a fresh contract which commenced at the seventy-fourth mile and extended to Walton junction.

In February 1849 the work on Brassey's contract was speeded up. Boring the tunnels up to this time had remained in abeyance, but £50,000 a month was now to be spent on construction. By September the board had come to the conclusion that it could no longer delay getting on with construction of the remainder of the Towns lines. A contract was let to Thomas Jackson of Pimlico for the Corby-Hougham section (for the sum of £229,883), which included the heaviest engineering work, involving deep cuttings and boring of Stoke and Peascliffe tunnels. Jackson broke ground at the end of January 1850.

There were two applicants for the post of architect for the stations from London to Peterborough. The work was divided, Lewis Cubitt of 52 Bedford Square being appointed architect for the London temporary passenger station and the permanent goods station, while Henry Goddard of Lincoln was appointed for the other stations, and the hotel at Peterborough. In addition to the passenger and goods stations, Lewis Cubitt also designed the engine shed, carriage shed, granary, offices, etc. Jay secured the contract for the London buildings, and Brassey's tender for the intermediate stations was accepted. The station and hotel at

Peterborough formed the subject of a separate contract, let to F. W. Costar, it being deemed that the work should be undertaken by someone who was on amicable terms with Petos.

Early in 1849 Bury was called upon to explain the delivery of goods and stores from various firms; he had been authorised to order stores without requisition up to £500 and had apparently well exceeded this limit. Later in the year a series of minor accidents appeared to reflect upon Bury's capabilities as locomotive engineer and as superintendent, although many of them could be attributed to the inexperience of the staff. Two of these occurred in November, at Firsby on 27 and at Claythorpe on 30 November. In December there was one near Doncaster on the 3rd, at Spalding on the 4th, and at Boston on the 10th. The Doncaster accident took place at Chadwick Brick Yard, 'a siding built without authority'. A coal wagon had been detached from a L & Y goods train. While the driver, fireman and guard were pushing it into the siding a GN passenger train collided with other wagons, and derailed some into the path of a goods train, approaching on the opposite line. A third collision took place, when a light engine, sent to fetch Denniston, ran into the engine of the breakdown train. Another rash of minor accidents broke out in January, at Lincoln, on the 9th, Bardney on the 11th, Boston on the 14th, Doncaster on the 16th, Legbourne on the 18th, Bawtry on the 22nd, Shaftholme (south of Askern, the site of the later junction; see vol. II) on the 23rd when a train ran through the gates, and Spalding on the 31st.

During the same month Fox of Fox Henderson complained that although his tender was lower he did not get the business for wheels and axles, the award being given to Burys, and Vernons. He went on to allege that in fact Burys supplied to Vernons the goods they in turn supplied to the GN. He was asked to put his allegations in writing and it was arranged that Fox's letters and all papers in the case should be laid before the board on 17 January. Things were looking black for Bury. On 18 February he wrote resigning his position as locomotive superintendent and general manager. His resignation was accepted and it was agreed to pay his salary up to 31 March. He appeared reluctant to leave and a letter was sent on 8 March requesting him to go. Instructions were sent to the principal officers that from the date of Bury's departure they were each to be held responsible for their own departments and that they were to report weekly to the secretary for the directors' information.

The Cubitts were ready once again and Joseph proposed that E. B. Wilson & Co of Leeds should work the traffic. The conditions were that the GN should transfer its stock and plant at a valuation, the contractors to find tools and stores, and the company to provide engine sheds and offices. However the influence of the Cubitts was waning and the company had already advertised the post of locomotive engineer at £500 per annum. There were 41 applicants for the position. From these a short list of four was selected, George Harrison, F. H. Trevithick, Archibald Sturrock and John Dewrance. Although the other three were, or had been, locomotive superintendents to other railways, Sturrock was the successful candidate and was appointed on 27 March. The young Scotsman, only 34, had served on the GWR under Daniel Gooch for over ten years, and was works manager at Swindon. The board received word that Sturrock would be travelling down the line on Wednesday 24 April. The secretary was instructed to accompany him to Boston where he would be installed in his position. Minutes do not reveal how he travelled as far as Peterborough. It is just possible that the works were sufficiently advanced for him to travel over the GN, for the directors had been able to inspect them on Thursday 27 March. The company also advertised for a general manager. Again selection fell on a GW man, Seymour Clarke, then London traffic manager at Paddington. Engaged on 14 May at £900 per annum, he took up his duties soon afterwards.

Three directors resigned in February and their number was increased to 17 by the election of Graham Hutchinson of Glasgow, Charles Atticus Monck of Newcastle, Isaac Burkill of Leeds, and George Humphrys of Eardisley.

The Y&NM, who expected to have its Knottingley branch in use on 1 March 1850, and the YN&B, in January, were urging the GN to make arrangements with the EC to run GN expresses in both directions between Shoreditch and York when the line was opened. The next preference to this vital link was in a letter dated 13 April from the Y&NM, stating that the Commissioners had sanctioned opening of the Knottingley branch, subject to a pilotman being provided over the single line. At that time the Aire was crossed at Brotherton by a temporary bridge and it was the single line over this bridge to which the Commissioners referred. An arrangement was made early in May for running a goods, dead meat and cattle train between Edinburgh and London over the NB, YN&B, Y&NM, GN and EC. The train left Edinburgh at 3.0 p.m. and was allowed 32½ hours for the journey including some lengthy stops. This allowed for the meat to be pitched into the London market (then at Newgate) by 2.0 a.m.

Provided that the GN was willing to give up its own line to York, the Y&NM was prepared to provide running powers on the following terms. The GN was to run from Knottingley to York paying 60% of gross receipts, and £1,000 a year for station accommodation including all services except booking clerks. An agreement on these terms was signed on 6 June 1850. The directors were not unanimous. Graham Hutchinson, supported by some north country shareholders, protested against any arrangement with the Y&NM, implying abandonment or unnecessary delay in construction of 26 miles of GN from Askern to York, arguing that these could be constructed and maintained so cheaply as to leave a large profit beyond paying 6%. As the distance to Edinburgh would thus be 3½ miles less than by the west coast route instead of exactly the same, he was of the opinion that the GN would receive considerable advantage, including carriage of mails, and considered that it would be in the interests of the Y&NM, Y&NB, and NB, to act harmoniously with the GN, and resist offers by Euston Square. The majority of the directors supported their chairman in his view that the small amount of capital remaining unexpended was already earmarked for other essential purposes, and that it would not be prudent to raise fresh capital for construction of the York line. They, especially Alderman Meek of York, besides Denison himself, thought it was highly desirable to cultivate the friendship of the Y & N M, and the Y & N B, and not antagonise them by building a separate station at York. In the following January, Baxter advised the 'quiet and judicious' cancellation of engagements with the landowners between Selby and York. Despite the threat of a 'Mandamus' in the Queen's Bench in July 1851, the line was never built by the GN.

Early in May 1850 the GN believed that the Commissioners had sanctioned opening of the Leverton branch for passengers, and asked the MS&L and the Commissioners if this was so. James Allport, manager of the MS&L, had intimated that he would bring the branch into use for goods on 28 January. His company held running powers over the GN from Sykes Junction to Lincoln in return for GN powers from Retford to Sheffield. The GN had intended to use the Leverton branch from Monday 1 July 1850, and had named that day in timetables. However the MS&L blocked its lines with trucks, set up red flags, and got men to lie across the metals, so the GN had to continue to send its traffic round via Gainsborough. At the end of the month came a notice from the MS&L that it would run from Sheffield to the GN station at Lincoln on 1 August. In return the GN advised the MS&L that it would run passenger trains between Lincoln and Sheffield commencing 7 August. This latter date is the one which is accepted as that for the opening of the Leverton branch for passengers, so it is likely that the two companies commenced their services simultaneously. Plans for an engine shed at

Lincoln were approved in August, and two months later it was resolved to erect another on GN ground at Retford. The MS & L paid £500 a year rent for the use of Lincoln station, while the GN paid £650 per annum for use of Grimsby and Gainsborough.

Relations with the MS & L were deteriorating, as its officers refused to allow GN engines to take water at Retford, and were obstructing GN trains at Grimsby, despite agreements of 7 April and 13 May 1848. Thus in August it was resolved to take Chancery proceedings. On 16 December 1851 Vice-Chancellor Parker granted an injunction against the MS&L by which the rights of using the line to New Holland were secured to the GN. This was a hollow victory, for it does not appear that through running was resumed, as the GN failed to get a running power clause inserted in one of its Acts. Meantime, MS&L engines ceased to work through to Louth from 8 July 1851, and on 18 October, Allport wrote that after 1 November all traffic between Grimsby and New Holland would be worked by MS&L engines and servants, and all passengers from Hull would have to book at his company's office there. These arrangements were subsequently deferred until 1 December. The GN had acquired offices and a warehouse in Hull in 1849. In October 1850, Clarke made an agreement with James Audus of Selby for employment of a steam packet to convey goods between Grimsby and Hull.

Advertisements inviting tenders for construction of the remainder of the Towns line were issued in April 1850. The Helpstone Corby contract went to Warren & Denroche of Cardiff for £87,000. Elisha Wright Oldham of Poppleton, York, was successful with his tenders of £39,000 and £73,000 for Hougham to Newark, and the Trent to Retford respectively. The tenders were low, and the GN made enquiries about the standing and competence of these firms. Warren & Denroche had miscalculated their tender, and on 4 June the Helpstone to Corby contract was let to Pearce & Smith who quoted £97,800. The contract for works at the Trent, which included diversion of the river, remained in abeyance until 3 December when it was awarded to Rennie & Logan of Newport, Mon., for £16,925. The two final contracts were let in 1851, Pearce & Smith undertaking Werrington junction–Helpstone for £7,615 on 4 March, and Fox, Henderson & Co the wrought iron bridge to cross the Newark Dyke on 27 May, the price being £9,748.

In May 1850 Baxter called attention to subtraction of traffic, and damage caused to the banks, by steamers on the Witham. Sturrock was told to convert six cattle wagons into passenger vehicles without seats. This was done at a cost of £7 10s 0d (£7.50) per wagon. While at first they were labelled 'wagons', it was considered prudent to paint this word out. One or more were attached to the slower trains between Boston and Lincoln, at a fare for the 'fourth class' of ½d a mile. It was hoped by this competition to drive the boats off the water, but it was 11 years before competition on the river ceased, and it was not until 1 August 1863 that fourth class fares were withdrawn. To be fair to Bury, it must be recorded that in 1849 he had proposed an inferior class to compete with the steamers.

Although Boston works had been extended by the addition of repair shops for wagons and carriages, it had still not been decided where the permanent works should be. In August 1846 the board had received a memorial from the mayor and inhabitants of Doncaster praying for the establishment of the 'Plant and Workshops' of the GN there. Two months later the townsfolk of Huntingdon (supported by Godmanchester) requested that the repairing station should be at Huntingdon. Grantham was another town which petitioned for the works to be located there. As we know, Bury had drawn up plans for works at Doncaster. Sturrock, however, favoured Peterborough, which he regarded as a central point, more or less midway between London and Yorkshire, and close to the junction with the Lincolnshire lines. He considered that almost every engine would visit Peterborough often enough for him to keep his watchful eye on them. He argued that all engines could work a train in either direction when they visited repair shops at Peterborough, whereas if the works were at one end of the line, considerable light mileage would be incurred. Surely he must have regarded Peterborough in the light of a Swindon. He went on to list the proposed allocation of the stud of engines, given as follows: 10 at York, 6 at Leeds, 49 at Doncaster, 2 at Lincoln, 8 at Grimsby, 14 at Boston, 32 in London, 58 at Peterborough with another 62 undergoing repairs there in the works. He almost succeeded in persuading the directors, for on 27 August it was resolved to purchase 28 acres of land, and to obtain estimates for a works at Peterborough. Behind the scenes, other counsels must have prevailed, for on 3 June 1851, Doncaster was definitely selected for the new shops.

The winter of 1849/50 produced exceptionally bad weather which held up some works between London and Peterborough. On 6 January a slip of earth at Yaxley cutting, near Peterborough carried away one of the piers of the bridge over the cutting and caused the fall of four of the five arches. Brassey encountered considerable difficulty in laying his line over the soft undrained fens north of Huntingdon, and engaged the services of Stephen Ballard, a young engineer who had experience of the fen country. Ballard devised the system of sinking alternate layers of faggots and peat and forcing out the surplus water by gradually increasing the weight, and in this way, secured a solid foundation for the permanent way. Jay's task in London was complicated by simultaneous construction of the East & West India Docks & Birmingham Junction, which passed overhead by a viaduct at Belle Isle. Some delay was caused in 1850 when one of the arches of this collapsed.

The complete line, as laid out by William Cubitt, had a ruling gradient of 1 in 200, but due to it passing just under the Regent's Canal he had to tolerate a rise of 1 in 108 from the future terminus to level at Holloway. Thence the formation undulated until at 4½ miles a rise of 1 in 200 was encountered, which continued unbroken to a summit at Potters Bar, where the line fell with stretches of 1 in 200 till beyond Hatfield. Another rise of 1 in 200 took the line up to Welwyn viaduct, and after a brief level, the same gradient continued to the north end of Harmer Green (later Welwyn North) tunnel. Apart from a slight hump at Stevenage it was now downhill practically all the way to the valley of the Ouse, with a long stretch of 1 in 200 through Hitchin. Beyond Huntingdon a rise of 3 miles at 1 in 200 gave way to a descent of nearly 6 miles at the same gradient followed by a level section through Holme. There was one more sharp rise before Yaxley, and then the final stretch through Peterborough to Walton junction had easier grades.

The line was inspected by Captain Wynne who was well satisfied with the state of the works. As there were about 250 bridges and culverts it is not surprising that he confined his remarks to the most important engineering features, eight tunnels and two large viaducts. The tunnels, in order from London, were Copenhagen (594 yd), Tottenham (705 yd), East Barnet (605 yd), South Enfield (384 yd), North Enfield (232 yd), South Mimms (1,214 yd), Locksley Hill or Digswell (446 yd), and Harmer Green (1,046 yd). The last two were driven through chalk but all the others passed through clay. With the exception of Copenhagen, these names have all changed over the years and latterly were more familiarly known as Wood Green, Barnet, Hadley South, Hadley North, Potters Bar, Welwyn South and Welwyn North in the same order. The magnificent viaduct at Welwyn (often known as Digswell) a lasting memorial to the skill of Brassey, was 1,490 ft long and 89 ft high at its highest point. Built of brick, it consisted of 40 arches each with a span of 30 ft. The viaduct over the Nene near Peterborough had three arches of cast iron with spans of 66 ft over the river, flanked by 12 brick arches at the south end, and three more at the north end, which crossed the EC and Midland. The line, double, with similar materials to those used on the earlier lines, measured 79 miles 34 chains from Maiden Lane to Walton junction.

The line emerged into open country on leaving Copenhagen tunnel. It was originally intended that the first two stations should be Barnet and Hatfield, with others at Welwyn, Stevenage, Hitchin, Arlsey, Biggleswade, St Neots, Huntingdon, Holme and Peterborough. Colney Hatch was added in order to serve the new lunatic asylum, and Sandy as the nearest point to Bedford. Although the inhabitants of Hornsey had petitioned against a station, this was put on the list, as were Potters Bar and Offord. Completion of Offord was delayed owing to a dispute with the Ouse Navigation. It first appeared in Bradshaw in September 1851, and had a siding, for a Mr Bowyer, who was in business in a large way. Arlsey station was called Arlsey & Shefford Road. Refreshment rooms were provided at Hitchin and Peterborough, where there was the Great Northern hotel. The Holloway ticket platform was first mentioned in August 1852. A payment to Brassey in December appears to have been in settlement of his account for its erection. Ticket platforms were also provided in the 1850s at Peterborough, Boston, Lincoln and Doncaster.

Colney Hatch was originally intended to be called Betstile, the earlier name of the locality. It was at first called Colney Hatch & Southgate, and later, Southgate & Colney Hatch, according to Bradshaw in January 1855 and the company's timetable in June 1856. Nevertheless the station and locality were often referred to as Southgate in GN records. Even after the name was altered to New Southgate several years later, handbills advertising alterations in the local services were issued which named the station as Southgate. The asylum authorities manufactured their own gas, and for many years supplied the station with gas, and water, and were one of the earliest GN coal customers.

The London engine shed had been re-designed by Bury and was not completed when the line was opened, engines being temporarily put under cover in the goods shed. The first locomotive foreman here, John Budge, aged 35, who had served on the GW, was appointed as from 23 July 1850 at a salary of £170 per annum, and remained in charge of the district until he retired. There were also engine sheds at Hitchin and Peterborough, the temporary shed at Walton junction being removed to Boston yard early in 1851.

On Monday 5 August 1850 the directors and guests totalling about 400 passengers boarded a train at Maiden Lane station, and set off to view the line to Peterborough. Passes had been issued to representatives of the London and local press. The train, 17 carriages drawn by two engines, left at 9.0 a.m. Hornsey was passed, but the train stopped at Southgate where the 'large and handsome' lunatic asylum was admired. Halts were made at most of the principal stations. A lengthy stop was made at Welwyn to enable passengers to descend to the Mimram valley and obtain a good view of 'the splendid viaduct'. Peterborough was reached just after 1.30 p.m., where the party was entertained by Brassey, who observed in his speech that this was the 'most perfect line he had ever opened'. There were no free passes for shareholders, the directors ruling that it would be invidious to make a selection.

Public opening took place on the following Wednesday, without any celebrations. Passenger traffic only was dealt with at first, eight trains in and out of Maiden Lane on weekdays and three on Sundays. The best time to Peterborough was about 2½ hours.

On 8 August, GN trains first began to run to York, now a distance of 210 miles from Maiden Lane. It is convenient to distinguish the temporary terminus as Maiden Lane, but the company referred to it as King's Cross. The station was put in charge of John Carruthers, formerly stationmaster at Louth, who was appointed Station Inspector.

The Y&NM promised to turn all possible traffic on to the GN, and provided a ticket office for GN use in the centre of its own office at York. The GN made arrangements for bookings to London from Wakefield, Pontefract, and Knottingley, also for collection and delivery of goods independent of the L&Y. The general manager reported that he had arranged excursion trains with the Y&NM, and other companies, at about 25% less than one double fare, which was approved, but not at less than one single fare.

An improved timetable appeared on 2 September. The 7.40 a.m. from Maiden Lane gave a through service to Edinburgh in 12 hours. On the route worked by the GN, the train stopped at Hatfield, Hitchin, Biggleswade, Huntingdon, Peterborough (2½ hours from London), Spalding, Boston, Kirkstead, Lincoln, Retford, Doncaster, Knottingley, Milford Junction (connection to Hull), and Church Fenton (connection for Harrogate) reaching York in 7 hr 10 m. Two trains leaving at 10.30 a.m. and 6.0 p.m. had Leeds and York portions. The latter was slightly faster than the 7.40 a.m. between Peterborough and Doncaster. The distance to Leeds was 206 miles, the same as by the competing LNW–Midland route from Euston. Only a 6.0 a.m. 'parliamentary' train, stopping at all stations, conveyed third class passengers.

Another fast train at this stage was the night mail to New Holland for Hull. This still started at Shoreditch, EC, and was handed to the GN at Peterborough, which it left at 1.43 a.m., and reached New Holland, with five stops, at 4.55 a.m.

The 7.40 a.m. from Maiden Lane was soon accelerated to run nonstop to Hitchin, about 31⅓ miles in 42 mins—45 mph, a very good speed for those days.

Throughout its history the Doncaster St Leger race meeting was the most important event in the GN calendar. A special train for the races was run from London at 10.45 a.m. on Monday 16 September. A blow was dealt to GN prestige when it arrived at Doncaster nearly 2½ hours behind time. It was a sorry tale of incompetence. Driver Moon and his mate lost time to Boston in consequence of their engine not getting steam, although Sturrock afterwards asserted that it was in perfect order. A pilot, attached at Peterborough, had a 'green' fire, and further delay took place. At Boston the engines were replaced by engines 57 and 15, although neither of them were fit to work an express, for 57 had taken in bad water, and 15 was new out of shops and required 'running in'. Finally the passenger pilot at Lincoln, which should have replaced No. 15, had been sent away by the station master to shunt, contrary to orders. A special train to Doncaster was booked for 18 September, St Leger day, and orders were hastily given that it should be divided if necessary. The conclusion was drawn that 5 hours was insufficient for a heavy train.

Goods traffic was advertised to commence from London on 18 November, but had to be postponed for lack of engine power. Merchandise actually began to be carried on 12 December. On 16 October, Edward Sherman of the Bull & Mouth, St Martin-le-Grand, proposed a permanent office there and to collect and deliver merchandise for the GN, when goods services began. With the board's authority, Seymour Clarke agreed to this. Two days later Clarke made a contract for collection and delivery of goods at Leeds with William Holland, who had been a company's servant, and had resigned to go into business on his own behalf. A contract was arranged with W. H. Smith (the famous firm), who agreed to pay £500 a year for the privilege of selling newspapers, and also secured advertising rights at the stations.

A letter arrived on 1 October from the R&H, enclosing Board of Trade sanction for opening, provided that strong fixed buffers were put up at Royston temporary terminus. It was resolved that Joseph Cubitt should take charge of the Shepreth extension and complete it as soon as possible, making arrangements with Locke who was engineer to the R&H.

The 12¾ miles from Hitchin junction to Royston were opened on 21 October 1850. The route was hilly. Soon after leaving Hitchin, there was a fall on 1 in 200 for about ½ mile followed by a rise of 1 in 161 for 1½ miles. The line then fell at 1 in 244 to the level through Baldock station. Beyond, the line climbed at 1 in 197 for 1½ miles, and then undulated slightly to another level through the only other intermediate station at Ashwell. Thence it was downhill to Royston at 1 in 183, 1 in 142, and finally 1 in 163, to another short level formation. Beyond Royston the line (under construction) fell at 1 in 175, 1 in 120, and 1 in 100 until it levelled out approaching the future terminus at Shepreth. The line served a purely agricultural district, but a connecting bus service ran between Royston and Cambridge. The Newmarket Railway (from there to Great Chesterford, south of Cambridge) was having one of its numerous disputes with the EC, and proposed an extension to Royston to join the R&H there. If this had come about, the GN might have had, at an early date, what it long desired, and obtained many years later, a route into East Anglia, but nothing came of it.

The extension of 5 miles 4 chains to Shepreth was brought into use on 3 August 1851, with one intermediate station at Meldreth. A turntable, an engine shed and carriage shed were provided at the terminus. The line and stations were built by Brassey, double track, laid with 72 lb rails. The sleepers were 'Payanised' (sic) Scotch fir, 10 in by 5 in, and the ballast consisted of chalk and light gravel. All bridges were brick. The omnibus service to Cambridge now plied to and from Shepreth. Other omnibuses provided feeder services to various stations. Early examples were Hatfield–Luton, Hatfield–St Albans, Colney Hatch–Finchley, and Colney Hatch–Southgate.

The smaller stations on all lines so far opened were spartan affairs, almost devoid of shelter, with primitive sanitary arrangements. There was not a single footbridge on the system. In early years it almost always took the recommendation of a coroner's jury to jolt the directors into providing them at stations, and busy level crossings. Some stations including Colney Hatch, Barnet and Biggleswade had staggered platforms.

Third class carriages were run only in Parliamentary trains. The principal express was first class only, while others conveyed first and second class. The carriages of all classes attracted favourable notice, especially the thirds, said to be as good as seconds on some other lines. (The carriages are more fully described in chapter XIV.) Company's servants were not allowed to accept gratuities. There were instances of dismissal for pocketing 3d tips. On the other hand honesty was encouraged. With the directors' approval, servants were allowed to accept rewards for finding and returning of valuables. Finders of money not claimed were allowed to retain a proportion, the balance going to a provident fund. From November 1850 a general order prohibited sale of spirits in refreshment rooms to company officers and servants. With the exception of those employed in the locomotive and engineering departments, all servants were interviewed and engaged (and sacked) by the directors. The appointment of John Budge was a rare exception to this.

The MS&L was encouraged in its recent anti-GN activities by the influence of Captain Mark Huish. Since the eclipse of Hudson, a new star had arisen to dominate the railway scene, in the person of Huish. One time general manager of the GJ, he had been appointed general manager to the L&NW, on its formation in 1846. With his chairman, George Carr Glynn, immersed in banking affairs, Huish probably wielded more power than his contemporaries. Besides being an expert administrator, he was dedicated to preserving the monopolies his company enjoyed, and was prepared to crush all opposition by fair means or foul. He was undoubtedly the most skilful and ruthless of all railway diplomats.

Opening of the GN's alternative route from London to Yorkshire and the north had already broken some of the monopolies which the L&NW held. The junction at Retford threatened a possible GN invasion of Lancashire via the MS&L's main line. When the Towns line was completed, the GN would provide the shortest route to a number of principal towns and industrial areas, and in consequence could offer lower rates and fares, which would attract traders and travellers. Since Hudson's departure, the Midland had become somewhat dependent on the L&NW. These two had been joined by the L&Y in a traffic pooling arrangement, concocted by Huish, with the object of denying through traffic to the MS&L, as it struggled to expand. The new circumstances, occasioned by the rise of the GN, forced Huish to change tactics, and woo the MS&L. With the offer of a division of goods traffic, he succeeded in persuading that penurious company that an alliance with Euston Square would be to its immediate and greater advantage than any benefits which future friendship with the GN might offer. Thus was born the Euston Square Confederacy, as the alliance of the four companies was soon nicknamed, whose object was strangling the infant GN. The confederates refused all facilities for exchange of competitive traffic, so the GN was practically confined to working traffic over the rails it owned or leased. Even the EC had been encouraged to exchange traffic at Peterborough with the Midland in preference to the GN. Although hemmed in to the west and to a lesser extent in the east, the GN was at least in communication with Edinburgh, but beyond, the key to Glasgow, Perth and Aberdeen was held by the Edinburgh & Glasgow, at that time allied to Euston Square.

Representatives of eight railways met at Normanton on 2 August 1850 to discuss competition for Scotch traffic. The companies were the L&NW, L&C, Caledonian, GN, Midland, Y&NM, YN&B, and NB. The outcome of this and subsequent meetings was that proposals were drawn up to divide the traffic between London and places north of York. The GN received an inadequate share of the traffic between York and Edinburgh, and no share beyond, but having not yet got thoroughly established, was not in a position to become involved in a contest. It was with the greatest reluctance that Denison consented to the GN becoming a party to this Octuple Agreement, which came into force on 1 January 1851, and was limited to a period of five years.

Soon afterwards, on 18 February, Clarke drew the attention of his directors to the unsatisfactory state of traffic arrangements with the Midland and the L&NW, and suggested a similar pooling of competitive traffic to York and some towns south thereof. Negotiations were commenced with a joint committee of the Midland & LNW general managers, the GN naming the percentages to which it felt it was entitled for traffic to York, Doncaster, Lincoln, Leeds, Sheffield and Wakefield. To these figures the joint committee was unable to agree and named others, likewise unacceptable to the GN. By common consent Mr Gladstone, lately President of the Board of Trade (and future Prime Minister), was chosen to arbitrate in the matter.

This was the year of the Great Exhibition, to be opened on 1 May. Harmony between the companies in view of the heavy traffic anticipated was especially needed. However the talks were soon brought to a standstill, for the joint committee declined to proceed with the arbitration unless the GN abstained from competition in fares to Bradford and other places not contemplated by reference. To this the GN refused to accede, unless Euston Square would abandon articles of treaty with other companies which precluded interchange of traffic with the GN. The joint committee reduced fares from Normanton from 15s to 10s, whereupon the GN retaliated by lowering the Knottingley fare to the same standard. At this point the Midland and GN chairmen proposed equal passenger fares, but were overridden by the L&NW.

Cheap excursions for the Exhibition commenced on 2 June. At first equal fares from competitive towns were advertised, but after a fortnight, a rate war set in and fares rapidly and progressively cheapened. Another meeting was held before Gladstone on 19 July, but the joint committee still declined to proceed with the arbitration as it stood. On the same day they reduced the fare from Leeds. The GN followed suit and in a few days the fare had shrunk to 5s (25p). At the end of the month the GN advertised a Leeds to London excursion with a third class return fare of 4s 6d (22½p). The train was timed to leave Leeds at 10.15 a.m. and arrive at Maiden Lane at 7.30 p.m. Still the joint committee refused to restore trains and fares to ordinary standards unless the GN either joined in a reference for division of territory, or abstained from competition at lower fares from places where it was shut out by L & N W and Midland treaties with other companies. The GN board decided that it was impractical to make a territorial agreement until the whole of its system was open.

Nevertheless, hostilities cooled off sufficiently for Gladstone to continue his deliberations. Shortly afterwards, on 26 August, he announced his award, with separate percentages for passenger and goods traffic. The award was fairly satisfactory to the GN at that time, for the percentages set out below were in the aggregate slightly higher than those to which the company felt it was entitled (indicated in parenthesis):

	Passenger		*Goods*	
York	(80%)	80%	(66%)	75%
Doncaster	(85%)	95%	(85%)	90%
Lincoln	(85%)	85%	(75%)	70%
Leeds	(66%)	65%	(50%)	35%
Sheffield	(66%)	60%	(50%)	30%
Wakefield	(66%)	75%	(50%)	60%

The award was back-dated to 4 April 1851 and was to remain in force until 1 January 1856. Students of railway history will have observed that almost before the ink was dry, companies which signed agreements were often looking round for means to circumvent them. Thus the joint committee adopted the expedient of keeping their fares low to intermediate stations and encouraging passengers to re-book. The result was that discerning travellers soon found that they could journey to one of the six towns named at a lower fare than that charged by the GN, and the receipts obtained by this artifice were taken out of the pool. The GN had printed bills advertising the St Leger with first class fares at £2 6s (£2.30) and second class at £1 11s (£1.55). Almost immediately its rivals stated they would run to Doncaster on 15 September (St Leger day) at £1 and 10s (50p). Such competition was sheer malice, for by the Gladstone Award, the joint committee would be entitled to retain but 5% of the receipts, and out of this they would have to pay the SY toll over its line from Swinton to Doncaster. Following further reference to Gladstone by the GN, the terms of the award were amended to prevent evasion by the rebooking artifice.

To revert to the Exhibition, despite the low fares the volume of passengers during the season was so heavy that the receipts were highly satisfactory. The GN had withdrawn from competition for excursion passengers from Sheffield, for the toll due to the MS&L more than swallowed the fare, which had been cut to 5s (25p). So far, the GN had not installed the electric telegraph. Consequently, running the excursions was chaotic, for the authorities in London could never be sure of the extent of the traffic with which they would have to cope, or when the trains would arrive. Officers and servants received from three to five days leave and free travel in order that they and their families might have opportunities of visiting the Exhibition. E. B. Denison, when attending it, was attracted by the great clock made by Frederick Dent of the Strand, and was struck by its suitability for use at King's Cross station. Having contacted the maker, he wrote to his father, suggesting that the GN should buy the clock when the exhibition closed, and install it in the tower at the terminus at the price of £200 exclusive of the three new 9 ft dials which would be necessary. Within a few days Mowatt was instructed to write to Dent and accept the terms for purchase of the clock. In connection with his duties as one of the Commissioners of the Exhibition, William Cubitt received a knighthood.

In early days of operation, the GN was bedevilled by some minor accidents, caused by failure of various component parts of rolling stock. At one period it would be tyres, at another axles, at another wheels and so on. Each led to the use of safer and more durable materials. Cast iron wheels were responsible for two accidents in February 1851. First a broken wheel threw three trucks of a cattle train off the road near Colney Hatch. Within three weeks a similar failure caused an accident at Water Orton (near Birmingham) on the Midland, who held the GN responsible. The truck was new, built by Adams of Birmingham, and was being delivered to Boston. The wheels were manufactured by Rayne & Burn of Newcastle and had been supplied to Adams by the GN. The decision was taken immediately to substitute wrought iron wheels for unreliable cast iron.

Other measures designed to increase safety, taken about this time, included provision of red side lights on brake vans, and fitting of lamp irons on all coaching stock in order that tail lamps could be properly displayed on the rear vehicle, in practice not always a brake van. Side lights on brake vans showed a white light forward which enabled the driver to be sure that his train was complete. Nevertheless, generally speaking, the GN provided steady and punctual running, and there were no serious accidents at this period. Also, Clarke insisted on civility and good attention by all members of the working staff. The GN, indeed, soon was regarded as the popular line to the north.

In June, Sturrock wrote to the board explaining that his engines had to run tender-first in one direction between Leeds and Wakefield, Royston and Hitchin, and Gainsborough and Lincoln because there were no turntables at Knottingley and Royston, and the one at Lincoln was not large enough. The same applied between Louth and Grimsby, where there was no suitable turntable. In Sturrock's view the practice was dangerous. The board concurred, for Clarke was required to report at which stations turntables capable of turning engines and tenders should be provided. Meantime, it was ordered that all tenders should be fitted with 'lifeguards'. The recommendation that 40 ft tables should be provided at Hitchin, Lincoln and Knottingley, and 16 ft turntables at Hatfield, Biggleswade, Huntingdon, St Ives and Shepreth was approved. The 40 ft turntable was moved from Louth to Grimsby.

Next Sturrock drew attention to siting of distant signals. He considered that on gradients as severe as 1 in 200, or on curves, these should be placed 1,000 or 1,200 yards in advance of stop signals to allow coal trains at 20 mph or heavy passenger trains at 45 mph to be brought to a stand in safety. He also said that the distant signal at Colney Hatch needed raising, and reminded the board that Clarborough tunnel on the MS&L near Retford was still not signalled. He called for provision of carriage sheds at Peterborough, Barnet, Hatfield and Doncaster, and extra accommodation at Boston. He requested cover for the one or two engines stationed at Sheffield. Allport was agreeable to the provision of this, but demanded the exorbitant annual rental of 10% on the outlay. The matter was deferred.

Soon after his appointment, Sturrock suggested that enginemen should be paid premiums for economy in consumption of fuel below a stated average. His recommendation was approved and thus Sturrock was responsible for the nickname of 'starvers' for six-coupled saddle tanks, which worked the south London coal traffic in more recent years. To qualify for substantial premiums, it was the practice of drivers and firemen to transfer coal from trucks behind them to the engine bunkers. When carried to extreme, some of the engines appeared to be burning so little fuel that it was said that they were 'starved', hence the term 'starvers'. Farringdon Street station platform was a favourite and convenient place for coal to be 'won'. Other engines in earlier days must also have been 'starved', for Clarke was soon complaining of pilferage of coal and coke by enginemen. Although Sturrock defended his men the edict went forth that under no circumstances must coal or coke from trucks be used in the engines.

Early in December 1850 Henry Fowler resigned, as he had obtained a position in India. W. M. Brydone was appointed Resident Engineer in his stead at £500 per annum. Mowatt's salary was further reduced to £600 in March 1850 while P. M. Middlemiss, the coal superintendent at Doncaster, had his pay raised from £150 to £250 on the following New Year's day. During the next six months there was a general review of salaries and from 1 July 1851 many officers received a rise in salary:

Secretary	from £600	to £800
General Manager	£900	£1200
Locomotive Engineer	£500	£900
Superintendent of the Line	£500	£600
Goods Manager	£400	£500
Accountant	£500	£700
Storekeeper	£300	£400
Inspector at King's Cross	£100	£140
Inspector of Police	£100	£140

Sturrock also received a present of £200 for supervising the carriage department during the previous 12 months.

Stations were divided into five classes, and salaries of the clerks in charge were fixed according to the class. However the most important arrangement resolved by the board and ratified by the proprietors, was a system of bonuses. The minute was as follows, 'That to induce the best exertions on the part of the officers to encourage traffic, and at the same time to promote economy in the working expenses and general management (after dividends have been paid to the shareholders at the rate of 3% on the original shares or stock of the company and upon the declaration of every 10s of dividend) there be paid to all officers in receipt of salaries of £75 per annum and upwards, and to all clerks in charge of stations, though receiving a salary of less than £75 per annum, a gratuity of 5% of the amount of salary for the previous half year, being the half year in respect of which such dividend is paid, but that such gratuity be paid only till dividends are declared at the rate of 5%'. The dividends declared for the first and second half years of 1851 were 15s (75p) and 25s (£1.25) respectively.

Towards the close of 1855, the directors 'expressed altered feelings on the subject and decided objection to continue an allowance of such gravity. The engagement having been made in good faith and sanctioned by the shareholders it can only be dealt with by compromise'. The gratuity had amounted to over 7% in 1853, 12½% in 1854, and would be 20% on a yearly dividend of 5% in the foreseeable future. It was left to the secretary and general manager to provide an acceptable answer to the problem. Their solution, which was adopted, was that 'in future 15% on salary should be paid at the end of each year, in lieu of the gratuity to every officer and servant now so entitled, and until he should obtain by promotion an increase of salary greater than 15%'. The gratuity was to cease in the case of new appointments and would thus gradually become extinguished.

Denniston's health began to break down in August 1851. He was given leave of absence and Walter Leith, district agent at Peterborough, was brought to London to act temporarily as superintendent of the line. Leith received a grant of £50 nine months later as he was still deputising. When Denniston returned to duty Leith was appointed District Agent at Grantham.

Two Acts were obtained in 1851. No. 1 Bill, which passed on 3 July, empowering the company to raise £750,000 new capital and borrow £250,000, authorised construction of new joint stations with the L & Y at Knottingley and Wakefield, enlargement of the London station, and diversion of Old St Pancras Road. No. 2 Bill, which became an Act on 24 July, empowering the company to raise £60,000 capital and borrow £20,000, authorised GN access to the tidal basin and docks at Grimsby for fish and goods traffic, GN running powers from Bole to Gainsborough, and two curves at Retford and the junction with the MS&L at Durham Ox, Lincoln. The GN was also authorised to construct a short branch and goods station at Sheffield, but these works were not undertaken.

EXPANSION IN THE WIND

Early in 1851, the GN was making arrangements to take over the East Anglian, a small and penurious system of 67½ miles, formed by an amalgamation in 1847 of the Lynn and Dereham, Lynn and Ely, and Ely and Huntingdon. At Dereham, there was a junction with the Norfolk, and at Ely, one with the EC. From Watlington Road junction, 6 miles south of Lynn, there was a branch to a station in the south east of Wisbech where the East station now is. The EC had made a connecting line from that point to a junction just outside its own station, later the goods station. The Ely-Huntingdon section, despite its name, only extended from the EC at St Ives to its own station at Huntingdon (renamed Godmanchester in 1882) and so was isolated from the rest of the system.

Denison and Baxter had been busy with views of extending the GN into Norfolk, and creating a route from the north to Cambridge. Despite protests from Graham Hutchinson against arrangements being made with the EA, negotiations continued. In February, GN officers inspected the line and rolling stock. A traffic agreement for 21 years was signed on 16 May. The GN was to have at least 40% of the receipts and maintain the plant and lines. The EA agreed to make permanent bridges on the Wisbech branch, and complete a junction with the GN at Huntingdon.

The GN had to advance the money for this, £3,500 for works, and £1,109 for the land. The ¾ mile was inspected by the Board of Trade on 27 September, and the opening postponed for one month because the inspecting officer was not satisfied with the signalling arrangements. It was double until it reached GN property at Huntingdon where the two lines converged to form 'Godmanchester Junction', with the GN up line 13 chains south of the station, facing towards London. Without further application to the Board of Trade, it was brought into use on 29 October.

It was resolved to commence working the local traffic as from 25 May

1 Sharp single in original condition, 1848

2 Grimsby Station in 1855, showing the Postmaster, J Read, the Station Master, Mr Robinson, and E H Clarke of the Loco Dept.

3 Bardney Bridge, October 1848

5 The line at Spalding, October 1848

4 Boston, October 1848

6 The line at Peterborough, August 1850

7 The North London viaduct and junction, Maiden Lane, November 1851

8 The station at Huntingdon, August 1850

9 Kings Cross passenger station exterior, 1853

10 Kings Cross goods station exterior, 1852

11 Queen Victoria and Prince Albert at Maiden Lane (described as Kings Cross) August 1851

12 Sir William Cubitt

and general traffic from 1 July. Accordingly, the GN gave notice to the EC of its intention to work over its line from Peterborough to Wisbech under the provisions of an agreement between the EC and GN on 29 May 1849, under which the EC had granted the GN running powers, in return for the GN abandoning its powers for construction of its own line from Stamford, via Peterborough, to Wisbech (inherited from the Boston Stamford and Birmingham which it had absorbed). It was unreasonable to have two parallel Peterborough–Wisbech lines at this stage. The EC accepted the notice, and promised co-operation of its officers. The EC must have viewed GN's designs on Cambridge with some apprehension for it advised Seymour Clarke of its intention to single the line from St Ives to Cambridge.

The new arrangements were not put into operation until Thursday 10 July. But when the first GN train, intending to travel over the EA to Lynn, reached Wisbech EC, it found the junction points blocked against it by vehicles chained to the rails. The same obstacle faced a train in the other direction from Lynn. Wentworth Claye, manager of the EA, was prepared for something of this nature, for he had omnibuses ready to convey passengers between the Wisbech stations, about ½ mile apart.

But of course the traffic could not be satisfactorily worked while the junction remained blocked, so the dispute was referred to the Railway Commissioners. The EC maintained that the EA had departed from the authorised line, and that it had no right to join the EC where it did; that in granting powers to the GN, it expected the trains to work into its Wisbech station and not to a junction just outside, and that anyway the powers did not cover the connecting line to the EA station; and that this had only been provided to give the EA a route to its isolated section at St Ives. The Commissioners would probably have ordered removal of the obstruction until they discovered that the connection had not been approved by an Inspecting Officer, and when this procedure was carried out, they washed their hands of the matter. The GN then applied to the Court of Chancery for an injunction to compel the EC to keep to the agreement and remove the obstruction. Confident in its cause, the GN provided temporary accommodation at St Ives and comtemplated erection of its own station at Wisbech, while the EA prepared plans for a permanent station at St Ives. The case was heard before Vice-Chancellor Turner. He was disposed to find that the EC was bound under the agreement to allow the GN to use the connecting line. But he decided against the GN on different grounds—that the GN-EA agreement was really a lease, invalid without parliamentary sanction, and refused an injunction.

In consequence, there were further GN-EA negotiations, the EA proposing a modification of terms, so that the GN would pay money for the plant instead of paying an annuity as stipulated in the existing agreement. The new terms meant that the GN was to buy the plant at a valuation of £52,000. The bridges and works were to be paid for out of this sale and bonds given for the balance. An Act would be sought to enable the EA to grant an immediate working contract to the GN for 25 years, substantially on the terms of the previous contract, including a specific guarantee of £15,000 per annum. In the interim the GN was to work the line.

Almost immediately the EA used this draft agreement to bargain with the EC. In a sharply worded letter to its solicitor, Baxter informed the EA that the GN did not intend bidding against the EC nor would it allow the terms to stand over, and the plant would be handed back as soon as the EA settled its accounts with the GN. On 25 November arrangements were made to re-transfer working the line to the EA. Early in December the plant was restored to it. To the dismay of many proprietors, the poverty-stricken concern had now no option but to come to terms with the EC, which leased it from 1 January 1852.

The eleventh GN half-yearly meeting on Friday 27 February, was a stormy one. Angry shareholders, already disgruntled with the burden of guarantees to the EL, the R&H and the Lincolnshire navigations which almost swallowed up such profits as the company could then earn, left Denison in no doubt that they resented his signature being appended to another guarantee without their authority. It can be surmised that the chairman and solicitor had been looking even further east, as it was minuted that Baxter proposed that the GN, and Eastern Union should show interest in a line projected from Norwich to Dereham.

Unknown to the proprietors, Denison and Baxter were looking for opportunities of expansion in the north. In Yorkshire, a small company possessed powers to construct a railway from a junction with the Leeds & Thirsk at Arthington to Skipton, a town already served by the Leeds & Bradford Extension (leased to the Midland) and the (little) North Western. Incorporated on 16 July 1847, as the Lancashire & Yorkshire North Eastern, it submitted a Bill for a 55 mile line from Skipton to York via Ilkley and Tadcaster. Only the portion from Skipton to Arthington, 22 miles, was authorised (subsequently renamed the Wharfedale) and now attracted the chairman's and solicitor's attention. The 'North Western' was almost invariably prefixed by 'little' to distinguish it from the L&NW.

In April 1851, Denison proposed to the L&T, and East Lancashire, that they should join the GN in construction of the Wharfedale. The project fell through as probably neither of the other two were in a position then to undertake fresh liabilities. The Wharfedale, as such, was never made although later the NE and Midland constructed a line over an almost identical route.

However it is interesting to conjecture how the possession of such a line could have extended GN scope. The L & T had powers to Stockton, where it would connect with the Stockton & Darlington, and the Stockton & Hartlepool, and also had powers to absorb the Clarence, and the Stockton & Hartlepool, although it failed to implement them. From Skipton, the (little) N W ran to Lancaster and Poulton, and had a branch from Clapham to Ingleton, also of some importance, for it was authorised to continue to join the L&C near Tebay. From Skipton, the Midland had a line to Colne where it formed an end-on junction with the EL. It would have been fascinating to have read Denison's mind, as he must have had visions of arrangements with the L&T and the ELR, thus providing the GN with extensive access to north Yorkshire and north Lancashire and even a back door entrance to Manchester.

Yet another project in the north was considered, the abortive Northern Counties Union, Thirsk to Penrith. In March preliminary

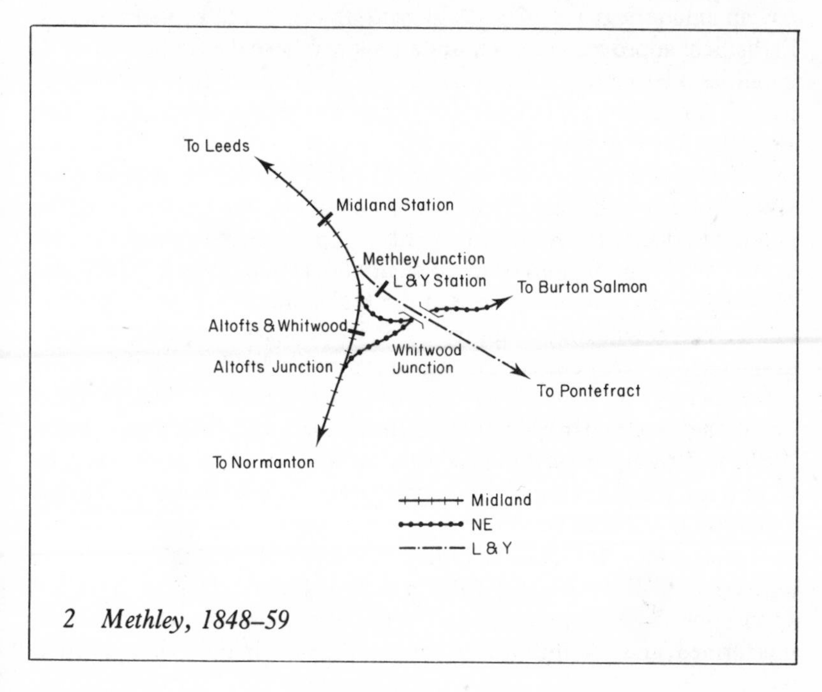

2 *Methley, 1848–59*

discussions were opened with the L&C with a view to arranging future GN services to south-west Scotland via the (little) North Western or the Northern Counties Union. The Glasgow & South Western and the Caledonian were informed of these. In August 1851, the GN undertook to pay one-third of the Northern Counties Union's Parliamentary expenses, provided running powers were secured. But the line was not built, and the Midland soon gained control of the (little) NW.

The records state little about a proposed alliance with the Y&NM, which was discussed at a directors' meeting on 27 July 1852. In August negotiations were broken off, because the Y&NM would not treat on any other basis than a fixed rent or guarantee.

In April 1851, the L&NW and the Midland, acting together, offered the 'Ambergate' a working agreement and eventual lease, proposing rental of £2,750 for 1852, £5,500 for 1853 and £6,850 per annum for the years 1854 to 1858 inclusive, with an option to fix it at 4% on the Ambergate's capital before the end of 1854. To the surprise of the directors, who agreed to the terms, the offer was rejected by the shareholders. Negotiations were re-opened with the GN, a meeting being held on 31 March 1852, at which it was agreed that the GN should work the Ambergate from 1 July and, after deducting working expenses, pay an amount equal to 4% on the paid-up capital, to be guaranteed if Parliament approved. The GN undertook to relieve the Ambergate of all liabilities relating to the Nottingham and Grantham Canals, and would pay off Ambergate shareholders at par on six months notice at any time after the Act was passed. This offer was accepted by the Ambergate proprietors at a meeting on 19 May. The GN was indebted to Graham Hutchinson for the success of the negotiations, for he, realising the potential value of the Ambergate to his company, had obtained a corner in the shares, and by his influence secured rejection of the L&NW and Midland terms, and acceptance of the GN's offer.

The agreement was contrary to Parliamentary Standing Orders, designed to prevent one company guaranteeing a dividend on the capital of another. At Midland instigation, two shareholders of the Grantham Canal (then engaged in a lawsuit with the Ambergate), John Simpson and William Wright, applied in Chancery for an injunction to restrain the GN from implementing the agreement. Vice-Chancellor Turner delivered judgement on 28 June, ruling that the payment of a fixed guarantee on the Ambergate's capital was not a 'toll' within the meaning of Section 87 of the Railway Clauses Act, 1845, and that the 'intended application to Parliament was not one of the purposes for which the GN was formed, and that the funds of the company ought not to be applied to such a purpose'. The injunction was granted and the ruling prevented the working agreement being carried into effect from 1 July 1852 as arranged, and the GN from applying for powers to work the line. Joseph Cubitt had been instructed on 25 May to arrange with John Underwood, engineer to the Ambergate, for construction of the connecting line at Grantham, authorised by the Act of 2 July 1847.

The Ambergate had powers to construct a railway from a junction with the Midland at Ambergate to Nottingham, (the last four miles of which were to be joint with the Midland) then to use three miles of the Midland's Lincoln branch before proceeding to Grantham and Spalding. With short branches to Sleaford and Boston, a total of 92½ miles had been authorised. In the event only 22 miles 44 chains had actually been constructed, from the canal basin at Grantham to Carlton junction with the Midland at Colwick. From this point the company had running powers over the Midland to Nottingham, and use of its station there. Opening for passengers had taken place on Monday 15 July 1850, with local goods one week later. A temporary station was erected at the Grantham canal basin, where there were engine and carriage sheds. Intermediate stations were at Sedgebrook, Bottesford, Elton, Aslockton, Bingham, and Radcliffe. Sidings and a warehouse were built at Colwick. There were four passenger trains each way on weekdays and two on Sundays. E. B. Wilson & Co were the original contractors for working the line, but more recently Neale & Wilson of Grantham had taken over.

The railway was double. From Grantham the formation undulated to the east end of Gonerby tunnel (561 yd) where it fell at 1 in 176 to Sedgebrook. It next climbed at 1 in 330 for 1½ miles, and then descended again at 1 in 176 to Bottesford. After a further fall of 1 in 165 the line levelled through Elton, fell at 1 in 264 and levelled once more through Aslockton. A final climb of 1 in 176 to the 16¼ mile post and then a descent of 1 in 220 and 1 in 132 took the line down to the Trent valley. The remainder of the line from Radcliffe to Carlton junction undulated gently. Two viaducts crossed the Trent valley, one 417 yd long, consisting of a cast iron bridge with a span of 107 ft over the river, three arches of brick faced with stone, and long timber gearing on timber piles spaced 30 ft apart, the other, separated from the first by an embankment, constructed wholly of timber and 263 yd long. A third structure was a flat cast iron girder bridge with a span of 40 ft. There were earthworks near Gonerby where the tunnel passed through blue clay.

While the negotiations with the Ambergate had been taking place, the SY had become within an ace of being absorbed in the GN. By an agreement between them signed in February 1851, the GN would pay the SY a dividend of 3% for which the GN would be entitled to carry 200,000 tons of coal, the tonnage at that time. The dividend was to increase by ½% upon each additional 100,000 tons until 800,000 tons should be carried and 6% paid, to be the maximum dividend even if this tonnage was exceeded, but with a provison that once 4½% was reached the dividend should never exceed from that figure.

Meetings of both companies were called. The GN shareholders approved the proposal, but the SY proprietors were now not so happy about it. Most of them were large coalowners, and putting that interest first, showed a marked reluctance to accept, for naturally they preferred to retain freedom to send their coal to whichever markets promised the best return. A temporary arrangement was made whereby the SY would receive 10d a ton as its share of the through rate.

Although stalemate had apparently been reached, the GN directors continued to urge the SY board to accept the terms. Baxter, solicitor to both, who had set his heart on the fusion, worked hard to achieve it. Success came early in 1852 for on 26 February it was resolved to seal the agreement with the SY, work it for 21 years, or transfer it to the GN. When a Bill for this, lodged in the autumn of 1852, reached the Commons Committee stage, it was strenuously opposed by the Midland, which objected to the SY coalfield being made a GN monopoly. Impressed with the Midland's arguments, the Committee insisted on insertion of a clause providing for free interchange of Midland traffic at Swinton upon the principle of a mileage rate. This meant that the Midland was put on equal terms with the GN without undertaking any liability, and the success of the Midland intervention was a disaster for the GN. Although the far-reaching results could not be seen in 1852, they will become apparent as this history unfolds. What Denison could see plainly was that the bargain with the SY had been transformed into an unsatisfactory one, for complete control of the railway (and the coal) which had been envisaged would now be impracticable. Denison, never fully convinced of the value of the SY to his company, now had second thoughts. Nevertheless, the Bill was allowed to go to the Lords and became an Act on 21 June 1852.

Almost immediately the SY called for meetings of both companies to implement the amalgamation upon the terms of the 26 February agreement. At the same time the SY demanded that the GN should waive the right of voting at SY meetings which it possessed by its holding of SY shares. The GN refused to accept this demand or proceed with the amalgamation until it was withdrawn. Denison now took the view that if the agreements with the Ambergate were *ultra vires*, as the

Vice-Chancellor had so recently declared, the agreement with the SY must also be.

Soon another bone of contention arose for in July the general managers and accountants of the two companies were unable to agree about the SY dividend. The SY contended that the GN must pay on the quantity of coal carried calculated at 20 cwt to the ton, instead of, as usual in the coal trade, 21 cwt. The difference worked out at ¼% for the dividends would by 3¾, or 4%. The SY maintained that the quantity of coal carried south of Doncaster for the half year to 30 June 1852 amounted to 200,000 tons and that the toll to be paid was £12,544. The GN was not satisfied with the accuracy of these figures and disputed the calculation of a 20 cwt ton, although Baxter's opinion was that, unless otherwise defined, 1 ton by law meant 20 cwt. To aggravate matters, the SY retained the dividend of £2,209 on shares held by the GN to 31 December 1851 as a set-off against a balance of toll of £2,982 claimed up to the same date. The GN directors were now in a dilemma. They could not withhold payment, for that would imply repudiation of an agreement but, on the other hand, to settle the account in full would commit them for the future. Accordingly on 25 August it was resolved to pay £9,000 without prejudice. Denison now convinced his board that the Amalgamation Bill was merely permissive, not compulsory and the decision was taken not to proceed further with the amalgamation. In the autumn, supplies of coal decreased to a mere trickle, Grantham and other places on the line reporting that they were without coal, while Coles Child, in London, complained that he was unable to fulfill orders.

The directors discussed the SY problem again on 1 November. The chairman urged his colleagues not to consent to any arrangement like that of 26 February, stating that the value of the SY might possibly depreciate, owing to the Midland interchange at Swinton. Baxter explained his views, directly in opposition to Denison's, stating that he felt he was seriously implicated and his personal honour and character were impugned. He continued that, with the chairman holding the views he did, it would be impossible to carry out the agreement which must therefore fall to the ground, and having made the agreement he would be no party to 'un-making' it. He concluded that in consequence he had no alternative but to tender his resignation of the office of solicitor to the GN. Denison carried the day and the meeting broke up after the decision was taken to adhere to the resolution of 25 August.

For many years Baxter and Denison had collaborated. In the first instance, they had together endeavoured to persuade Hudson to include Doncaster in his plans to connect York with the south. The efforts of no other two men contributed more to GN success. Baxter had united with Barker, Rose & Norton and formed the firm of Baxter, Rose & Norton previous to GN incorporation, played a major role in the development of the railway and worked hard to further its success and extend its enterprise. This was not lost upon the directors, for in the summer of 1850 they formed a committee to confer with him as to the practicability of securing his individual services for the company's benefit generally, otherwise than professionally as solicitor. All this Denison very unwisely threw away, and now and for many years to come the directors would have bitter cause to reflect on Baxter's skill in legal and Parliamentary business, henceforth turned against them. His firm formally resigned on 15 February 1853. The other joint solicitors, Johnson, Farquhar & Leech, took over the whole legal and Parliamentary business. Ten days later Denison relinquished his seat on the SY board.

In the meantime the SY applied to the Court of Chancery to restrain the GN from paying dividends until SY claims for toll, etc. were satisfied. The injunction was refused by Vice-Chancellor Stuart on 8 February. An appeal was made to the Lords Justices of Appeal who, on 17 February, refused the injunction without calling on the GN's counsel. Almost immediately a notice was sent to the GN that on and after Tuesday 22 February 1853 its trains would not be allowed to run over the SY except under the terms of the February 1852 agreement. The SY also issued a writ for recovery of £3,544. An offer was made to pay a toll of 1s 6d (7½p) per ton without prejudice, but the SY declined to accept an offer made under protest, and duly stopped the trains. This dispute also came before Vice-Chancellor Stuart, who granted an injunction to prevent stopping the trains on condition that the GN paid 1s 6d per ton without prejudice—the terms King's Cross had offered. The trains began to run again during the Thursday. Baxter denied that he had played any part in these SY manoeuvres.

Some landowners in the Thorne area obtained a 'Mandamus' in the Queen's Bench, to compel the GN to construct the 'Axholme extension', which was served on 14 May 1852, so soon afterwards modified plans were drawn up for the line. Joseph Cubitt estimated that the least sum for which it could be made, commencing at Gainsborough, would be £252,127 for a single line with timber bridges, including cost of permanent way and stations. In July it was resolved that it should be made, but no further action was taken pending the hearing of an appeal, which was successful. In May 1853 the decision to build the line was reversed, the SY being given an offer to make it. A few weeks later it was minuted that no further action would be taken, but despite the decision not to construct it, a crossing for it was laid on the MS&L at Gainsborough on 2 July 1853.

In May 1853 the company was served with a writ for recovery of £13,116, the amount of toll claimed by the SY for the half-year ending 31 December 1852. A lawsuit with the SY about the validity of the agreement dragged its expensive course from one court to another. In June a decision was given by the Court of Exchequer in favour of the SY, but the GN appealed, and the case sent back for re-hearing. Notice was given to the SY that the GN would cease to work the goods and passenger trains between Doncaster and Barnsley on and from 1 August 1853 as they were not remunerative (according to the SY chairman the GN continued to work one passenger train). On 1 February 1854 the Exchequer Chamber (then the appellate Court) confirmed the Court's decision but still the obstinate Denison would not submit, and his board resolved to appeal to the Lords. Fortunately, before any more money was wasted on useless litigation, a proposal arrived from the SY which put an end to the dispute. The SY was prepared to cancel all agreements with the GN at the close of the current year, except that relating to Doncaster station, provided that the GN would settle all accounts, on the basis of the February 1852 agreement, up to 31 December 1854 so as to allow time for the SY to procure plant to work its own traffic. Thus a regrettable episode in the early history of the GN was brought at least to a temporary close.

In the West Riding things began to look brighter for, in the autumn of 1851, a Bill was deposited for the Leeds, Bradford & Halifax Junction, wholeheartedly supported by the GN, for here was the opportunity to run its own trains into Bradford and Halifax. The scheme was almost identical with the principal portion of the earlier West Riding Union, which the L&Y had absorbed. Only a small portion of the Union's authorised lines had been constructed, connecting Halifax, Bradford and Low Moor with the old L&Y line at Mirfield and Sowerby Bridge. The L&Y had neglected to proceed with the principal part from Halifax to Leeds to the intense disappointment of two WRU foremost promoters.

These same two Yorkshiremen, Edward Akroyd and William Firth, now came forward with the new project, acting with Henry Nelson, a Leeds solicitor and John Hawkshaw, the engineer. GN relations with the L&Y had already deteriorated under Huish influence. Now with the prospect of what it regarded as GN invasion of its territory, the L&Y adopted a hostile attitude. Captain Laws resigned from the GN board on 25 November, writing that his resignation was 'induced by his inability to promote more favourable arrangements with companies with which they work in Yorkshire'. Soon afterwards his company threatened to stop GN trains running north of Askern, unless full Parliamentary toll was paid, maintaining that the agreement of 1 May 1847 required this, and offering a fresh agreement. An injunction was obtained in January 1852 restraining the L&Y from interfering with GN trains.

In December 1849 a meeting had been arranged with the EC to complete a traffic agreement. Negotiations continued for six months but in June 1850 these broke down, because the terms stipulated for coal traffic could not be conceded. From that time the EC had tended to support Euston Square. In the summer of 1851 it was constructing its truncated Bedford branch from Shelford to Shepreth, and notified the GN that it intended to work its own traffic over the line, but was prepared to carry GN traffic to Cambridge. Seymour Clarke's reaction was to arrange cheap fares on the buses between Shepreth and Cambridge.

Having taken the EA off the GN's hands, the EC next proposed to lease the R&H. Agreement was reached in February 1852 that the EC, from the date of opening of its branch, would pay £16,000 per annum guaranteed rent and interest on the R&H. The GN agreed to pay 60% of any earnings in respect of King's Cross/Hitchin traffic to and from Cambridge and stations east of Ashwell on the R&H, and arranged to pay a bonus of 20% of the earnings from EC traffic exchanged at Peterborough for Newark, Lincoln, Hull and some other places north thereof. The R&H lease was to last for 14 years during which time the Railway Clearing House referred to it as the 'Shelford & Hitchin Railway'. The GN agreed to cease running from Peterborough to Wisbech as from 14 February. Thus for 14 years the GN avoided the liability of what was no better than an agricultural branch, and also secured peace on its eastern flank.

The EC opened its branch on 1 April 1852, with works constructed for double line, although only a single line was laid, 5 miles 28 chains from Shelford junction to an end-on junction with the R&H down-line 200 yd east of Shepreth station. The Inspecting Officer was apparently unaware of the arrangement between the companies, for he sanctioned opening only on condition that the EC could use the turntable at Shepreth. It seems that through carriages were worked between King's Cross and Cambridge. The EC paid £300 per annum for use of Hitchin station. When Seymour Clarke, looking round for additional revenue, sought to charge it for the expense of the junction, the EC rightly claimed that rent of the station included charge for the junction. It was allowed to remove the carriage shed from Shepreth and re-erect it at Ashwell, as a warehouse, at its own expense. The EC was always well behind in payment of rent, as was its successor, the Great Eastern.

Although the Midland and L & N W had come close to amalgamating, it was apparent that the former had tended to become less dependant on Euston Square. Moreover the L & N W had turned its attention to the GW and was engaged in discussions suggesting fusion with that company. Denison judged that the time had come to approach the Midland which was anxious to associate with some other company with London as terminus. He urged upon his colleagues the importance of considering a policy of amalgamation with the Midland, and on 16 August 1852 he wrote to John Ellis, the Midland chairman, proposing a union of the companies. He pointed out that they competed with each other in the south and north and crossed each other in two or three places, with double stations at several towns, and duplicate trains run when single ones would suit the public equally well. He said that a large annual expenditure would be saved which would improve dividends, and the real value of both companies' properties. Unfortunately ties between the Midland and Euston Square were still too strong, and when Ellis replied a few days later he informed Denison that, while his board was fully alive to the serious evils of needless competition, it had received a further proposal from Euston Square about amalgamation. A Bill for such an alliance was submitted for the 1853 Session but Parliament was not prepared to sanction large scale amalgamations until a Select Committee had investigated the problem in all aspects. As no further action could be taken then, the Bill was withdrawn.

The Midland lodged a Bill for the same Session reviving its Leicester to Hitchin line. The GN decided to oppose this with a Bill for a branch from Sandy to Bedford but withdrew it when the Midland promised that its goods and passenger trains would connect with GN services at Hitchin.

THE TOWNS LINE COMPLETED

Work on the Towns line proceeded slower than planned. Slips in the deep cuttings caused considerable delays and the work of two contractors was below standard. Oldham failed and had no funds to pay his men. Work stopped on his contract in March 1852. Solicitors on behalf of the Yorkshire Banking Co, his trustees, took over his plant. Joseph Cubitt paid the men, and work was resumed. In July however, following near riots at Retford, he took over the contract, because the trustees had not paid the men. The company took over Jackson's contract on 2 June. A short-lived Brick Tax (imposed by an Act in 1850) had adversely affected his calculations, and placed him in financial difficulties. He was already in the GN's debt by as much as £16,753, and protracted litigation resulted. The Trent took its new channel in July 1851, and the Newark Dyke bridge was completed in time. Captain Wynne inspected the line in the middle of June, and put off opening for one month by letter from the Board of Trade dated 19 June, reminding the directors that the penalty for opening without sanction was £20 a day. The directors were impatient to open the line, for, under the Octuple Agreement, once this was accomplished, the GN would be entitled to 63% of the passenger receipts from traffic north of York instead of 33%, and a slight increase in the percentage of receipts from goods traffic. Clarke was instructed to open the line on Thursday 15 July 1852, provided Captain Wynne approved. Next followed a letter from a perturbed Joseph Cubitt who wrote that Wynne required to travel over both lines between Werrington junction and Retford at express speed, and he feared he would not be able to open the line until the 16th. Notices had been posted at the stations advertising a service commencing 15 July. Traffic did commence on this day but only for goods. It was not until Sunday 1 August that passenger trains were allowed, and from that day the express trains between London and the north were diverted from the Loop to the new main line. From the same date expresses ceased to call at Huntingdon. The journey time to Retford and beyond was reduced by at least half an hour, and the

GN gained a distinct advantage over the old route by the L&NW and Midland, over which competitive traffic steadily declined.

The new line added 59 miles 13 chains to the system, and commenced with a junction with the Loop at Werrington. This junction must not be confused with that connecting the GN with the Midland at Walton or Werrington, which was now taken out. From this point to Helpstone (alongside the Midland station; there was no GN station there) the line was level, and then began a steady rise, which became 1 in 200 before Little Bytham, which continued to the GN's main line summit at Stoke (347 ft above sea level), broken only by a short level breather by Corby. From Stoke the line dropped at 1 in 200 through Stoke tunnel (880 yd) and almost to Grantham where the gradient eased until beyond Peascliffe tunnel (968 yd). Another fall of 1 in 200 and 1 in 300 past Hougham, followed by easier gradients, took the line to the level of the Trent valley at Newark. Here the Midland was crossed on the flat, and level continued until the site of the future Crow Park station, where the final rise was encountered, first at 1 in 300 and then at 1 in 200 up to a summit close to Markham. The line then descended at 1 in 200, threading the short Askham tunnel (55 yd), and then more steeply at 1 in 178 until the level was reached just before Retford where the MS&L main line was crossed on the flat. Immediately beyond the crossing a junction was made with the 7 chain radius 'Lincoln Curve' from the MS&L station at Retford. A 10 chain radius south to west curve was laid which allowed traffic from the south to proceed direct to Sheffield, the GN paying the MS&L £70 per annum for use of this 'Retford Curve'.

Besides the tunnels, the principal engineering feature was the Newark Dyke bridge which crossed the water on the skew and had a span of 262 ft. The design chosen by Joseph Cubitt was unique to this country, (although there was at least one example in the United States), and was known as the Warren Truss. It was in duplicate, separate bridges carrying the up and down lines. Captain Wynne was impressed with the soundness of construction. There was a brick viaduct near by over the Trent measuring 310 yd, and another, 100 yd long at Little Bytham. Bridges were all of brick, or brick and iron girders.

The stations, designed by Goddard, were built by Kirk & Parry of Sleaford. That at Retford was just north of the Lincoln Curve. The intermediate stations were at Tallington, Essendine, Little Bytham, Corby, Great Ponton, Grantham, Hougham, Claypole, Newark, Carlton and Tuxford. Grantham, Newark and Retford had refreshment rooms. Buses soon provided feeder services to Tallington from Bourn and Stamford. A few years later the proprietor of a hostelry at Newark, who already performed local cartage, commenced a bus service to Ollerton.

The GN had the misfortune to lay its line at Tallington through Lord Lindsey's estate. His ability to wring money out of railway surpassed that of any other landowner with whom the directors had to treat. Litigation alone soon ran up to over £2,000. Also, in an agreement for purchase of his land the directors of the Direct Northern had promised that all trains should stop at Tallington. When traffic commenced, the GN disputed the agreement's validity. Lord Lindsey secured an injunction on 13 March 1853, which compelled the GN to stop all trains at Tallington to his requirements from 1 April. Not only were trains stopped for himself and his family but also for his servants. At one time hardly a day went by without one or more expresses being stopped. When, many years later, in 1883, a minor member of the household appeared at King's Cross and demanded that the 8.0 p.m. Scotch express should set him down at Tallington, the directors decided to do something about it. The company paid £1,000 to have the right extinguished.

From Monday 2 August 1852 the Ambergate's trains commenced to use the joint station at Grantham, and the one at the canal basin was henceforth used only for goods. On this day the GN advertised a through service between London and Nottingham via Grantham in less time than that by the L&NW cum Midland route. What happened to the first train was pure comedy. When it, with a through carriage off the 11.0 a.m. from King's Cross, headed by a GN engine, drew into Nottingham station, the Midland officers were ready to apply drastic action. On instructions from the Derby authorities, who took the view that this was defiance of the injunction, a number of Midland engines were used to force the GN engine into the disused Midland Counties shed. The rails leading to it were then taken up! The intended return working had to be cancelled and the engine was not released for many days. Grinling alleges that it was held captive for seven months. The GN brought proceedings against the Midland for seizing the engine, but the Court held that the Midland were entitled to remove the engine if it was 'wrongfully encumbering their lines'. In fact, the engine was legitimately hired to the Ambergate, was driven by their men, and the GN held a receipt for it. The Midland applied for an injunction to restrain the Ambergate or GN from using GN locomotives on its line into Nottingham. Vice-Chancellor Wood decided that the Midland's agreement allowed this, but granted an injunction preventing the Ambergate from running engines over the Midland line until their fitness had been certified. The engines already in use were excepted from this restriction, save two, one of which was the one which caused the trouble.

The Midland refused to accept at Nottingham parcels and goods for destinations beyond Grantham. Through goods traffic from the GN to Nottingham began on 19 August, but had to be carted from Colwick. Passenger traffic continued, for the Ambergate held indisputable right to work into Nottingham with its own engines. For the York race meeting in August the GN advertised a special from Nottingham with a first class fare of 17s (85p) and third class of 7s (35p) returning the same day. The Midland replied with a train with fares at 8s 6d (42½p) and 6s (30p) with a two day limit, and in November began to carry second class passengers on expresses to Sheffield. In both instances the GN was forced to offer similar fares and facilities. The warfare at Nottingham was brought to an end by an agreement on 24 May 1853. This extended the pooling arrangement for division of competitive traffic to four more towns, and gave the GN the following percentages:

	Passengers	*Goods*
Nottingham	50%	30%
Newark	80%	55%
Stamford	70%	30%
Peterborough	90%	33%

Another most important event of the year 1852 was the completion of King's Cross passenger station. Work on demolishing the hospital buildings was not authorised until May 1850 and it was not until 11 months later that Jay began excavation of the site. The new terminus, designed by Lewis Cubitt and built by Jay, was opened to the public without any festivities on Thursday 14 October and from that day passenger trains ceased to use Maiden Lane station. King's Cross consisted of two huge sheds covered with glazed arched roofs, each shed being 800 ft long, 105 ft wide and 71 ft high, separated from each other by an arched wall. Present day architects are inclinded to discount Grinling's story that the design for the roof was borrowed from a riding school in Moscow, but it is a fact that Lewis Cubitt had to re-design the roof when it was discovered that the one at Maiden Lane was none too safe. There were only two platforms, one for arrival and one for departure (the present Nos 1 and 8), which were separated by 14 tracks inter-connected by turntables. The intervening tracks were used for storage of rolling stock. The two platforms were sufficient for the traffic of the period, about a dozen trains each way a day. The façade was 216 ft wide and faced on to Old St Pancras Road which was later diverted. Above it was the clock tower, 112 ft above rail level. The tower was 16 ft square, surmounted by a gilded vane. The width of the station was 305 ft.

The eastern wall abutted on to York Road (Maiden Lane until the previous October) and a block of offices occupied the western side, built above the usual series of waiting rooms, refreshment rooms, booking and parcel offices.

The station cost £123,500. £65,000 was paid for purchase and demolition of the hospitals, besides further large sums spent on purchase and demolition of property in adjoining streets, which were stopped up. Two others, Congreve Street and Battle Bridge Road were carried over the station by bridges. In answer to criticisms of extravagance, Edmund Denison claimed that it was 'the cheapest building for what it contained, and will contain, that can be pointed out in London'. It was the largest terminus in London at the time and, apart from extra platforms, the main part of it remains substantially the same today as when it was built.

Three bells were bought from John Murphy at a cost of £255 and installed in the clock tower, being tenor, bass and treble. The largest weighed 29 cwt and also came from the Great Exhibition where it had received a medal. For two years the clock struck the quarter hours as well as the hours, Denison thinking that since the clock was not visible to the interior of the station it would be useful for the quarter chimes to be heard. In 1853 Dent supplied a double-faced clock for the departure platform.

The opening of King's Cross added about ¾ mile of new line, which included passing through Maiden Lane tunnel (527 yd). Curiously, for 15 years engines proceeding from the shed in the goods yard had to back into the station over the down line, for it was not until 1867 that a crossover was laid between the two tunnels at Belle Isle. At the station a small signal hut was provided west of the south portal of the tunnel, and the signals were controlled from it by wires, the points being moved by hand levers. Two fire engines were purchased for the station. King's Cross was lit by gas, supplied from the Imperial Gas Light & Coke Co works, west of the station yard. An experiment with electric lighting was tried in a portion of the station in May 1854, but was reported a failure at the end of June. Carruthers resigned on 3 June 1852 and was succeeded as station inspector by James Fisher who thus took charge of the new station on opening.

In the early hours of the morning before Kings Cross opened, the Towns line was blocked by a heavy slip of earth in Spittlegate cutting, Grantham. Trains were diverted by the Loop, but Seymour Clarke quickly arranged for a temporary track, with special pointsmen, round the obstacle for single line working. Normal double line working was not resumed until the following 19 March.

The Great Northern Hotel, designed by Lewis Cubitt, was being constructed by Jay, west of the station. Owing to strikes among the bricklayers and plasterers, it was not opened until 17 May 1854, and cost about £35,000. J. Dethier of Brussels became tenant of the hotel and the refreshment rooms at the station for a term of 22 years. Besides hotels, the company was interested in some inns, built at Hornsey, and various country stations. Like the refreshment rooms, these were let to tenants. The GN also acquired the Albion in Maiden Lane. The temporary station there was converted into a potato warehouse. The company encouraged many trades, and erected warehouses, granaries, sheep and cattle pens, etc. where there was need for them. In 1852, hydraulic machinery was installed in King's Cross goods depot.

In February 1852, the directors decided that when Sherman's contract finished at the end of the year, the company would itself undertake collection and delivery of goods in London from 1 January 1853. Half of Sherman's horses were bought in September. There was already stabling for about 70 horses in King's Cross goods yard, but this accommodation had to be increased. Premises for road vehicle maintenance, and for shoeing horses, and an infirmary for sick horses, were built. The GN was becoming one of the largest owners of horses in the country. Further, the animals became noted for their splendid quality and well-being. Apart from London and one or two other places, collection and delivery was by local contractors, and shunting horses at country stations were hired. The first reference to a company owned horse was a report of the death on 30 October 1849 of 'Tinker', a black horse bought from Petos for £26. The stud of draught horses, over 200 in December 1852, increased to 879 at the end of 1867. Handling of goods at Leeds passed from Bolland to J. Pepper at the end of 1852, Seymour Clarke reporting that Bolland was intolerably rude and he had great difficulty in dealing with him.

From September 1852 the GN made an arrangement with the GW for joint rental of the Bull & Mouth, leased for 14 years at an annual rental of £1,900. In the next few years joint receiving offices were established at Holborn, Strand, Regent Street, Crutched Friars, Parliament Street, King Street, Bridge Road and Fish Street Hill. An Oxford Street office had been leased since June 1848.

The company thoroughly engaged in the coal trade, for not only did it act as carrier but also bought coal from the owners, carried it, and then sold it to merchants and the public, retaining the profits. Some coal began to be moved into Lincolnshire early in 1850. In August of that year Coles Child, a partner in Coles Child & Co, Belvedere Wharf, near

Lambeth, was appointed manager of London District coal traffic. He was sent to visit the South Yorkshire coalowners and make a report, and a month later advocated encouragement of coal from Durham. It was now decided to proceed with accommodation at King's Cross for the company's coal trade. Sidings and coal drops took about four months to construct, so London trade began on 1 March 1851. Middlemiss estimated that 66 trains of 30 wagons weekly would be required in the winter, exclusive of the London trade. A few days later a further estimate stated that six or seven out of 11 trains daily from Doncaster would be required for coal between Boston and London in winter. Coles Child's salary was fixed at £500 per annum on an estimated annual turnover of 100,000 tons with an additional £100 for every further 100,000 tons. Later on he had some explaining to do, because several customers complained that although they had ordered coal from the GN they had been supplied from Belvedere Wharf.

London trade had barely begun when a memorial was addressed to the Railway Commissioners by Charles Cooper of Peterborough, about GN dealing in coals. The Board of Trade wrote to the company enquiring if the allegations were correct, and the secretary replied implying that the company was not selling coals on its own account. It remains a mystery how the GN got away with this, and continued to do so for another nine years. Apparently the profit on the sale of coal was disguised as additional profit on carriage. The company purchased 2 and 4 ton road vehicles for London coal delivery. Charles Cave Williams, now the principal in the carriage building business at Glasshouse Yard, built some of these, and was the first contractor to undertake delivery of coal, supplying horses, harness and carmen. Information was received during the summer that some of his carmen were distributing leaflets advertising coal from rival firms. Williams was warned to give up all orders as coal merchant to the GN and lost the contract at the end of the year. From 1 January 1852 it went to Edward Wiggins of Long Lane, West Smithfield, who undertook to supply horses, harness, weighing machines and weights, and carmen, it being agreed to find him stabling, an office, a granary and a haystore.

At the close of 1852, with completion of the permanent London terminus, opening throughout of the Towns line, and GN trains running through to York, the aims of the original promoters of the London & York may be fairly said to have been accomplished. At this period, there were four trains from King's Cross to York, one express first class only, two first and second class, and one Parliamentary. In the opposite direction, there were five first and second class, and a Parliamentary.

The down express, 9.30 from King's Cross, reached Peterborough in 105 minutes, with a Hitchin stop, Doncaster in 3 hr 53 m., York in 4 hr 50 m., and Edinburgh in 11 hr. The best up train was slower, 11 hr 50 m. from Edinburgh, and 5 hr 20 m. from York. From 1854, the down express had a Leeds portion, which got there in 4 hr 50 m. The distances were now 191 miles to York, 186½ miles to Leeds, and just over 400 miles to Edinburgh, much the same as the rival west coast route from Euston. The Parliamentarys took as much as 9 hr 20 m. to York. At this stage, a few trains, besides the 'Parlys,' were shown as conveying third class passengers, making local journeys, but the fares were slightly more than 1d a mile. Early in 1853, one of these ran from Peterborough to York, and another from Doncaster to York. At this date, on Sundays, there was a 'Parly' from King's Cross to York, and two, first and second only, in the opposite direction.

From 18 July 1853, a night express to and from Edinburgh was introduced. The down train left King's Cross at 9.15 p.m., arrived at York at 2.25 a.m., and Edinburgh at 9.0 a.m. The up train left Edinburgh at 9.15 p.m., reached York at 3.35 a.m., and King's Cross at 9.15 a.m. At that period, and for many years, the best up trains from Scotland were always timed slower than the down, to allow a 'recovery margin', in case of serious delays in the north. The new night trains were originally 'first and second' only, but at the instance of the NB, third class passengers were soon admitted on two days a week. In the following June, Huish demanded that the east coast companies should discontinue carrying third class passengers by this service, failing which he threatened that the west coast would carry third class passengers by fast trains from 1 July. He did not carry out his threat, which was rather an empty one, as the best west coast trains for first and second class passengers were taking about 13 hr by day and 12 hr by night to Edinburgh and Glasgow. However, this was the thin end of the wedge of competition which later led to third class passengers being conveyed on some of the faster trains. This particular facility for the third class passengers was only available for a short time, as by 1855 the best services for them took 10 hr 50 m. to Edinburgh (see p. 88). For this year the holders of the original stock received a dividend of 2¼%.

Sir William Cubitt resigned on 21 June 1852, but consented to remain as consultant engineer. At the end of the year, with the major part of his work behind him, Joseph Cubitt proposed altered terms. It was agreed that his out of town expenses should cease on 31 December, and his salary for 1853 fixed at £2,000, 1854 at £1,600, and 1855 and subsequent years at £1,200. George Walker, of Osgarthorpe, was elected to the board in August 1852 in the place of George Humphrys, resigned for health reasons.

From 1 January 1853 Clarke's and Sturrock's salaries were raised to £1,500 and £1,000 per annum respectively. The inspector of police received a rise to £160 and was granted use of a house. Invariably referred to as 'Mr Inspector Williams' he held a responsible position, for in addition to police duties he investigated minor claims for injury and was authorised to make cash settlements on the spot. When necessary he was accompanied by a surgeon. At the same time, upon the opening of Doncaster Works, Frederick Parker received £350 as Works Manager, and John Coffin, lately carriage foreman, £265 as Carriage Superintendent, both with free houses. John Denniston's health broke down again in November; he was allowed three months' leave and advised that if he recovered he would have to take a lighter position. Walter Leith was brought back to London and appointed Superintendent of the Line at £400 from 1 December. By early January Denniston's health had totally failed, so he was paid to the end of 1853, plus a further £600.

As previously mentioned, the decision to build the permanent repairing establishment at Doncaster was taken on 3 June 1851. Wilsons, who had been undertaking some engine rebuilding and heavy repairing, realised that they would lose this business, and wrote to King's Cross, offering to repair engines by contract. The proposal was declined, but Wilsons wrote again with a further offer to undertake heavy repairs, also turned down.

A small wagon-repair shop was first built nearby at Hexthorpe, and a mineral office on S Y land. Plans for the new workshops were drawn up by William and Joseph Cubitt, and Sturrock, at an estimate of £45,000. In November it was resolved to include carriage repair shops, and next month the plans were approved. Tenders for construction were invited. On 23 March 1852 the contract was awarded to A. and G. Holmes of Liverpool who offered to undertake the work at 10% below the schedule of prices. Sturrock was allowed a budget for the purchase of the necessary tools and machinery, most supplied by Nasmyths. But orders were given to other firms which manufactured specialised appliances, and for months Sturrock was frequently seeking authority for the purchases. By May the following year, the engine erecting shop, smithy and iron store were completed, and the roof of a new, larger wagon repair shop nearly finished. Engines were brought in for repair at the end of June, and the plant was in full use by 9 August. Two fire engines were stationed at the new works, which were extended in 1855. Sturrock, whose reports to the board had been addressed from Peterborough since September 1851, took up his headquarters at Doncaster a year later.

Staff were gradually transferred from Boston until at the end of the year about 900 workmen, and their wives and children, had moved to Doncaster. With the population of his home town rapidly rising, Denison was disturbed at the lack of facilities for worship and education. Since the GN had been responsible for the influx, he felt justified in urging the proprietors to provide a church and schools. While the majority of shareholders were prepared to vote money for schools, building a church out of funds of a trading company was another matter. The sum of £2,000 was proposed for the schools, but an amendment that only half this amount should be spent was carried. The schools, built by C. Lister & Son of Doncaster, and designed by Henry Goddard, were attended by 246 boys and girls when opened in January 1855. The Rev. J. Campion, who was already devoting much of his time to the spiritual welfare of the workers and their families, took charge of them. The cost of the buildings exceeded the sum allowed by £212, and later the shareholders voted to repay this amount to Denison who had personally settled the account.

Building a church required an Act, and despite howls of dissent from many shareholders, the Denisons grimly determined to steamroller a Bill through, but opposition was so great that it had to be withdrawn. A subscription list was opened among the shareholders and a few friends. When by May 1857 the fund had reached £5,641, E. B. Denison moved that time had come to begin construction of the church. The list was headed by Lord Fitzwilliam, chairman of the SY. The GN provided land for the church and arranged for free conveyance from Ancaster of stone for its construction. E. B. Denison supervised the building and was supplied with a free pass between London and Doncaster. The church, St James, capable of holding a congregation of nearly 700, was ready for consecration in October 1858. A cheque for £1,000 was drawn on the fund for endowment. In April 1862, Edmund Denison and his colleagues bought an organ (from St George's, Doncaster) for £350 out of their allowances.

Immediately after the decision that the workshops should be at Doncaster, the directors turned their attention to land purchased for the same purpose north of Peterborough. In 1851, they acquired additional land, and provided a large engine shed, a turntable and sidings. Orders were given in August 1853 to extend the shed to hold more engines. Sturrock at this time was having difficulty in obtaining and retaining staff at New England (as the place became known) because there was a dearth of living accommodation in the locality, then open country. He recommended that the company should either build cottages, or have them built. The board was slow to move. It was not until 25 April 1854 that a contract was let to Kirk and Parry for building 50 cottages. More cottages were built later. Sturrock still had to press the vital need for housing accommodation. At his suggestion, a bakehouse was provided at the growing village (later described as a general store, bakery and coffee house). The workmen's children needed a school. So in November 1856 it was resolved to build one at New England for 50 boys, 50 girls and 75 infants. G. Holme & Co of Peterborough began this work in the following May, and completed it by the end of the year. This firm constructed an erecting shop and stores, finished in the spring 1858 at a cost of £6,000—the space previously occupied in the running shed by engines under repair becoming available for stabling.

A committee of directors was authorised in August 1851 to proceed with an agreement with the Electric Telegraph Co for installation of the electric telegraph over the system. In the following month, it was resolved that it should be put up at every station where Clarke considered it necessary. Almost immediately, the trains were worked through the longer London tunnels by the telegraph, which was installed between the principal stations as far as Doncaster in March 1852 and completed to York in April. Evidently only one shift of operators was provided at first, for in October Sturrock requested that the offices should be opened at night as well as by day.

In February 1854 Clarke informed the board that from the experience of working the telegraph through the tunnels he could adapt it to working all traffic between London and Hatfield. The recommendation was approved, and Joseph Cubitt was instructed to proceed with the installation. In the next year block telegraph was installed through Doncaster, at Peterborough, and, as a result of an accident in the London goods yard, between Copenhagen tunnel and a new box near Maiden Lane Bridge. The block system was extended from Hatfield to Hitchin in 1856. In January 1859, it was decided to continue it to Peterborough. Instructions were given for signal huts to be erected at Arlsey, Biggleswade, Sandy, St Neots and Holme but the system was not adopted on this section for many years.

Although no further construction was contemplated, the company urgently needed additional capital. In order to develop its business, warehouses, granaries, coal depots, sidings, and carriage sheds had to be built or enlarged throughout the system. More engines and rolling stock would be required when the time came to work the Leeds, Bradford &

Halifax Junction (see chapter V). In January 1852 figures were produced which showed that out of borrowing powers totalling nearly £2,500,000 all but £168,070 had been raised. Out of this amount £30,000 was reserved for the Axholme line and the board resolved to borrow the remainder. Later in the year the proprietors consented to a Bill for raising another million, which became an Act on 28 June 1853, empowering the company to raise £750,000 in shares and borrow £250,000.

A Sick and Funeral Fund open to station inspectors, guards, policemen and porters, instituted in the summer of 1853, received contributions from 4 September and gave benefits from the following 1 January. Later, other grades were admitted to the fund. Although no new members have been accepted since the 1923 grouping, there were still, in 1970, old GN men enjoying excellent benefits from this fund. A year later a system of bonuses to signalmen was approved, 50s for each half-year of satisfactory service.

The East & West India Docks & Birmingham Junction had, under its Act, authority to construct a junction with the GN near King's Cross. It was Baxter who had drawn the directors' attention to this, and to the fact that no effort was being made to form the junction, which would provide access to the docks. This small company with a long name, under the dominating influence of Euston Square, declined to proceed with construction of the junction, arguing that it could put the land to better use. The GN took the dispute to Chancery, and on 23 July 1852 Vice-Chancellor Parker ruled that the E&W&BJ must afford junction facilities to the GN as laid down in the Act. The GN laid the junction itself from the goods yard. In June 1853 Cubitt reported that the work was completed, and it only remained for the small company to put in the actual connection, which was known as St Pancras junction. The small company had by this time changed its name to the less cumbersome North London.

The first week of 1854 was remarkable for severe snowstorms which swept across the country and disrupted the services of nearly all railways, particularly those whose lines extended northwards from London. By Wednesday morning the main GN line was blocked by snowdrifts from Peterborough to Newark, and by 8.0 p.m. the Loop was impassable. One line of the Loop was cleared during the night. No trains from York reached London from Tuesday until Thursday afternoon, while one train from York was 8½ hours on the road. Snowdrifts were deepest in the cuttings south of Stoke tunnel, a stretch of line not cleared until Friday evening. Soon afterwards Sturrock set about constructing snow ploughs at Doncaster, which were ready for use by the following winter.

In the autumn of 1854, a quarrel between the Caledonian and the Edinburgh and Glasgow resulted in the latter becoming more friendly towards the NB and its East Coast allies. From 1 January 1855, through bookings and services became possible beyond Edinburgh to Glasgow, and, in conjunction with the Scottish Central, to Perth, by the junction at Greenhill with the E&G (south of Larbert). Negotiations followed with the Scottish Midland Junction (Perth to a junction north of Forfar) and the Aberdeen, which completed the route from there to the 'Granite City'. Through coaches and bookings were even extended to Aberdeen. Agreements with these Scottish companies included payment of a bonus of top of the normal mileage charge.

In consequence, the 9.30 from King's Cross was accelerated in the summer of 1855. It was only allowed 40 minutes to Hitchin, a remarkable speed for those days, and then stopped, on the GN worked section, at Peterborough, Grantham, Newark, Retford, Doncaster, Knottingley and Milford Junction. Doncaster was reached in 3¾ hr, York in 4 hr 50 m. and Edinburgh in 10 hr 50 m. Second class passengers were admitted for through journeys from King's Cross to Scotland, but not for other journeys until 1860. The night train was accelerated to 11 hr to Edinburgh. But third class passengers had to leave earlier and take 12 hr 50 m. Again, the up trains were slower, the best day train taking 11 hr 40 m. from Edinburgh, and the best night, with third class passengers, as much as 13 hr. A practice soon developed of providing Glasgow and Perth through carriages on the best day train, but Aberdeen carriages only on the best night train. In September, there was a further improvement, as a 10.30 a.m. from King's Cross was accelerated by 20 minutes to reach York at 4.50 p.m., this change enabling the North Eastern and NB to work the train through to Edinburgh the same night, thus giving a second day service to Edinburgh. The departure of the best train varied for some years after this, as it sometimes left at 9.0 or 9.15 instead of 9.30, but maintained the 10 hr 50 m. schedule to Edinburgh. The overall time to Aberdeen by the night trains was 17½ hr down and 18½ hr up. The North Eastern had been formed in 1854 by the amalgamation of the YN&B, Y&NM, and the Leeds Northern (late Leeds & Thirsk).

The condition of the locomotives and rolling stock of the NB around this time had become so deplorable that without assistance its services would have practically come to a standstill. The GN lent it six goods engines and drivers for two months from 4 December 1854. In the first week of the New Year Sturrock visited Edinburgh and on his return, recommended the immediate loan of two passenger engines. He was of the opinion that, failing the loan, the NB would be unable to maintain the east coast service between Berwick and Edinburgh.

Towards the end of 1855 a Joint Committee of the Aberdeen and SMJ applied to the GN for the loan of goods engines to enable the through goods trains run in connection with the east coast companies to work with greater regularity. Sturrock's view was that the loan would be inconvenient, but that it could be arranged if the object to be gained was very important to his company. The board considered that it was objectionable to lend engines, but as a matter of policy it was left to Clarke and Sturrock to deal with the application as they deemed best. Their decision is not recorded.

Carriage of day mails to Hull, Lincoln, Leeds and Wakefield began in April 1853. The Post Office offered £1,500 per annum for this service while the GN required £2,000. The dispute was referred to the arbitration of John Hawkshaw, who in 1856, awarded that the sum of 10d per bag per mile should be paid on the main line, and 3d per bag per mile on branches. By then, the day mails were also carried to York, and receipts from Post Office traffic under the award amounted to £2,557 per annum. Lineside mail bag exchange apparatus was in use about this time, being installed at Post Office expense.

In order to encourage fishing at Grimsby, the MS&L in 1854 decided to construct a fish dock. Later in the year the Midland and the GN joined the MS&L in formation of the Grimsby Deep Sea Fishing Co. Several vessels were purchased. The dock was equipped with an icehouse, and fishermen's cottages built. After two years, each of the three companies had lost about £2,000, so in 1858 the GN board recommended that the company be wound up and the vessels and plant sold.

Despite the losses a valuable fish trade developed. Increasing quantities were sent by rail to London and other towns. From 1 February 1856 the GN worked its own traffic at Grimsby, appointing a staff of six there including a drayman. Fish traffic from Hull to Billingsgate via Milford Junction also began to expand. Containers, transferable to road vehicles, were soon built for this traffic.

Early in 1854 a change of coal manager occurred. Coles Child, who only gave part-time service, was retired on 30 April. Herbert Clarke, the general manager's brother (lately superintendent of the South Devon), was appointed, on 14 March, Manager of Coal Traffic at all stations from London to Peterborough inclusive, at £350 per annum, and was also allowed by the coalowners half of 1% on cost price of all coal sold. In 1854 GN gross receipts from coal carriage amounted to over £300,000, and in the same year the total coal sold reached 525,334 ton composed of 113,675 ton in Lincolnshire, 46,716 ton on the Peterborough line, and 281,559 ton in London. It was principally obtained from pits in Yorkshire and Durham but a small quantity came from Derbyshire, the Butterley Co supplying 600 ton a week, the Pinxton Colliery 500 ton, and Loscoe Colliery 12 trucks a day. Bearing in mind that it had stated through its secretary that it was not selling coals on its own account, the GN found it embarrassing to enforce payment for coal, but found a solution in July 1855 by appointing Herbert Clarke as Commission Agent at 1d per ton.

The Ambergate obtained an Act on 31 July 1854 which empowered it to agree with the GN to work or use its line and to sell its rolling stock to it, and also permitted lease or sale to it with consent of three-fifths of the shareholders present at a general meeting. The Midland station at Nottingham was not to be used by the Ambergate or the GN (except for traffic working through to the west of Nottingham) after five years from the passing of the Act or when the Ambergate's own station was opened. Agreement between the Ambergate and GN was signed on Friday 30 March 1855, and three months later, the engines, rolling stock and plant were handed over.

A Bill for an extension into Nottingham, thrown out by the Lords in the 1853 session, passed on 3 July 1854, empowering the Ambergate to construct a line, 2 miles 61 chains, from just short of Carlton junction, Colwick, to a station in East Croft on the east side of London Road (then Flood Road). A junction diverging 26 chains from the terminus and joining the Midland at Sneinton was also authorised, the whole being estimated to cost £120,500.

The new station was brought into use on Saturday 3 October 1857, and the arrangement for rent at the Midland station ended. Called London Road, the station consisted of two platforms with four intervening lines. The buildings included new offices for the Ambergate (previously at Petergate), a small refreshment room, an engine shed, warehouse, cattle dock and stable, all completed in March 1858.

New sheds for Ambergate engines and carriages were built at Grantham in 1855 at a cost of £2,450 including permanent way, the old buildings then being demolished. The warehouse at Colwick was removed in March 1856, and the sidings and embankment in July 1857. On 1 August of that year the GN board approved extension of the electric telegraph from Grantham to Nottingham. Sidings were laid in at Gonerby, with necessary signalling, completed in June 1857.

From the opening of London Road, the GN operated an omnibus

service between there and the Midland station, and performed its own cartage. In December 1858 Seymour Clarke found a cab proprietor who took over the bus service. A contract was made with J. Pepper who undertook goods collection and delivery.

The Ambergate changed its name to the Nottingham & Grantham Railway & Canal Co by its Act of 15 May 1860. Soon afterwards the GN exercised its option to lease it. The terms agreed were a fixed annual rental of 4⅛% on capital of £1,014,000 from 1 August 1861, with the right to purchase outright on repayment of capital at par. The N&G preserved its identity until 1 January 1923, when it was absorbed into the London & North Eastern.

Denison's son-in-law, Charles Wilson Faber of Doncaster, was elected to the board in March 1854 in the place of Colonel Colquhoun who had died in the previous September. Walter Leith received a rise in salary of £100 in January 1855 and on the following 1 July J. Coffin's pay was increased to £315 and F. Parker's to £450. Leith's salary was again raised by £100 on 1 January 1856 and Pulford's was increased to £500 at the same time.

There were changes among the engineers. In April 1853 Walter Brydone was appointed for the Loop and East Lincolnshire lines, and Henry Carr for the King's Cross–Askern main line, both appointments carrying a salary of £400 per annum. Carr resigned on 18 January 1855, and Brydone took over Carr's duties too, but on 23 May he also resigned. As it was intended that Joseph Cubitt should retire at the end of the year, a temporary arrangement was made for W. C. Graves to take charge of the main line and Richard Johnson the Loop and East Lincolnshire, both receiving five guineas a week. In November the company advertised for a successor to Cubitt at £800 per annum. Of 48 applicants, the names were whittled down to ten, then seven, then three, with a final choice between Brydone, and Whitton of the Oxford, Worcester & Wolverhampton. Brydone was successful and took up appointment on 1 January 1856. Cubitt had agreed to retire from this date and took over the position of consultant engineer from his father. Brydone continued to employ all Cubitt's staff, except Burleigh, the London resident engineer, who was given three months' notice and after leaving, became engineer to the Three Counties Asylum which was to be built near Arlsey. Upon his departure three district engineers were appointed, all to receive five guineas a week, R. Gastenau London–Peterborough, W. Graves Peterborough–Askern and the Ambergate line, and Richard Johnson the Loop and East Lincolnshire, and the Horncastle branch. From this time the engineers department employed its own architect, Silas Bolton.

The Leeds, Bradford & Halifax Junction was opened on 1 August 1854, the Horncastle & Kirkstead Junction on 11 August 1855, and the Stamford & Essendine on 1 November 1856. These were all worked by the GN, and will be described in later chapters. In 1854 the promoters of the Barnet & Willesden, which proposed a main line from Barnet to the West London and sundry branches, put plans to the GN directors, who were not impressed, and resolved not to support the scheme.

The original Gladstone and Octuple Agreements made provision for an additional allowance in the event of any company working traffic in excess of its allotted percentage. Clarke does not seem to have exercised much foresight in agreeing with the other general managers that this should be a mere 20%, not even sufficient to cover working expenses. In the long run, the pooling was not advantageous to the GN, for with its shorter routes and faster services it had increasingly carried traffic in excess of the percentages apportioned. On the other hand the confederates had settled down to drawing their percentages without offering serious competition. Railway Clearing House returns show that the GN had, during the twelve months ending 30 June 1855, paid the Midland and L & NW £8,355 on a traffic of £94,251 (without terminals) on goods, and £16,883 on a traffic of £169,183 (without terminals) for passengers, in respect of the Gladstone Agreement. With a somewhat similar result from the Octuple Agreement, £61,000 was the total paid out for the year 1855. It was small wonder that Denison bitterly complained that his company was paying away more than a £1,000 a week from its earnings, and looked forward to an equitable division of receipts when the agreements were revised.

The Octuple Agreement was replaced by an English and Scotch Alliance, which was reasonably satisfactory to the GN and its east coast allies. It was complicated by the allotment of percentages between many intermediate towns in England to places in Scotland as well as from London. Traffic to places beyond Larbert junction (south of Stirling, where the rival routes then met) was equally divided between the east coast and west coast routes, and to places south thereof the division was fair. The unjust aspect of the new agreement which came into force on 1 January 1856 was that, for the 14 years it was to last, it ignored the potential claims of a central route, then being formed by the Midland, which was building its Leicester & Hitchin line and had leased the (little) North Western.

Clarke opened negotiations with Huish for revision of the Gladstone Award, and in the light of what transpired later, it should be noted that in his letter of 23 July 1855 Clarke emphasised that any conclusions reached would be 'subject to the approval of the three companies'. He, of course, expected to negotiate only with the L&NW and Midland, but found that the confederates had included the MS&L in the talks. Allport had by this time left the MS&L to become general manager of the Midland and had been succeeded on the MS&L by Edward Watkin. Several meetings had taken place before Clarke even informed his directors that he was faced by Watkin in addition to Huish and Allport. Clarke's main object was to obtain a realistic division of the traffic, but he also optimistically hoped to secure a share of the traffic west of Sheffield, a proposal with which the opposing managers would be most reluctant to agree, for one of the principal objects of the confederacy was to preserve Lancashire traffic to Euston Square. His arguments for increased percentages to the competitive towns had to be admitted, but the extent of the increases could not be agreed. Clarke then claimed a fresh reference to arbitration, while the confederate managers insisted that any such reference should be extended to the whole area of competition. The series of meetings ended in December with Clarke persuaded (hoodwinked would be a better term) into putting his signature to proposals to form the basis of a new reference to arbitration.

Two days later, on 19 December 1855, the GN board thoroughly discussed Clarke's conclusions. Denison summed up the recommendation as 'precluding the GN for 14 years from any participation in traffic arising between London and any town on the MS&L lying west of Sheffield, or from any new railway west of the Midland, while the L&NW and Midland would participate in the traffic arising at or between London and nearly every town east of Sheffield'. As usual, the majority of the directors supported their chairman, and it was resolved not to confirm the document which Clarke had signed. In view of Clarke's letter to Huish of 23 July, the board was quite entitled to adopt this attitude, although the opposing companies regarded the action as repudiation.

The Midland and L&NW boards were only too ready to support their managers, and did so within a few days. The GN refusal to adopt the recommendations was tantamount to a declaration of war, and, while a month's armistice was arranged during which no solution to the dispute was forth-coming, from 1 February the confederates put on new fast trains and cut fares to competitive towns by approximately half. Passengers deserted the GN, which was forced into retaliation. On Friday 8 February advertisements were inserted in the newspapers that from the following Monday the GN would lower its fares. Additional down trains were arranged from King's Cross at 9.45 a.m. and 5.45 p.m., arriving at York at 2.55 and 11.0 p.m., and up trains from York at 10.0 a.m. and 5.40 p.m., reaching King's Cross at 3.30 and 10.0 p.m. Fares were reduced to competitors' level except in the cases of Nottingham and Sheffield to which they were considerably lower. One reduction followed another until the first and second class fares between London and York fell to 5s (25p) and 3s 6d (17½p) respectively, and between London and Peterborough to 2s (10p) and 1s (5p). After three weeks' hostilities, agreement was reached that Gladstone should be asked to frame a fresh set of percentages, leaving the GN's claim to a share of traffic west of Sheffield in abeyance. Accordingly it was arranged that from 1 March the low fares would be withdrawn. The news leaked out that only one week remained for the public to take advantage of these. They did so in thousands, for Seymour Clarke reported that in the last five days of competition, ending 29 February, 21,843½ passengers were carried in GN cheap trains producing a total of £3,756. He added that there were no complaints and no accidents. The competition did not extend to goods traffic, but the Midland was accused of receiving goods at Leeds, addressed via the GN, and invoicing them through Derby and Peterborough to Norwich. The GN, prevented from forwarding goods over the L & Y beyond Wakefield in April, acquired an office, stables and a warehouse at Huddersfield, and a few months later rented a coach-house and stables at Dewsbury.

Robert Baxter, who had previous cognizance of the Gladstone Awards, was engaged to conduct the new arbitration on behalf of the GN. On 29 April 1857 he advised the directors of the result of Gladstone's deliberations. The percentages allotted to the GN for passengers and goods were as under and it was intended that the award should be back-dated to 1 March 1856:

York	90%	75%	Peterborough	90%	55%
Leeds	75%	48%	Newark	90%	55%
Wakefield	85%	85%	Halifax	85%	57%
Doncaster	95%	88%	Bradford	80%	42%
Sheffield	80%	42%	Hull	92%	87%
Lincoln	85%	75%	Grimsby	95%	90%
Nottingham	50%	25%	Gainsborough	95%	90%
Stamford	95%	70%			

The GN fell in with a proposal by the L & N W that with the Midland the three companies should subscribe to a present for Gladstone which should cost 500 guineas.

In the 1856 Session, the (little) North Western submitted a Bill seeking to obtain running powers over the Midland, and L & C, to enable it to work an Anglo-Scottish service in conjunction with the GN. Opposed by the confederates, and supported by the GN, the contest raged over many days, and reports of the proceedings filled several issues of the *Railway Times*. The Bill failed on a technicality, but so far the GN was concerned, a most important outcome was that E. B. Denison Q.C. during cross-examination, extracted a full confession of an illegal common-purse agreement between the L & N W and Midland, which had been secretly operating for two years or so. This had been one of the factors in the development of the Midland's coal traffic, which originated principally in Derbyshire and passed to the L & N W, which conveyed it to London. Thus did the GN lose supremacy in the coal carrying trade, although it could not know the reason at the time.

V

THE WEST RIDING

The Leeds, Bradford & Halifax Junction received its Act on 30 June 1852, authorising a line from Bowling junction with the L&Y (¾ miles south of Bradford) to a junction with the Leeds & Dewsbury (by now part of the LNW) where it crossed the Leeds & Bradford, about ½ mile from Central Station. Running powers were granted into Central, and over the L&Y from Bowling to Halifax. The L&Y received reciprocal running powers over the LB&HJ. In October, Denison and Firth agreed terms for the GN to work the line. On 4 August 1853, the LB&HJ obtained a further act sanctioning these, and construction of two branches from Laister Dyke (sometimes spelt Leicester Dyke), one to an independent station in Bradford, and another to Gildersome, to serve Adwalton coalfields.

The small low level station was not large enough to deal with the anticipated additional traffic. The directors had to go, cap in hand, to the Central Station board for permission to return to Central. In June 1854 it was agreed that the GN would use a portion on payment of £12,000, a quarter of the cost of works up to that time, £48,000. The GN would have use of the viaduct from a point just south of the Leeds and Bradford line—close to the LB&HJ's intended junction with the Leeds and Dewsbury—to Central, on payment to the L&Y of £20,000. Thus a junction with the Leeds and Dewsbury, and use of its metals by GN trains, was avoided. The GN and LB&HJ also obtained rights to use the short curved viaduct from the low level station to Central. These arrangements were sanctioned by an Act of 2 July 1855, which authorised £1,000,000 new capital and £330,000 loans.

The LB&HJ directors viewed their line on Tuesday 11 July 1854 and, although the stations were incomplete, expected to open it in three weeks' time. The government officer who inspected it on 27 July was satisfied that the works were forward enough for safe public use, and sanctioned opening on 1 August as planned. Final agreement for the GN to provide rolling stock, plant and staff was made on 14 July. Seymour

Clarke was appointed Traffic Manager. The L&Y arranged that its traffic from Halifax and Bradford to Leeds should pass over the line. Also on 1 August the GN ceased to use the 'low level' for passenger trains, which returned to Central.

The line, laid out by John Hawkshaw, ran for 8 miles 66 chains from Bowling junction to the junction outside Leeds. It was double line, as was the Bradford branch opened on the same day, which added a further 1 mile 11 chains. The gradients were steep. Laister Dyke was approached by stiff climbs from both Bowling and Bradford. Thence the line fell at 1 in 100 through Stanningley tunnel (455 yd) and then steepened to 1 in 50 to Holbeck, threading Armley tunnel (80 yd). Stations were at Bowling (1 mile from the junction), Laister Dyke, Stanningley, Bramley, and Armley & Wortley. The exchange (high level) station at Holbeck (above the Midland station) was not brought into use until 2 July 1855. Signals were disc and crossbar.

Ten trains were run each way on weekdays between Leeds and Bradford, and eight each way between Leeds and Halifax. Except those including King's Cross through carriages, Halifax trains were L&Y. There were four each way on each service on Sundays. Huish agreed to division of traffic between Halifax and Low Moor to London, the GN to receive 65% of passenger receipts and 50% of goods, and fares to be the same as to Bradford. But the GN soon discovered that its rivals were re-booking at Huddersfield, giving lower fares to Halifax, Bradford, Leeds and Wakefield.

Through goods traffic began from Monday 7 August, but the local goods services were delayed by the incomplete state of stations. Goods sheds were provided at Bramley and Stanningley by the end of November, but months elapsed before the Bradford Adolphus Street station was ready for merchandise (which continued to be handled at the L&Y station). Adolphus St station included office accommodation for the LB&HJ, removed from premises occupied at 27 Park Row, Leeds. About this time Edward Ackroyd succeeded Firth as chairman, although the latter remained on the board.

The LB&HJ obtained a further Act on 10 July 1854 for an extension from Gildersome to Ardsley, to form a junction with the Bradford, Wakefield & Leeds, authorised on the same day. The latter was closely allied, had been projected by the same parties, with Hawkshaw as engineer and Fraser as resident, and was authorised to construct a Wakefield–Leeds railway. The promoters expected to serve several collieries. Offices were at Bradford. Although the first chairman was Samuel Smith, (mayor of Bradford), he was soon replaced by Akroyd.

The Gildersome branch was formally opened on Tuesday 19 August 1856, the directors and guests taking a trip over the line and then having lunch at the Sun Hotel, Bradford. Passenger services began next day over the 5 miles 7 furlongs, stations being provided at Dudley Hill, Birkenshaw & Tong, Drighlington & Adwalton, and Gildersome. By the end of September five coal trains a day, carrying an aggregate of 1,000 tons were working from Adwalton coalfield to Bradford. Passenger traffic was satisfactory, although the local population was small—about 300 people were using the Saturday market trains. Warehouses were built at Birkenshaw and Drighlington, and goods trains began on 1 May 1857. The branch was extended to Ardsley on Saturday 10 October 1857, with an intermediate station at Morley on the 4½ mile section and another at Tingley, first shown in the May 1859 Bradshaw. This branch, double track, formed an alternative route between Wakefield and Bradford, but was even more heavily graded than the route via Holbeck, with banks of 1 in 40. From 1 December a through carriage from King's Cross to Bradford was diverted over it. Tunnels were at Birkenshaw (106 yd) and Gildersome (156 yd).

Due to the impending opening of the BW&L, the engine shed at the low level yard at Leeds was removed to a fresh site at Wortley junction, where a triangular piece of land, joint property of the GN and L&Y, was available.

On Saturday 3 October 1857 the BW&L was formally opened, a special train leaving Central at noon and returning from Wakefield at 5.0 p.m. after some junketing in the Music Hall there. Public opening followed on Monday when local trains, operated by the GN and L&Y, (which had obtained running powers) began. Unfortunately the engine of the 9.15 a.m. from Wakefield got off the line at Holbeck junction, but it was soon re-railed and, no harm being done, the train proceeded. The new line left the L&Y main line ¼ mile west of Wakefield (Kirkgate) station at Ings Road junction and joined the LB&HJ at Holbeck junction, 9 miles 66 chains. GN trains could now run direct into Leeds Central without reversal. There was a sharply curved south to west spur from Wortley South junction to Wortley West junction, allowing through running from Wakefield to Bradford. The BW&L had running powers over the LB&HJ, and into Central. The GN worked the line, and appointed the staff at BW&L expense. Seymour Clarke acted as traffic manager. From 1 November the GN turned its long distance trains over the line instead of the route via Methley, and goods traffic began 11 days later. The line, double, on leaving Wakefield climbed almost continuously to Ardsley, first at 1 in 100 and then at 1 in 122. Ardsley was on a short level stretch, but then the line dropped through Ardsley tunnel (297 yd) for three miles at 1 in 100, followed by a slight hump and a final steep fall of 1 in 50 towards Holbeck. Stations were at Wakefield (Westgate), Lofthouse, and Ardsley.

In July 1855 the Central board agreed to GN plans drawn up by Joseph Cubitt for a new station and offices at an estimate of £20,000. The work was undertaken by Kirk & Parry and took about a year longer than anticipated. Cubitt supervised these works just before he retired. The buildings were sufficiently complete by 18 November 1856 for the electric telegraph to be moved from the old offices, and the station was finished in August of the next year. Approval was given on 22 August 1855 for a three signal gantry at the station entrance, hence the oddly named Three Signal Bridge junction. Until this was provided the man at the junction controlled the approaching traffic, converging from three lines, with one semaphore, entailing risk of a sidelong collision. Coal sidings for the two Yorkshire companies were built in the low level yard in 1858. The GN acquired some more ground at Leeds, always known as 'Gott's land', on which a large goods establishment was built. Also in 1858 the GN bought the junction line from Wellington Road to the high level from the NER.

Relations between the GN and the two small companies were frequently strained. One source of dis-satisfaction was the competition in 1858 between the GN and its rivals, thought to have affected adversely LB&HJ, and BWL passenger receipts. The LB&HJ was also incensed at the GN conceding running powers to the Midland between Hitchin and King's Cross. Seymour Clarke resigned from the management of both in April. In October an agreement was made with the LB&HJ that from 1 January 1859 it would provide its own staff on the Gildersome and Ardsley branches and the GN would not provide stock, or plant, for branches. This lasted until June 1863. The directors were not satisfised with GN's handling of their coal traffic, as they were anxious to enter the trade, buy coal at the pithead and sell it to potential customers on the L&Y. To these proposals the GN, already skating on thin ice with its own coal trade, turned a deaf ear. Towards the end of 1856, the LB&HJ proposed to hire engines from the GN and L&Y for developing its coal trade. Eventually it acquired engines of its own, put in charge of F. Rouse and housed in a shed at Bradford. The company discontinued sale of coal on 1 April 1860.

From November 1857 the GN complained about permanent way conditions between Wakefield and Leeds and threatened to return its traffic to the Methley route. In October the BW&L gave notice that from 1 January it would appoint its own staff. The GN, for reasons not apparent, abruptly withdrew its engines and coal wagons. The BWL hurriedly had to acquire engines and wagons of its own. For a few months it hired wagons from the GN. In the following May it retaliated by withdrawing passes issued to some GN directors and officers. A year later there was an abortive proposal that the LB&HJ and BW&L should amalgamate.

Although the LB&HJ held an advantage in mileage over the Midland, about 9 miles to 13½, it failed to capture more than about 30% of the Leeds–Bradford traffic. It was thought that if the trains were diverted to the better situated L&Y Bradford station an improved result might be obtained. But in 1859 an arrangement was made with the Midland whereby for five years the LB&HJ would receive 35% of receipts on all traffic between Leeds and Bradford, and for the following five years, receive 40%. From 1 November, despite much grumbling by the public, the service on both lines was reduced, and the fares raised.

The BW&L proprietors learned at their August 1860 meeting that cottages and an engine shed at Ardsley and a small Beeston station would complete their main line. The station, serving the Low Moor Co's new works there, was first shown in the February 1860 Bradshaw. The company obtained an Act on 23 July 1860 for a branch to Ossett. It was single line, and left the main line at Wrenthorpe junction and at first ran for 2 miles 29½ chains to Flushdyke, however called Ossett until the line was extended two years later. General traffic commenced on Monday 7 April 1862, but minerals had been carried between Wrenthorpe and Roundwood Colliery sidings since 6 January. There were two occupations overbridges and four underbridges. The permanent way was laid with 80 lb rails. A turntable suitable for tender engines was provided at the temporary terminus.

The remainder of the line to Ossett was sanctioned for public use by Captain Rich when he inspected the works on 12 March 1864, and opened for traffic on 7 April (single line, 65 chains long). There was a viaduct with three brick arches of 30 ft span and two underbridges. A new platform, at a higher level, was provided at Flushdyke, although to reach it passengers had to cross the old rails. Captain Rich was satisfied that there was no public danger as these were to be removed. Flushdyke station did not appear in the timetables until March 1865. No turntable was provided at Ossett, and so trains had to be worked by tank engines. The branch was operated by train staff.

Both the BW&L and the LB&HJ obtained Acts in 1861 to extend to Batley, the former on 17 May and the latter on 7 June. The last was the first to reach Batley, opening a branch from Adwalton junction (between Drighlington and Gildersome) to a temporary station at Upper Batley on Wednesday 19 August 1863. The line, 2 miles 31 chains, was double except at the temporary terminus which was on a 1 in 41 gradient. In the absence of a turntable, the Board of Trade insisted that tank engines were employed. There were three overbridges and six underbridges. The remainder, on to the L & N W Batley station, where the trains used the east platform, was brought into use on 1 November 1864. This extension, authorised by an Act of 30 June 1862, was mostly on a gradient of 1 in 50, with heavy earthworks, and the sharpest curves of 13 chains radius. The L & N W was crossed by a substantial bridge. There were three other underbridges and two overbridges. The line was double except the short Upper Batley section. The permanent station here was opened about October 1866. The old one was removed to Howden Clough to provide a station there on 1 November.

The B W & L single line to Batley, 3 miles 55 chains, started with an end-on junction at Ossett and made a junction with the L B & H J line. Works were considerable, involving the Chickenley Heath (47 yd) and Shaw Cross (209 yd) tunnels, seven overbridges and nine underbridges. The line was opened on 15 December 1864, but passenger services were first shown in the February 1865 Bradshaw. There was a station at Batley, just south of the junction with the L B & H J. The combined branches formed yet a third route between Wakefield and Bradford.

In the 1863 Session the B W & L sought powers for branches to Methley and Low Moor, and to change its name to the West Yorkshire. The Methley branch and change of title were sanctioned by the Act of 21 July but the other branches was rejected. The Act also authorised running powers over the N E from Methley to Castleford and over the L & Y from Wakefield to Barnsley. By a further Act of 23 June 1864 the Methley line became W Y, L & Y, and N E joint property. A Methley Joint Committee was set up, each company appointing two directors with Firth and Isaac Knight representing the W Y. The first meeting was on 8 August 1864. Henry Nelson was appointed Secretary, and Fraser was confirmed as Engineer. A contract for construction was let to James Bray & Sons. Stations were to be at Stanley and Methley, also at Lofthouse, (at the junction with the main line), and sidings provided at Lofthouse Alum Works, and at several collieries. A fixed toll on all traffic would be paid into a joint fund. Up to 18 March 1867 each company had subscribed £34,500 for the joint line.

The railway diverged from the W Y at Lofthouse North junction, was 5 miles 3 chains long, and joined the N E's old Y & N M line at Methley

Joint Line junction. At Methley High Level junction it bifurcated, platforms being provided on both forks at Methley station, and a 30 chain spur connected with the L&Y at Lofthouse junction. This was a confusing name for the eastern end of the line, as there was a triangular junction at the western end, a 25 chain curve from Lofthouse East junction to Lofthouse South junction on the WY. Lofthouse Joint station was built on this curve and was on a 1 in 90 gradient. The line, double, was inspected for the Board of Trade three times in 1865. On 19 September it was passed for passenger traffic. Goods traffic began in August but a regular passenger service was not put on for another four years. R. Robinson, GN Leeds district agent, managed the line, and the GN maintained it. The GN's account for working it for the first half of 1867 was £510. The NE stated that the charges were 20% too high, to which the GN retorted that if the NW desired to work the line for 20% less it was welcome to do so. None of the companies was anxious to provide passenger trains, although the local inhabitants became impatient. Lofthouse South fork was not in regular use in early years.

By 1863 accommodation at Bradford Adolphus St station was hopelessly inadequate to deal with the expanding goods traffic. The arcade and platforms were choked with sheets of wool, waiting to be collected by merchants who used railway premises as a free warehouse. Under these chaotic conditions, room was barely left for the passengers, and extra staff had to be employed. Additional sidings were completed in 1864, but a scheme to spend thousands of pounds on additional accommodation was deferred. To relieve congestion, it was resolved to transfer passenger traffic to the L&Y station (later known as Exchange, but then referred to as St George's), which the L&Y proposed to enlarge. An Act was obtained on 14 July 1864 authorising the LB&HJ to construct a line from Hammerton Street junction on the Bradford branch to Mill Lane junction on the L&Y. The contract for construction was let to S. Pearson & Son for £17,700. The line was double, 57 chains long, but in that short distance there were four small overbridges, one small underbridge and Wakefield Road tunnel (132 yd). The steepest gradient was 1 in 50 descending to Bradford and the sharpest curve was 11 chains radius. The line was brought into use on 7 January 1867, and Adolphus St station was given over to goods and mineral traffic. Use of 'St George's' cost the GN £1,500 per annum plus toll. The arrangement was not satisfactory, for accommodation was cramped, GN down trains had to cross the L&Y up line twice, while a tunnel (subsequently opened out) created a bottleneck at the station entrance.

Meantime, despite strenuous L&Y opposition, both the small

Yorkshire lines passed into GN possession. By an agreement of 8 April 1863 LB&HJ proprietors received a dividend of 6%, or the same dividend as paid by the GN, whichever was greater. A bill to authorise absorption failed in 1864 but was successful on 5 July 1865. The GN took over working of the WY on 1 January 1865, and by another Act of 5 July the WY and a third share of the Methley Joint line became GN property from 5 September. The shareholders were guaranteed a minimum dividend of 6%.

Both the small companies had installed the electric telegraph. On 21 April 1866 the GN resolved to put the block system on all its West Riding lines. A goods warehouse at Batley was ready on 1 April 1866. Work was proceeding on construction of an engine shed, a coke stage, pits and a turntable at Bradford, all brought into use on Monday 11 February 1867. Sidings for Balaclava Colliery were laid near Tingley late in 1867.

Back in March 1851, it had been arranged with the L&Y that Wakefield (Kirkgate) and Knottingley stations should be rebuilt at joint expense. Contracts were not let until September 1853. Knottingley station was completed in March 1854. Up to that time the GN had expended £43,590 on the two stations, including half the cost of the original structures. Three more years elapsed before final payment was made for the Wakefield works, although the station was in partial use before then. The buildings included an engine shed, granary and a goods shed. A Joint GN and L&Y Committee was set up to manage the stations, the GN administering Knottingley and the L&Y providing staff and stores at Wakefield. Management of Halifax station was included in the joint arrangement in 1854, and in 1867 that of Bradford, which appeared in GN timetables as 'Bradford near St George's Hall' until March 1867, thereafter as 'Bradford Exchange'.

The GN paid half rent of an engine shed at Halifax from January 1855. A goods depot and stables were built for the LB&HJ. When in 1862 it was proposed to enlarge Halifax station, plans to move the shed and stables were discussed, but were not approved until 1865, and another two years went by before works were completed.

Reluctantly the directors, in response to memorials, agreed that from 1 April 1860 one or two trains to Bradford and Halifax should run via Wortley junction instead of via Holbeck. But they were not well patronised so from 1 May 1861 they again ran via Holbeck. Seymour Clarke, who was inclined to keep the mileage down to a minimum, also withdrew the through Halifax carriages. Not only did Halifax passengers have to change at Laister Dyke, but on the last train at night they were kept waiting until the engine returned from Bradford to work their train to Halifax. He chose an unfortunate time to introduce this economy. From 16 July the L & Y began to work goods traffic, from Huddersfield, Halifax and Wakefield, handed to the Midland at a new junction at Oakenshaw. If letters from irate Halifax traders, in the local press, are any indication, Clarke's policy of reduced mileage must have lost considerable business to the GN.

Some years later, through carriages were again provided between King's Cross and Halifax, some being worked via Bowling, and others by different routes.

THE FRAUDS OF LEOPOLD REDPATH

Although accidents on the GN were neither frequent nor serious, in 1856 a disaster of another nature was to throw the shareholders and directors into consternation. On 7 July 1846 the registration department had been placed in the charge of W. H. Clark, who had been secretary to the Direct Northern and was appointed Chief Registrar to find him a position in the united company. A solicitor by profession, he was not familiar with the work and so was content to rely on his clerk, Leopold Redpath, who had gained experience of the procedure in the service of the Brighton & Chichester and then the London & Brighton. Redpath had been temporarily engaged by the GN at 42s (£2.10) a week on 27 October 1846, and confirmed in the position at £130 per annum on the following 4 May. His salary was increased to £160 from 1 January 1848 as a reward for efficiency and good conduct, and from 1 July 1851 he received £180. On 28 June 1853 the board discussed the expense of the registration department, deciding that costs were too high and should be reduced. Besides Clark and Redpath there were only three other clerks. Two of them each received £109 per annum, and the third, Charles Kent, had actually served in the department throughout 1847 without pay. For this he received a gratuity of £25 and was taken on the strength at £75 per annum from 1 January 1848, a salary now increased to £90, while Clark was requested to find other employment. Redpath tendered his resignation on 8 December, but not to take effect before 30 June 1854, which was accepted. Clark made no signs of leaving, and in February was instructed to retire on 30 April. Redpath withdrew his resignation on 10 May, offered himself in lieu of Clark, and was appointed Clerk in Charge of the Registration Department 13 days later, salary £250 per annum. Unknown to the directors, he had already robbed the company of upwards of £120,000. He had even had the impudence to lend some of the money back at 4½% interest.

Discrepancies between the amounts paid in dividends, and due to be paid on registered stock, came to light early in 1854. Then came a curious incident, which may have had a bearing on these events. On 30 March a Mr Turner Townsend wrote to Francis Parker, a director, calling attention to a mistake in sending him a dividend warrant for £1,250 A Stock, although he did not hold any GN stock. Clark had already begun investigations into these matters, but left before he could complete them, leaving Redpath to continue them! That dividends were regularly being overpaid was obvious to some senior clerks, who, after conferring, put their suspicions to Thomas Reynolds who had succeeded Mylne as accountant in August 1847. Reynolds, however, had such confidence in Redpath that he was content to wait for the statement the latter had promised to produce. On 29 January 1856, two years after the first hint of fraud had come to light, the secretary received a statement by Redpath which showed that dividends had been overpaid on some stocks. The chairman was informed, but even he was convinced that Redpath, by continuing investigations, would soon discover the 'errors' which gave rise to the 'apparent discrepancies'.

Incredibly, matters were allowed to slide until September when Redpath was again pressed to produce a satisfactory explanation. This he was unable to do and tendered his resignation which under the circumstances could not be accepted. Independent investigations by other officers proved that stock to the amount of £137,000 was registered in excess in the company's books. Further enquiries exposed Redpath's system of fraud and forgery. By coincidence a somewhat similar fraud on the Crystal Palace & West End of London Railway had just become known.

Redpath fled to Paris, but returned almost immediately to face the case against him. He and Kent, accused in complicity in the frauds, were charged before the Clerkenwell Magistrate on 15 November 1856. The simplicity of the frauds was exposed. For over eight years Redpath had created fictitious stock almost at will. After this, conversion of the stock into cash through brokers had only been a matter of inventing a few names and forging signatures on forms to hand in his office. Although he had joined the GN with good credentials from the London & Brighton, it now appeared that he had been a bankrupt, and that there were discreditable episodes in his past. It was unfortunate that so recently as the twentieth half-yearly meeting on 23 August the chairman, when already aware of the serious irregularities in the registration department, allowed himself to devote a portion of his speech to an expression of the utmost confidence in every officer and servant of the company. On 16 January 1857, at the Old Bailey, Redpath was sentenced to transportation for life. Kent was acquitted and was taken back into the company's service, retiring in 1885 aged 74. Three clerks were dismissed for minor complicity, by allowing their addresses and those of relatives to be used by Redpath.

Even at the time of his appointment as Chief Clerk, Redpath owned a town house at Regent's Park and a country place at Weybridge. He kept a staff of servants, indulged in rich entertaining, was noted for generosity, and was on intimate terms with peers and wealthy people. All this on less than £4 a week, so that although he had acquired a reputation for successful speculation, one wonders how he could have possibly escaped suspicion from the very moment of the discovery that something was radically at fault in the registration department. It is even more surprising that he hoodwinked his superiors for another two and a half years.

A firm of accountants, Deloitte & Greenwood, was called in to unravel the tangle. They brought a staff of 52 clerks for whom they charged a guinea and a half a day (profit of half a guinea), and three guineas a day for the principal's attendance. With fares for clerks and cab fares for principals, in a couple of months they ran up a bill of £4,407, including £687 for books. In this time they had only examined two out of the seven stocks and merely reproduced the results which Henry Oakley, William Grinling, and others of the senior staff had achieved by working far into the nights. In these circumstances, the board decided to cut expenses, and dispense with these professional accountants. They paid for the books and offered Deloitte £3,000, ultimately settling by payment of £3,937.

The company now had to face the problem of how the loss of over £220,000 should be met. Legal opinion was sought. The directors were advised that the loss must be treated in the same way as any other calamity and be paid for out of revenue, not out of capital. An Act was obtained on 10 August 1857 authorising the company to purchase and cancel stock equal to the amount of that fraudulently created, which was £221,070, including £18,000 East Lincolnshire stock. The value of bogus dividends was estimated at £15,000. The expenses of prosecution were put at £8,000 making a total of £224,070. The amount of net revenue available for dividend at the half-year ending 31 December 1856 was £243,925.

A great deal of indignation was ventilated by the shareholders at the half-yearly meetings in 1857, the chairman and directors being roundly abused for their lack of supervision of the registration department. It was even suggested that they should be made personally responsible for the loss. This resolution was defeated, but it was agreed that a committee of investigation should be set up to inquire into the company's accounts. Two directors and four shareholders were elected to the committee. One of the latter failed to take part, but the other three, Giesler, Malins and Waters, worked independently of the directors and carried their enquiries into every aspect of the company's affairs. Without authority they hired a secretary and had their findings printed and circulated among the shareholders at the company's expense. They found practically nothing, except what was already known—that the board had been extremely lax in supervision of the registration department. There was some excuse for the directors, for the system adopted was based on that in use in the LNW's corresponding department. In those days no one would have conceived that a clever rogue could have manipulated the books and robbed the undertaking of a fortune. The expenses incurred by the committee plus the very futility of their report stung Edmund Denison (some said it was E. B. Denison) into compiling a lengthy reply, circulated with the report sent out in advance of the adjourned twenty-second half-yearly meeting due on 1 December. In it he put matters into their proper perspective. Thus with regard to the loss in 1856 of £13,635 on the Lincolnshire canals, he reminded the proprietors that the Witham and Fossdyke had found the land for nearly 40 miles of railway, which would have cost a great deal more money. The GN Act might not have passed, but for adopting these canals. Although there was a loss of £36,000 on the EL guarantee, he considered that the GN would have been worse off if the line had fallen into the hands of another company (meaning the MS&L). He pointed out that the annual sum paid to the EC had nothing to do with the least of the R&H as the committee had wrongly concluded, but was a valuable bonus paid in respect of traffic exchanged at Peterborough, formerly turned over to the Midland.

With their report the directors issued a warning which read as follows:

> 'If the peaceful and rational majority of the proprietors think the character of the company worth preserving, and that the time is come to make an end of the business which has caused so much ill-feeling, it is neither prudent for themselves, nor fair to those who have to fight their battle for them, to leave their opponents in even apparent command of the meeting. It is impossible to foresee what course may be taken at the approaching meeting by those who have created the disturbance at the last two. But the time is coming when no company will get persons of character to serve them as directors, if they are to be insulted by their constituents whenever they meet them publicly, and not even allowed to make the speeches necessary to conduct the

business without interruptions. If the proprietors think their business would be better done by such persons as those who usually distinguish themselves by imputing the worst possible motives to the present directors in all their acts, it is easy for them to say so, and so soon as that opinion is deliberately expressed it shall be immediately acted upon. But they must make their choice, and the proceedings of the ensuing meeting will probably be taken to indicate that choice in one way or the other.'

This report and warning was well received by most of the shareholders. At the meeting a proposer of a vote of censure on the directors 'for their long mismanagement and neglect of the registration department' was heard with impatience. Other speakers appealed to the meeting to 'bury the story of Redpath's frauds in oblivion', and to leave the company's affairs in the hands of the board which, with this one exception, had served them so well in the past. Edmund Denison, in a spirited speech said he believed the great majority of shareholders had full confidence in the board. This was clearly the case, as the censure motion was easily defeated.

The loss was met, as the Act authorised, out of revenue. But the Chancery Court had decided, on application by preference shareholders, that this class had to receive their dividends, so the ordinary shareholders, instead of a reasonable dividend, received nothing for one half-year, and very little for the other: But it was a remarkable tribute to the company's position, that it could meet such an appalling loss out of a half-year's profits.

Clark, Mowatt and Reynolds had all been contenders for the position of secretary when the GN's officers were first appointed. Clark was the former DN secretary, while Reynolds claimed that he was one of the originators of the London & York scheme and had been closely engaged in the work since the autumn of 1843. It appears that Mowatt was appointed over the heads of the other two by the influence of his brother Francis, one of the principal promoters of the original Great Northern scheme and in consequence there was no love lost between Reynolds and Mowatt.

Reynolds had performed his work as accountant extremely well and as each balance sheet was produced the auditors invariably remarked in glowing terms upon the 'assistance afforded to them by the company's able accountant'. But as accountant he did not have the authority over the registrar which the secretary possessed. He tendered his resignation on 20 July 1857 whereupon Mowatt took the opportunity of writing a damning letter to the directors. He alleged that Reynolds had 'instigated' Redpath's appointment although he knew that he had been a bankrupt in 1840 under discreditable circumstances, and was not to be trusted. He had been dismissed by Wilcox & Anderson (founders of the Peninsular & Oriental Steam Navigation Co) for embezzlement. He had resided with the late Major Sherman, whose daughter he married a few weeks before his bankruptcy. After Redpath's frauds had been discovered, Reynolds had first mentioned Redpath's antecedents to him. He told him that he had lent Redpath small sums and was then unexpectedly repaid but did not disclose that he later borrowed larger sums from Redpath, which between March 1854 and October 1856 had amounted to over £12,000. Reynolds had alleged that these were for Williams, in connection with contracts for the Oxford, Worcester & Wolverhampton and that he had merely acted as a friendly agent. Finally Mowatt stated that he had discovered that Reynolds had been a bankrupt in 1844, the solicitors concerned in the case including Baxter & Rose, the predecessors of Baxter, Rose & Norton. A dividend of 2s 6d (12½p) in the pound was paid on Redpath's estate and 1s 8d (10p) in the pound on Reynolds', after he was in the company's service. The late Major Sherman was a creditor of both.

Reynolds promptly wrote to the directors in his defence. He denied that he instigated Redpath's appointment; the company needed a clerk understanding registration, he had mentioned him as having the necessary knowledge. He denied that he had concealed he had been bankrupt himself, but after this time he could not assert that he had stated that Redpath had been one. He was sure he had stated that Redpath had been in a mess and needed a berth, and that for his wife's sake he would be glad to get him employed. He denied that he knew of Redpath's discreditable circumstances until November 1856 and did not know that he had been guilty of embezzlement. All that he knew of him over four or five years had been good accounts from his wife's family. He was never intimate with him. He knew nothing of him before his marriage and as he failed and broke up house his wife returned to her parents a few weeks after marriage. His information all came from Redpath's in-laws, Major and Mrs Sherman (friends of his own father). He asked for confirmation from Williams about the loans from Redpath. He said his own bankruptcy was in the spring of 1843, not 1844 as Mowatt had declared. He had been offered a partnership with a relation, a merchant, who became insolvent three years later, so he himself was ruined. He claimed that, as soon as he had the means, he paid 20s in the pound.

Denison's opinion was that Mowat's report was correct and that Reynolds knew of Redpath. The board accepted Reynolds' resignation on 4 August and made provisional arrangements for Oakley to undertake the accountant's duties. Reynolds remained until 9 September. Mowatt's turn was to come.

On 22 December the board passed the following resolution: 'The investigation of the Redpath frauds now being completed, and no further light being likely to be thrown on the subject, the board feel bound to record that although Mr W. H. Clark, the registrar of the company, during six years of the continuance of Redpath's frauds, was most culpably negligent of his duty, and, but for such negligence, the frauds must have been at one detected, if they had ever begun. And although the board are also of the opinion that Mr Reynolds, the late accountant, ought to have noticed and reported to the directors much sooner than he did the discrepancies between his own accounts and the statements given by the registrar, nevertheless the board is clearly of the opinion that the frauds must have been discovered long before if the secretary had not signed the dividend warrants sent to him by the registrar, from time to time, without taking any measures whatever to check or record the amount for which he signed, and that he herein failed in the performance of a most important duty.'

Mowatt wrote an injudicious letter defending himself. A fortnight afterwards, on 19 January 1858, the directors discussed the letter, and asked themselves these two questions. First, whether the duties of the company's officers were to be defined by them or the board? Secondly, whether the directors were to be at liberty to censure any officer for what they may consider neglect of duty, or misconduct, without the risk of the officer complaining of their interference of expressions of their opinion and of disregard of his feelings? The resolution continued that such an issue could only be determined in one way by any board who meant to remain directors, instead of servants of their own officers—therefore there was no alternative but to decide that Mowatt should not continue as secretary. He could resign, and retire within a reasonable time.

Mowatt, however, still had friends among the directors. On 2 February it was minuted that Mowatt should be allowed to withdraw his letter. This did not suit Denison, who regarded Mowatt as below the standard of other great companies' secretaries, who were capable of conducting critical negotiations which, on his own admission, Mowatt was not. Denison afterwards stated that Mowatt had a violent temper, was obstinate and indiscreet, and was particularly hostile to Robert Baxter. Denison resigned the chair on 1 March. This was concealed from his colleagues and the proprietors by Packe, who was forced into the position of choosing between the secretary and the chairman. Thus on 30 March Packe (doubtless prompted by Denison) tabled a motion that as no notice of resignation had been received from Mowatt, his appointment should be cancelled. The motion was carried by five votes to four, the remainder of the directors present declining to vote. Mowatt thereupon left the room. Seymour Clarke was deputed to go and inform him that the board had no intention of dismissing him summarily and that he could continue his duties until 30 June. Mowatt would not accept this verbal message and left the building, so a letter was sent after him. He replied that he considered his appointment ceased the moment the resolution was passed, and offered assistance and information to his successor.

Henry Oakley was appointed Secretary on 13 April, and became a Freeman of the City of London at the company's expense. The board decided that Oakley's name should be inscribed on the goods vehicles and Herbert Clarke's on the coal carts. Thus was Henry Oakley, who had joined the company as a clerk on 13 July 1850, set on the long road which was ultimately to bring him to the position of general manager, then caused to provide him with a seat on the board, and his name to be inscribed on one of the company's locomotives. James Church Grinling was appointed Accountant on 11 May. Oakley received £600 per annum from 10 September 1857, the date he had undertaken the accountant's duties, while Grinling's pay was increased from £280 to £500 from 22 May 1858, (salaries increased by £200 and £100 respectively from 1 January 1860). The way was clear for Denison to return. On 13 July 1858 (in response to a request), he resumed the chairmanship. It had taken him ten years and two resignations to get rid of Mowatt.

Mowatt brought an action against the company for wrongful dismissal and injury to character, which was tried at Chelmsford on 22 and 23 July 1858. He was awarded £200 for wrongful dismissal, no more than the equivalent of a quarter's salary he could have had for the sake of asking anyway. The other issues were decided in the company's favour, but he might have derived some satisfaction, because it had to pay his costs, £750.

The GN took over Redpath's estate and paid the small creditors. Some £50,000 was realised. The last echo of the Redpath frauds came on 18 January 1866 when a final dividend of about £1,100 was declared. In the furore of the Redpath affair the embezzlement of nearly £1,000 by William Snell of the accounts department passed almost unnoticed.

CONSOLIDATION

The first improvements in the London area were in 1854, when £255 was spent on Hornsey and £450 on Colney Hatch stations. Holloway cattle siding came into use on 3 April, built on the up side just north of Caledonian Road bridge. About a year later the City Corporation removed the live cattle market from Smithfield to a new site on Copenhagen Fields. Soon afterwards the GN built a private road from the siding up to the cattle market through an arch in the bridge. It was illegal to drive sheep and cattle through public streets on Sundays, so Clarke issued a notice drawing the attention of the drovers to this facility, especially for Sundays, and in consequence received blame from Alderman Meek and other strict Sabbatarians among the directors.

A new coal depot, built by Jay, was opened at Holloway in the spring of 1855, sited just south of Hornsey Road bridge on the up side of the line and including stabling for horses. Apart from Leeds Central station, Cubitt's last task before retiring was planning additional up lines at Holloway. The scheme, approved on 9 June 1855, involved moving Holloway ticket platform, and use of the down siding there as part of the down main line, part of the existing down main line becoming part of the up main line. When work was complete there were four tracks. The most westerley was the down main line which had to carry all down traffic; the next, the up main line, was for passenger traffic only; the third was a loop for cattle, goods and coal which left the up main line at Seven Sisters and rejoined it at the mouth of Copenhagen tunnel where a new signal box, Caledonian Road junction, was built; the fourth branched out of the third at Seven Sisters and rejoined it at Holloway and was intended for standage of Holloway coal trains. Seven Sisters box, on the up side just south of the bridge over Seven Sisters Road, was thereafter kept open by night as well as by day. The final cost of this work was £46,403.

Passengers holding tickets for London could alight at Holloway ticket platform from August 1852, but were warned that there were no porters for luggage. A staircase was built from Holloway Road and the passengers had to scramble over two sets of running lines. As the platform was narrow and dangerous, it was a precarious procedure. Largely for the benefit of visitors to Colney Hatch Asylum, Holloway became a regular station, brought into use on Friday 1 August 1856. Four years elapsed before a proper down platform with waiting shed was erected, and it was 1864 before a staircase was built leading directly to the platforms.

Two former directors were re-elected early in 1857. Colonel Duncombe took the place of Graham Hutchinson, resigned, and Archibald Frederick Paull replaced C. A. Monck who had died in the previous December. In the spring events rapidly occurred. The new Gladstone Fifteen Town Award was announced in April. The Midland, following disclosure and subsequent abandonment of its common-purse arrangement with the L&NW pursued a more independent course, and on 5 May signed an agreement with the GN whereby on payment of toll it was to use the line from Hitchin to King's Cross. On 19 May Huish arrived at King's Cross for an interview with Clarke. Without any regard for his former allies he suggested that if the GN would forego all claims to traffic west of Sheffield for the 14 years that the new pooling was to last, he would give more liberal terms to the competitive towns than the new award allowed. This time, Clarke was not to be caught napping. He rapidly deduced that the break-up of the Euston Square confederacy was an opportunity which his company might turn to good account. Ignoring these proposals, he made preparations for a conversation with Edward Watkin.

Watkin had spent much of his early life under Huish at Euston Square, and nobody knew better than he of the Captain's capacity for double-dealing and of the unscrupulous and oppressive tactics he employed in his efforts to crush weak neighbours. Watkin was as sharp as Clarke in realising the implication of Huish's volte-face, for no agreement with Euston Square was now worth the paper on which it was written, and a carve-up of traffic between the L&NW and the GN, to the exclusion of his own MS&L, spelt disaster for it. Accordingly, he was ready to listen to the proposition which Clarke put to him. Before they parted, they had sketched out the basis of an alliance between their companies, which would allow for complete interchange of traffic.

After further conferences about details of the new treaty, which became known as the Fifty Years Agreement, both companies held meetings. Arrangements of the circumstances in which the GN could use or work all or any part of the MS&L were confirmed. Following an assurance that MS&L agreements with the L&NW were at an end, the

GN agreed to give the MS&L a bonus mileage on the division of joint London traffic, and guaranteed a gross traffic of £10,000 per week. Neither company could make an agreement with a third party, which might affect the other's traffic, without prior agreement. Unfortunately (as later events showed) the GN would not obtain running powers unless it could show that the MS&L was obstructing its traffic. A Bill to authorise the agreement was prepared.

A joint committee of GN and MS&L directors was set up, including the chairmen, meetings being attended by the general managers, and on occasions other officers. The first was held on 9 July 1857. It was decided to establish a 'Special Service' of passenger trains between King's Cross and Manchester. Instructions were given for advertisements in the press, announcing that the service would begin on 1 August. Other arrangements included co-ordination of MS&L passenger trains between Penistone and Huddersfield to connect with the Special Service (the MS&L held running powers over this L&Y branch), and organising goods trains between King's Cross and Manchester. Clarke reported that he had spoken to the manager of London Victoria Docks and the chairman of the Hertford & Welwyn Junction Railway, and was of opinion that arrangements could be made for traffic over the EC from Hertford to the Docks when the Hertford line was opened. He mentioned that as the GN was joint owner with the GWR of London receiving offices it would be necessary to make separate collections for goods for Manchester. But the GW withdrew from the joint arrangments in the following March, because of competition for goods traffic in the north-west.

The Special Service, which commenced on 1 August, comprised two expresses each way, calling at Hitchin, Peterborough, Grantham, Retford, Sheffield and Penistone. The down trains left King's Cross at 10.0 a.m. and 5.30 p.m. while the trains from London Road, Manchester, departed at 9.55 a.m. and 5.20 p.m. The King's Cross–Hitchin schedule was 40 minutes (48 mph) and Hitchin–Peterborough 58 minutes (45 mph), good going for those days. The journeys occupied 5hr 20m. The trains consisted principally of GN carriages, acknowledged to be superior to those of the MS&L. Guards were appointed for the joint service. Retford was a serious handicap, as the trains had to reverse at the GN station, back to the junction south of the crossing, and reverse again. The passenger and goods stations at London Road were joint L&NW and MS&L, but some time since, the former had offered to perform all station services for a moderate annual charge, an offer the penurious MS&L had been glad to accept. This it came to regret, for the L&NW now behaved as though the premises were its own property. A subsequent statement by E. B. Denison, Q.C. has often been quoted and since no other words can better describe the strife which took place it is repeated here. He was speaking as counsel on behalf of the MS&L:

> 'The North Western authorities began to take people into custody for coming by the Sheffield train into the Manchester station, they frightened an old lady out of her wits, and distracted several feeble people, who showed them they had "caught a tartar"; so after that no more passengers were apprehended. We had painted up our names over our shop, but they, being in possession, which is nine points of the law, swept them out with their brush. They kept a truck standing in front of the platform, and left timber trains in front of our express trains. They turned our clerks out of the booking office, indeed they nailed up the part which the Sheffield company had been accustomed to use, and when one of the clerks, acting under instructions, made his way in through the window, they ejected him by the same way, "not I hope", wrote their solicitor, "with un-necessary violence".'

The second meeting of the joint committe was on 4 August. Brydone was authorised to purchase land for an easier junction south of Retford, and instructed to make this as quickly as possible, expense to be charged equally to the two companies. Joint accounts would be settled by the companies' accountants, not by the Clearing House—four clerks to be employed in an office at King's Cross, two from each company. Clarke reported that the L&NW was running expresses between London and Manchester at ordinary fares in 35 minutes less than the joint service, so acceleration was ordered from 1 September. He said that the L&NW was obstructing London traffic at London Road and that he and Watkin had seen examples of this in the passenger department. He cited a case where the MS&L and GN had lost 23 ton of goods as the L&NW kept them, and did the MS&L's work. The L&NW had stopped through rates with the MS&L, and was diverting Manchester and Liverpool traffic with Midland and MS&L stations away from the MS&L route, contrary to agreement.

Throughout August reports were received from the Clearing House of fresh traffic diversions, until the only section of the MS&L still carrying L&NW traffic was the few miles between Guide Bridge and Staley Bridge (as then spelt), the rest being diverted via Normanton, or Crewe and Derby. Watkin reported that the L&Y and NE boards were determined to adhere to their agreements with the L&NW, had offered

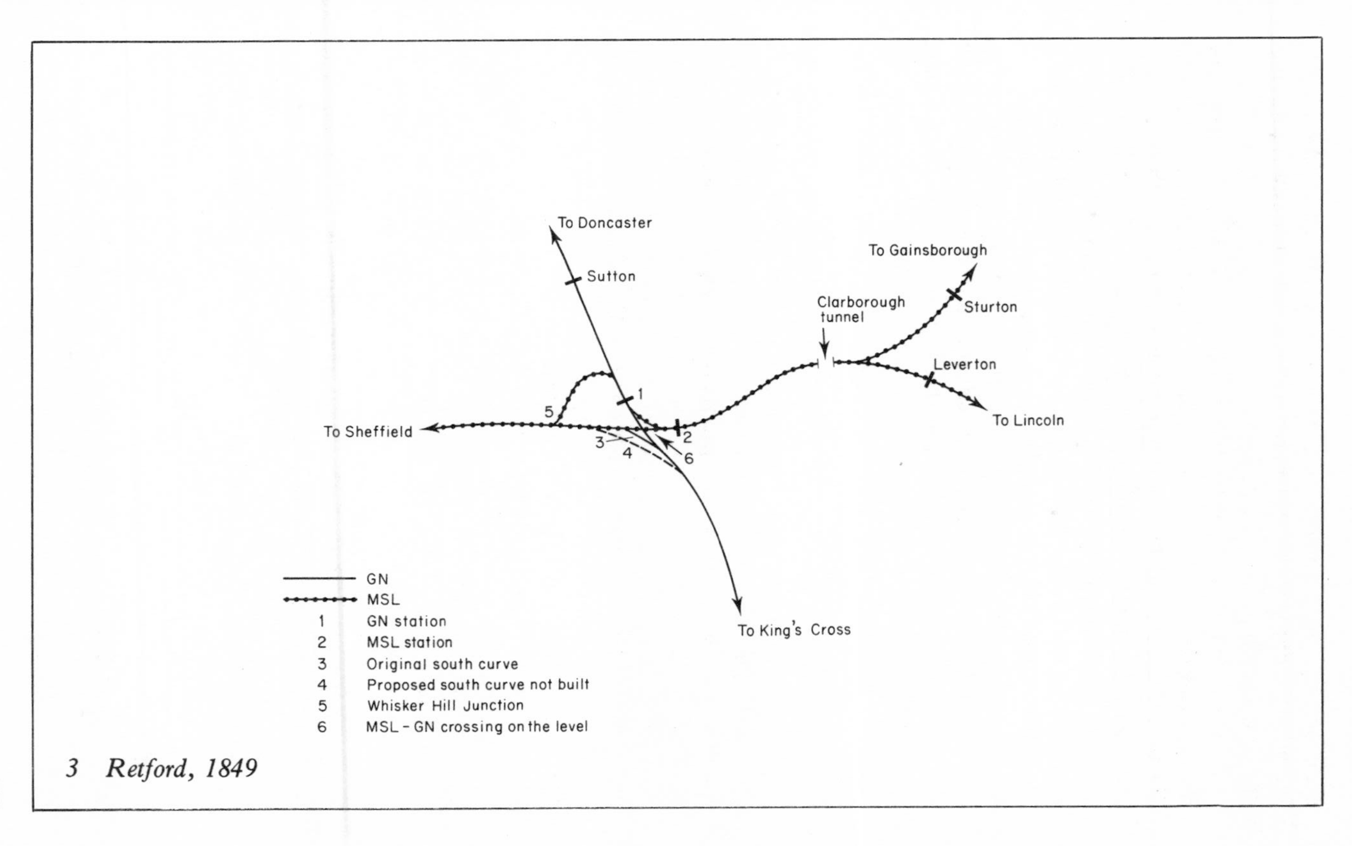

3 *Retford, 1849*

their services as mediators between the L&NW and MS&L, and intended to approach the Midland, to request it to withdraw from aiding the competition against the MS&L.

By the time the fourth meeting was held on 17 August, Clarke and Watkin had been over the ground, and considered an extension from Garston to Liverpool. The joint committee thought that this should be made quickly, and that it could be built at comparatively small cost. The chain by which the MS&L reached Garston consisted of three links. The first was the Manchester South Junction & Altrincham, which it jointly owned with the L&NW; from Timperley on this line extended the second link, the Warrington & Stockport. At Warrington this formed an end-on junction with the St Helens Canal & Railway, the last link. Of these two latter, the MS&L was at that time working the W&S, and running trains over the St Helens. They were soon swallowed up by the L&NW. But by the links, through carriages from King's Cross reached Garston in 1858, with a connecting bus into Liverpool.

Leith submitted his timetable for September which allowed for the Special Service trains accomplishing the journey in 5hr and this was approved. The schedule King's Cross to Hitchin came down to 38 minutes (50.5 mph). It was arranged that three instead of two excursions between King's Cross and Manchester should be run each week, in connection with the Art Treasures Exhibition then being held at Manchester. The accelerated service was further discussed at the next meeting on 27 August. As the trains were not timed to stop at Retford from 1 September, and the awkward reversal there was avoided, it was resolved that GN engines should work the trains to and from Sheffield and that in compensation the MS&L should work an equivalent mileage elsewhere on the GN.

The L&NW increased the number of its expresses from eight to eleven each way, and its best trains had timings of 4 hr 40m. Its 'Parliamentary' trains were accelerated to a 7 hr timing. It abolished express fares and advertised cheap excursions for the Exhibition. The route to Manchester via Retford was 15 miles longer than the L&NW's and the gradients were stiffer. The MS&L's permanent way over the Pennines between Sheffield and Manchester was in poor condition and was to remain so for several more years, so the timing for the 40 miles could not be reduced to less than 80 minutes. The new allies could not equal the best trains from Euston Square, but thanks to comfortable carriages and punctuality, patronage was gained. Upon the GN fell the burden of fast running; it already held the reputation of the fastest services in the country and now ran the 162 miles between London and

Sheffield in 220 minutes.

When the Exhibition closed on 15 October, Watkin was anxious that the excursion trains should continue, for he considered that while his company was denied proper use of its own station in Manchester he could not expect much traffic unless cheap facilities continued. So the excursions still ran. The MS&L began construction of a goods shed at Ardwick which came into use in December. Watkin arranged collection of goods in Liverpool for transmission via Garston to King's Cross and other places on the MS&L and GN. The arrangements were soon extended to Warrington, Stockport and other places. Next the allies commenced competing for the large Liverpool cattle traffic for Peterborough and London via Garston; so it was necessary to supply additional cattle trucks. The proportion agreed was 75 to be provided by the GN to 25 by the MS&L. Actually, the GN supplied 80, while those provided by the MS&L were too small.

The allied companies then explored possibilities of Irish traffic. An agent was established in Dublin and arrangements were made with the owners of S.S. *Nicolai I* for transport of passengers, goods and cattle across the Irish Sea. In March 1859, it was agreed with the Dublin & Liverpool, and the City of Dublin Steam Packet Companies that they, when the contract with the *Nicolai* owners expired, should carry GN and MS&L traffic on equal terms and conditions with that of the L&NW and L&Y as to through rates and fares, and provide daily communication with Ireland.

Naturally the L&NW did not take kindly to these incursions into its territories. It slashed rates and fares in all competitive directions; reductions followed step by step by the allies. An MS&L clerk reported that he had been offered bribes by a L&NW servant to disclose the weight of goods sent daily between London and Manchester by the GN and MS&L. By February 1858 excursion passengers were being carried between London and Manchester for 5s (25p) return, and 'giving them fifteen inch seats, stuffed cushions and backs to lean against', to quote a disgruntled GN shareholder. Mason, general manager of the Birkenhead, Lancashire & Cheshire Junction (soon to be known as the Birkenhead), in November suggested granting running powers to the MS&L over his line from Warrington to Chester and Birkenhead. A few days later he withdrew, saying 'in consequence of the discovery through its Law Clerk of its total inability to proceed without breaking an honourable and binding agreement'. Again, on the following 1 March, Underdown, MS&L assistant manager, reported that on that day the superintendent at Chester station had taken a rail up and prevented the passage of MS&L trains there under W&S powers. The rail had been put down again and 'the service of the Joint Companies between Chester and King's Cross was complete'. Surely Huish's influence can be detected in these instances.

Other companies soon began to complain of the reductions in rates and fares. The Midland chairman attempted, without success, to mediate between the hostile companies. At his request deputations of chairmen and directors from his own, the NE, L&Y, and ELR companies attended the 'Derby Conference', held at Euston Hotel on 11 March 1858. These peace-making efforts met with no reponse from Euston Square. A month later the Derby Conference attempted once more to find a solution to the strife. There was a slight easing in the situation for the L&NW restored the rates and fares between Lancashire and Peterborough.

Further success came in June when rates between London and Manchester were increased, it being agreed that equal rates and fares should be charged. By then the battle was raging in the Commons Committee Room. The allies were represented by Edmund Denison and E. B. Denison who again found themselves ranged alongside Baxter (now Parliamentary agent of the MS&L) and Serjeant Wrangham. Stoutly opposed by Euston Square and with all big guns brought to bear, the fight occupied 21 sittings. The concluding rhetoric delivered by Serjeant Wrangham is well worth recounting.

> 'A decision in favour of the petitioners will tell the world that their obstructive agreements for locking up the trade of a commerical country are looked upon with distinguished favour by a tribunal such as this, and that the sanction of the legislature has been given to that which legislation has previously sought to control. It is for you to say whether, yielding to the arguments of my learned friend, you shall denounce competition in the free passage of commerce between, perhaps, our largest emporium and the greatest and wealthiest of the world's capitals. With you it is to say whether that route existing, constructed, in which untold millions are invested, shall be rendered available for the public, or shall be inflexibly closed against it. It is for you to choose between the two courses laid before you—to give to commerce that which is her life—freedom, or if you please, to make monopoly immortal.'

After six hours' suspense, the Committee found in favour of the GN and MS&L Traffic Arrangements Bill. Further opposition was encountered in the Lords but the allies emerged victorious and the Bill passed on 23 July 1858. Thirteen days earlier, notice was received at King's Cross that the L & N W had determined the Gladstone Award, which it was entitled to do, once the GN had gone west of Sheffield.

The way to peace was made easier by Huish's resignation on 11 September. He had brought his company into disrepute, and his policy of rate wars was not compatible with good dividends. There had been a growing movement against him by shareholders and directors and he went before he was asked to go. He was succeeded as general manager by W. Cawkwell. On 12 November peace was signed, it being agreed to apply through rates, and make arrangements for interchange of traffic. This must have been an immense relief for the MS&L, which had suffered a deficiency in receipts of £28,516 in the half-year to 30 June 1858, and borrowed £10,000 from the GN. It deposited a Bill for the 1859 Session for powers to sell or lease its undertaking to the GN, L&NW, Midland, L&Y, or EL, or any combination of them, but it was withdrawn. The agreement came into force on 1 January 1859 and the fares were settled at 10% less than those before hostilities began. From December the MS&L resumed some of its rights at London Road, and regained them all by an Act of 21 July 1859, which settled partition of the station.

Another result of the agreement was that the Special Service trains were allowed an extra 15 minutes overall. It was soon decided to re-insert the Retford stop instead of one made at Newark, attracting little traffic. As the trains had again to back in and out of Retford station, it was agreed that the MS&L should construct a new curved junction, north of the station and, in compensation, would have free use of the GN station. Although Brydone had reported purchase of land for the improved curved junction, proposed south of the station, no more was heard of it, and the Manchester trains were traversing the earlier very sharp curve. The new ½ mile curve from Retford North junction on the GN to 'Whisker' (a corruption of West Carr) Hill junction on the MS&L was brought into use on 1 July 1859, and the old junction, south of the station, was taken out. The shortest radius on the Whisker Hill curve was 7 chains, and a severe speed restriction has always been imposed. On the same day the MS&L closed its Retford station for passenger business, which it transferred to the GN station.

Until February 1859 the GN paid £1,500 per annum for use of Sheffield station but now, for £25,000, secured permanent half rights to use it jointly with the MS&L. The GN staff was withdrawn.

The St Helens agreed to make the Garston & Liverpool with the allied companies' financial support. The Bill was rejected by the Commons, so another was prepared. At this juncture, the L&NW proposed an alternative line from Edge Hill to Garston, which would give the joint companies access to Liverpool, so for the time being the Garston & Liverpool project was shelved. From 1 September 1859, through carriages and goods vehicles from King's Cross reached the L&NW Liverpool Lime Street station. Accommodation in the passenger trains, run to and from London Road over the ex-Liverpool & Manchester, and the South Junction, was confined exclusively to allied companies' traffic, and Euston Square took good care that local passengers did not use them. In Liverpool, the allies established a staff at several goods and passenger stations, including Old Hall Street, Waterloo, Park Lane, and Lime Street.

In January 1860 the allied companies considered providing passenger and goods services between Lancashire and Leeds, Bradford and Halifax. Carriages for the West Riding were attached to the 10.0 a.m. from London Road. Goods services began on 1 May, but 'peace' was so uneasy that soon it was reported that West Riding traffic was meeting delays, and that accommodation at Waterloo and Park Lane was insufficient. Complaints were made of want of organisation and arrangements by the L&NW at Liverpool. After 18 months' working the GN was incurring loss on some traffic and not much gain on the remainder, so the service was soon discontinued.

Another result of the settlement between the opposing companies was that they agreed to divide the London and Lancashire traffic between themselves in agreed proportions, to the exclusion of the Midland. For this purpose they deposited a 'Three Companies Bill' for the 1859 Session, but it was thrown out on Midland opposition. For the next Session a fresh 'Three Companies Bill' was lodged, and also an alternative 'Four Companies Bill' which made provision for inclusion of the Midland, but both were rejected on Midland and North Staffordshire oppositiom. After this failure to exclude the Midland from Lancashire, Huish methods were adopted, and the junctions at Beighton and Stockport were blocked against competitive traffic.

The Midland now recalled James Allport to the general managership. (He had resigned his position in 1857.) Almost immediately he formed an alliance with the L&Y, and thus obtained access to Lancashire. The GN and MS&L feared Midland competition in June 1861. Rumours of a possible fusion of the Midland, and L&Y were circulating. In these circumstances the MS&L came very close to being absorbed jointly by the GN and L&NW. Heads of Agreement had been reached by the three general managers (meeting at Euston Hotel on 20 December 1860) which allowed for the MS&L being guaranteed a dividend of 1½% in

1861, to increase annually by ½% until in 1866 it reached a permanent 3½%. By a majority of 25 to one, the L & N W directors agreed to the terms. The only dissenter was none other than the chairman, Lord Chandos, who resigned his position, and wrote a private explanatory letter to Edmund Denison, which reached him at Doncaster where he was laid low with one of his periodic attacks of gout. He discussed it with his son (E. B. Denison) and they drew the same conclusion as Lord Chandos, that an amalgamation on the proposed terms would not be in GN shareholders' interests. The GN board was in agreement with its chairman when the matter was dicussed next month, so on 23 January 1861 the MS&L directors were informed that the GN declined to proceed further with amalgamation upon the terms proposed.

The MS&L complained that it had suffered a loss of £4,525 on towards the loss. The W & S was leased to the St Helens, and L & N W, by towards the loss. The W & S was leased to the St Helens, and L & N W by an Act of 13 August 1859, and on 1 July 1860, the portion of the St Helens from Warrington to Garston was leased to the L & N W. In the same 1860 Session the L & N W withdrew its Garston & Brunswick Dock Bill, which prompted Denison to propose revival of the Garston & Liverpool project. After a meeting in Liverpool in support in March 1861, an Act was obtained on May 17 with a terminus near Parliament Street and Queens Dock (altered next year to one near Brunswick Dock) despite strong L & N W opposition.

The subsequent story of events west of Sheffield will be related in chapter XI, dealing with the Cheshire Lines Committee. Meantime, it is necessary to go back a few years, for the Midland opened its line from Leicester to Hitchin for minerals on 15 April 1857, one week later for general goods, some of which was worked to and from King's Cross by the GN, an operation described by an indignant Euston Square as 'surreptitious'. The LB&HJ was not amused either, for some of the traffic originated in Bradford. The line was formally opened on 7 May, a train of 18 carriages leaving Hitchin at 7.33 a.m. for Leicester. Public traffic commenced next day with four trains each way on weekdays and two on Sundays. The Midland agreed to pay £500 per annum for the use of Hitchin station, constructing its own goods yard to the west of the GN line.

On 1 February 1858 Midland trains began to run over the GN between Hitchin and King's Cross. Full agreement had been reached for the Midland to pay the normal two-thirds gross receipts and from 1 January 1859 a minimum annual toll of £20,000. The agreement, terminable upon seven years' notice by either company, included a clause providing for the Midland, the MS&L and GN to abstain from aggression, and promote each other's interests. The Midland paid £1,500 per annum for use of King's Cross (where the GN provided accommodation for booking and parcels) and had use of Holloway coal depot and part of King's Cross goods yard. The GN anticipated spending about £30,000 on the provision of facilities for the Midland. The potato shed, (once Maiden Lane station) became a goods shed, ready on 1 July, and a roundhouse was built adjacent for Midland engines. The soil excavated from the site of this was deposited beside the line at Holloway, and a crossover laid at Seven Sisters to facilitate this. The Midland agreed to pay 6% per annum on the cost of the roundhouse as rent. Similar terms were arranged for occupation of goods offices, stabling for horses, and coal drops. The GN insisted on a minimum toll of 1s 9d (8p) per ton of 20 or 21 cwt of coal over the 32 miles from Hitchin to London. This high rate forced the Midland to continue to send much of its coal traffic via Rugby. Midland passenger trains were not allowed to stop at intermediate stations except of necessity or by consent, the GN arranging to carry local traffic.

A signal hut, completed at Welwyn Junction for the Hertford line, was brought into use in time for the additional Midland trains. Another box was opened at Wymondley, between Stevenage and Hitchin, in April 1858, both boxes being telegraph stations. With but one up and one down line between Hitchin and London, the extra Midland traffic plus a growing number of GN trains soon brought about congestion. This was felt most between the two London tunnels where all up traffic destined for the goods yard had to cross the down line on the level. There were also insufficient refuge sidings in which to shunt slower trains to allow faster ones to pass. Some sections between signal boxes were too long.

The origin of Wood Green station was unusual. In December 1857 Harrison Rhodes and other proprietors of the late Thomas Rhodes' Tottenham Wood Estate, who were developing it, proposed to the GN directors that they should build a station at Wood Green, and when it was completed, convey it to the railway. It was to be sited at the level crossing at the north end of Wood Green Common. In March, it was settled that they should provide the land and contribute £4,000 towards cost of the station, which was opened on 1 May 1859. Culshaw of Biggleswade was the contractor. Additional coal sidings were laid and the station illuminated by gas in 1862. The platforms were extended in 1863.

Part of Rhodes' estate was developed as pleasure grounds. In 1860 it was proposed to erect a People's Palace on Muswell Hill. A plan was made for a double line branch from the main line north of the station, almost to encircle the palace. The up line would be carried across the main line by a fly-over. That particular palace, and therefore the branch, were not built, but the grounds, called Alexandra Park, were used for a World's Fair, opened in May 1864. Flowers, dogs and poultry were conveyed free of charge for shows held in July and August. The station was renamed Wood Green (Alexandra Park) on 1 August 1864, and considerable expenditure was approved for providing additional sidings on each side of the line for stabling empty trains, and a short bay on the east side of the up platform. It was also intended to erect waiting rooms, lavatories, a booking office, and a roof over the up platform; however the waiting rooms went to improve Holloway. The engineer was instructed to prepare plans for four lines, although this was deferred.

At King's Cross an excursion platform was approved in 1857, and completed about the end of the year. This occupied the position of the present numbers 2 and 4, and a portable booking office was provided at the south end. It is not apparent when the stepped platform, the equivalent on No. 3 (now filled in), was brought into use, but it was shown on a plan of the station dated 1865. Also in 1857 Culshaw built a roofed extension to the departure platform. The excursion platforms were not designated arrival platforms until October 1867.

The branches to Hertford, Dunstable and St Albans were all promoted by independent companies, which purchased land and constructed overbridges for double but built their lines single. The first of these was the Hertford & Welwyn Junction, incorporated on 3 July 1854, capital £65,000, borrowing powers £21,600, and authorised to construct a railway between the two points in its title. It measured 7 miles 30 chains and ran from a junction with the EC at Hertford to a south facing connection with the GN at Welwyn Junction. The line curved sharply as it approached the main line, for the last 300 yards paralleled it, and doubled as it formed the junction. There were six overbridges and nine underbridges, and the only station was at Hertford. A turntable was available at the EC station. The H&WJ undertook to provide a turntable, or a triangle for turning at Welwyn Junction within six months, an undertaking not kept. Colonel Yolland sanctioned public use on 26 February 1858, insisting that the line should be worked by tank engines until the turntable was ready, and (because of the sharp curves) on a speed limit of 20 mph. A ballast engine from Stratford worked to Welwyn Junction at the end of October 1857. This may have caused the railway press to state that traffic had begun, but since there were no intermediate stations or sidings, and the junction at Welwyn was not completed it is difficult to accept this. General traffic commenced on 1 March 1858, jointly worked by the GN and EC, who arranged through bookings between some of their respective stations. The GN opened a station and some sidings at Welwyn Junction on that day. The station had a short life, for it closed on 1 October 1860. The H&WJ opened stations at Cole Green and Hertingfordbury, first shown in the timetables for December 1858. The line formed an early useful route for dock traffic. Wagons for the main line were attached and detached at Welwyn Junction sidings. The EC worked a night goods trains with dock traffic from 1 March 1858 to 31 August 1860.

W. F. Cowper, M.P. was chairman of the H&WJ, and of the Luton, Dunstable & Welwyn Junction, whose Act on 16 July 1855 empowered £120,000 capital, borrowing £40,000, and a line from a junction with the L&NW at Dunstable to the GN at Welwyn Junction, also a north facing junction with the GN there, and a connecting line near Digswell Lodge Farm with the H&WJ. A further Act of 7 July 1856 authorised a deviation at the junction with the L&NW. The portion from Dunstable junction to Luton was opened for goods on Monday 5 April and passengers on Monday 3 May 1858, 5 miles 45 chains, worked by the L&NW. A turntable was provided at Luton, then the only station.

The company amalgamated with the H&WJ by an Act of 28 June 1858, as the Hertford, Luton & Dunstable. Six months' notice was given to the EC in 1860 to terminate the Hertford line working agreement. The remainder, 12 miles ½ chain, from Luton to Welwyn Junction, where it made a connection 2 chains south of that from Hertford, was opened on Saturday 1 September 1860. The GN then took over working the completed line. The L&NW continued to exercise running powers between Dunstable junction and Luton until 1866, when it withdrew its service, but restored it in 1881 (see vol. II). Colonel Yolland inspected the line on 11 August, but as no turntable had been installed at Hatfield he could not recommend public use, and was also concerned about a down gradient of 1 in 56 approaching Welwyn Junction. Eighteen days later he re-inspected the line, and as the turntable would be ready that day or next, sanctioned opening, but urged moderation in speed because of the sharp curves. Stations and sidings were at New Mill End, Harpenden, and Wheathampstead. There were nine overbridges, 13 underbridges, and two small viaducts over the Lea. Five trains ran each way on weekdays and two on Sundays. The first train left Dunstable at 7.55 a.m. and reached King's Cross at 9.30. While it seems certain that the station at Dunstable (Church Street) was opened on 1 December 1860, the L&NW paid rent for it from 1 September.

The HL&D was absorbed by the GN by an Act of 12 June 1861. The terms were that the GN paid a fixed dividend of 3% on the original capital of the LD&WJ for the first year, 4% for the second and third years, and 4½% for each subsequent year, and 10% on the original capital of the H&WJ until April 1866 and 3½% subsequently. The GN later abandoned the short curves proposed at Welwyn. A deputation of directors visited the line in the following February and approved alterations to stations, as recommended by Clarke, estimated to cost £18,900. The work was given to Kirk & Parry, who completed new stations at Luton and Hertford in 1863, and Harpenden and New Mill End in 1864. Luton had a refreshment room. At the small company's expense the GN had to insert 6,000 new sleepers on the Dunstable branch. Too few per length of rail had been laid by the contractor, and rails were frequently breaking at the fish plate holes due to insufficient support. The Dunstable branch was worked by staff and ticket from 16 October 1865, and Welwyn Junction signal box was fitted with locking apparatus in December 1867.

The LD&WJ had arranged to build a new station at Dunstable for the L&NW. The GN had to honour this liability. The station opened in January 1866 and the GN was credited with the materials from the original station. GN Sunday trains ceased to run beyond Dunstable (Church Street) in the following June. They did not reappear at the L&NW station on Sundays until July 1914!

In 1860 the down engineers' siding at Colney Hatch was lengthened and transferred to the traffic department as a refuge siding, and an additional signal box called 'Nineteenth Mile' was opened between Hatfield and Welwyn Junction. At the close of the year the board authorised Clarke to relax the system of signalling between King's Cross and Hitchin 'owing to the crowded state of the traffic'. The new code of rules actually applied between Holloway box and Wood Green station, Potters Bar station and Welwyn station, and Knebworth box and Hitchin station (and also on the up line between Stoke Tunnel and Essendine station). Thus the traffic through the tunnels near London was worked (or intended to be) by a proper block system. The remainder of the line to Hitchin was operated by a combination of time interval and space interval, controlled by electric telegraph. The rules were complicated and not very intelligible, but in effect permitted a signalman, after passage of one train, to allow a second into the section, without any prescribed time interval, merely by sending the appropriate message on the telegraph instrument, and cautioning the driver by word of mouth. The driver was thereby prohibited from exceeding 15 mph until he received an 'all right' at another signal station. Trains halted by signal had to stop with the last vehicle inside the signal, and were given permission to proceed by the signalman ringing the starting bell. But if an up and a down train were halted at the same time, the signal man had to go and tell the appropriate guard that he might go on. This rule was apparently thought sufficient to provide protection from a rear-end collision. An accident to a Midland train at Southgate in 1865 brought the directors up with a jerk, and a proper block system was again enforced.

At the end of 1860 the board approved the following recommendations by Clarke:

1. Down shunting siding and new station, at Seven Sisters Road.
2. Half the carriage shed at Southgate to be a waiting room, and cattle accommodation there.
3. Up and down shunting sidings at Barnet.
4. Signal station at 'North Enfield' (later renamed Ganwick).
5. Two sidings at Welwyn.
6. Up shunting siding at Bell Bar.
7. Up shunting siding at Wymondley.

Seven Sisters Road station was opened on 1 July 1861, the nucleus of the large junction called Finsbury Park (familiarly known to long suffering suburban travellers of later generations as 'Pneumonia Junction'). As built the station consisted of two draughty wooden platforms perched up on the embankment, replaced by island platforms in 1867, ready to accommodate the new Edgware line services.

In the 1860s numerous railways were projected to serve and stimulate residential areas north of London. One of the few which obtained Parliamentary sanction and built its line was the Edgware, Highgate & London, authorised to join the GN near Seven Sisters Road, incorporated on 3 June 1862 with capital £220,000 and powers to borrow £73,300. The Act empowered the GN, which was to work the line, to subscribe £73,300 to the capital. In anticipation of this line the GN negotiated for purchase of land at Seven Sisters. The vendor offered the required 4½ acres at £1,000 per acre but if the company would buy the complete parcel of seven acres he was prepared to sell it for £800 an acre. Wisely the larger parcel was bought, and some of it came in very useful later for sidings.

An Act of 19 April 1859 authorised an improvement to the junction line with the NL, easing the sharp gradient. The work was completed in 1862 by construction of a rising brick viaduct, the line being 29 chains. The expense of some catch sidings and new signalling was later shared by the Midland, which began to send goods traffic over the NL. The same

13 Archibald Sturrock (right) with H A Ivatt (Locomotive Superintendent 1896-1911) in 1902

14 (*above*) Stamford Station (Stamford and Essendine)

15 Sharp 2-2-2 on the first day of Long Sutton Station on the Norwich and Spalding, July 1862

16 The exterior of Bourne Station

17 Welwyn Viaduct

18 An artist's impression of the Great Northern Railway in 1853 – this drawing contains technical inaccuracies, but is a lively contemporary record of the railway's earliest years

No.52
46

19 (*above*) Royston Station, about 1900

20 Finchley (later Church End) Station, about 1900

21 'The Night Mail' by Howard Geach passing Doncaster, about 1856

22 Thomas Brassey, the Contractor, 1850

23 Edmund Denison in 1856. On the right is the portrait of Edmund Denison which was attached to the front of the engine of the Centenary Special in 1950

Act sanctioned widening the NL viaduct over the GN main line. About this time new coal sidings were put in at Goods & Mineral junction.

After many complaints of delays to the 5.30 p.m. down Midland express, the GN altered the timing of its 5.05 and 5.10 trains in September 1861, the 5.10 being shunted to Southgate and a slip carriage attached to the 5.05 p.m. To reduce light engine movements between King's Cross and the goods yard, it was resolved in 1860 to put in a large turntable. A year later it was decided to provide a coke stage and alter the carriage repair shop, west of the station, to an engine shed. A contract was let to Kirk & Parry for construction of an additional engine shed, a machine shop and a carriage repair shop. A platform for the short trains was made on the west side of the departure platform, and a crossover laid for Midland trains to pass GN trains at the departure platform. After the new 45 ft turntable was installed, Midland light engines continued to pass through Maiden Lane tunnel. It was found that Budge, or Sturrock, or both were preventing the Midland from making use of it. The engine shed in the goods yard became known as the 'high level' shed but for many, many years it has been known familiarly as 'top shed'.

Cemetery box, just over 7 miles from King's Cross, serves as a reminder of the nearby site of the original burial ground laid out by the Great Northern London Cemetery Co to provide cheap burial facilities on the outskirts of London. The Cemetery company made arrangements with the GN for conveyance of coffins and mourners to the cemetery at East Barnet. In September 1858, a request was made for the starting point of the funeral trains to be at the west side of King's Cross passenger station, adjoining the carriage repair shop. This was refused, so the Cemetery company accepted a site on GN ground for its London terminus east of the line at Belle Isle, Maiden Lane. This building resembled a chapel, and consisted of a mortuary and a covered station from which a track led down to the main line with which it connected at the south end of Copenhagen tunnel. The building on cemetery ground at East Barnet was substantial, with chapels for various denominations, and a station for the funeral trains which the GN agreed to run in June 1859. To serve the cemetery, a long siding was laid on the up side from Colney Hatch station. The funeral trains commenced in 1861, (run, it is believed, once or twice a week). In April it was agreed that two carriages for the mourners should be altered in appearance. In July the GN directors were invited to inspect the Cemetery company's arrangements, but declined. From 1 November the charge of £1 per journey for use of the coffin carriage was reduced by one half owing to inconsiderable traffic. An application for special funeral trains to be run at 2.0 p.m. on

Sundays was refused in January, the directors reminding the Cemetery company that no Sunday trains were run between 10.0 a.m. and 3.0 p.m. The enterprise was not a success, for in April 1865 Clarke reported that the Cemetery company had ceased to use the station and buildings erected for it at Belle Isle and asked instructions to terminate the agreement. It seems, however, that the stations were occasionally used until 1867, and closed by 1873. In October 1875 the company relinquished the siding rights at Colney Hatch and rights to part of the land at Belle Isle. The latter was required in connection with boring the duplicate tunnel, and the west side of the building was demolished. The remainder stood for about another 80 years, and frequently excited speculation as to what had been its purpose. The site is now occupied by a concrete plant. The building at East Barnet disappeared about the turn of the century, and a similar siding now serves the Standard Telephones & Cable Co works.

More interruptions to traffic occurred. A portion of Stoke tunnel fell in on the evening of Thursday 25 October 1855, the 5.0 p.m. down express having to be sent back to Werrington and routed via the Loop. Repairs to the tunnel were completed by 6.0 a.m. on the following Monday, and meantime traffic was diverted via the Loop. At 9.0 p.m. on the Sunday a coal train broke down at Stixwould with a broken wagon axle, and some wagons telescoped. Both lines of the Loop were blocked until Monday afternoon. Severe gales at the end of February 1860 caused disruption of traffic all over the system. Signal arms were blown off posts, signal and telegraph posts were blown down, roofs and chimney stacks extensively damaged and the goods shed at Firsby flattened. A bridge at Wood Walton failed on 14 November 1861. Until repairs were made traffic was sent over the Midland and L&NW, via Luffenham, Syston and Leicester.

In the engineers' department re-ballasting the main line with gravel was completed early in 1858. Near London the line had originally been ballasted with burnt clay, and with sand on other stretches of the line. Sand was covered with a thin layer of gravel, for Sturrock complained of the detrimental effect it had on engine moving parts. Experiments were made with fishplates for joining rails on the new lines at Holloway in 1856 and also near Hatfield. The result had been so satisfactory that large quantites of fishplates and bolts were purchased, and the practice spread all over the line, £15,000 being spent on fishplates by 1859. Creosoting some sleepers commenced in 1851, the work being undertaken by a man named Bethel, becoming more general in 1857, so Bethel was allowed to set up a creosoting plant at Boston at no expense to the company. Once the main line was completed, no more triangular sleepers were purchased, but replaced by conventional rectangular pattern, about 8 ft 11 in long by 10 in by 5 in, costing around 3s 3d (16p) apiece.

The heavy coal trains wore out the rails more rapidly than expected. On the down gradient after Barnet the life of the rails had only been about 3½ years. In 1857 82 lb rails were tried. Brydone advised the board of the approaching necessity for relaying the main line from London to Askern, and suggested that the expense should be spread over five years at the rate of about £30,000 per half year. The proposal was agreed to in principle. It was arranged that the cost should be charged to revenue and spread in equal portions over five years from 1 July 1860. By this time 82 lb rails and heavier chairs were being used for replacements, at an additional cost of about £500 per mile.

The wooden viaduct at Bawtry required renewal in 1856, designs for its reconstruction in more durable materials being drawn up by both Brydone and Cubitt. That of Cubitt was the more suitable and Brydone was willing it should be adopted, in preference to his own, for reconstruction in iron and masonry. Much difficulty was experienced in securing proper foundations. Delays were caused by unexpected requirements of local landowners and authorities. The ultimate cost was £18,592. The company also had to pay for repair of W. Marrison's wharf at Bawtry, alleged to have been damaged by diversion of the Idle when the viaduct was rebuilt. The remains of the wooden viaduct were removed in the summer of 1858. Three timber bridges near Scrooby were reconstructed in brick or masonry about the same time.

In January 1858 Brydone reported on the Welwyn viaduct, in which longitudinal cracks had appeared in the arches' brickwork. He said that drivers of up coal trains were running over it at speed in excess of 40 mph. The trouble was arrested by insertion of tie rods, and a speed restriction of 15 mph was imposed on goods and mineral trains.

Many timber structures on the Lincolnshire lines required extensive repairs or renewals. Some long viaducts, such as Longwood, tackled in 1855, were partly replaced by embankments alongside the old line, thus reducing the length of the new spans (of masonry and iron girders). Bardney bridge had been patched up but in 1858 it became necessary to renew it. Brydone decided to divert over a 1,440 ft long embankment making the length of the new bridge 745 ft with two spans of 60 ft and one of 90 ft with fixed girders resting on cylinders sunk in the waterway, and the other shorter spans on brickwork. The contract for reconstruction went to F. Rummens on 26 January 1859, with plate girders by Butler & Co of Stanningley, whose procrastinations delayed completion until the end of 1860. Sincil Dyke bridge was rebuilt soon afterwards.

Brydone resigned on 24 June 1861, to go into business on his own account and was succeeded on 30 June by Richard Johnson who had been with the GN since 1846 (when he worked on the Loop), spent almost his entire working life with the company, and for the next 35 years was its chief engineer. Appointed at £600 per annum his salary was increased to £800 from 1 January 1864. C. Ogilvie moved from Boston to Peterborough vice Johnson at £300 and W. Kirby was appointed at Boston at £250 per annum. R. Gastineau resigned and was succeeded in London by J. Macdonnell (from the Bristol & Exeter) at £300 from 1 February 1862. A nasty piece of work this one, he later wrote letters to the board containing unfounded allegations against his chief.

A three year agreement was concluded with the SY on 5 May 1855 which took effect from 1 June. For 300,000 tons of 20 cwt of coal, including back carriage, the SY would receive 1s 6d (7½p) per ton, decreasing by ½d per ton for every additional 50,000 ton to 1s 3d (6p) per ton for 550,000 tons or more. By the close of 1857 it was decided that this contract would not be renewed in 1858. It was reported that the SY owed £3,316. A new agreement applied from 1 June 1858 which allowed each company 8d (3p) for terminals, 4d (2p) to the GN shunting and 9d (3p) for the use of wagons, 1s 1d (6p) for the City of London dues, and the remainder was divided on mileage of coals for London while the SY was allowed a mean toll of 1s 5d (7p) for coals for country places. At the end of the month the GN advanced £10,000 to the SY, but in October, the latter gave notice that it intended to determine the agreement as from 31 December. The SY opened a branch to Thorne on 11 December 1855 which diverged from the GN at Milethorne (later Marsh Gate) junction just north of Doncaster station. It was single, and did not carry passengers until the following 1 July. Three years later it was extended to Keadby on the west side of the Trent. From 1 January 1857 the SY paid an additional £50 rent for use of Doncaster station, plus another £50 in respect of the Thorne services making a total of £550 per annum.

The GN policy of being both buyer and seller of South Yorkshire coal in London was attacked by Samuel Plimsoll at the half-yearly meeting in August 1854. He was endeavouring to establish a trade with steamboats and gas companies, and advocated the trade being set free, by which he meant that anyone should be allowed to buy Yorkshire coal and have it transported to London in his, or the company's wagons, or coalowners should send coal to London and find their own markets. He had been trying to buy coal from some South Yorkshire pits which did not trade with the GN and had been frustrated by Clarke. He purchased his own wagons, but Clarke declined to run them until their fitness was certified by Sturrock. When this formality was complete, he was informed that the colliery sidings were not ready, yet when he went to see for himself he found that they had been used for three weeks. It was a scathing speech, but he had got into the meeting by a subterfuge, for he had already disposed of the small amount of GN stock he had formerly possessed. He did not obtain satisfaction until 1 November 1856 when he was offered carriage of 1,000 tons of coal a week in GN wagons from Doncaster to London at 8s 7d (43p) per 20 cwt, inclusive of freight, city dues and labour. In December he was not allowed further credit; nevertheless he prospered and later set up depots at King's Cross and the Elephant & Castle.

Similar criticisms were levelled from time to time, which culminated in a deputation of South Yorkshire coalowners at King's Cross in May 1859, complaining that the GN was the only seller in the market. They contended that the practice of mixing coal from various collieries was injudicious and unjust. The GN directors held an extra-ordinary meeting at Doncaster on Saturday 4 June to which they were invited. The company proposed to become merely carriers and offered to charge 6s (30p) per ton wagon hire between 1 March and 31 August and 7s (35p) between 1 September and 28 February between Doncaster and London. The coalowners were to pay dues on the SY, City of London dues, and expenses attending screening, loading, and advertising in London. They would have the option of using Herbert Clarke's services or separate agents. The figures for January 1859 disclosed that the L&NW had taken the lead by carrying 52,413 tons of coal to London against 37,217 tons by GN. The firm of E. & A. Prior failed during the year owing about £4,500 for coals; it was thought there was a possibility of recovering about 3s 9d (18p) in the pound. However the company made the mistake of detaining some trucks belonging to Thomas North and hired by Priors. North took legal action and the GN had to pay £915 compensation and £566 costs.

In June of 1860 information filed by North resulted in a Chancery suit which compelled the GN to cease selling coals on its own account. Vice-Chancellor Kindersley described the set-up with Herbert Clarke as agent as a 'crafty and tricky contrivance'. Accounts for sale of coal were finally closed on Saturday 30 September. Herbert Clarke tendered his resignation on 26 July, but it was not accepted to take effect until 1 October when he left to go into the coal business on his own account, his name being a familiar sight on London coal carts for nearly a century.

Wiggins' accommodation in the goods yard was altered to offices. These and other offices were let to coal merchants, the carts hired to merchants, and the sacks sold. J. C. Palmer was appointed Coal Manager at King's Cross and Holloway at £300 per annum and when he retired through ill health three years later he was not replaced. Middlemiss had his district extended as far south as Hornsey and then in April 1861 he was removed from his position at £500 and a house, to be agent in the colliery districts at £350. This demotion did not suit him and he resigned on 24 August, nevertheless his salary was paid up till 1 October and he was given a present of 100 guineas. He was succeeded at Doncaster by John Ashley, who took over the house.

Early in February 1859 Seymour Clarke was authorised to 'stop running coal wagons over the SY from such date as he may decide'. In November 1860 a notice was sent to the SY that from Tuesday 1 January the GN intended to run to Elsecar and other collieries with its own engines and wagons at ½d toll. MS&L trains had commenced to run over the SY and into Doncaster on 1 December 1859. Following the breakdown of the proposed joint takeover of the MS&L by the GN and L&NW, Watkin had opened talks with Baxter with a view to drafting an agreement whereby the MS&L might absorb the SY. On 12 February 1861 Edmund Denison explained to his colleagues that ten days earlier he had been interviewed at his Doncaster home (where he was again laid up with gout) by John Chapman and George Gamble of the MS&L who informed him of their company's intention to lease or purchase the SY and hoped that the GN would take equal shares in the acquisition. They called on Denison, gave him a full account of what had happened and was proposed, but then proceeded to the SY offices in Doncaster, where heads of agreement were signed. Then they returned to Denison, and informed him of the transaction, to which he raised no objection. Apparently it took a day or two for it to sink in that Watkin had stolen a march on him, for not only would the MS&L control the coalfield traffic, but also acquisition of the SY would give Watkin a lever to manipulate additional bargaining power in any future negotiations with the GN. Denison gave vent to his feelings and, according to Grinling, described the proceedings as a 'dirty trick'.

The terms the SY accepted were that the MS&L guaranteed a dividend of 4½% for 1861 and 5% thereafter. It was agreed that until Parliamentary approval was obtained, the railway should be managed by a joint stock committee and worked by the MS&L. It was also arranged with the GN that the MS&L should have running powers from Doncaster to Retford in return for the GN running to the South

Yorkshire collieries at ½d toll. During March all three companies held meetings which approved a joint lease. Although Denison was of the opinion that the MS & L had made an improvident bargain, he attended the SY meeting to protect GN interests, and objected to the agreement with the MS & L as too hasty. Needless to say, his motion was defeated. Denison had no more enthusiasm for part ownership in 1861 than he had had for full ownership in 1852. This was reflected in meetings between Clarke and Watkin, who failed to agree on an arrangement for a joint lease.

In the summer of 1861 Watkin was granted three months' leave of absence by the MS & L owing to his indifferent health. During this break from MS & L matters, despite his health, he accepted an invitation to investigate the embarrassed affairs of the Grand Trunk Railway, and set sail for Canada. While he was away his chairman, Chapman, took a step which angered both Watkin and Denison and led to the former resigning his position. The story of a chance meeting between some MS & L's officers and Allport and the Midland officers who were surveying a line of their own from Buxton to Manchester has been told in the *Midland Railway* by F. S. Williams. At all events Chapman became aware that the Midland was determined on its own line. He offered the Midland running powers from New Mills to Manchester if the Midland was to limit new construction to a connecting line from Miller's Dale, near Buxton, to New Mills. Heads of agreement were signed on 11 October by J. Allport and R. C. Underdown, (who had succeeded Watkin as MS & L general manager), providing that until the Midland built its new line, exchange of traffic should be at Beighton from 1 November or earlier.

Chapman's action was contradictory to the spirit and letter of the Fifty Years Agreement, so recently signed with the GN. However, he was in a cleft stick. The Midland was determined to get a good route to Manchester. He had either to risk introduction of a new trunk line through MS & L territory, or give running powers which would at least bring substantial tolls to his impoverished company. Denison and his colleagues were understandably furious when news of the agreement reached their ears. An application was made in Chancery for an injunction to prevent the Midland and MS & L from carrying out their treaty. On 13 December Vice-Chancellor Wood refused this, and an appeal to the Lords Justice was dismissed.

From the start through trains between King's Cross and Edinburgh were largely composed of GN carriages, for it was accepted that the condition and comfort of those vehicles was superior to those owned by the NB, or the motley collection inherited by the NE. In March 1860

Walter Leith proposed that the three companies should provide common stock in proportion to the mileage each company worked between the two capitals. He estimated that 50 vehicles costing £13,450 would answer the purpose and meticulously worked out the proportions as under:

		No.	Vehicles	Cost
GNR	191 miles	8	First class carriages	£310 = £ 2480
		3	Second class carriages	£245 = £ 735
		5	Third class carriages	£230 = £ 1150
		4	Composite carriages	£300 = £ 1200
		4	Brake vans	£215 = £ 860
		24		£ 6425
NER	151 miles	4	First class carriages	£310 = £ 1240
		1	Second class carriage	£245 = £ 245
		5	Third class carriages	£230 = £ 1150
		6	Composite carriages	£300 = £ 1800
		3	Brake vans	£215 = £ 645
		19		£ 5080
NBR	58 miles	4	First class carriages	£310 = £ 1240
		2	Second class carriages	£245 = £ 490
		1	Brake van	£215 = £ 215
		7		£ 1945
	400 miles	50		£13,450

The scheme met the approval of all concerned. Designs were got ready, and it was agreed that the carriages should be built and repaired at Doncaster works. Orders for construction were given in September. They were all in service by the end of 1861. GN guards began to work through to Edinburgh in August of that year and it may well be that this duty coincided with introduction of the new stock in time for the 'Glorious Twelfth'. The 50 carriages, built in the proportions listed above, finished in varnished teak, and inscribed 'East Coast Joint Stock' were used only on the through trains between London and Scotland, not on intermediate services.

The so-called 'central' route to Scotland began to take definite shape in the 1860s. The Lune valley route between Ingleton and Low Gill on the

L&C was opened for goods on 24 August and passengers on 16 September 1861. An express ran each way over this route, Midland, L&NW and Caledonian from 1 March 1862, between Leeds and Glasgow, about two hours being cut off the former journey time. Soon afterwards the NB opened its Border Union between Hawick and Carlisle, goods on 24 June and passengers on 1 July 1862, completing the 'Waverley Route' over which it could work Midland trains from Carlisle to Edinburgh. But such trains did not run until 1876, on the completion of the Midland's Settle and Carlisle line (see vol. II).

[illegible] RAILWAY.—LONDON (King's-[illegible] MANCHESTER, WARRINGTON, GARSTON, and LIVERPOOL.

[illegible] FROM LONDON.—KING'S CROSS STATION.

Leave King's Cross.	Arrival Manchester.	Arrival Liverpool.	Leave King's Cross.	Arrival Manchester.	Arrival Liverpool.
[illegible] 0 a.m.	}		10 [illegible]5 a.m	8 45 p.m.	11 30 p.m.
7 [illegible]0 „	} 4 [illegible] p.m.	6 50 p.m.	1 45 p.m.	10 20 „	—
[illegible] 15 „	}		5 0 „	10 0 „	11 30 „
1[illegible] 0 „	[illegible] 0 „	4 30 „			

T[illegible]AINS FROM MANCHESTER.—LONDON ROAD STATION.

Leave Liverpool.	Leave Manchester.	Arrival King's Cross.	Leave Liverpool.	Leave Manchester.	Arrival King's Cross.
	[illegible] a.m.	4 15 p.m.	1[illegible] 15 a.m.	1 45 p.m.	[illegible] 30 p.m.
	[illegible] 1[illegible] „	4 0 „	3 25 p.m.	5 0 „	10 0 „
[illegible] 30 a.m.	[illegible] „	2 [illegible]5 „	7 0 „	9 30 „	[illegible] 30 a.m.
[illegible] „	1[illegible] 30 „	6 0 „			

SUNDAYS

Leave King's Cross.	Arrival Manchester.	Arrival Liverpool.	Leave Liverpool.	Leave Manchester.	Arrival King's Cross.
[illegible] 0 p.m.	10 0 p.m.	11 30 p.m.		7 0 a.m.	7 45 p.m.
			3 25 p.m.	5 0 p.m.	10 0 „

Express Omnibuses run between 12, North John-street, Liverpool, and Garston, in connection with Through Trains between Garston and London, King's-cross Station.

RETURN TICKETS at 21s. First Class and 12s. 6d. Second Class, available for seven days, and at 37s. First Class and 17s. Second Class, available for twenty-eight days, are issued by all Trains between [illegible]ondon (King's-cross [illegible]tation) and Staley Bridge, Ashton, Guide Bridge, Manchester, Warrington, Garston, and Liverpool.

[illegible] must be taken at London-road Station, Manchester, to ask for Tickets viâ the Great [illegible] route.

[illegible] at the above fares can be obtained at the King's-cross Station, and (for Manchester only) at the Great Northern Receiving Offices, Bull and Mouth, St. Martin's-le-Grand; 16, Fish-street-hill; 264, Holborn; 32, Regent-circus, Piccadilly; 62 and 63, Bridge-road, Lambeth; 269, Strand; 38, Charing-cross; 27, King-street, Cheapside; 351, Oxford-street; George Inn, Boro[illegible]; 43 and 4[illegible], Crutched-friars.

For [illegible]ther particulars see the Time Tables of the Company and the Handbills.

King's-cross Station, February 19, 1858 By order

GREAT NORTHERN and MANCHESTER, SHEFFIELD, and LINCOLNSHIRE RAILWAYS.—CHEAP [illegible]XCURSION TRAINS between [illegible]ONDON (King's cross Station) and MANCHESTER, commencing THURSDAY, 25th FEBRUARY, until further notice, as under:—

EVERY WEDNESDAY AND SATURDAY.		Morn.	EVERY MONDAY AND THURSDAY.		Morn.
King's-cross	dep.	10. 0	Manchester	dep.	10 25
Guide Bridge	arr	4.40	Staley Bridge	„	9.10
Ashton	„	5 31	Ashton	„	9.15
Staley Bridge	„	5.35	Guide Bridge	„	10.45
Manchester	„	5. 0	King's-cross	arr.	5.40

FARE 5s., CLOSED CARRIAGES,

For the Double Journey to or from the above-named Stations and King's-cross.

Tickets issued [illegible]rom King's cross on Wednesdays and Saturdays are available for return either o[illegible] the Monday or Thurs[illegible]ay in the following week.

Tickets issued from Manchester, Staley Bridge Ashton, or Guide Bridge, on Mondays, are available for return either on the Wednesday or Saturday following; [illegible]nd those issued on Thurs[illegible] are available for return either o[illegible] the Saturday or Wedn[illegible]sday following.

The Tickets are not transfer[illegible], and are only available by the above Trains.

[illegible] King's-cross Station [illegible]2n[illegible] February, 1858, By order.

(Courtesy Illustrated London News)

COUNTRY BRANCH LINES

A coal wharf and a warehouse was set up by the GN on the canal at Horncastle in 1851, goods and coal being sent by canal from Dogdyke. In 1853 a company was formed to build a railway from the Loop at Kirkstead to Horncastle. The title first adopted was the Horncastle & Kirkstead Junction but it became the Horncastle. The Horncastle's Act was passed on 10 July 1854, with powers to raise £48,000 capital, and borrow up to £16,000. Brassey was contractor, and built the line between March and September 1855. Earthworks were light. The line was single, 7 miles 28 chains long. The junction at Kirkstead, south of the station, faced Boston, entailing a reversal of branch trains. As a turntable was not provided, a tank engine was employed by the GN which worked the line by 'one engine in steam', sent out daily from Boston shed. A small intermediate passenger station with one platform was provided at Woodhall Spa, then a very small place, though it developed later, as will be described in vol. II. The railway was opened for passengers and light goods on 11 August and for heavy goods and general traffic on 26 September 1855. The Horncastle contrived to remain independent until it became part of the L&NER on 1 January 1923.

Lord Exeter, it is said, had been largely responsible for preventing the GN main line from passing through Stamford. If so, in due course he came to regret his opposition and anyway played the leading part in promotion of the Stamford & Essendine, which received its Act on 15 August 1853. The line was single, 3 miles 67 chains long, leaving the GN by a trailing junction at Essendine where it used the western face of the down platform. A small intermediate station was at Ryhall and a turntable and an engine shed were provided at Stamford. The line crossed the Welland by a viaduct with four openings, spanned by a continuous cast iron plate girder. Captain Wynne first inspected the railway on 12 September 1856, but was not satisfied with the ballasting, and the opening was postponed. Final arrangements having been made for the GN to work the line for 50% of the gross receipts, and Captain Wynne being in agreement, public opening took place on Saturday 1 November 1856. At first there were four trains each way on weekdays, soon increased to five each way on weekdays and two on Sundays.

Stamford station was a handsome stone structure in Elizabethan style in keeping with historic buildings in the town. The large timbered booking hall contained a gallery which gave access to the company's offices. For the first 40 odd years of its existence the interior was unsullied by soot and smoke, for engines of arriving trains were detached at the ticket platform and the carriages towed in, while the engines of departing trains stood clear of the roof.

By the autumn of 1859 a second line of rails had been laid from Stamford station, where there was already a line each side of the platform, to a point 400 yd from Essendine. Captain Wynne went down to inspect this on 19 September, and found that a second connection with the GN had been laid, apparently without the Board of Trade sanction. He decided that this new connection rendered working the single line unsafe, and refused to sanction the second line. On his third inspection he reported that the Bourn & Essendine, then under construction, would cross the GN and the S & E on the level on its way to the platform allotted to it at Essendine. His fourth visit took place on 17 November. He then reported that one crossover with the GN had been removed, and that a pair of points had been connected with the B & E which was still under construction. Again he refused to sanction the second line, and no further reference to it appears in records.

Lord Exeter soon discovered that as the junction at Essendine faced the wrong way for through running towards Peterborough and London, and the route was indirect anyway, passengers, to avoid changing and waiting at Essendine, still used the Midland to Peterborough to reach the GN. The company decided to seek separate access to Peterborough, with another junction with the GN there. But there were financial difficulties. An attempt to borrow £6,000 from assurance companies, on security of debentures, failed. Eventually the company obtained an Act on 25 July 1864 for a line from Stamford to a junction with the LNW's Northampton–Peterborough line at Wansford, 6½ miles from Peterborough. This, 8 miles long, was known as the Sibson extension, as the Act stated it ended at Sibson, a village closer to Wansford station than Wansford village is. Unfortunately, the junction was authorised and constructed, again the wrong way for through working towards Peterborough.

The GN's agreement with the S & E was due to expire on 1 November 1864, and as it had lost £1,700 a year on working the line, the board declined to continue on the original terms, and offered Lord Exeter a rental of £2,000 a year until the Sibson extension was built. He then decided to work his line himself, and was informed that if he did, the nominal rent at Essendine station would be £10 per annum. The GN refused to sell him the engine which was working the line, so he had to make arrangements to obtain his own stock. He temporarily hired an engine and rolling stock from the GN to take over the working on 1 January 1865. His coat of arms was emblazoned on one or two sides of the carriages he obtained. The GN repaired his engine and stock.

The 'Sibson' extension was opened on Friday 9 August 1867, a single line of 8 miles 22 chains. It diverged from the Essendine line 16 chains from Stamford station, and after crossing the Midland by a bridge near Uffington, had stations at Barnack, Ufford Bridge, and Wansford Road. The latter was later the smallest GN station. There were eight bridges. The trains terminated at Wansford station by arrangement with the L&NW. Later, there was trouble about the junction there, and a station was in use for some time just short of the junction, called Sibson. (These events will be described in volume II.) There were five trains each way on weekdays only. Sunday trains between Essendine and Stamford were withdrawn in February 1867. The little company continued to work itself until 1 January 1872 as will be seen in volume II. At one period, Lord Exeter hired engines from the L&NW. A descendant of Lord Exeter now maintains that his ancestor did not oppose the GN original main line plan to pass through Stamford!

The Boston, Sleaford & Midland Counties, incorporated on 20 August 1853, was authorised to construct a line from a junction with the GN at Barkstone to another junction with the GN at Boston. It thus covered much of the intended route of the 'Ambergate' east of Grantham, which had been abandoned. The point for the railway to diverge from the main line was Jericho Wood, near Barkstone, 4¼ miles north of Grantham. The first portion was ready for inspection early in June 1857, Captain Tyler reporting that it was single, with four bridges under the railway, and one timber viaduct. The line was re-inspected by Colonel Yolland on 13 June, who (apart from the incomplete state of Honington station) was satisfied that it could be opened, provided tank engines were used until a turntable was installed at Sleaford. The line to the temporary terminus there was formally opened on the same day, the event being celebrated by the proprietors who entertained the Sleaford townsfolk. Public traffic began on Tuesday 16 June, worked by the GN at 50% of the gross earnings. There were stations at Honington and Ancaster but the former was not opened until 1 July. The line, engineered by Brydone and built by Smith, Knight & Co, was laid with 72 lb rails and was 11 miles long, leaving the GN at the

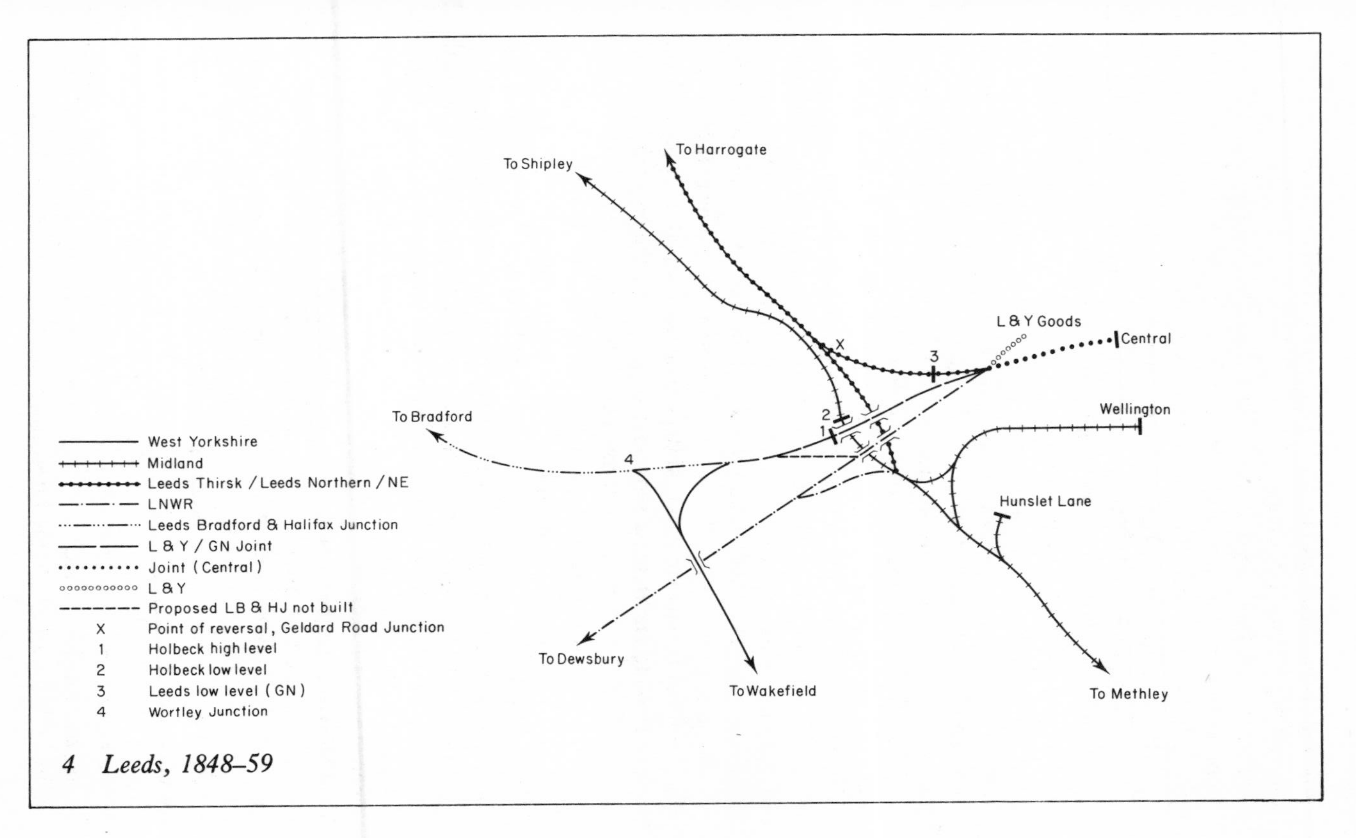

4 Leeds, 1848–59

junction (later Barkstone) by a 17 chain curve. Goods and mineral traffic did not begin until 1 September.

The second, final, section from Sleaford to Sleaford junction with the Loop at Boston was formally opened on Tuesday 12 April 1859. Public traffic began next day. The single line was 16¾ miles, with stations at Heckington and Swineshead. Earthworks were comparatively unimportant, with three underbridges. The railway was inspected by Captain Tyler on 31 March, but he was not satisfied, requiring the electric telegraph to be installed, the junction and signalman's stage at Boston to be completed, clocks at stations, a ballast pit near Sleaford to be fenced, contractors' gear removed, a safe method of working to be determined by the GN, and iron spikes instead of wooden trenails used to secure chairs to sleepers. On his second visit he was satisfied that these conditions had been fulfilled. The single line was to be worked in two sections by staff and ticket. The staves, of different shapes and colours, came from the L&NW. The opening day was marred by a mishap when the 3.10 p.m. from Grantham ran into some coal wagons at Sleaford, being shunted from one side of the line to the other by coal merchants' men without railwaymen's authority. In May 1860 an additional station was opened at Hubbard's Bridge, a name soon altered to Hubbert's Bridge, according to the October Bradshaw. An exchange station at Barkstone was opened at the junction on 1 July 1867, to facilitate passengers' journeys from the Newark direction for Sleaford and Boston, platforms being staggered on either side of the level crossing, separate from the down main line and branch.

The BS&MC was absorbed by the GN on 1 January 1865 by an Act of 25 July 1864. By this Act, the GN also took over the B&E which is the next railway to be described, the undertaking being transferred as from the date of the Act. For over 30 years Bourn was spelt with or without the final 'e'; in fact both varieties of spelling appeared on the same page in GN timetables for a month or two after the Sleaford and Bourn line was opened.

The B&E has been mentioned in connection with the S&E. It was incorporated on 12 August 1857 with powers to construct a railway between the two places in its title, and was empowered to raise £48,000 capital, and borrow £16,000. It had been intended to open the line on 1 May 1860, but the inspecting officer's requirements delayed opening until Wednesday 16 May, when the GN began to work the line. Land was purchased, and the bridges constructed, for double, but it was built, and remained, single. It connected with the S&E on the west side of Essendine, and ran for 6 miles 51 chains to Bourn, where the company purchased Old Red Hall (a fine Elizabethan mansion) for use as offices. Stations were at Braceboro' Spa, Thurlby and Bourn. There were two underbridges, one overbridge and two viaducts. The earthworks were light and the permanent way was laid with 62 lb flat bottomed rails in 21 ft lengths. As a turntable had not been installed at Bourn, the line had to be worked by a tank engine. The little company was always floundering in the red, and after the GN had given notice in 1863 that it would discontinue working, it was persuaded to carry on for another year at 60% of the receipts instead of the previous 50%. However by an Act of 16 May 1864, the GN absorbed the concern. Powers were obtained for a direct spur at Essendine to allow direct running to and from the south, in July 1865, but this was never built.

The Edenham and Little Bytham was first mentioned in GN records on 17 March 1856, when Clarke reported that Lord Willoughby de Eresby had constructed a line from Bytham to Edenham at his own expense, and was requesting permission to form a junction with the GN at Bytham. This request was acceded to at a board meeting on the following day. A passenger service was advertised in December 1857, and shown in GN timetables. In 1864, there were five trains each way between Edenham and Little Bytham which conveyed all three classes. Lord Willoughby worked the line with his own plant, but occasionally had to hire engines and rolling stock from the GN, e.g. a carriage, from 2 May until 30 June 1868, and at the end of the year. His engines were repaired at Peterborough in 1858 and at Doncaster in 1859. One called *Havillah* was repaired in 1868, and Lord Willoughby was charged with the cost of getting it back on the line after a derailment. He offered to sell his railway to the GN in 1867, but the directors were not interested; he had paid the cost of extending the telegraph from Essendine to Little Bytham in 1857. The junction at Bytham was 7 chains north of the station and faced Grantham. Edenham passengers had to alight there and walk to the GN station. The only record of a GN train on the line was on Thursday 4 August 1870, the occasion being a St Pauls Sunday School treat when about 500 passengers were conveyed from New England 'to Bytham and thence to Edenham'. However, the little line got in a bad state. The passenger service last appeared in Bradshaw for February 1872. By this time, the two engines were beyond repair. Goods was worked by horses for some years, but the railway was abandoned early in the '80s. The Midland and Great Northern joint line cut across its route near Bytham in 1893.

The Sandy and Potton was opened for goods on 23 June 1857. It was constructed by Captain Peel R.N., who was allowed by the GN to form a connection at Sandy. Here the line began in the GN yard, and ran through it for a little way, the GN allowing this if Captain Peel would remove it if the GN required the site. A passenger service began in April 1858, the month when Captain Peel died on active service in India. A few years later, the line was bought by, and became part of, the Bedford and Cambridge, opened on 7 July 1862. It crossed the GN by a bridge north of Sandy Station, and then paralleled the GN before turning away to Cambridge. The GN up platform was altered to an island with Bedford trains using the eastern face, and a new junction was made between the two companies' lines south of the station. The layout of the GN sidings had to be altered, the original S & P line being removed as arranged, and an up refuge siding was laid in north of the station. The Bedford and Cambridge was worked, and soon owned by the L & N W. While the Potton line was independent, the GN hired engines and carriages to Captain Peel's executors on one or two occasions.

The Ramsey was incorporated on 22 July 1861 and opened on 1 August 1863 with the GN as working company. Land had been bought for double line, but it was single. There were two underbridges. The line made a junction with the GN at Holme, where there was a curve of 13 chains radius, and ran for 5 miles 58 chains to Ramsey. An intermediate station and sidings were provided at St Mary's, and in the absence of a turntable the line was worked by a tank engine.

The first constituent of a series of small railways which was ultimately to become the Midland & Great Northern Joint Committee was the Norwich and Spalding. It was incorporated on 4 August 1853 with powers to construct a line from Spalding to Sutton Bridge, and a branch from Long Sutton to the EA station at Wisbeach (not spelt Wisbech until 1879)—the spot which had caused the dispute between the GN and EC two years before. There were hopes of extending from Sutton to Lynn and Norwich later. Traffic facilities were contemplated via the EA and EC to the Norfolk, and The Eastern Union (Colchester, Ipswich, Bury and Norwich). Mr J. C. Cobbold of Ipswich, a director of the EU was on the N & S board. Capital of £170,000 had been authorised, but money was difficult to raise, and at first the line was built only as far as Holbeach. Arrangements were made for the GN to work the line and it apppointed staff on 28 July 1858. The line was opened for goods on 9 August, passengers being conveyed from Monday 15 November. The line was single, 7 miles 52 chains long. Leaving the GN by a junction south of Spalding station, it turned eastwards and ran through stations at Weston, Moulton and Whaplode to Holbeach, where an engine shed was provided.

Powers were revived by an Act of 13 August 1859, and the line was extended by 8 miles to Sutton Bridge. Traffic began on Tuesday 1 July 1862 with the GN continuing as working company. There were stations at

Gedney and Long Sutton, while that at Fleet, although completed, was not brought into use until the following November. Three trains were provided on weekdays only and the line was worked with a train staff. The engineering works were unimportant and the permanent way was laid with 65 lb rails. The 1859 Act unfortunately provided that no dividend could be declared unless the company proceeded with promotion of the branch from Sutton to Wisbech. But powers to construct this were refused in 1860 and 1862.

The next link was the Lynn & Sutton Bridge, authorised on 6 August 1861, also single, and opened on Thursday 1 March 1866 for passengers, arrangements for goods not then completed. From a junction with the GE's Lynn–Ely line (just south of the junction of the Harbour Branch at Lynn) it ran for 9 miles 51 chains to a junction with the N&S 15 chains west of that company's Sutton Bridge station. The Ouse was crossed by a 150 yd viaduct, and the Nene by the Cross Keys swing bridge. The company obtained an Act on 25 July 1864, repealing the previous Act requiring it to build a separate bridge parallel to the Cross Keys swing bridge. It was now authorised to adapt this road bridge and its approaches, to carry the railway over the river. Thus, road and rail traffic both used the same swing bridge. It was small wonder that Captain Tyler, reporting on his inspection of the L&SB, was constrained to remark 'working of Cross Keys bridge unprecendented'. The bridge company was bought out for £22,500, purchase being completed on 28 February 1866 by Waring Bros. & Eckersley. Stations were at West Lynn, Clenchwarton, Terrington, Walpole, and Sutton Bridge. The steepest gradient was 1 in 100 and the sharpest curve was one of only 9 chains radius at Sutton Bridge, where a severe speed restriction was imposed. The line was operated by train staff. It was at first intended that the Midland should be the working company, but temporarily the line was worked by the contractors with engines hired from the GN.

In 1861, there was a scheme called the Mid-Eastern and Great Northern Junction, to extend the N&S all the way to Bury, but it came to nothing.

Yet another railway to Sutton Bridge was approaching completion, the Peterborough, Wisbech & Sutton, incorporated on 28 July 1863, and leased to and worked by the Midland. It was first inspected by Captain Rich on 26 April 1866, but owing to incomplete state of works, he refused sanction for public use. He re-inspected the line in May and again refused, mentioning in his report that on his first visit a connection was being put in with the GN at 'Wisbech junction' near Peterborough, but the points had been taken out. The next inspection was on 11 July but as the Midland refused to install proper signals at Wisbech junction he again declined sanction. The Midland, at this period, inclined to flaunt requirements of Board of Trade officers, then put in the required signalling, and reconnected the points with the GN. The connection was called Westwood junction, and there the GN opened a 'large glazed' signal box. Good trains had been running since 1 June and the passenger service began on Monday 1 August. The line, 26¾ miles long, commenced at Wisbech junction with the Midland and after diverging to the west, turned eastwards and crossed the Midland, and the GN, by the New England bridge. Passing through stations at Eye, Thorney, Wryde, Murrow, Wisbech St Mary, Wisbech, Ferry, and Tydd it ended at Sutton Bridge junction with the N&S. This junction faced Lynn, and was about 18 chains west of the L&SB Sutton Bridge station. Land was bought and the overbridges constructed for double lines but the railway was single. Turntables were available at Peterborough and Sutton Bridge. Midland trains began to call at the GN Peterborough station on 1 August 1866, when it closed its own Peterborough (Crescent) station which had been in use since 1 February 1858. As this line provided a Wisbeach–Sutton line, the N & S was relieved of the obligation to promote it, and was allowed to pay dividends, by an Act in 1867.

Also on 1 August 1866 the Midland & Eastern opened the line between Spalding and Bourn, authorised by an Act of 29 July 1862, which incorporated the Spalding & Bourn company. The undertaking was closely associated with the L&SB. Henry Tootal was chairman of both, while James Brunlees was engineer, and Waring Bros. & Eckersley were contractors and principal proprietors. Commencing by a junction with the GN south of Spalding, it measured 9 miles 30 chains to an end-on junction at Bourn with the GN branch from Essendine. Land had been bought by the company at Bourn with the intention of building its own station, but this was not done. It was a lightly constructed single line with flat bottomed rails weighing 65 lbs to the yard, with eight level crossings and no road bridges. There were five viaducts over streams which comprised 48 openings, the widest of which was 36 ft on the skew. An engine shed and a turntable were provided at Spalding where the company also built a goods shed. There were hardly any villages on the route, but there were intermediate stations at North Drove, Counter Drain, and Twenty. The last two were named after local drainage ditches! A new signal box was erected at Spalding junction, the first GN box equipped with inter-locking apparatus. Eckersley informed the directors that he and his partners had provided rolling stock and were prepared to work the line.

While the L & S B was under construction it made an arrangement with the GN which undertook to lease it at 4½%, on an expenditure of £117,000. A Bill was submitted for the 1864 Session to authorise this but it was not successful. Two years later the L&SB and the S&B promoted a Bill in which they sought to amalgamate, lease the N&S, and construct a line from Bourn to the Midland at Saxby. The Bill was supported by the Midland, which expected to work the concern, and opposed by the GN. In response to an offer by the GN, the Saxby extension was withdrawn, but the remainder of the Bill became an Act on 23 July 1866, and the little system adopted the title of the Midland & Eastern. With S&E co-operation, the GN proposed that if the Bourn to Saxby line was given up, it would provide running powers over the existing lines from Bourn to the Midland at Stamford via Essendine. It was an unlikely route with several reversals, but the proposal was accepted, provided that the undertaking was worked jointly by the Midland and the GN. Many years later, a Saxby line was built.

Agreements were signed in July which provided that the Midland and the GN would work the Bourn–Lynn line, the Midland to make a junction at Stamford and give the GN running powers into its Stamford station. Both were to have running powers over the S&E, and the GN was to give the Midland powers from Essendine to Bourn and from the junction to the station at Spalding. Arrangements were made with the GE for use of its lines and station at Lynn, all this being authorised by an Act on 12 August 1867. The GN and Midland set up a Bourn & Lynn Joint Committee, R. A. Dykes being appointed Superintendent on 19 December 1866. The M&E was guaranteed a minimum rental of £15,000 a year, 11½d (4½p) a mile being charged by both companies for working the trains. The Midland did not regularly exercise its powers except between Spalding junction and the station; indeed in later years the GN accountant expressed a doubt that the Midland had ever worked between Stamford and Bourn. However, it appears that the Midland occasionally worked excursions over this section from Lynn to Matlock and Buxton, and on at least one occasion had been allowed to divert its traffic over the GN via Essendine when its own line between Peterborough and Stamford was under water. A regular weekly Midland cattle train from Lynn was worked by a GN engine from Bourn to Stamford.

GN through trains between Stamford and Lynn commenced on 1 August 1866. The GN had to reinstate the connecting line at Essendine between the B&E and the S&E (removed after it took over the former company) and run the Bourn trains into the up platform. This had been sanctioned by the Act of 5 July 1865 which also permitted an improved junction at Spalding with the authorised line from March (see chapter IX); empowered the Midland and the GN jointly to construct a junction line and a branch to the Trent at Newark; and authorised £150,000 capital, borrow £54,000 and subscribe one-third of the capital of the Liverpool Central Station Railway (see chapter XI). The junction at Newark was really a siding connection providing the GN and M with access to the maltings. In 1867 it was under construction by the Midland, and in 1868 the GN paid its proportion of the expenses.

The eastern end of the junction at Stamford had to commence on the viaduct owned by the S & E. The Midland, awkward as ever, was not satisfied with its condition and insisted on an embankment under part of it. This Lord Exeter agreed to do, the junction being brought into use on 1 July 1867. At this period, three mixed passenger, goods and coal trains ran daily between Stamford and Lynn. One started from the Midland station, the second did likewise and called at the S & E station, while the third commenced its journey there.

The M & E way and works were maintained by the GN from 1 August 1866. The M & E paid £50 rent annually to the GN for the use of Bourn, and £150 for Spalding stations, and £32 to the GE for use of Lynn station and harbour lines. The Midland paid the M & E £75 for use of Sutton Bridge station while the GN paid annual £24 rent for the engine shed at Spalding.

On 5 December 1866 it was decided to pull down the wooden engine shed at Holbeach and lay in a passing place. At the same time it was resolved to move the points of the PW & S nearer to the junction of the N & S and the L & S B so that they could be worked by rod by the junction signalman. It was not necessary to retain the older station at Sutton Bridge and on 23 January 1867 instructions were given that it should be abolished. The buildings were converted to platelayers cottages but the platforms continued to be used by passenger trains for many years in times of heavy traffic. The receipts of some wayside stations were very meagre at this time. Several narrowly escaped closure, that at Weston being in the charge of a platelayer's wife.

The Bourn and Lynn Joint Committee had its own staff and uniform, but rarely met—apparently only in 1866 and 1867, and then not till 1880, Mr Dykes looking after the line with joint meetings with GN and Midland officers. As Midland trains were so rare on the Sutton–Bourn section (besides those mentioned above there was a daily goods from Sutton to Spalding) only the Lynn–Sutton section was really worked jointly. Some trains had GN and Midland coaches, but at other times passengers had to change at Sutton Bridge. There were no Sunday trains for passengers between Bourn and Lynn, or between Peterborough and Sutton.

THE EARLY 'SIXTIES

Following the 1852 truce, relations with the EC remained unruffled until the GN took over the HL&D, which established it at Hertford. A further cause of discontent was GN interest in the N & S, which appeared to Shoreditch as the spearhead of invasion from the north.

The Great Eastern Railway came into being by an Act on 7 August 1862, sanctioning amalgamation of the EA, EC, Eastern Union, East Suffolk, Newmarket and Norfolk. Before long, the GE planned to break out of its agricultural confines, and construct a line to the north over which it aspired to compete for London coal traffic. A Bill for a line from March to Askern via Lincoln failed in the 1862 Session. So a Bill was submitted for the 1863 Session in which the GE sought to construct a line from March to Spalding, and secure running powers thence to Doncaster over the GN. In opposition the GN lodged a Bill for its own Spalding–March line, and proposed to exchange traffic with the GE at March, also applying for variation of the Gainsborough to Rossington, on this occasion planned to run from Owston to Cottam. The GE and the variation Bills were rejected, but the GN was successful with its Spalding–March Bill, although it had to concede running powers over it to the GE, by an Act of 21 July 1863, empowering also £225,000 new capital and £75,000 loans.

In anticipation of again taking up leasing and working the R&H, the GN prepared a Bill for its own line from Shepreth to Cambridge. The threat of this was sufficient to bring the GE to terms. An agreement was signed on 2 May 1864. In consideration of the GN withdrawing its extension Bill, the GE conceded running powers from Shepreth to Cambridge and undertook to double its line from Shelford junction to Shepreth junction before 31 March 1866 when its R&H lease would expire. GN trains were to call at intermediate stations, while the GE undertook to provide facilities at Cambridge for booking, parcels, goods and shedding engines by GN servants.

Having at last given way on GN entry to Cambridge the GE was exceedingly bitter when its 'Great Eastern Northern Junction' Bill was thrown out in the 1864 Session. Projected by a nominally independent company, the proposed line, including branches, was to have been 134 miles long, and would have cost over £2,000,000. It was to have left the GE at Long Stanton, between Cambridge and St Ives, and joined the West Riding & Grimsby (page 160) near Askern. Connections had been proposed with the NE projected York to Doncaster line, the L&Y, SY, MS&L, and Midland. Primarily as a coal carrying line, it was laid out by Fowler and Hawkshaw with a maximum gradient of 1 in 400. It was claimed that, provided coal was handed over in trainloads of 400 tons, these could be profitably worked at one farthing per ton per mile. For half its length it would have run within three miles of existing railways. Opposed by the GN, the Bill was rejected after a long and expensive fight. The GE had been supported by the WR&G, and SY, while its Parliamentary adviser was none other than Robert Baxter who had entered the contest with enthusiasm.

By an Act of 25 July 1864 the GN at last obtained powers to build its Gainsborough–Doncaster line, and to raise £408,000 capital and borrow £136,000. While the Bill was before the Lords, the GE pressed for running powers, but had to be content with facility clauses. Another Bill in the same Session was the Lincoln & Bourn, in which the GN sought powers for a line from a triangular junction at Honington to Lincoln, another from Sleaford to Bourn, and for absorption of the BS&MC, and the B&E. The motive behind absorbing these two, and providing a Sleaford to Bourn line, was to block GE aspirations. The Sleaford–Bourn was rejected, but the remainder of the Bill became an Act on 25 July 1864, with new capital at £310,000 and borrowing powers £103,000. The Sleaford–Bourn was re-submitted for the next Session and was authorised by the Act of 29 June 1865, with powers to raise £190,000 capital and borrow £63,000.

George Thompson, whose salary was advanced to £650 from 1 January 1858, was called to resign in favour of a younger man in the autumn of 1862. Despite appeals, he had to go at the end of the year, but was allowed to take his old position of canal manager of £300 from 1 January 1863. He died towards the end of the following year. Ashley became Goods Manager and was succeeded as mineral manager at Doncaster by William Newton who had been district agent at Boston.

The 10.0 a.m. express from King's Cross to Scotland began to run in June 1862. The corresponding up day express had been leaving Edinburgh Waverley at 10.0 a.m. since 1859. These trains later became famous as the 'Flying Scotsman'. The down express was much the best

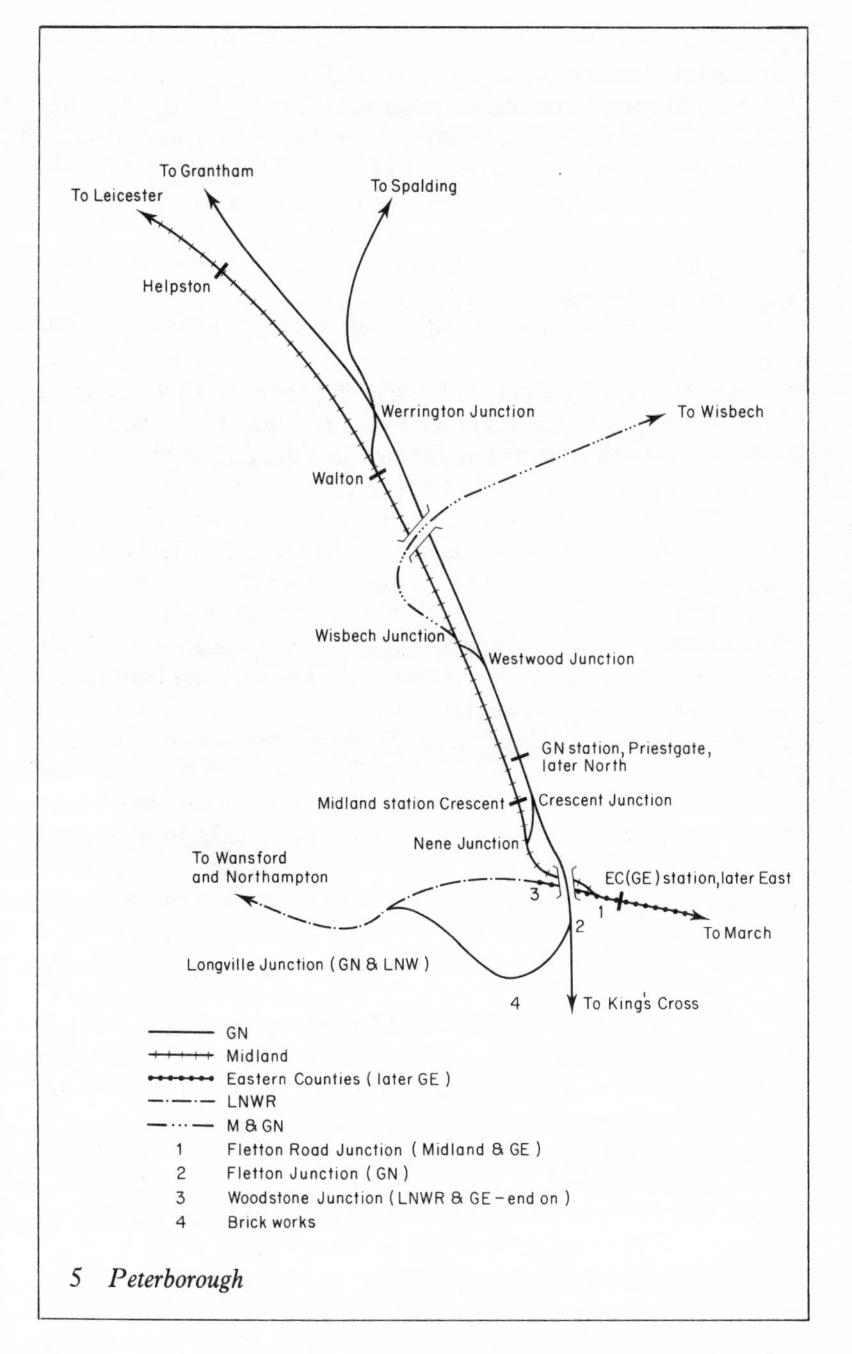

5 *Peterborough*

train between London and Scotland so far, and so remained for many years. It ran non-stop to Peterborough in 95 minutes, 48.2 mph, and then stopped only at Grantham and Retford to reach York in 4 hr 35 m. The overall schedule to Edinburgh was 10½ hr, an improvement of 20 minutes on the old 9.30 service. There were through carriages to Glasgow and Perth. The Retford stop gave a connection to Manchester. The train was 'first and second' only. There was a 30 minute stop at York 'for refreshments' so the overall schedule was better than it looked. Again the up train was slower, 11½ hr from Edinburgh.

The 95 minute schedule to Peterborough was found to be rather stiff, so in the summer of 1864 it was increased to 97 minutes, without affecting the overall schedule to Edinburgh. The rival 10.0 a.m. from Euston also began to run in the same month, June 1862. It was much slower than the east coast train to Edinburgh, taking 11 hr 10 m., but of course had a great advantage to Glasgow thanks to the shorter route.

In 1867, the 10.0 from King's Cross was given a Doncaster slip, to provide a West Riding connection. This became a stop in 1868, and the schedule to York made 4 hr 40 m., again without affecting the 10½ hr time to Edinburgh.

The origin of the name Flying Scotsman—or Scotchman— is difficult to discover. A practice was developing on the east and west coast routes (and later on the Midland) for the staff and public to refer to all Scottish expresses as Scotsmen or Scotchmen. The name 'Flying Dutchman' was already in use for the best train in the GWR from Paddington. The name, in the 'Scotchmen. or 'Scotsman' form, seems to have been in use for the train quite soon, as the name 'Flying Scotchman' actually appears in a Board of Trade report, 1873, (see vol. II, chapter 2). Bradshaw, however, in the '70s and '80s, called the 10 o'clocks (and the best night trains) 'Special Scotch Express'. The term 'Flying' was frequently used for the 10.0 from King's Cross when the train raced to Edinburgh in 1888 (see vol. II).

Acworth, describing the race in 'The Railways of England' published in 1889, called it the Flying Scotchman, and once 'The Flying Scot'. The *Railway News*, of July 29 1893, in a favourable description of the train called it the 'Flying Scotsman' as if that term was accepted. Certainly it was in general use for the 10 o'clock from King's Cross and Waverley by the early twentieth century, and can be found on postcards of the train dating from the 1890s. But the name was not officially used by the company, nor to be found in Bradshaw, until LNER days.

Charles Dickens was a passenger on the train one day in the late 1860s, and as he was then a very sick man it was stated that one of the royal saloons was provided for him.

1862 was also the year of the International Exhibition and a heavy excursion traffic was run. Between 1 May and 31 October, 280,943 additional passengers had been carried compared with the same period in 1861. When all was over, and the vast additional traffic had been accomplished in safety a very relieved board loosened its purse strings and voted £4,000 to be distributed between the staff. The senior officers declined to take a share. The money was divided between 1,923 servants, in the grades of clerks in charge, porters, guards, drivers and firemen. While the traffic was at its height Clarke's health broke down and he was given leave, his duties being performed by Leith. Fisher also suffered from the strain, and took a lighter position as station master at Bourn, where he died soon afterwards. He was succeeded as station master at King's Cross by Vizer, his assistant.

Clarke returned to duty in the early spring, and soon afterwards Leith was appointed Assistant Manager with a salary of £1,500 with effect from 1 July 1863. Charles Currey (Leith's chief clerk) was appointed Superintendent of the Line. Currey left on 13 February 1865 to take up a position in India, and Leith resigned 11 days later whereupon Clarke's salary was increased to £3,000. Twelve months later C. H. Turner, GE chairman, offered Clarke the 'lucrative' position of general manager to his company and in order to retain his services the GN directors increased his salary by £1,000 from 1 April 1866.

The most important event of the period, however, was the retirement of Edmund Denison, aged 77. His drive, determination, and tenacity of purpose which bordered on obstinacy had been among the major forces which resulted in the London & York plans being carried through almost in entirety, even if it appeared at times that the direction of the company had been something in the nature of a one man band. The railway press, which had so frequently employed the terms 'aggressive, abusive, bellicose, or despotic', now paid tribute to his 'singular ability, vigour, and prudence'. He was a martyr to gout and fated to have been laid low all too often with it at his house at Doncaster, when crises developed. He had been taken ill early in 1864, did not take his accustomed place at either half-yearly meeting, and on 17 December wrote tendering his resignation from the chair and the board. Colonel Packe moved up to the chairmanship, and was succeeded as deputy by Colonel Duncombe.

While Denison blundered in handling the South Yorkshire affair, and consequent severing of association with Baxter, the increase in the profits available for distribution spoke eloquently of the success of his fighting policy. Dividends paid on the original stock rose from £2 in 1851 to £7 2s

6d (£7.12½) in the year of his retirement and only looked back in 1856/7 by reason of the Redpath frauds:

	£	s	d	£ p		£	s	d	£ p
1851	2	0	0	(2.00)	1858	4	15	0	(4.75)
1852	2	5	0	(2.25)	1859	5	6	9	(5.34)
1853	3	12	6	(3.62½)	1860	5	8	9	(5.44)
1854	4	0	0	(4.00)	1861	5	15	0	(5.75)
1855	4	2	6	(4.12½)	1862	6	10	0	(6.50)
1856	1	15	0	(1.75	1863	6	10	0	(6.50)
1857	2	19	3	(2.96)	1864	7	2	6	(7.12½)

The shareholders subscribed £1,500 to purchase a testimonial to their late chairman, who expressed a wish that £1,000 should be devoted towards building a church at New England, and the remainder used for purchase of a present of candelabrum.

There were several changes among the directors. Following the retirement of T. Wetherel in February, and the company having services to, and joint lines in Lancashire, Charles Turner of Liverpool was elected to the board. The Act of that year approved that the minimum number of directors might be reduced to ten. Thus when Francis Pym died in 1860, and A. F. Paull retired and James Arbouin died in 1861 they were not replaced. Isaac Burkill resigned in 1862 and was replaced by Edward Christopher Egerton, M.P. Alderman Meek and Francis Parker died in 1862, and were replaced in the following year by Samuel Waterhouse, and Lord Colville of Culross, who was elected to the board on 3 February, and was a future chairman. Also in 1863 Robert Tennant was elected in the place of Paull, which brought the board's numbers to 14. In 1865 Christopher B. Denison was elected in place of his father. Another change then was the election of William Firth following the death of John Barff, particularly appropriate, for Barff had had the company's interests in the West Riding under his wing, while Firth, as we know, had been one of the leading spirits in promotion of the Yorkshire railways which the GN had just absorbed.

A notable appointment was made on 4 April 1865, when Francis Pickersgill Cockshott was engaged as Superintendent of the Line, a position he was to hold for 30 years. Then aged 41, he had made railways his career. He was apprenticed to Joseph Pease Junior in 1841, and entered Shildon works four years later. From there he moved to the Edinburgh, Perth & Dundee where he was successively goods manager and passenger superintendent. After six years in Scotland he went to the South Devon in December 1851 where he was traffic superintendent.

From 1858 his duties included superintendence of the Cornwall. Engaged by the GN at £1,000 per annum his salary was increased to £1,200 from 1 January 1867.

At the plant, John Coffin died on 20 April 1858, and was succeeded by John Griffiths who, after a trial period, was appointed Assistant Carriage & Wagon Superintendent on the following 1 April, salary £300. He made good for successive rises of £50 took him up to £450 on 1 January 1867, and his designs for new carriages soon earned praise in the railway press. Frederick Parker's salary was raised to £500 from 1 January 1863 but he resigned on 2 October 1865 to take up an appointment with John Fowler & Co of Leeds. On 1 January 1864 Sturrock's rate of salary was increased to £1,500.

The position of manager of Doncaster Locomotive Shops was advertised and there were seven applicants. One of the Stephenson family, Patrick Stirling, Montgomeries, Kitson, Griffiths and Davis were interviewed by the Executive Committee on 1 December 1865; the seventh candidate, Irving, did not attend. After discussion, the candidates were called in again, and informed that the matter was postponed and that only Stephenson and Kitson need apply again. No doubt there was backstage work, for at a board meeting on 9 January 1866 the directors were informed that Sturrock had announced his intended retirement, and were introduced to Patrick Stirling. Colonel Packe stated that Stirling 'was at present the locomotive engineer of the Edinburgh & Glasgow' (the howler of 1866), 'was qualified by his attainments and experience to meet the company's requirements and had charge of the locomotive carriage and wagon department of the Glasgow & South Western'. Stirling was of course the latter's locomotive engineer, and had no connection with the E&G. Sturrock's views were that Stirling should be appointed Assistant Locomotive Engineer until he himself retired, that his salary should commence at £1,000 and be increased to £2,000 when he became locomotive engineer, on an engagement for three years. Sturrock proposed to retire at the close of 1866, but on 1 October handed over to Stirling and remained only as a consultant. At a gathering in the erecting shop at Doncaster in the following February Sturrock was presented with a plate of £200 value. On 7 August 1866 John Shotton, from Stephensons, was appointed Works Manager at £400 on Stirling's recommendation.

For reasons not made clear Pulford, the storekeeper, was reduced to canal manager at £200 from 1 October 1866, and W. Nicholls succeeded him at £350. John Ashley became goods manager and in April 1867 it was arranged that he should receive £900 from 25 March 1867 and £1,000 from 25 March 1868. S. L. Mason resigned as assistant superintendent of the line in April 1867 on being appointed Goods Manager to the NB, and was succeeded by Henry Conder at £400. James Grinling replaced his brother, William as accountant early in 1865.

As already mentioned 1862 was International Exhibition year, and with both the GN and the Midland running numerous excursions, congestion intensified. There just was not sufficient accommodation at King's Cross to handle more than normal traffic, and to the intense annoyance of the Midland its excursion passengers were often loaded or unloaded on the ballast. Complaints poured in about detention of Midland goods and coal trains, particularly at Holloway. Each instance was investigated by GN officers, who pointed out that a train, claimed by the Midland as a fast goods, was shown in its time books as a coal train, that trains arriving late at Hitchin lost their paths in consequence, and that trains were held at Holloway because the Midland sidings were full up. There is no evidence that the King's Cross authorities ordered or encouraged hindrance to Midland traffic, but plenty that GN trains were also suffering delays. Complaints were made to the Midland that some of its drivers were running by distants at 'caution' too fast.

The Midland had already obtained powers to construct its own goods yard at St Pancras, adjoining the GN's. Four hundred slum houses in Agar Town were swept away to make room for this. In June 1861 the Midland estimated that it would evacuate the GN sidings early in 1862. Two months later the GN instructed Jay to proceed immediately with excavation of land up to the Midland boundary so that connecting lines might be laid. While no doubt the GN was anxious to resume use of its sidings, Clarke and Leith, in a most undiplomatic manner, bombarded the Midland with demands for removal of its coal traffic, and on 5 July 1862 an ultimatum was delivered 'Move coal tonight'. Small wonder that the Midland complained of 'eviction in the night'; however it was still allowed to handle some coal traffic in GN sidings for another year.

In view of frustration to regular working of its traffic, hostility between the companies, and the unwise campaign by Clarke and Leith, it is not surprising that the Midland began to think seriously about its own line into London, to run southwards from Bedford and pass through Luton, St Albans and Mill Hill, all served, or about to be, by GN branches. The GN was reluctant to lose the Midland tolls (£47,000 in 1861), and did not want another competing trunk line into London. Whatever Denison subsequently chose to tell the shareholders, on one occasion he did offer the Midland perpetual running powers between Hitchin and London. However, when the Midland applied for such powers, the GN declined to grant them, offering more permanent powers, provided the minimum toll was raised from £20,000 to £60,000 per annum. It was prepared to put down one or two additional lines between Hitchin and London if on an arbitrator's opinion the two companies' traffics could not be carried on the existing lines, but in this event the guarantee was to be increased by 5% on the money the GN might spend. In return the GN required running powers to the Leicestershire, Nottinghamshire and Derbyshire coalfields.

The Midland was not impressed, and presented a Bill for its London Extension. Despite GN opposition, this became an Act on 22 June 1863. Earlier this year, the Midland had given the necessary seven years' notice of its intention to cease running over the GN. On 25 July 1864 it obtained another Act, authorising construction of a short branch to connect its new main line with the Metropolitan at King's Cross. A third Act of 30 July 1866 authorised the Midland to deviate 32 chains of the GN, Luton & Dunstable branch between the 10½ and 11 mile posts. The new Midland line bridged this branch, and those to St Albans and Edgware. It began to carry goods traffic on 9 September 1867, and passenger trains in the following year. St Pancras goods station in King's Road, Agar Town, had been opened on Monday 2 January 1865.

When the Exhibition closed, the Midland continued issue of seven day return excursion tickets, a course which Leith had to follow. This was the weapon chosen by Allport to try and force the other companies to revise the terms of the 1856 English & Scottish Alliance, so that his company might recieve a more adequate share of the receipts of the Anglo-Scottish traffic it was developing. Since the Midland trains were using King's Cross, this competition was less damaging to the GN than to others. Left to itself it is probable that it would have been in favour of an adjustment to Midland benefit. However it was only one of a number of companies, and had to support its east coast ally, the NE, which firmly opposed any revision, for it stood to lose the most if the Midland transferred its Scotch traffic from the old route via Normanton and York to the central route via the Lune valley and Carlisle. Not only was the Midland denied what it regarded as a just share of Anglo-Scottish traffic, but since April 1860 the Clearing House had, on the other Alliance signatories' direction, collected all central route receipts and held them in suspense. This was because the Midland had attempted to evade the pooling by dividing these receipts between the companies over whose lines the traffic passed.

At a GN directors' meeting on 3 August 1863, when £45,500 was held in suspense, it was resolved that the time had come to withdraw traffic from division by the English & Scotch committee. To force the issue, notice was sent to the committee that until the matter was settled the GN would object to any further division of any receipts whatever. When informed of this notice the Clearing House began to collect all the receipts of traffic on all the routes, and similarly hold them in suspense. While its action did not have any immediate effect, it was reported on 11 April 1865 that 75% of the disputed money had been divided and that the amount due to the GN was £42,823.

Meantime, the Midland, on 22 July 1864, brought an action in the Chancery Court against the other members of the Alliance. When Vice-Chancellor Kindersley delivered judgement on 28 July 1866, victory went to the Midland, for he declared that the construction which the west and east coast companies sought to put upon the Alliance was *ultra vires*. If that was not enough to spell the doom of the Alliance, a decisive move by the Midland certainly was, for on 16 July 1866 it obtained powers to construct a line to Carlisle from the (little) NW at Settle. These powers meant that when this, and its Bedford to London lines were completed it would run from London to the Scottish border over its own metals. Thus faded into oblivion the last vestige of the Huish protectionist policies, designed to stunt GN development.

Across the border, the NB absorbed the Edinburgh, Perth & Dundee in 1862. This was almost isolated from the main system and was not suitably connected until the Forth Bridge was completed nearly 30 years later. Its only means of communication with Edinburgh and Dundee were by ferries across the Firths of Forth and Tay between Burntisland and Granton, and Broughty Ferry and Tayport respectively. For the following Session, the E&G introduced a Bill in which it sought to amalgamate with, or sell its undertaking to, the NB, GN, and NE, or some of them. The Bill was rejected, but in 1865 the NB absorbed the line, and secured permanent access to Glasgow for the east coast alliance. It also obtained powers to bridge the Forth and Tay, which would give the east coast allies their own routes to Perth and Dundee. However the 1866 financial crisis caused abandonment of these schemes, but they were revived later, as will be seen in volume II. In 1865 the Caledonian absorbed the Scottish Central, and in 1866 the Scottish North Eastern, formed ten years earlier by amalgamation of the Scottish Midland Junction and Aberdeen. Both Caledonian Bills were opposed by the GN and NE, to protect the arrangements they had made with these companies for east coast traffic to Perth and Aberdeen. They were successful in securing insertion of 'facility' clauses, which bound the Caledonian to give equal priority to their traffic.

As ECJ carriages worked north of Edinburgh, the Caledonian, and the Inverness & Perth Junction (and its successor the Highland), began to pay a proportion of the expense of the joint stock. Construction of five brakes at Doncaster for the service was sanctioned in April 1866. The latest pattern GN carriages were used in the ECJ trains, so early the next year it was resolved that the joint stock should be replaced by more commodious vehicles. It was proposed that 53 carriages and 12 brakes should be built, all at Doncaster, and instructions were given that a pattern of each was to be built as quickly as possible for approval by the three EC companies.

At no time had the South Yorkshire coalowners provided the regular flow of coal the GN required to carry on its trade in an efficient manner, nor had a lasting agreement for coal carriage been effected between the SY and the GN. The position was unlikely to improve with the MS&L in control, while the comparative figures for December 1861 showed that the L&NW had forged ahead with coal carriage to London. The figures were 74,953 ton against the combined GN and Midland total of 42,843 ton. As an alternative, the GN determined to establish an increased trade with Derbyshire where many new pits were being opened. The high toll which the Midland exacted on coal passing through the junction at Nottingham (2s 2d, 11p a ton from Clay Cross, taken as the centre of the field) precluded a profitable business being built up by that route. On 28 October 1862, Cubitt was instructed to survey a line from 'Nottingham into the Midland coalfield'. Within a fortnight Allport intimated that his company was prepared to negotiate on coal; nevertheless a Bill was deposited, but subsequently withdrawn, for a line from Colwick to Codnor Park in the Erewash valley. In the absence of Clarke on sick leave Leith undertook negotiations with Allport. The Midland agreed to give the GN free access to Derbyshire coal on condition that it withdrew the 1s 9d (8p) minimum toll on the coal the Midland worked from Hitchin to London. That was fair enough, but the Midland also insisted that the rates from Yorkshire, Nottinghamshire, Derbyshire and Leicestershire should be equitably adjusted to each other on a geographical basis, a condition which was to store up trouble for the GN in future. But Leith was no more gifted with foresight than his chief, and on 23 January 1863 he signed the Coal Traffic Agreement. In 1863 the GN carried 560,000 ton of coal to London, 770,000 ton in 1864, and 975,000 ton in 1865. It was considered that the increase would have been 25% greater in 1864 if the company had had sufficient engine power and siding accommodation.

The Act sanctioning MS&L lease of the SY passed on 23 June 1864.

Almost immediately the GN sent a notice to the MS&L, demanding £1,400 rent for use of Doncaster station. Underdown offered £650 which was unacceptable and it was agreed to submit to arbitration. Huish was chosen as arbitrator, and making a brief emergence from retirement, awarded the GN £1,250.

The next railway to be considered is the West Riding & Grimsby, incorporated on 7 August 1862, authorised to build a line from a junction with the BW&L (shortly to become the West Yorkshire, see chapter V) at Wakefield to a junction with the SY near Stainforth, a branch to Doncaster, and a junction line to the Midland. Ever since the GN had deposited its original Bill, in London & York days, it had desired to construct its own line from Doncaster to Wakefield. It had lodged Bills for this on several occasions, including one as recently as the 1861 Session, but almost inevitably, opposition by its neighbours led to their rejection. That Parliament should not turn about and sanction such a line to an independent company would seem surprising, but it was no doubt influenced by the fact that the WR&G main line would provide a new route from Yorkshire industrial towns to Grimsby. Although nominally independent, the company was backed by the SY, and MS&L, which guaranteed a minimum of 4½% on capital of £360,000. Borrowing powers were £120,000. Fowler was appointed Engineer (and Fraser as Resident) in August 1862. A contract for construction was awarded to Smith Knight & Co.

Captain Tyler, early in November 1865, found the line very incomplete. He reported that the main line from Wakefield to Barnby upon Don was 21 miles 40 chains, the 'so-called Doncaster branch' (Tyler's sarcasm) 4 miles 32 chains, and the branch to the Midland 46 chains. From Wakefield (later West Riding) junction to Milethorne junction the line was double, but from Adwick junction to Haggs Wood junction at Stainforth it was single. At Haggs Wood junction it was to make a connection with a double line deviation which the SY was building to replace the 1855 single line which followed the canal's sinuous curves. This old line, shortly to be abandoned, was crossed on the flat by the WR&G. There was a viaduct of 1,200 yd near Wakefield, the widest span of which was 163 ft. Tyler found fault with some cast iron girders in this and other bridges, and demanded their replacement, also requiring strengthening of a swing bridge by which the Stainforth line crossed the Don. He re-inspected the line on 29 December and was satisfied that his requirements had been carried out on the Wakefield–Doncaster line. Seymour Clarke had written that the electric telegraph would shortly be installed between Milethorne junction and

Westgate junction, and Tyler thereupon sanctioned opening of this section which, however, did not take place until 1 February 1866 (definitely not 1 January as was stated in the railway press, and sometimes even now repeated).

In 1864, the GN wished to buy the WR&G, but actually it became joint property of the GN, and MS&L, who took possession on 1 February 1866, authorised by an Act of 28 June. This also provided for GN running powers from Stainforth to Grimsby over the MS&L, SY, and Trent, Ancholme & Grimsby, and for MS&L powers over the WY, LB&H, and into Leeds Central. The GN promptly diverted its West Riding trains over the new line which finally reduced the distance between King's Cross and Leeds to 185¾ miles and enabled the journey time to be cut by 20 minutes. From 1 March the L&Y, which paid £300 per annum for the use of Doncaster station, worked all local trains between Doncaster and Wakefield via Knottingley.

Captain Tyler's next inspection was on 5 June, when he declined to sanction opening of the remainder. With regard to the branch to the Midland, he stated that the Midland would not exercise running powers over it until the new goods station at Wakefield was ready in some months time. He eventually sanctioned the use of this, which ran from Sandal junction to Walton junction on the Midland, on 31 July, and was opened on 1 September. The final section between Adwick junction and Haggs Wood junction, (doubled on GN insistence) was opened on 1 November. A station had been built at Barnby Dun but apparently it was never used for regular passenger traffic, although it was handling goods by 1867. From the early '70s it was occasionally used by excursion trains. About 1888, it was renamed Bramwith to avoid confusion with the station at Barnby Dun between Doncaster and Thorne; about 1901 it reverted to goods only. Many years later the section had regular passenger trains. The other stations, all between Doncaster and Wakefield, were Hampole, South Elmsall, Hemsworth, Nostell, and Sandal. Adwick was opened on 1 March 1866, renamed Adwick-le-Street & Carcroft 13 months later, although the inhabitants had expressed a preference for Carcroft. From Doncaster to Adwick, the line was practically level and then rose at 1 in 440 to Hampole, then steepened to 1 in 200 to South Elmsall and next at 1 in 150 until nearly Nostell, where it fell at the same inclination until before Sandal, thence a final rise to 1 in 150.

The WR&G obtained an Act on 23 June 1864 authorising a new Westgate station on the WY, for joint use of the Midland, WY, MS&L, and SY, all of which subscribed to its cost. The old station was partly demolished in April 1867 and the new passenger station was brought into use on 1 May. The new goods station, joint Midland and MS&L, approached by their 24 chain branch from Balne Lane junction, was opened on 1 July 1868. The company sponsored a Bill for an Althorpe-on-Trent & Lincoln which passed on 5 July 1865. This was conceived by Watkin to counter joint GE and L&Y aspirations, shortly to be mentioned. Powers to abandon it were obtained on 25 June 1868 by the GN, which did not exercise its powers to Grimsby (other than for excursion and other special traffic), which was unfortunate, as their use would have helped the GN, when there was a dispute about Grimsby traffic later.

A company was formed in 1863 to build a railway along the Thornton valley, to connect Halifax with Keighley. As the Halifax & Ovenden, it was incorporated on 30 June 1864, with capital of £90,000, and borrowing powers £30,000. The GN and L&Y each subscribed £30,000 towards the capital. Powers were restricted to a line a little over 2½ miles from a junction with the L&Y at Halifax to Holmfield. Akroyd was chairman, and Fraser was engineer. Ten years elapsed before the line began to carry traffic (see vol. II).

The NE obtained powers on 23 June 1864 to construct a direct line from York to a junction with the GN at Shaftholme junction, ¼ mile north of the end-on Askern junction. This spot became very well known later as the end of the GN main line (see vol. II). An agreement was signed with the GN on the previous 15 March, which arranged for the NE to have running powers from Askern to Doncaster, and to St James's junction with the SY. The GN received powers over the new route, and it was agreed that there should be no competition. Four GN engines were to be stationed at York, and two NE engines at Doncaster.

J. Pepper's cartage agreements with the GN in the West Riding, extended to Barnsley and Huddersfield in 1858, Wakefield in 1861 and Ossett in 1862, lapsed on 31 December 1866, but were renewed for 12 months or longer, terminable by six months' notice, until 1 July 1868.

The L&Y had been unable to prevent the GN taking possession of the LB&HJ, and the WY, and was also in the unfortunate position of steadily losing the GN traffic, which produced considerable revenue from tolls. It had already lost the tolls on the traffic via Methley, and would lose those on that via Wakefield when the WR&G opened. The GN arranged to turn the bulk of its traffic running via Knottingley to the new NE line when completed. That the GN had become so firmly established in the West Riding was entirely due to the L&Y's neglect to complete the West Riding Union, but it now turned hostile, and joined forces with an equally disgruntled company in promoting, in the 1865 Session, a project entitled the Lancashire & Yorkshire & Great Eastern Junction. This was to commence at Long Stanton and as far as Sleaford follow the route of the Great Eastern & Northern Junction, and then take a more easterly course until it joined the L&Y at Askern. It was supported by a Goole, Keadby & Haxey, to connect with it at Haxey and join the L&Y at Goole. On this occasion it was intended to be not only a coal line, but also a brand new trunk railway between London and Yorkshire and Lancashire and thus threaten the MS&L as well as the GN. However it made little progress in Parliament, that felt the subject had been sufficiently discussed the year before. The Bill was thrown out on Commons second reading on 14 March 1865, whereupon the Goole, Keadby & Haxey was abandoned.

The sequel to all this was that the GN opened talks with the GE about providing the latter with the route to the north it coveted. The GE agreed to pay half the cost both of the Loop line and construction of the new GN Spalding–March and Gainsborough–Doncaster lines. The GE would have running powers to Wakefield over the WR&G (which the GN and MS&L were about to take over), and over the MS&L across Trent Bridge and between Sykes junction and Retford. Lancashire traffic would be exchanged at Lincoln with the MS&L. A GN&GE Arrangements Bill was deposited for the 1866 Session, but then there was a change in the board of directors at Shoreditch. The new board had to face the hard facts that the kitty was empty, and there was not the remotest chance of finding the money which their predecessors had so rashly undertaken to pay the GN. So the Arrangements Bill had to be withdrawn.

If they had not realised it already, the GN directors were soon to learn how flat broke was their neighbour. In December 1865 GN and GE engineers made an inspection of the R&H. The stations and permanent way were in a state of dilapidation, as there were insufficient sleepers to each length of rail. The GN's engineer demanded that 11,400 sleepers should be renewed. When the line was handed back on 1 April 1866, the sleepers were provided, but it was left to the GN to put the road in order. Eleven miles had been relaid and 5,000 new sleepers inserted within three months, but on 3 July a fatal derailment occurred (see chapter XIII). It was anticipated that relaying would take three months to complete, and in compliance with Captain Tyler's (the inspecting officer) recommendation, trains were allowed an extra ten minutes between Hitchin and Cambridge until repairs were finished. The GE section was in no better shape, for on the previous 31 May, the 7.10 p.m.

from Cambridge was derailed between Shelford and Shepreth, but there were no serious casualties. This piece had not been doubled as promised, nor was the accommodation provided at Cambridge, where there was no shelter for GN passengers. W. Bell & Sons, the contractors for these works, ceased operations when the GE was unable to pay them, leaving the GN to advance £5,000 for the work to proceed. From 1 January 1868 the GN provided its own staff at Cambridge for passenger traffic. Doubling the line between Shelford and Shepreth junctions was passed by the Board of Trade early in May 1867, and the electric telegraph was set up between Hitchin and Cambridge a few months afterwards.

Negotiations with the GE recommenced in January 1867 when the general managers worked out a new agreement. This time the GE was to have powers to Doncaster (as soon as the GN new Spalding–March, and Gainsborough–Doncaster lines were ready) and would pay a minimum toll of £25,000 per annum for this. It could exchange West Riding traffic with the L & Y at Doncaster, but traffic for Liverpool and Manchester had to be worked over the MS & L via Sykes junction and Retford, or Doncaster and Penistone. When the chairmen met on 12 March to complete arrangements, they were unable to agree about L & Y exchange of traffic. In consequence the agreement fell to the ground, for in fairness to its MS & L ally, the GN could not agree to allow the GE any further facility.

The three Lincolnshire lines authorised in 1863 and 1864 were completed in 1867. They were all engineered by Fowler and Brydone, and built double. The electric telegraph was installed on all. The first was that from Spalding to a junction with the GE at March, 19 miles 10 chains long. Opening was delayed first by an extensive slip of earth, and then by a fault in the plate girders of the Nene bridge at Guyhirne. Just when it was decided to open the northern end in January, it was discovered that the Ouse bridge at Spalding would have to be raised, owing to a mistake in the levels. Local goods traffic began on Friday 1 April, but there was no hurry to introduce a passenger service, for the line was not submitted for inspection until June. Captain Tyler refused sanction because the turntable at March was not finished, while that at Spalding was not large enough to turn GN tender engines. Upon his third visit a month later the turntable at March was complete, but nothing had been done about the Spalding one, installed by the S & B, only 23 ft diameter. Tyler not only thought that it was too small, but also that it was inconveniently situated for GN purposes. Normally the GN was quick to satisfy government officers' requirements, but on this occasion Seymour Clarke was awkward; thinking that since the turntable had been approved by Captain Rich for the S&B in 1866, Captain Tyler's demands were unreasonable. By this attitude, Clarke delayed commencement of passenger services, until 2 September, when three trains each way on weekdays only were provided. The line was laid with 82 lb rails and was almost flat, but did include a few short banks of 1 in 200. It crossed the Peterborough, Wisbeach & Sutton on the level at Murrow. There were five bridges and eight viaducts. The stations were at Cowbit, Crowland, French Drove, Murrow and Guyhirne. The GN used an engine shed at March belonging to Jackson Bros, contractors for the line.

The branch authorised by the 1864 Lincoln & Bourn Act was opened on 15 April. It measured 18 miles 2 chains and was constructed by Kirk & Parry for £121,533. From a junction with the Sleaford line at Honington it had stations at Caythorpe, Leadenham, Navenby, Harmston and Waddington, and joined the Loop at Pelham Street junction, Lincoln just before the flat crossing with the MS&L. The steepest gradient was 1 in 132 and the sharpest curve was 16 chains radius near Lincoln. There were 19 overbridges and seven underbridges, the longest span being 37 ft. The permanent way was laid with 72 lb rails. Sanction was given for opening provided that a 5 mph speed limit was observed over Fulbeck bank where a slip was giving trouble, and on condition that ALL trains over Pelham Street crossing had a pilotman. Captain Tyler withdrew this condition on 2 August, as a satisfactory signalling and locking system had been installed there. The train service consisted of five each way on weekdays between Grantham and Lincoln and two on Sundays. Construction of this branch involved provision of a new station at Honington, built slightly to the west of the old one, and with a refreshment room. Colonel Packe, who lived at Caythorpe, received the privilege of having the trains stopped at the station as he required. Some time later he commenced working ironstone deposits, discovered on his land.

When the line was constructed a 13 chain spur was laid at Honington, connecting with the down Sleaford line. Some years earlier a refuge siding had been constructed at Barkstone, intended later to form part of a second line on the Sleaford branch. The company undertook doubling with its own staff, and to a point 1 mile 60 chains from Barkstone junction and brought it into use on 1 February 1866 without Board of Trade sanction. Kirk & Parry used the materials from the Honington spur in an extension of the second line to Sudbrook Crossing. About the same time Barkstone junction box was equipped with locking apparatus. In December 1862 this box had been staffed by men, instead of boys, who had worked the signals and electric telegraph. An east-to-north curve at Honington, for direct Sleaford–Lincoln running, was certainly partly constructed. But it appears doubtful if it was ever completed or used. It would be of little value after the direct Sleaford–Lincoln route was opened (see vol. II).

The Act which authorised the Gainsborough–Doncaster line also provided for flattening the old line from Sykes junction to Gainsborough. This section, including Marton and Lea stations, was closed to traffic on 1 December 1864. Connection with Gainsborough was maintained via Retford. The new line was to have a bridge over the Trent, but to save considerable expense an agreement was made with the MS&L for the GN to use its bridge at Bole, an arrangement and the necessary deviation sanctioned by an Act of 28 June 1866.

The new line from Trent West junction to Black Carr junction with the Towns line near Doncaster, and the rebuilt line from Sykes junction to Trent East junction were brought into use for goods on 1 July 1867 and for passengers two weeks later, the total distance being 26 miles 36 chains. Construction involved unusually heavy earthworks, to keep the formation almost level, the steepest gradient being 1 in 300. There were seven overbridges and nine underbridges. Of 11 viaducts, the most important was one for Trent floodwaters which had 18½ spans of 30 ft. South of Gainsborough, a few of the nine original bridges were rebuilt. Although the gradients had been largely ironed out, there was still a long bank of 1 in 200 between Lea and Marton. As far as Misterton, new construction roughly followed the route planned for the 'Axholme' Extension. It was laid with 82 lb rails, the old 72 lb rails being, it seems, re-laid on the reconstructed section. Marton and Lea stations were re-opened, and new ones were at Gainsborough, Beckingham, Walkeringham, Misterton, Haxey, and Finningley. The train service consisted of four each way between Lincoln and Doncaster on weekdays and one each way on Sundays. There was a ballast pit at Finningley, and the main line signals at Balderton were taken down and re-erected to serve the siding for it.

About 17 daily coal trains were promptly diverted over the new line. The GN ceased to exercise its powers between Sykes junction and Retford in 1868, (goods traffic on 30 June and passenger on 31 July). The MS&L made a claim for diverted traffic. The matter was referred to the arbitration of T. E. Harrison, (engineer of the NE), who awarded £25,450 for loss of traffic, and a toll for Trent bridge use, equal to 1 mile's receipts for all traffic over it.

Smith Knight & Co received their final instalment for constructing the

Gainsborough to Doncaster line in 1868, bringing the total payment to them to £258,404. Soon afterwards they went bankrupt.

By the time the final section of the Loop was complete, the gradients over waterways on the older Lincolnshire lines had been eased. The works, approved in 1864 at an estimated cost of nearly £10,000 involved 55 chains approaching the Witham at Bardney, 44 chains over the Horncastle Canal at Tattershall, 24 chains of the EL and 36 chains of the Loop over the Witham at Boston, 20 chains over the Glen at Surfleet (where the bridge was rebuilt), and 30 chains over Vernatts Drain at Spalding.

A siding was put in at Skellingthorpe, between Lincoln and Saxilby, early in 1863 to serve a manure works set up by a Mr Footitt who paid £700 towards the cost. A station was opened here on 1 January 1865 but was closed on 1 June 1868, as Footitt's works closed, the siding however remaining in use.

Also at Lincoln there was a short single branch line which the MS&L built across Holmes Common to link the Midland with the GN at West Holmes junction, about ¾ mile north of Lincoln station, brought into use in January 1859. Subsequently the MS&L built a goods station on it, and that portion of the line between the new depot and the Midland was abandoned.

The GN might have obtained access to Hemel Hempstead, as in 1866 a small company named after that town was authorised to build a line from the town to junctions at Harpenden both with the Midland's authorised London extension and the GN Luton branch there. But the line was only built to the Midland junction, not to the GN, and the little company was absorbed by the Midland.

MAINLY THE LONDON AREA

In June 1851 a scheme was set on foot for construction of a large central London station, the principal promoter being Charles Pearson, solicitor to the City Corporation, who endeavoured to enlist support of all railways having termini in London, but the necessary support was not forthcoming. The GN, for one, was not disposed to raise the large amount of capital necessary to join this project, but this was an error of judgement which it would come to regret. Pearson's scheme, however, aroused interest. Plans were made for a railway, to be constructed by cut and cover, under the New Road, from Paddington to King's Cross, there to join the City terminus Line, planned to run through the Fleet valley to Holborn. This 'North Metropolitan' obtained its Act in 1853, but then dropped the City Terminus part and decided on an eastern terminus at the General Post Office, St Martin-le-Grand. It was reconstituted as the 'Metropolitan', and decided on Farringdon Street as the terminus, obtaining powers to construct junctions with the GN at King's Cross. The GN was empowered to subscribed to its capital but failed to do so. Difficulty in raising capital delayed building the Met. but it was eventually opened between Bishops Road, Paddington, and Farringdon Street on 10 January 1863. The line was worked by the GW with broad gauge stock as mixed gauge had been laid.

Jay was the contractor for the eastern end, and was allowed to tip the spoil from the tunnels of the east side of the GN line between Hornsey and Wood Green. He hired GN engines, brake vans and guards and was charged 2d per ton toll on the spoil. He constructed an 'East branch', connecting the Met up line with the GN on the east side of King's Cross station, and from it the 'West branch' to connect with the Met down line, completely in tunnel, both single line.

The GN was authorised by an Act of 23 July 1860 to construct the single line Hotel Curve connecting the Met down line with the west side of King's Cross station yard, and intersecting the West branch, with Jay as contractor. Property was acquired in Edmund Street and

Northampton Street to provide room for the Hotel Curve junction. Much of the line was in tunnel, and property overhead was so disturbed that the Denison Arms and other buildings above had to be bought.

A dispute arose between the Met and the GW in July. The latter gave notice that it would cease to operate the Met traffic from 30 September 1863, and then suddenly advanced the date to 10 August. The embarrassed Met had then to look for help, the L&NW and the GN agreeing to lend carriages, while the GN also lent some engines. Sturrock had prepared some with condensing apparatus ready for GN services later in the year, and hastily improvised others for working underground. Despite short notice, they were ready in time for the Met service to continue uninterrupted, 3d per mile profit on engine mileage being charged, plus interest on engine cost and hire of carriages. The loan was at first intended to terminate at the end of the year but continued into the summer of 1864 when the Met took delivery of its own. The GN engines concerned are described in chapter XIV.

Colonel Yolland inspected the 'East branch and the 'Hotel curve' on 1 September 1863. The East was 30 chains, through two tunnels of 68 and 288 yd. The steepest gradient was 1 in 46 and the sharpest curve was of less than 8 chains radius. The Hotel curve measured 26 chains of which 350 yd were in tunnel, the steepest gradient 1 in 48, with two curves of less than 8 chains radius. He was not satisfied with the signal for backing trains into the main line station, and required that it should lock the points leading to the engine shed. Captain Tyler carried out a further inspection on 26 September and sanctioned opening on 1 October. The Hotel curve was laid with steel rails, the first instance of their use on the GN, whose own trains commenced to run to and from Farringdon Street on 1 October 1863, one month later than intended. The West branch was never used for regular traffic. From 1865 the track was removed. The up trains for Farringdon Street ran into King's Cross main line station and then set back into a dead end before continuing. The layout at that time did not permit through running. Only a portion of some trains went through to Farringdon Street. Similarly, down trains on arriving from there, ran into a dead end and then set back into the short departure platform before proceeding. The station plan of 1865 showed a crossover from the middle of the dead end to the down main line.

The London, Chatham & Dover had been authorised to build a line from Herne Hill to Blackfriars, and obtained powers to continue it to a junction with the Met at West Street, near Farringdon Street. By this line the GN hoped to run passenger and goods services to south London. The LC&D was unable to raise enough capital for this expensive extension on its own and appealed to other interested railways for assistance. On 21 July 1863 Clarke wrote to his chairman reporting on the LC&D's difficulties and advising that, if the Met would subscribe £250,000, the GN should do the same, if Parliamentary powers were obtained for the loan, and running powers. The Met declined to subscribe, preferring construction of an additional double track between King's Cross and West Street, the 'Widened Lines', sanctioned by an Act of 11 July 1861. By a further Act of 6 August 1861 the Met were empowered to extend (including the 'Widened Lines') from Farringdon Street to Moorgate Street. In 1864 the Earl Street (now the Elephant and Castle) to West Street junction section of the LC&D's extension was constituted a separate undertaking with a capital of £1,000,000, to which the GN contributed £300,000 at 3½% interest secured by rent charge. The GN obtained running powers to Crystal Palace and Victoria while the LC&D was to use King's Cross.

By August 1865 the LC&D was ready to open its connection with the Met, 25 chains, half on a gradient of 1 in 40, which has always involved the necessity of heavy goods trains being assisted in the rear by a banking engine from Farringdon Street. For many years the GN attached an extra brake to provide additional power. The few chains of Met track from Farringdon Street to West Street junction were not ready until the end of the year and were sanctioned by the Board of Trade on 30 December.

These lines were opened on 1 January 1866, and GN trains were extended from Farringdon Street to Ludgate Hill. In August they were further extended to Herne Hill, and next month, four LC&D trains commenced to run beyond King's Cross, terminating at Wood Green, Southgate and Barnet. In July 1865, building a platform at York Road for the use of the 'Chatham' (at an estimated expense of £1,888) was approved. Called York Road (King's Cross), the station (which had cost £2,502) was first shown in the GN timetables for March 1866 with only LC&D trains using it. GN trains began to run to Victoria in April 1867, and LC&D trains to Hatfield. By this time the Met Widened Lines were nearly ready so the GN junctions had to be altered to connect with them, including re-alignment of the Hotel curve. The junctions were taken out on the night of 30 June and from 1 July 1867 the LC&D trains terminated at Farringdon Street and the GN trains ceased to run beyond King's Cross. The LC&D had been on the point of starting its Continental trains from York Road and the GN had resolved to employ a French-speaking booking clerk there. Spoil from the new works was used to fill in the moribund West branch. The new junctions were complete and the services restored, early in 1868. Up till now the LC&D had made no effort to enable the GN to start coal traffic at its south London stations, letters from King's Cross being parried, for no money was available. The GN had been fortunate in being so soundly established that it weathered the 1866 financial storms which brought about the collapse of banks, financial houses, and contractors (including Petos) interested in railway construction, and placed the LC&D, the GE, the NB and several other railways in direst difficulties.

Increasing congestion of traffic between Hitchin and London caused severe holdups to GN traffic as well as Midland, as has already been mentioned. A census of engines taking water at Hitchin on Thursday 23 November 1865 throws some light on this:

Down	Up	
37	36	GN goods and coal.
17	17	GN passenger.
10	12	Midland goods.
8	8	Midland passenger.

Besides, several main line trains did not take water there and locals did not run out so far. On 2 November ten Peterborough goods or coal drivers were delayed at Holloway by an average of over 7 hr and worked an average of more than 18½ hours. The worst case cited was that of a driver who had stood 9 hr 25 m. at Holloway and was on duty for 30 hr 20 m.

The cost of duplicating tunnels was considered too expensive for the company to go ahead with doubling the existing tracks. As an alternative, a loop line was considered. An Act was obtained on 19 June 1865 for a Hornsey to Hertford line (empowering £650,000 new capital and borrowing £216,000), to build a line from the main line near Wood Green to the Hertford branch at Hertingfordbury. A Bill was prepared for another line from that point to rejoin the main line at Stevenage. Until this was complete a northern spur should have been provided at Welwyn junction. But this Bill did not proceed. The Hornsey–Hertford was eventually reduced to a branch from Wood Green to Enfield (opened in 1871, see vol. II). An Act of 28 June 1866 authorised duplicating Copenhagen tunnel, but this was also deferred, and the tunnel was not brought into use until 1877. Capital was being frittered away on the unrewarding 'Cheshire Lines' which would have been better spent on improving GN property, particularly elimination of these bottlenecks.

The GN made an agreement with the London & Blackwall (worked by the EC) for use of its goods station at Royal Mint Street from 8 December 1858, and leased a warehouse from the Victoria (London) Dock Co. Arrangements were made for the NL to fulfill its obligation and work the traffic between St Pancras junction and Royal Mint Street. Business exceeded expectations. On 1 February 1861, the goods station became GN property. In September 1867 arrangements were made with the GE and NL for accommodation at Poplar, the latter building a warehouse for which the GN paid 6% of the cost as annual rent, but the full cost of installing hydraulic machinery.

When it became known that the 1862 Exhibition building was to be re-erected by Kelk & Lucas in the grounds of Alexandra Park as Alexandra Palace, the EH&L sought powers for a branch from Highgate to serve it in anticipation of lucrative traffic from expected crowds of pleasure seekers. It was decided that the main line from Seven Sisters Road to Highgate should be double instead of single and the branch should be double. It was authorised by an Act of 13 May 1864, the GN being empowered to subscribe £32,000 to the £96,000 capital. Borrowing powers were £32,000. The part of the line inside the Palace grounds was sanctioned by an Act of 30 June 1866 obtained by the Muswell Hill Estate Co, new capital of £70,000 being authorised.

In the 1863 Session a Bill for an independent 'Barnet & Great Northern' had been defeated. The GN, which opposed it, undertook to serve High (sometimes called Chipping) Barnet with its own branch and obtained powers by an Act of 14 July 1864, which, sanctioning raising of £200,000 capital and borrowing £66,000, also authorised improvements at King's Cross, and arrangements with the Met and LC&D. Two years later it introduced a Bill for a line from Potters Bar which would pass through Barnet and join the EH&L at Finchley, which conflicted with a new branch which the EH&L proposed from Finchley to Barnet. At first the GN opposed the EH&L Bill but after consideration discarded its own branch (which would have served as a useful loop) and supported the EH&L, whose Bill became an Act on 28 June 1866. This provided for new capital of £75,000 and borrowing powers of £25,000 and permitted the GN to abandon its Barnet powers of 1864. The EH&L obtained an Act on 29 June 1865 to build a branch of 1¾ miles to the Tottenham & Hampstead junction, but this was not built.

In 1865, a concern called the North London, Highgate and Alexandra Park, despite vigorous GN opposition, obtained an Act for a line from Caledonian Road on the NL through Stroud Green and Archway to a junction with the EH&L south of its Highgate tunnel, with running powers over it thence to Alexandra 'Park'—presumably 'Palace' was intended. Such a line would have provided a more direct route to the City than the GN's. Fortunately for the GN, nothing was done towards construction but it was clear to King's Cross that the EH & L was flirting with the NL. Relations remained fairly friendly until the dispute about the Barnet line, but then the GN decided it was high time that it took full control of the ambitious little line. By an Act of 15 July 1867 it was absorbed by the GN. At the same time the GN took over the authorised undertaking of the Watford & Edgware junction. This would have been 6½ miles through Brockley Hill under the LN&W main line to a junction with the Rickmansworth branch. This was not constructed, although the scheme was frequently revived.

A few weeks later, on Thursday 22 August 1867, the Edgware line was brought into use. Fowler and Brydone were engineers, and the contractors were Smith Knight & Co. Land had been bought for double line and most of the underbridges and all the overbridges had been so constructed. The permanent way was laid with 72 lb bull-headed and 69 lb flat-bottomed rails, all of which were fishplated. The railway was 8 miles 70 chains, was double from the junction with the GN to Alexandra Park junction, 22 chains beyond the station at Highgate, and thence to Edgware was single. Approaching Seven Sisters Road the up line was carried over the main line by a bridge and there was a curve of only 7½ chains radius at the junction. A new box, Edgware Branch junction, equipped with locking apparatus, was built at the north end of Seven Sisters Road station. Earthworks were heavy and much difficulty was experienced in stabilising some of the embankments. Gradients were severe, the steepest 1 in 59. There was a brick built viaduct of 13 arches over the Brent valley. There were two pairs of single line tunnels at either end of Highgate station, the western 332 yd long and the eastern 139 yd. Stations were at Crouch End, Highgate, East End, Finchley, Finchley & Hendon, Mill Hill, and Edgware. There were no sidings at Crouch End, Highgate and Mill Hill. Wellington sidings, just west of Alexandra Park junction, were brought into use by September, when a loop was laid between the platform lines at Highgate for trains' reversal. Signal boxes were at Crouch End, Highgate, Alexandra Park junction, Finchley & Hendon, and Edgware, and soon, at Reservoir, (near the site of the future Stroud Green station), all connected to the main line by electric telegraph later in the year. The single line section was worked with a train staff, square-headed, painted red, and inscribed 'Go to Edgware' and 'Go to Highgate'. Edgware had an engine shed and turntable. A substantial train service was provided. Highgate had 18 trains each way on weekdays, ten of these running through to Edgware. On Sundays there were four each way, two of which served Edgware. In December the Highgate trains were reduced to five and extended to East End Finchley; the Sunday service was cut to three trains, all for Edgware.

The down line was extended by about ¾ mile to a point beyond East End Finchley station, for use by passengers' trains on 1 December 1867 without prior Board of Trade sanction. The government officer revisited the line in January and discovered that Clarke had jumped the gun. As penalty, he insisted on alterations to the signalling, and arrangements at Wellington Sidings which Clarke estimated would cost £800.

Towards the end of 1863 a coal tumbling platform was built at King's Cross goods yard, enabling coal to be transferred into barges on the Regent's Canal. Later Jay built a wooden viaduct, which led up to the Cambridge Street coal depot, the property of Plimsoll who, now in a large coal trade business, paid the expense of the viaduct, completed in September 1866. In 1866 a large waiting shed and waiting rooms, originally ordered for Wood Green, were fitted to the up platform at Holloway. At the same time the coal depot there was extended, and the down sidings were ready for use, accommodating 156 trucks and costing £2,200, including erection of a new signal box. A plan of this period showed a footpath along the 6 ft way from Caledonian Road bridge to the station.

Mansfield undertook to construct an additional down line from the north face of Copenhagen tunnel to Seven Sisters. This involved widening bridges at Caledonian Road, Holloway Road, Seven Sisters Road, and Stroud Green Lane. Negotiations with local authorities were so protracted, that the line was not fully in use until 1867. From Holloway Road to Stroud Green Lane was ready in the summer of 1864, £50,365 had been spent, exclusive of £1,192 for widening Stroud Green Lane bridge. The signals were fixed at Caledonian Road junction in January 1867, but a new down platform at Holloway was not in use until the following September. When this was completed, there were three tracks between the platforms with the down main line in the centre.

Up and down sorting sidings at Hornsey were being laid, five having been completed on the up side by the close of 1866. A small engine shed was constructed, on the down side, and although called Hornsey shed it was rather nearer Wood Green. Hornsey viaduct and the bridge over the New River at Wood Green had to be widened.

Land at Whetstone was developed for housing, and sidings were laid. Building started in 1864 but it was not until September 1866 that the sidings and a signal box were brought into use. Two 300 ft platforms were also built, but completion of the station was deferred until a specific number of houses had been built, which took another ten years.

The third Hatfield line was the Hatfield & St Albans, with Lord Ebury a promoter of several lines in the area as chairman, incorporated on 30 June 1862 with capital of £70,000 and power to borrow £23,000. The Act empowered the GN, which had arranged to work the line, to subscribe £20,000 to the capital, and stipulated that the GN should build a bridge at Hatfield over the St Albans road, and abolish the level crossing. The single line measured 5 miles 76 chains, commencing at St Albans Branch junction, 400 yd north of Hatfield station, and ending by a junction with the L&NW about 350 yd outside its St Albans station. There were eight bridges, (one under the line). The steepest gradient was 1 in 100 and there was a curve of 12 chains radius near Hatfield. A passenger service began on 16 October 1865 to the GN station at St Albans (where there were 15 chains of double line) ½ mile short of the junction with the LNW. Sidings were at Springfield (later Smallford) and Nast Hyde where there was a level crossing. The passenger service was extended to the L&NW St Albans station on 1 November 1866 but goods trains must have used this service earlier. A conditional stop at Springfield first appeared in the February 1866 timetable. The company was never a financial success, whatever chance it had of paying its way being killed by the advent of the new Midland line. It was unable to pay £937, the expense of the Hatfield junction, which the GN eventually wrote off as a bad debt.

To accommodate the additional traffic Hatfield station was rebuilt at a cost of £9,500. The down platform was moved westwards and became an island, leaving room for three sets of metals between the platforms with the up main line in the centre. The layout was peculiar. There was a through road from the St Albans branch, allowing the trains to run into the up platform but stopping trains on the up main line had to run by the station and then set back into the platform. Similarly down trains, to be dealt with on the west side of the platform, had also to run by and then set back. The work was completed towards the end of 1864. Then it was decided to extend the platforms and provide a refreshment room and additional waiting rooms, all completed by September 1866. The engine and carriage sheds had been built in 1854.

Additional signal boxes were opened at Hawkshead and Red Hall (between Potters Bar and Hatfield) late in 1866, and at Woolmer Green and Langley on 1 November of the same year, while that at Hitchin was fitted with an interlocking frame early in 1867. Hitchin engine shed was extended in 1865. Two new platforms were built at Huntingdon, and two long sidings were laid in at Holme in 1860. A new station, complete with goods sidings and a signal box, was opened at Tempsford on 1 January 1863, and sidings and a signal box were brought into use at Abbotts Ripton in mid-1864.

Orders were given in March 1853 for improvement of Arlsey station (altered to Arlesey in March 1860), a waiting room being built on the up side and a small covered shed on the down platform. Arrangements were made with Pearts Patent Brick Co in 1852 for a siding at a brickworks brought into use on 1 May 1853, about 1¼ mile south of Arlsey station. Arlsey Siding station at this spot was officially opened for passengers on 1 April 1866 although trains had been calling for some time. From 1860 the gatekeeper issued tickets. From April 1862 the 8.10 a.m. from Peterborough stopped there once a month to pick up the Management Committee of the Three Counties Asylum there. The 1864 timetables showed one up train calling on Tuesdays only. Four goods and four passengers trains stopped daily in 1866, coal traffic increasing from 2,281 ton to 5,311 ton for March compared with 1865. General traffic also increased. The asylum sidings got so choked with other people's traffic that the Committee complained that on occasions their men and horses were wasting a whole day in vain attempts to handle their traffic.

Godmanchester junction with the GE at Huntingdon appears to have fallen out of use after July 1862. Until then, Ely flour and coal traffic had used it. A new junction was formed at Huntingdon in October 1866 by the Kettering, Thrapstone & Huntingdon, worked by the Midland, a single line, burrowing under the GN main line about a mile south of Huntingdon and then running alongside it. Near the station it forked, one arm crossing the GE by a bridge and making connection with the GN Huntingdon station, the other linking with the GE. The GN offered free use of its station, but the Midland operated a through service from Kettering to Cambridge via St Ives and thus did not need to call at the GN station. The line was brought into use for through goods on 21 February and passengers on 1 March 1866. When Colonel Rich made his report on the KT&H, he disclosed that the old connection at Huntingdon, made by the EA in 1851, had never had Board of Trade sanction, and that most of the short line had been singled.

A wharf for transhipment of traffic with the Nene near Peterborough, brought into use early in 1855, built by Culshaw, was on the south bank, down river from the main line, so an approach line curved round to serve it.

Ticket platforms were provided at Peterborough in June 1856 and new junctions with the Midland, north and south of the station, were brought into use on 1 August 1866. If only the Midland had consented to move its tracks, Peterborough station would have been rebuilt with four sets of metals between the platforms. In 1860 a permanent way shop was built at Peterborough for manufacturing switches and crossings. The engineers' stores there were destroyed by fire on 7 June 1864. The loss was estimated at £600 for the building and £800 for the stores, the building being replaced and handed over to Pulford on the following 25 March. Between New England and Werrington junction a pair of additional tracks were built, and on completion the main line traffic used them and the old lines were confined to goods traffic. The box at Werrington was replaced by a larger one, equipped with locking apparatus. These works, including additional sidings, were completed in mid-1866.

At New England the locomotive premises were extended. In 1863 a gasworks and a boiler shop were completed, and two years later a big programme was approved to include a shed for spare engines and painting, a tender shop, a turning shop and a coppersmith's shop. There were then 72 goods engines and 22 passenger engines stationed there. With new engines on order, it was anticipated that the stud would be increased by 35 goods and five passengers engines. Peterborough station shed held eight and New England 36, the new shed being intended for 18. The works, by Rudd & Son of Grantham, were completed by the summer of 1866. There were now over 6,000 employees at New England and housing accommodation was continually being increased. A fire engine was provided in 1863 and a Mechanics' Institute was built about the same time. For some years there was a little known platform at New England, apparently used for market trains and other specials which did not appear in the timetables.

Water cranes and pits were ordered for Peterborough in February 1862 to enable engines from London to take water and run through to Grantham at an estimated saving of £2,000 a year. In the following October the conversion of the carriage shed at Grantham to an engine shed was authorised. So a new carriage shed was required, besides a water crane, a new turntable and an engine lift, all completed in the summer of 1863.

Grantham and Retford stations received improvements in the 1860s, and in common with one or two other principal stations, were provided with additional W.C.'s, particularly for passengers travelling in crowded excursion trains. The only alterations in the line between New England and Doncaster were the provision in 1853 of a down shunting siding at Corby and an up shunting siding at Hougham.

In October 1864 the board authorised £42,000 for rebuilding of Doncaster station, including removal of the goods depot to another side, which was completed early in 1866. But in March 1865, almost all of the rest of the scheme was deferred. The money was spent on the purchase of 46 acres at Balby Bridge, to provide sorting sidings on either side of the main line. The down and up sidings were ready in January 1866, and March 1867 respectively. Two months earlier, the South Yorkshire junction signals were altered, to be worked by levers instead of stirrups, the only reference in GN records to this rather uncommon method of operating signals.

Nothing was done about increased cover for engines at Doncaster. Of the 112 stationed there in 1865, only 30 could be housed and 33 new ones were expected from those on order. There were two fires at the Works, one on 11 December 1864 causing damage to the extent of £400. The second, more serious, started in the paint shop of the carriage department in the early hours of 4 July 1865 and destroyed the roof, the directors' saloon, a first class carriage and a brake van. The damage was assessed at £1,665. New carriage and wagon shops were already under construction. An additional boiler shop and a gas works were completed early in 1867.

Johnson continued replacement of the timber bridges on the Lincolnshire lines. That over the Witham at Grand Sluice near Boston was dealt with in 1862, No. 2 South Drive bridge in 1863, and that over the Welland at Deeping in 1866, all reconstructed in brick or masonry with wrought iron girders. On the Nottingham branch part of the Radcliffe viaduct was filled in by embankment in 1864.

Bessemer steel rails and tyres were first purchased in 1862. The rails cost £18 10s (£18.50) a ton, about three times the price of iron rails—so at first only small quantities were bought, used for switches and crossings. On the Hotel curve (as mentioned above) additional expense would be justified by the heavy traffic expected to be worked up the steep gradient and as the track was almost entirely in tunnel and difficult of access, the steel rails would be advantageous as they would need less repairs. Their use was extended in 1865 to the up lines through Doncaster, Retford and Peterborough, then to both lines through Grantham and through Copenhagen and Maiden Lane tunnels, and in 1866 from the 3½ mile post to Copenhagen tunnel.

The GN was not greatly troubled by the agitation among the staff for shorter hours and higher wages which became apparent on many railways in the middle 1860s. Inspector Williams did send one of his men to report secretly on a meeting of the United Amalgamated Operative Society held at Bradford on Saturday 29 September 1866. The founder and secretary was an ex-L&Y employee, Charles Bassett Vincent. The objects of the society were to grant annuities to railway servants when past work, give them pay when sick, shorten hours of labour, and improve their conditions, partly by strikes on one railway at a time. A paper called *The Train* circulated among railway servants, price 1d per copy.

One concession was made, in 1866 three days annual holiday being granted to all uniformed staff. Sturrock had not been in favour of conceding better conditions to footplatemen, but soon after his retirement a memorial was received from the drivers and firemen. Their requests (rather than demands) were:

1. A ten hour day.
2. Time and a half pay for Sunday duty.
3. A minimum of nine hours' rest between turns of duty.
4. 150 miles on main line passenger, or 120 miles on local or branch passenger or main line goods, or 100 miles on branch line goods trains to constitute a day's work.
5. Daily rates of pay:

	London		Country	
	Drivers	Firemen	Drivers	Firemen
First six months	6s (30p)	3s 6d (17½p)	6s (30p)	3s 6d (17½p)
Second six months	6s 6d (32½p)	4s (20p)	6s 6d (32½)	3s 6d (17½p)
Subsequently	7s 6d (37½p)	4s 6d (22½p)	7s (35p)	4s (20p)

All to be increased by 6d (2½p) a day after three years.

Drivers and firemen of engines fitted with steam tenders 7s 8d (40p) and 5s (25p) a day respectively.

6. Lodging allowance to be increased from 1s (5p) to 2s 6d (12½p) a day.

It was left to Stirling to negotiate with the men. In less than a month he reported a settlement. He agreed to items numbered 1, 2, 3 and 6 but did not accept the terms for mileage, agreeing instead that the men should not run more than 210 miles in one day, and should be allowed half a day each week. As regards daily rates of pay, all drivers and firemen should receive 5s 6d (27½p) and 3s 6d (17½p) respectively in the first year, 6s (30p) and 3s 9d (18p) in the second, and 7s (35p) and 4s (20p) in the third and subsequent years. They were to receive an extra 6d (2½p) a day in London after five years. In due course, the directors received a courteous letter from the enginemen thanking them for the concessions granted.

Letters of appreciation were always received by the board after the running of the annual free trips, began in 1861 for the men employed in Plant and their wives and sweethearts. It was the pleasant duty of the locomotive engineer to make application to the directors every year for this facility and name the place the men had chosen. Occasionally Scarborough was selected, and if so, a charge of 6d (2½p) per head was made to cover the toll over the N E. A similar facility was later granted to the employees at Boston works and the Sunday School children at Doncaster and New England were given a day's outing every summer.

THE CHESHIRE LINES COMMITTEE

Two railways were incorporated in 1860 which became GN jointly owned when the Cheshire Lines Committee was set up. These were the Stockport & Woodley Junction, authorised on 15 May, and the Cheshire Midland (Altrincham to Northwich) authorised on 14 June. They were promoted by landowners, but supported by the MS&L. Another line backed by the MS&L was the Marple, New Mills & Hayfield Junction authorised 15 May 1860, promoted as an independent venture but in reality an extension of the MS&L, which finds its place in this history because later it was the line by which the Midland entered Manchester. It was absorbed by the MS&L in 1865 and transferred to the Sheffield & Midland Joint Committee in 1869.

The ambitious Watkin now continued to weave his web of new lines in Cheshire and Lancashire. Unfortunately the GN got entangled in this, and eventually sunk millions of money in unremunerative railways. It was agreed to participate in promotion of the Stockport, Timperley & Altrincham Junction and the West Cheshire, which were incorporated on 22 July and 11 July. The first had a capital of £150,000 of which the GN and MS&L proportions were each £50,000. The second line, from the Cheshire Midland at Northwich to Helsby had capital of £200,000. The allies' proportions were each £65,000. The MS&L would work these lines and the Garston and Liverpool. Should it fail to do so 'faithfully and efficiently', the GN would have the right to work over the MS&L west of Retford.

The GN directors did avoid getting involved in another of Watkin's schemes in 1860. He had the idea of creating a rival resort to Blackpool, on the east coast at Cleethorpes, and invited the GN to join in construction of the Cleethorpes Railway. After consideration, the GN informed Watkin in 1862 that it had decided against the venture. Later, however, there was considerable excursion traffic from GN stations to Cleethorpes.

Since the great frost of 1861 the Special Service trains had been allowed an extra 15 minutes to Manchester. In March 1862, the time of 5¼ hr was restored due to competition by the Midland whose trains took a little over 5 hr. From 1 July the allies put on additional expresses, departing from both termini at 3.0 p.m. Tried for three months, these trains remained permanently in the timetables.

The first portion of the CM was brought into use for passengers on 12 May 1862. The line, double track, left the MSJ&A at Altrincham (later Bowden) junction and extended for 6 miles 65 chains to a temporary station at Knutsford. The bridges were 12 over the line and 4 under it. Intermediate stations were at Bowden, Ashley, and Mobberley.

The service of five trains each way on weekdays and four each way on Sundays was extended by 6 miles 8 chains from Knutsford to Northwich on 1 January 1863. Stations were Knutsford, Plumbley, Lostock, and Northwich, Lostock being renamed Lostock Gralam later in the year. Goods traffic began on 1 May.

Owing to its slender resources, the MS&L had to look around for financial aid in the construction of this, so on 11 June 1862 the GN and the MS&L agreed to subscribe equally to the CM's capital as well as the ST&AJ and the West Cheshire, an arrangement authorised by the Great Northern (Cheshire Lines) Act of 13 July 1863.

Passenger services began over the S&WJ on 12 January 1863. This diverged from the MS&L's Marple branch at Woodley Junction and ran for 2 miles 61 chains to a temporary station at Portwood, Stockport, merely a platform facing on to a single line which had a crossover, and a run-round line for engines. The line fell to Stockport, the steepest gradient being 1 in 64. Except at the terminus it was double. Works were heavy, including two short tunnels of 36 and 169 yd, high embankments, and a masonry viaduct near Woodley, built on the skew. There were no intermediate stations, and no accommodation for goods.

A 'Cheshire Lines' committee was now formed to manage the lines in Cheshire, and the Garston & Liverpool when opened. Three directors were each appointed by the GN and MS&L, those from the GN being E. C. Egerton, C. W. Faber and G. Walker. The committee's functions were decided when it first met at Manchester on 5 November 1863, and secondly a month later, at King's Cross. William English, manager of the SY, was appointed Manager of the CL at £600 per annum, to include his services as manager of the G&L, that day. Edward Ross, MS&L secretary, was appointed Secretary at £300, to include services to the G&L. John Rowson Lingard and Joseph Leech were appointed Joint Solicitors at £300, and W. H. Brydone became Consulting Engineer. A few days later, J. S. Wilkinson, from the GN, was appointed Resident

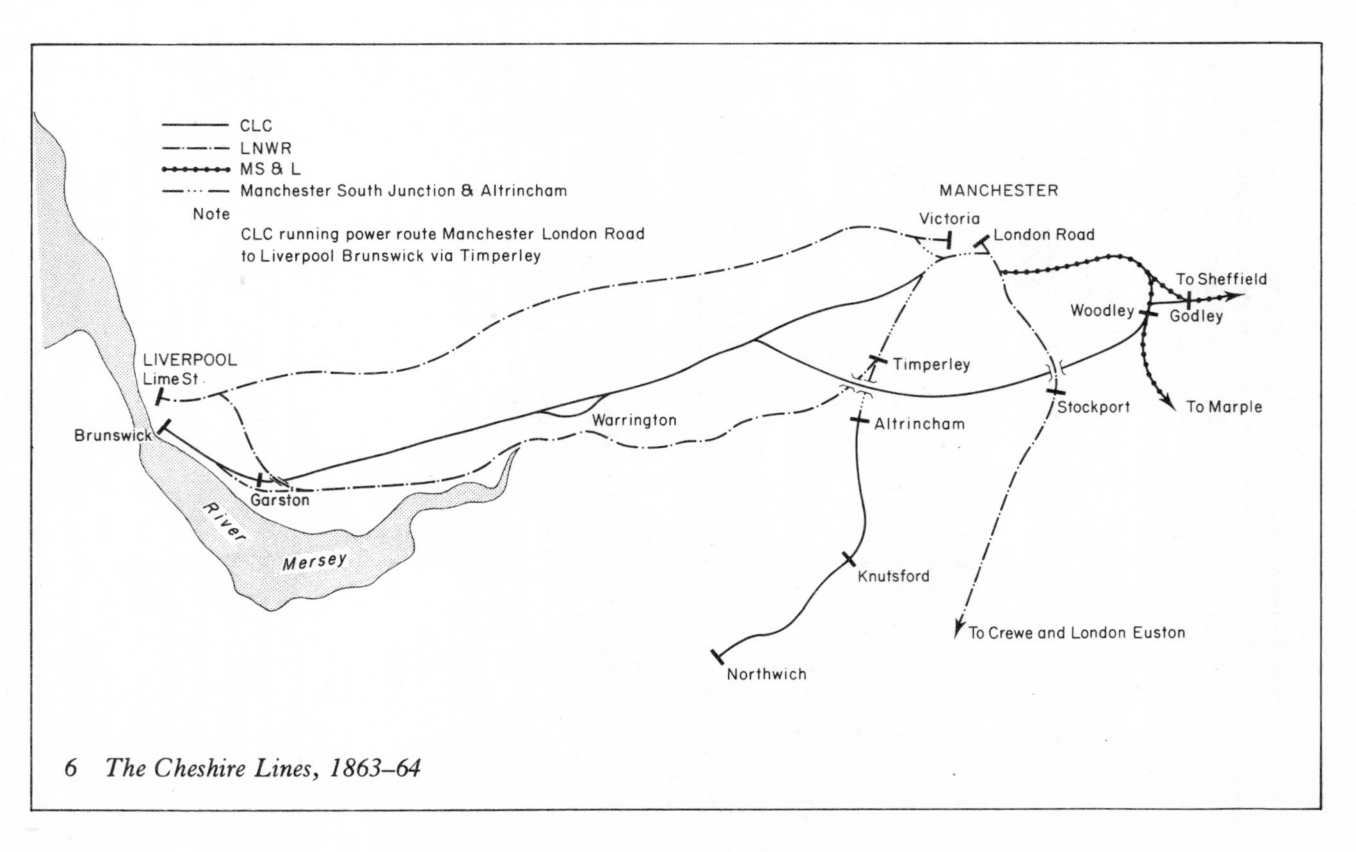

6 The Cheshire Lines, 1863–64

Engineer of the five railways from 1 January at £300, and an arrangement was made for engines to work them to be found by the M S & L at a price agreed by Sturrock and Sacré. For the time being, rolling stock was provided by the parent companies. Wilkinson soon resigned and was not replaced, his duties being taken over by Sacré.

Seymour Clarke looked at the ground east of the River Weaver at Northwich, and advised the committee that there was little chance of attracting the salt traffic away from the river unless branches were built to the salt works. He proposed that one branch should be extended to the Weaver Basin for traffic exchange with the Weaver Trustees. The committee inspected the locality, and powers were sought to construct these branches from the C M.

At this point Edward Watkin bounced back into power on the M S & L, being elected a director in February 1863 and becoming chairman 11 months later.

After delays from January, the G & L was opened on Wednesday 1 June 1864. Commencing by a junction with the St Helens at Garston it ran for 3 miles 73 chains to Brunswick passenger station in Northumberland Street, opposite Brunswick Dock, in Liverpool. Facilities for goods were not provided at the intermediate stations, Mersey Road, Otter's Pool and St Michael's, spelling of the second being altered to Otterspool in April 1866. All were in cuttings and, remarkable for the period, were each provided with a footbridge. The railway was double. The steepest gradient was 1 in 200 and the sharpest curve was 20 chains radius. Betwen St Michael's and Brunswick the line threaded the Dingle tunnel (1,320 yd). The Act provided that the allies have running powers from Timperley Junction on the M S J & A to Garston Junction over the L N W Warrington & Stockport and St Helens sections, thus giving a through route from London Road to Liverpool. The G & L purchased John Leigh's Wavertree estate in 1861 for £20,744 (equal to 6s (30p) per square yard); Here a cattle station was built, approached by a 26 chain branch, which formed an end-on junction with a spur from the L & N W's recently opened Edge Hill to Speke Junction line.

In Liverpool the L & N W soon made things awkward. On 14 October it locked up the offices at Waterloo goods station with the allied companies' books and papers, and prevented the joint clerks from carrying out their duties. At Park Lane it removed the office, and left the books and papers on the warehouse floor. When the allies remonstrated they were reminded that under the 1859 agreement, they were precluded from using any route other than that via Warrington for carrying traffic between Manchester and Liverpool or any place west of Ardwick junction, and that from the opening of the G&L they should have withdrawn some Joint staff in Liverpool. It followed this up on the following 3 January by removing the Joint companies' parcel clerk and books from Lime Street station.

Despite the formation of the new route, the allies' two Special Service trains each way continued to run in and out of Lime Street. They were only kept going on Watkin's insistence although they were unremunerative. The L&NW did not welcome them, did not show them in its timetable or allow them in Bradshaw, had ceased to light and clean them, and refused their use by local passengers between Liverpool and Manchester. Seymour Clarke proposed that they should be withdrawn, for they produced only small traffic from Liverpool to stations south of Retford. The GN was probably relieved when the L&NW insisted that they should be withdrawn from 1 October 1865. Then the through carriages from King's Cross were diverted over the 'running power' route to Brunswick. Up till now up excursions had continued to use Lime Street, but down excursion trains arrived at Brunswick. For the half year ending 31 December 1864 the loss in working the G&L was £8,151, the CM £158 and the S&WJ £1,400, making an aggregate of £9,711. Twelve months later the comparable loss had been reduced to £5,227.

Even before the G&L began carrying traffic it was realised that the Brunswick terminus would not attract many passengers as it was at the extreme south of the city. A Bill for a 1½ mile extension to a terminus in Ranelagh Street was lodged for the 1864 Session, and, as the Liverpool Central Station & Railway Act, passed on 29 July 1864.

Until this extension was brought into use in 1874, passengers and luggage were conveyed free in buses between Brunswick and Lower Castle Street in the city centre where the Committee had headquarters. On 1 April 1865 these offices were removed to premises in James Street where there was also sufficient accommodation for a booking office and waiting room.

With Watkin in power at London Road, the partnership was an uneasy one. GN relations with the L&Y, already strained by the resentment of the latter of the incursions of the former in the West Riding, were almost ruptured by Watkin's demand that the traffic from many East Lancashire towns routed via Wakefield should be sent via Manchester. The L&Y refused to allow traffic passing to the GN to travel by more than one route. Clarke then accused the MS&L of passing competitive traffic to the Midland, via Eckington, contrary to agreement. This was denied by Underdown, but soon afterwards Watkin endeavoured to pour oil on troubled waters by offering Colonel Packe a seat on the MS&L board, an offer not taken up.

Tenders were opened on 1 March 1865 for the construction of carriages which Sacré had been instructed to design for the CL. A contract was awarded to the Metropolitan Railway Carriage & Wagon Co for:

6 First and second class composite carriages
4 Passenger brake vans
4 Horse boxes

and to the Railway Carriage Co, Oldbury, for:

7 First class carriages
7 Second class carriages
5 Second class brake composite carriages
9 Third class carriages
5 Third class brake composite carriages

The total of 50 vehicles was made up by three carriage trucks.

From 5 July 1865, date of the Cheshire Lines Transfer Act, the CM, the West Cheshire, the S&WJ, the S,T&AJ, Liverpool Central Station, and the G&L were vested jointly in the MS&L and GN. The Act empowered the Midland to join as an equal partner, and sanctioned construction of the Northwich salt branches, 3 miles 71 chains, opened on 17 December 1867. The Midland was anxious to reach Liverpool, and in February, encouraged by Watkin, was willing to take equal shares with the allies in the railways west of Manchester. From December, Midland directors and officers attended CLC monthly meetings. On 18 July 1866 the Committee was reconstituted with nine members, the chairman and two directors from each of the three companies being appointed to it, the GN being represented by Colonel Packe, C. W. Faber and G. Walker.

A party of directors and officers inspected the works of the ST&AJ on 4 August 1864, and made some recommendations. Colonel Yolland inspected the works on 29 July 1865 but deferred the opening owing to their incomplete state, and required strengthening of four bridges with heavier girders. Sacré was then instructed to associate himself with Mawson, the engineer, in completing the works to the requirements of Colonel Yolland, and the directors' recommendation.

The line, which was double, was an extension of the Stockport & Woodley Junction and ran for 8 miles 8 chains from Portwood to Deansgate junction, between Timperley and Altrincham, on the MSJ&A. There was a 39 chain link from Timperley junction to the L&NW at Broadheath junction. The steepest gradients were 1 in 75, 1 in 83 and 1 in 86, the sharpest curves being of 10 and 15 chains radius near the junctions. There were four short tunnels, and 16 underbridges and 18 overbridges. Of the three viaducts over streams that over the Mersey was the most outstanding, consisting of two spans of wrought iron box girders measuring 140 ft supported in the centre by cast iron columns filled with brickwork. A large goods shed was built at Heaton Norris at the end of a 20 chain branch, probably completed and brought into use when it was named Wellington Road Goods in June 1866. Against the wishes of the GN directors, who would have preferred to have delayed opening until through services could be operated via Godley, Underdown insisted on a local opening to Altrincham on 1 December 1865 by extending the service from Portwood. The only station then ready for use was Tiviot Dale, Stockport.

Mawson, who was also engineer to the CM and the West Cheshire Railways, involved the committee in needless and unauthorised expenditure during construction of the S&T, and his services were dispensed with on 1 January 1866. The committee approved that Sacré and Richard Johnson should be joint engineers in charge of construction of the WC and the salt branches. From 1 January 1866 it was agreed that the GN should maintain the way and works of the WR&G Railway when it opened (chapter IX) and that the MS&L should maintain the CL.

Despite his company's chronic lack of money Watkin submitted a Bill for the 1865 Session for a new Manchester–Liverpool line, as an alternative to the 'running power route' over the L&NW. He correctly deduced that the GN and Midland, perturbed at a proposed alliance of the L&Y and GE, and wishing to consolidate their positions west of Manchester, would support the Bill and come to his aid with the vital finance. After a long and expensive Parliamentary contest against the L&NW, L&Y, and landowners' opposition, the MS&L (Extension to Liverpool) Act passed on 6 July 1865, authorising construction of a line from a junction at Old Trafford on the MSJ&A to a junction with the G&L near Cressington, and another leaving the former at Glazebrook and connecting with the ST&AJ at Timperley. By an Act of 16 July 1866 the powers to construct these lines were transferred to the CL. The MS&L (New Lines) Act of 16 July 1866 permitted deviation of the eastern end of the main line to connect with the MSJ&A at Cornbrook instead of Old Trafford, authorised construction of a loop line to serve Warrington by a more centrally situated station, and a junction line from the mainline at Hunt's Cross to the L&NW at Allerton.

Two further undertakings were transferred to the CLC by an Act of 10

August 1866, the Chester & West Cheshire Junction, incorporated on 5 July 1865, authorised to construct a line from Mouldsworth on the West Cheshire to Chester, and a junction with the Birkenhead Joint at Mickle Trafford; and the MS&L Godley to Woodley line authorised on 30 June 1862 and MS&L, opened on 1 February 1866. When building a station to serve Godley on this branch was considered, the GN was not prepared to pay half the cost as Watkin requested. This led him, having to find money from somewhere, to propose that the GN should become half owner, hence the line's transfer to the CLC. It was double, 2 miles 15 chains from Godley Junction on the main line to Apethorne junction, about ¼ mile north of Woodley on the Marple branch. The only station was that at Godley. Through working via Godley J, including the Liverpool carriages from King's Cross, began when this line opened on 1 February 1866. Simultaneously, the stations on the ST&A Junction at Cheadle, Northenden, and Baguley, and the link between Timperley junction and Broadheath junction, were brought into use. An up platform at Portwood, a local departure platform at Tiviot Dale and refreshment rooms there and at Godley were provided. The coal drops at Portwood were brought into use from 1865. On 1 August 1866 the L&NW formed a junction at Gatley (later Northenden junction) 14 chains east of Northenden station when it opened a line from Edgeley junction, Stockport.

In February 1867 the MS&L was forced to admit its inability to pay its share, £36,000, of the last call made upon the three companies. The GN and the Midland advanced the money in equal proportions, charging 5% interest, and had to come to the rescue when further calls were made. Watkin was prevented from attending the next CLC meetings by reason of important business or indisposition! The CLC instructed Benton & Woodiwiss to slow down work on the construction of the West Cheshire and ordered that the Manchester to Garston line was not to proceed until further notice. This meant compensation to Brassey who had received a contract for its construction by the impetuous Watkin a few months after the Act passed. About this period, Watkin was considering possibilities of expansion in Wales and had just failed to interest the CLC in a proposition to take over the Cambrian, Mid-Wales, and other Welsh railways.

The CL Act of 15 August 1867 gave statutory authority to the Cheshire Lines Committee providing for consolidation of all these joint lines, and their incorporation as a separate undertaking, with a seal and a separate management but joint control by the three main line companies.

The MS&L Marple, New Mills & Hayfield Junction reached New

Mills on 1 July 1865 and the Midland opened its line for goods from Millers Dale to the same point on 1 October 1866. Derby had planned to exercise its powers into Manchester from 1 November but a landslide cut its line near Bugsworth and a deviation had to be built. Midland through trains between King's Cross and London Road began on 1 February 1867, and on 1 July the allies reverted to five hours timing for the Special Service trains.

In the autumn of 1866 the GN was persuaded by its partner to co-operate in an early morning service. The November timetable showed an express in each direction, departing from King's Cross and London Road at 7.0 a.m. While the Mancunian might have been prepared to rise early for the pleasure of a trip to the metropolis, the Londoner apparently preferred to have another two hours in bed, for only one passenger was booked for the new down train in the first 14 days. Seymour Clarke reported that the down train was a 'failure, unproductive of much traffic', proposed that it should be withdrawn and a Manchester carriage attached to the 7.40 a.m. slow train to Retford, whence it would be worked fast. So it was deleted from the December timetable. From 1 August 1859, through Huddersfield carriages were attached to and detached from the Special Service trains at Penistone. Commencing 1 January 1865 a through carriage from Rochdale was run through to King's Cross via Oldham and Guide Bridge.

The GN would have been wiser to have spent more money on improving its own main line by widening, instead of investing, through Watkin's influence, so much in these lines in Cheshire and Lancashire. But it should be remembered that Lancashire traffic in those days was very considerable, and the attraction of building competitive lines, and breaking the L&NW's near monopoly, was great.

SOME ROYAL AND ORDINARY TRAIN ARRANGEMENTS

Prince Albert was the first GN royal traveller, on a special train from Grimsby on 18 April 1849, after laying the foundation stone of the new dock there. He went to Peterborough (EC) and back to London by the LNW route.

Queen Victoria and her entourage made use of the GN during the 1850s when travelling to and from Balmoral. Her Majesty's first journey was on 27 August 1851. Her special train left Maiden Lane station at 2.0 p.m. en route for Doncaster (via the loop) where the royal party spent the night at the Angel Hotel. The journey northwards continued at 8.45 next morning. The train worked to Stonehaven, for the remainder of the journey to Balmoral by road. The Queen returned by the west coast route.

The GN had prepared for her patronage, for in October 1850 it had requested Walter Williams to give an estimate for a royal saloon. On 7 November, he was instructed to alter a first class carriage into a saloon and build a new carriage instead. The saloon was completed and delivered shortly before the Queen's journey. Her train included three saloons. The third saloon had been converted from a 'first' for a journey Prince Albert intended in October 1850. When the account for the royal saloon was rendered, the business was in the hands of Charles Williams. The directors were staggered to find that the charges amounted to £1,531. Williams eventually agreed to reduce the account to £1,400, which was paid 'with reluctance'. Williams was left in no doubt that the board considered his charges excessive. Next came an account from Hindley & Co (of Oxford Street) for silk linings and upholstery for the royal carriages, of £881. The directors complained, but the firm declined to make a reduction of 10% and the matter was left to Clarke to settle on the best terms he could. He met with some success for an entry in April 1852 shows that a payment of £837 was made.

In 1854 the Queen again selected the east coast for her journey to Balmoral, commencing on 14 September. The schedule was:

	King's Cross	dep.	8.0 a.m.	
arr. 9.38 a.m.	Peterborough	dep.	9.40 a.m.	Change engines
arr. 10.39 a.m.	Newark	dep.	10.42 a.m.	Take water
arr. 11.21 a.m.	Bawtry	dep.	11.24 a.m.	Change engines
arr. 12.45 p.m.	York			Change to N E engine

The schedule advised passing times for all intermediate stations. Regulations provided that the road ahead was to be kept clear for 30 minutes before the royal train was due. Shunting ceased for the same period. A pilot engine was to precede the royal train by five minutes. A man was mounted on the tender of the train engine, looking backwards, with instructions to keep watch for signals from the train he might have to relay to the driver. There was also a cord communication between guard and driver. Two greasers accompanied the train, and like the guards, had to keep watch on either side of it.

On her return the Queen broke her journey at Hull and Grimsby. The empty GN royal train left York for Aberdeen on Wednesday 11 October, and was taken (on the Deeside railway) to Banchory next day, when the Queen entrained for the first stage, as far as Edinburgh. On Friday she travelled to Hull. The empty train was then worked via Milford Junction to Doncaster where it was overhauled. On Saturday morning it was taken to Retford, and handed over to the M S & L to work to New Holland. The Queen crossed from Hull to New Holland by water and then re-entered her train. The MS&L engine worked the train from New Holland to Grimsby, where she opened the new dock. A GN engine placed the train at the docks, where it was due at 12.5 p.m. The journey to London was set out as follows:

	Grimsby Dock	dep.	2.0 p.m.	
arr. 3.05 p.m.	Boston (through road)	dep.	3.10 p.m.	Change engine
arr. 3.55 p.m.	Peterborough	dep.	4.0 p.m.	Change engine
arr. 5.45 p.m.	King's Cross			

After arrival the Queen and her party drove to Paddington where they entrained for Windsor.

The outward royal journey to Banchory in the following year was marred by the overheating of axles on four vehicles, including the royal saloon. The Queen left this at Darlington, and continued her journey in one of the others. A greaser named William Haigh travelled on the footboard to keep the axle lubricated, but this plucky fellow met his death by being knocked from his precarious perch by the girders of a bridge near Ferryhill. Sturrock attributed heating of axles to grease consistency, somewhat thicker than that used the year before.

The Queen, much distressed at the greaser's death, informed the directors of her intention to allow the widow a life pension of £30 per annum. Sturrock was delegated to advise her to attend the Priory Gate at Buckingham Palace four times a year to collect her pension. The directors allowed 2s a week for each of her three children. The allowance for the youngest child ceased in 1864.

In 1856 the outward journey commenced at 8.0 a.m. on 28 August, the schedule being the same as for 1855. The arrangements for the return journey on 16 October were:

		York	dep.	1.35 p.m.	
arr.	2.28 p.m.	Doncaster	dep.	2.33 p.m.	Change engine
arr.	2.57 p.m.	Retford	dep.	3.01 p.m.	Take water
arr.	3.43 p.m.	Grantham	dep.	3.47 p.m.	Take water
arr.	4.24 p.m.	Peterborough	dep.	4.29 p.m.	Change engine
arr.	4.54 p.m.	Huntingdon	dep.	4.58 p.m.	Take water
arr.	5.38 p.m.	Hitchin	dep.	5.42 p.m.	Take water
arr.	6.30 p.m.	King's Cross Goods			Change to N L engine

The Queen requested use of the 'Branch Railway', to reach Windsor, without leaving her train. It was taken from King's Cross Goods by a N L engine via Willesden and the North & South Western Junction to Kew junction where it was handed to the London & South Western, to go to its Windsor station. The train consisted of Engine, Brake Van No. 61, 'First' Nos 80 and 81, Family Carriage No. 65, Royal Saloon No. 3, Royal Saloon, Royal Saloon No.2, Family Carriage No. 66 'First' No. 98, Carriage Trucks Nos 35, 45 and 40, and Brake Van No. 80. The Queen travelled in the central saloon which had no number. The Princes and Princesses were in the saloons on either side. The directors were in the 'first' towards the end of the train. The pilot now ran ten minutes before the royal train, otherwise arrangements were much the same as in previous years.

On 6 September 1858 the Queen started from Osborne (Isle of Wight), entraining at Gosport. Her train was worked over the N & S W J and the N L to King's Cross Goods. Then the royal train took the Queen to Leeds via Knottingley and Wakefield leaving King's Cross at 12.55 p.m and arriving at 6.15. Next day, she opened the new Leeds Town Hall and rejoined the royal train at York for Scotland. In 1859 the royal train left London on the evening of 29 August and travelled through the night,

24 (*above*) A horse dray of 1909

25 Louth Station (photograph taken in the early 1960s, the architecture little altered from the original building)

26 Large Hawthorn 2-2-2 express passenger engine, 1852, designed by A Sturrock

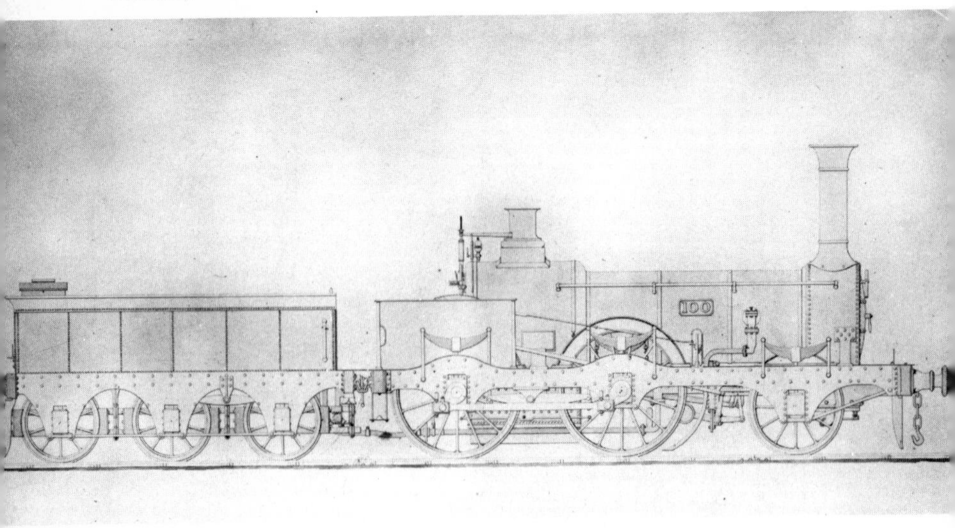

27 2-4-0 passenger coupled engine, 1856

28 Sturrock 0-4-2T, 1866

29 Sturrock 0-8-0T, 1866

30 *(above)* Sturrock 0-6-0 goods engine with steam tender

31 *(above)* Sturrock 0-6-0 goods engine, about 1860

32 Sharp single rebuilt as a tank, 1854

33 Sharp single rebuilt as a tank for branch work, about 1865

34 Peterborough bridges and Cathedral from the south-west, 1850

35 Sturrock 215 4-2-2, 1853

36 The exterior of Peterborough Great Northern station, 1850

timing as under:

	King's Cross	dep.	9.0 p.m.	(actual 9.05 p.m.)
arr. 10.0 p.m.	Biggleswade	dep.	10.04 p.m.	Take water
arr. 10.55 p.m.	Peterborough	dep.	11.0 p.m.	Change engine
arr. 12.06 a.m.	Newark	dep.	12.09 a.m.	Take water
arr. 1.04 a.m.	Doncaster	dep.	1.07 a.m.	Change engine
arr. 2.15 a.m.	York junction	dep.	2.20 a.m.	Change to N E engine

On 6 August 1860 the royal train had an identical timing except that the stop at Biggleswade for water was omitted. An entry in the cash book on 16 December 1859 analysed a payment received from the Queen for journeys to Scotland and back in August and October as: Her Majesty £480 17s 4d, The Prince Consort £37 13s 8d, The Prince of Wales £137 8s 0d, and Prince Alfred £13 13s 6d. Out of this sum the N L was paid £1 5s 0d, the N B £23 14s 6d and the Deeside £14 14s 7d.

In 1861 the Queen went north by the west coast route, but two saloons were attached to the 9.0 a.m. express from King's Cross on 22 August to convey the Princes and Princesses, who at her command, were accompanied by Clarke who regularly took change of the G N royal train. The royal party returned on 24 October and the train was timed as under:

	York junction	dep.	2.0 a.m.	
arr. 3.03 a.m.	Doncaster	dep.	3.08 a.m.	Change engine
arr. 4.05 a.m.	Newark	dep.	4.09 a.m.	Take water
arr. 5.08 a.m.	Peterborough	dep.	5.13 a.m.	Change engine
arr. 6.07 a.m.	Biggleswade	dep.	6.11 a.m.	Take water
arr. 7.15 a.m.	King's Cross Goods	dep.	7.20 a.m.	Change to N L engine
arr. 7.50 a.m.	Kew Junction	dep.	7.55 a.m.	Change to L S W engine
arr. 8.30 a.m.	Windsor L S W			

From 1862, the Queen always sent to Scotland by the west coast route.

In 1863 the Prince and Princess of Wales went by special train to Ripon where they were to stay before resuming their journey to Scotland. They were happy to travel at a higher speed than the Queen. So their train, on 5 August, was timed:

	King's Cross	dep.	10.30 a.m.	
arr. 12.00 noon	Peterborough	dep.	12.05 p.m.	Change engine
arr. 1.50 p.m.	Doncaster	dep.	1.55 p.m.	Change engine
arr. 2.17 p.m.	Knottingley	dep.	2.20 p.m.	Change to N E engine

arr.	2.33 p.m.	Church Fenton	dep.	2.35 p.m.	
arr.	3.45 p.m.	Ripon			

On 3 October the Prince of Wales had an offical engagement at Halifax. His special train had the following timing:

		King's Cross	dep.	10.00 a.m.	
arr.	11.35 a.m.	Peterborough	dep.	11.40 a.m.	Change engine
arr.	1.25 p.m.	Doncaster	dep.	1.30 p.m.	Change engine
arr.	2.20 p.m.	Wakefield	dep.	2.25 p.m.	Change to L & Y engine
arr.	3.10 p.m.	Halifax (via North Dean)			

The 10.0 a.m. 'Scotsman' ran ten minutes later.

Slip carriages began in 1861 when three ordinary brakes were converted. Others were added. In February 1866 the general manager requested construction of 15 more because he intended extending slip services. These carriages were fitted with sand boxes. The slip coupling consisted of a flat horizontal link with a hinged hook at the leading end, secured by a catch and trigger. The coupling was released by a pull on a cord, from the trigger over a pulley at the top of the end panel of the brake compartment at the leading end of the slip carriage, and the end of the cord hung down inside the brake compartment. Each slip brake or set of slip carriages had to have a slip carriage guard, travelling in the slip brake. The slip carriages were properly connected to the train by ordinary screw couplings and side chains until the train stopped at the last station before passing the station at which the carriages were slipped. From there, the slip coupling alone was used.

In 1867 carriages were attached to the 9.0 a.m., 12.0 noon and 5.0 p.m. to be slipped at Hitchin for Cambridge; to the 2.45 p.m. at Hatfield for Luton, Dunstable and St Albans; to the 5.0 p.m. at Essendine for Stamford and Bourne; to the 5.5 p.m. at Potters Bar; to the 5.25 p.m. at Hatfield for Hertford; and to the 10.0 a.m. and 9.15 p.m., at Doncaster. In the up direction the 4.28 p.m. from York slipped at Knottingley, and the train due at King's Cross at 10.0 p.m. slipped at Hitchin for Cambridge. The pattern of some of the slip services varied fairly frequently. Newark was sometimes served by both up and down expresses, and Bradford by a slip at Ardsley.

There were about 60 trains each way in and out of King's Cross on weekdays in 1867 including ten or eleven Midland; seven in each direction were Great Northern expresses as under:

Depart 9.0 a.m. for Nottingham, West Riding, York and Edinburgh.
10.0 a.m. 'Flying Scotsman' for Nottingham, Lancashire, West Riding, Edinburgh, Glasgow and Perth.
12.0 noon for Nottingham, Lancashire and West Riding.
2.45 p.m. for Nottingham, Lancashire and West Riding.
5.0 p.m. for Lancashire.
5.25 p.m. for Nottingham, West Riding and York.
9.15 p.m. for Nottingham, Lancashire, West Riding, Edinburgh, Glasgow, Aberdeen and Perth (connecting to Inverness).

Arrive 9.40 a.m. from Edinburgh and north of Scotland.
12.30 p.m. from West Riding, Lancashire and Nottingham.
3.0 p.m. from West Riding and Lancashire.
4.0 p.m. from Newcastle, West Riding and Nottingham.
8.0 p.m. from West Riding, Lancashire and Nottingham.
9.35 p.m. from Edinburgh ('Flying Scotsman').
10.0 p.m. from West Riding, Lancashire and Nottingham.

Best times were: To Nottingham 3 hr, Sheffield 3 hr 51 m., Manchester 5 hr, Leeds 4 hr 35 m., York 4 hr 40 m., and Edinburgh 10 hrs 30 m. The 7.40 a.m. down called at Hitchin and Peterborough, and then at all stations. It had connections for most places, and was the principal train for long distance third class passengers. Local trains running as far as Barnet had third class from the end of 1866.

In common with other railways, the GN included in its bye-laws a rule prohibiting smoking on its premises or in its carriages. Offenders were warned of a 40s penalty. The company fought a long and losing battle trying to enforce the regulation. In April 1852, on the subject of 'the nuisance of smoking' staff were reminded that the 'guard in charge of the train (or an officer) is authorised to eject offenders, but not the common porter', Clarke was instructed to clamp down on offenders who got more numerous. In February 1866 he pointed out that it was difficult to stop smoking in trains, since cigars were sold in refreshment rooms. He felt that the staff were turning a blind eye, and had a notice printed, implying that company servants would be held responsible if passengers were found smoking. Wisely, the directors banned issued of this. By this time they had to admit that smoking had become so universal in trains, that in October they agreed to smoking carriages on local trains as far as Hitchin. Twelve months later they sanctioned smoking carriages on the Yorkshire trains, but not on the Manchesters. However it was only a matter of time before there were 'smoking' carriages on all trains.

A system of periodical or season tickets was adopted in July 1850. In June 1851 it was approved that return fares at single prices should operate between Saturday and Monday at all stations from London to Doncaster and intermediately. From January 1862 new tickets were stamped with the fares. But in April 1866 instructions were given that fares were not to be printed on tickets.

Communication between guards and drivers, first fitted to passenger trains in 1854, consisted of an alarm bell on the tender, operated with a cord by the guard. All passenger trains were so fitted by 1857 when Sturrock estimated that the bells, wheels and frames would have cost £775. Twelve sets of this apparatus were supplied to the MS&L in January 1858 at £15 a set. The forerunner of the 'Train Following' board came into use in July 1853, a red target displayed on the rear vehicle of a train, to indicate to signalmen that a duplicate or other special, run without notice, should be expected. In July 1866 the general manager reported that all single lines were worked by staff and ticket, except the Ramsey and Bourn & Essendine branches, and recommended that they should be too.

To accommodate the vast traffic at Doncaster during St Leger week, it was the practice to commandeer all available sidings for the race specials, arrival and departure, including Plant, locomotive, and Marsh Gate engineers, sidings. Rolling stock had to be borrowed. For the meeting on 10–13 September 1867 there were the following loans, total 274 carriages:

L & SW	66
LC & D	60
L & NW	50
NL	28
NE	50
GE	22

The Midland and the GN ran specials from Nottingham, and in alternate years either on St Leger day or Doncaster Cup day (Friday). The Midland regularly ran specials from Bradford, and Leeds via Swinton, but that year arranged for the L&Y to cover Leeds with trains from Wellington via Methley.

The bookstall contract with W. H. Smiths, was renewed once or twice on increased terms, and was again on 18 December 1866 for five years from 1 January 1867 at £2,500 per annum.

A CHAPTER OF ACCIDENTS

Accounts of accidents serve to illustrate contemporary management and mismanagement; some had tragic results, a few were not without humour, but all were a drain on the funds. A review of a selection of those which occurred during the period which this volume covers reveals that the majority were caused by the failure of the human element, ranging from disregard of regulations and errors of judgement, to incompetence and downright foolishness; followed by failures of axles, tyres, boilers and permanent way. Adverse weather conditions also brought about a few collisions and a bad derailment.

The first running of a new cattle train from the EL on 21 September 1850 was marred by a collision which could have been a serious disaster. The train was well out of course. It was delayed at Firsby for four hours. When it reached Hatfield, it had 40 wagons, and three engines. The station master had it shunted to the down line to allow two up trains to pass. The signal for the down line was set to danger and a porter was sent 700 yd out with a red lamp. Nevertheless the driver of the 8.0 p.m. passenger train missed the warnings, and collided head-on with the cattle train with the result that he lost his life and his fireman was badly injured. His engine, 66, was seriously damaged, the leading van and a second class carriage were smashed, while the leading engine of the cattle train had its front stove in, the second capsized and the third also was damaged. There were no other casualties. Comparative immunity from injuries to passengers was a characteristic of GN accidents for some years to come. Since the dead driver was held responsible, the directors declined to make an allowance to the unfortunate widow.

Barnet was the scene of two collisions within months. A double-headed coal train struck the rear of a pick-up goods standing in the station on 3 December 1850. The drivers, running too hard, received a clear signal at Hadley Crossing and then failed to observe Barnet's caution signals, and a red light carried by a porter running towards them. There was heavy damage to the wagons, and the engines, 163 and 145, but 39, on the pick-up, escaped harm. Circumstances of a collision on 24 September 1851 were rather similar. The down train, due at Barnet at 4.30 p.m. detached six empty 'seconds'. While these were being manhandled by porters towards an up siding, partly on the down line and partly on the up, they were run into by an up coal train travelling at excessive speed, and unable to pull up although a caution signal was displayed. The driver, fireman and guard all jumped clear.

The awkward exit from Leeds Central high and low level, where trains were propelled out over a single line, and then reversed at Geldard Road junction, caused accidents in the days of primitive signalling. There was a mishap on 8 July 1851; when the 4.10 p.m. was being propelled towards the junction, a L & T 'luggage' train collided with it. An accident on 3 January 1854 had far graver consequences. About 100 yd from Central a L & Y line diverged with a pair of self-acting points and, as a GN train was being backed out, the brake van and a composite carriage became derailed there. The van met an obstacle, and the carriage was forced over the viaduct parapet, falling into the L & Y goods yard below. Three occupants were horribly injured, and unfortunately one was Mr. Hall, Recorder of Doncaster. Under Lord Campbell's Act, compensation to victims of railway accidents, provided that negligence was proved against the company, was related to their earning capacity. No doubt shareholders regretted that wealthy passengers did not pay more for their fares than poorer ones, for on 21 July, at York Assizes, Mr Hall was awarded £4,500. On New Years Day, failure of self-acting points caused a derailment at Doncaster. While the 4.10 p.m. express from York was passing from the main to the platform line, the points reversed under it throwing two carriages off the line. No explanation could be found for these points failures.

The reader will remember that the Y & N M had been allowed to open its Knottingley branch if a pilotman was provided on all trains over the single line temporary bridge. Robert Stephenson's design for the permanent bridge required two parallel tubes for the up and down lines. The up line tube came into use in July 1851. Although a single line still had to be worked over the river, the Y & N M installed a primitive signalling arrangement and dispensed with the pilotman. The second tube was ready towards the end of the year but the Inspecting Officer refused to sanction it (in January and in every succeeding month until October) stating that it was too narrow for passenger carriages, particularly the GN's which were wider. Since the first tube's clearance was identical and had been approved, the Y & N M was reluctant to incur the expense of alteration. The Officer explained that, when examining

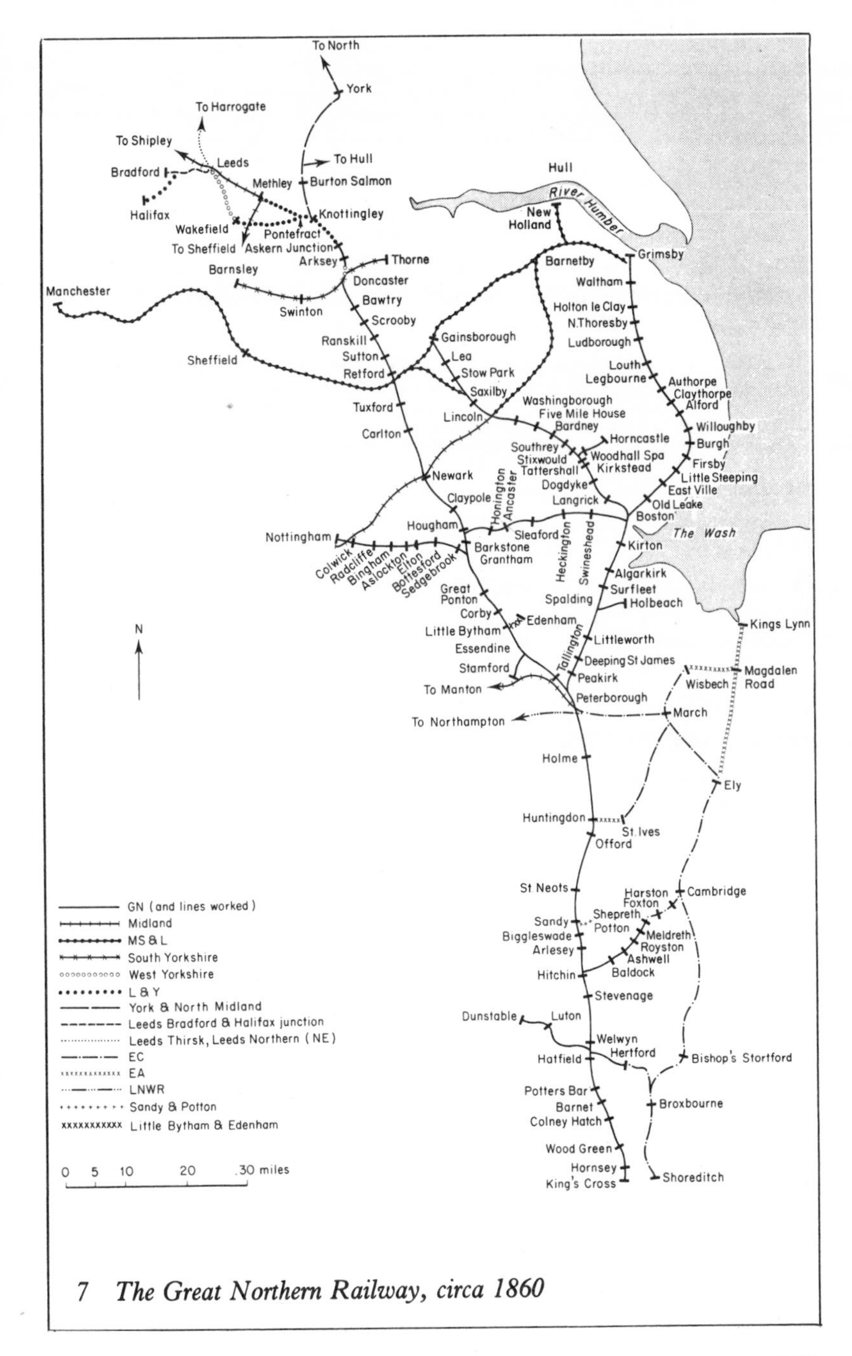

7 *The Great Northern Railway, circa 1860*

the original tube, he had been more concerned with other aspects, and omitted to observe lack of sufficient interior clearance. Thus in 1852 the Y&NM was making monthly applications for the second tube to be sanctioned, and the Officer adamant in confirming his original opinion. At length the Y&NM gave way and devised a method of clearance without too much expense.

Thus on 14 July 1852 only one tube was in use, and no pilotman provided, when an accident involving two GN trains occurred. An up coke train drawn by 135 passed through the bridge and was almost clear of the points when the 2.4 p.m. express from Doncaster ran into about the fifth last wagon. Fortunately the express had reduced speed so that little damage occurred. A nobleman, a passenger in the express, wrote to the Board of Trade drawing attention to the unsatisfactory method of traffic working, stating that he thought that, if the express had been running at higher speed, it might have finished in the river. Sturrock disclaimed the responsibility of his driver and stated his opinion that the signals were wrongly constructed and worked. But the Y&NM would not admit any responsibility for the accident and accused Driver Woodcock (of the express) of reckless driving. However, as the Y&NM was criticised by the Board of Trade for its failure to continue provision of pilotmen, it immediately made arrangements for them to resume duty. It proposed that the GN should appoint the signalmen and work the signals, while it would bear the expense. The two companies compromised and agreed to share losses caused by the damage.

The Midland was equally cantankerous at Newark where it resented the GN crossing it on the level. As first with its railway, it correctly claimed precedence for its traffic, although it was agreed that passenger trains should take precedence over goods. It insisted on installing a signal at the crossing normally showing 'clear' to its own traffic and 'danger' to GN trains. This was probably of disc and crossbar type. The Government Officer had been in favour of signals which would show 'danger' in every direction until 'clear' was required for an approaching train. On 4 October 1852 a GN up express was about an hour late as it approached Newark. The distant signal showed 'white', but the bridge superstructure then obscured the view until the train had crossed, when the driver observed that it had changed to red, and a Midland goods train was at that moment crossing his path. Although he made every effort to pull up, his engine hit about the third last wagon. The Midland goods driver had seen his signal at the crossing change to his favour, while on the crossing became aware of the express, had put on steam and almost managed to draw clear of the GN train which came to a stand 130 yd beyond the crossing. In those days it took an accident, even a disaster, to impress on railway managements the wisdom of recommendations of Board of Trade officers. The Midland was held responsible and reluctantly stumped up £250.

Stoke tunnel was blocked for six hours on 14 December 1853. Three trains had left Corby for Grantham at intervals of five and ten minutes. The first was a goods and the other two were coal trains. The driver of the second, knowing the goods would probably stop at Great Ponton, proceeded very cautiously into the tunnel, but was run into by the third. As a result of the inquiry, the GN intimated that it proposed to install the electric telegraph through the tunnel immediately. Another collision there on the following 7 March was almost a repetition, and the Inspecting Officer made pungent remarks on the absence of the telegraph, which the GN had promised to put in so promptly.

The first of three accidents in a few years at Hornsey happened to one of the Exhibition trains on 8 September 1851. A Grimsby train with Hull passengers off the EL was to be combined at Boston with a train from Leeds and Lincoln. But the Grimsby train was sent off by itself, as the Leeds was late. It was delayed outside Hornsey by the breakdown of a coal train and was run into by the second train, hauled by two engines. The Board of Trade inquiry revealed a curious story. The coal train had stopped at Hornsey and waited for a passenger train to clear. Then the driver was unable to restart because he had blown down the engine boiler and had neither water nor steam. He said that his engine was overdue for a wash-out and that the gauge glass had become cloudy. The Inquiring Officer thought that the driver had expected a clear run to London and that the impetus of his train would get him there without further steam, and he had blown down the boiler and raked out the fire, to save time when he arrived. The guard had been despatched to London to obtain a relief engine (presumably by Shank's pony). Meantime, a goods train from Boston had pulled up behind the coal train. An attempt was made to get the disabled train into a siding, but this failed. When the pilot arrived the two trains were joined together and sent away.

The station staff at Hornsey consisted of a station master and two porters, one of whom was engaged full time selling coal. The station master sent a labourer back with a red flag to protect the excursion which had stopped behind the goods, but he was not a railwayman and the station master failed to tell him how to display the flag. Meanwhile the first excursion had drawn up to the station signal, and two minutes later was run into by the Leeds train, the drivers of which had not seen the warning flag. Passengers in the Leeds train were unaware of the collision, but the last three coaches of the Grimsby train were damaged, and many passengers were injured. Forty six claims, amounting to £658, were settled by November with three outstanding. One victim was a curate, the Reverend Snell. After the accident he was taken to the company's hostel at Hornsey, and after about six weeks the general manager obtained lodgings for him nearby at £2 2s 6d a week and Mrs Snell was allowed £2 17s 6d a week for herself and her children. Snell was attended by two nursing sisters who gave free service, the company therefore giving two guineas annually to the Institution of Nursing Sisters of Bishopsgate. In December the company purchased an invalid chair (costing £22) for Snell, who declined to make a claim. In March 1852 his position as curate was filled, so the company leased a house for him and his family at £50 a year and later allowed him £4 a week. He lingered until January 1855 and was then buried at the railway's expense. His widow also declined to claim. The unique case of the Reverend Snell was closed by making her a present of £750. Another victim named John Jackson was eventually committed to Bethnal House Lunatic Asylum. The GN denied liablility, but contributed £100 to a subscription for maintaining him in the asylum, where he died five years later.

At Kirkstead, on Saturday 17 October 1851, the 9.15 p.m. return excursion ran into the rear of a standing train of empty coal wagons, the engine of which had been detached to take water. No harm came to any passenger, but the fireman was seriously injured and damage done to the engine and wagons. The *Railway Times* printed an exaggerated version of the accident in which it incorrectly stated that the fireman lost his life and the engine (84) was damaged beyond repair.

Hornsey again figured in an accident on 31 August 1853 when the 5.0 p.m. express crashed into a derailed tender. At Southgate the engine of an up goods had failed with a broken piston. A relief engine 205 was sent from King's Cross, and after the cripple had moved off with some cattle trucks 205 worked the rest of the train to Hornsey. Here six coal wagons had to be detached and shunted to the down side. The time was 4.56 and the driver considered that he had sufficient margin to shunt before the express would pass. But the tender came off the road on the crossover and fouled the down line. A telegraphic message, sent to King's Cross, came too late to prevent the express leaving. The station and distant signals were set to danger, and a man sent out with a red flag. Neither driver nor fireman saw the flagman who afterwards alleged that they were deep in conversation as they passed him. The signals were ignored. Although a 'second' was practically a write-off and other carriages damaged, no lives were lost. The engine of the express, 96, was damaged to the extent of £80, the tender of No. 205 £50, and 205 herself £20, total damage amounting to about £600. Compensation to injured passengers was considerable.

On Thursday 8 September Captain Wynne, Sturrock, and Leech, the solicitor, made test runs to ascertain if it was possible to stop a down express at ordinary speeds after sighting the distant signal. At 45 mph, shutting off steam and applying the tender brake only, the train stopped 65 yd south of the station, about 200 yd short of the point of collision. At 40 mph, applying all brakes and reversing, the train stopped in 510 yd at the distant. All this proved that the express driver had relied on the usual time interval, and failed to keep a proper look-out, besides vindicating the officers in siting the distant. Driver Pardenton and his mate were dismissed, and charged at Clerkenwell with negligently driving a locomotive. They were committed to the Old Bailey, where it was ruled that no offence at law had been committed. They ought to have been dealt with summarily by the magistrates under the 1842 Railway Regulations Act. However, in 1861, under the Offences against the Person Act, it became a serious offence, triable by judge and jury, to endanger the safety of railway passengers by unlawful act, or wilful omission or neglect. Pardenton got a job in the engineers department, but was found unsuitable, and sacked again.

Quick observation of a man in a nearby field prevented a third accident at Hornsey from developing into a crash. On 17 April 1854 this man attracted the attention of the driver, and one guard of the 10.0 a.m. from York who looked back to see the rear van off the rails. The train was brought to a stand before complications set in. The van left the rails owing to a broken tyre, and the other guard had been thrown out.

Luck continued to hold, for on 13 July 1855 the night express from Edinburgh ran into the rear of a breakaway coal train near Doncaster. The engine was thrown down the bank, and the line blocked for seven hours, but there were no claims for injuries. On the other hand £600 damages were awarded at Hertford Assizes to passengers in what appeared to be a mild collision at Hatfield on 12 January 1856 when an express ran into the rear of a coal train, slackening speed preparatory to shunting for it to pass.

A fatal accident at Darton on 5 December 1861 revealed the GN exercising running powers over the L&Y between Wakefield and Barnsley, obtained by the WY. A GN mineral train ran into a L&Y engine which, when shunting, had crossed to the wrong line. The station staff were too slow to protect it, and the distant was not put to danger until after the GN train had passed it, leaving insufficient time for the driver to avert a collision. The driver of the light engine was killed, and his fireman seriously injured.

On Christmas Eve 1862 a coal train, shunted into the long up siding at Barnet to allow other trains to pass, came out on to the main line again without the authority of the signalman, who had been advised by the Hatfield signalman of the approach of the 10.0 a.m. from York. He threw his signals to danger in the face of the express which, still travelling at over 15 mph, collided sidelong with the coal wagons. The express driver had braked and put his engine in reverse but had omitted to whistle for the guards' brakes. Twenty claims for injuries were received. Colonel Yolland strongly recommended the provision of continuous brakes, stating that the electric telegraph stations locally were Hatfield, Barnet and Southgate.

On 3 December 1863 there was a collision between two light engines. The early morning was pitch dark with high winds and heavy rain squalls as a pilot left New England shed, with a guard on the footplate as well as the enginemen. The pilot was followed by a goods engine, which overtook and collided with it so heavily it broke away from its tender, throwing the three men to the ground, and the guard was run over by the tender and killed. The driverless engine ran forward to Peterborough where it wrecked the brake van of a goods train and seriously injured the guard. Both engines were derailed and blocked the up main line.

Doncaster, on the evening of St Leger day, 14 September 1864, had dealt with 74 trainloads of departing race-goers. Two additional Bradford carriages were attached to the 5.0 p.m. from King's Cross. When it arrived at Laister Dyke, it was 65 minutes late and consisted of a brake compo for Bradford, a compo for Halifax, and two carriages (first and second) for Bradford. The engine and the normal Bradford carriage were sent up the Bradford branch to wait until an engine and van for Halifax came out of a siding, set back, and went away with the compo. Next the Bradford engine began to set back on the other two carriages, left standing in the platform without a tail lamp. The signalman at Gildersome Branch junction box had an empty L & Y train from Leeds waiting. He heard three whistles, when the Bradford man went up the branch and one, when the Halifax train departed. He was not in telegraphic communication with Laister Dyke box, nor could he see the carriages with no tail lamp, so he let the train go. It hit those carriages hard. They and their unfortunate inmates were cannoned backwards and forwards between the returning GN engine and carriage and the L & Y train. They were smashed, and a dozen passengers were injured.

About a month later there was a disastrous collision between two

Manchester goods trains, loaded with valuable merchandise. The first left Peterborough at 12.30 a.m., followed 20 minutes later by the second. The first was standing in Grantham platform when the other crashed into it at over 30 mph. The fireman was killed and the driver was so seriously injured that he was unable to give any reason for the accident. It was thought that he had lost control of his engine.

The relaxed form of signalling, introduced in the London area in 1860, was exposed and subsequently abandoned, following a collision involving a Midland train and a coal train at Colney Hatch on 30 August 1865. An up coal train stopped at the station to put off a wagon, and when re-starting, a drawbar broke and it had to be shunted into a siding. At this stage the signalman, who had kept his signals at danger, received 'Be Ready' and almost immediately 'Train Waiting' from Barnet. He replied 'Trains Out' and 'Line Blocked' which meant that the coal train had reached him and that the line at his station was occupied. Shortly afterwards he saw the Midland train before it entered Barnet tunnel, judged that it was running at too high a speed to pull up in time, and warned the driver of the coal train to get back into the siding. The Midland train, a return excursion from Derby, consisted of 19 carriages and three brake vans with three guards. Although all brakes were applied and the engine put into reverse, the train hit the coal wagons which in turn collided with the engine which had not quite managed to get clear. Seven passengers were seriously injured (one of them subsequently died) and there were 250 compensation claims. Evidence about the signals at Barnet was conflicting. The Midland driver, supported by his fireman and the second guard, said that the up distant was clear and the station signal at caution, and that after about ¼ mile he shut off steam because he had been shown a green light at Barnet. But the Barnet signalman maintained that his signals were at danger. If he had been 'cautioned', the driver had 2½ miles in which to bring his train to a stand, and if he had not, then he would still have had over 2,000 yd from sighting the Colney Hatch distant which would have been visible through the tunnel. There was a suspicion that, despite intervention of a tunnel, it had been the practice to allow more than one train in the Barnet Colney Hatch section.

About 9.30 p.m. on Sunday 7 April 1867 the driver of a light engine, proceeding north, put into a siding at Hatfield, to allow the 9.15 p.m. Scotch express to pass. The points to this siding were normally operated by a pointsman, but this man (who was inexperienced, and did not intend to stay with the company) had left his post to get his supper or something, and the fireman altered them. As soon as he was inside the siding, the driver whistled to indicate that he was clear of the main line, and oiled his engine. He heard a train pass (which he thought was the express), whistled twice, got no reply, so whistled again. He then saw a light moving in the box and told the fireman to alter the points. As he began to move, the main line signal at St Albans junction dropped, which he took as his own signal. He had no sooner got on the main than he heard and saw the express bearing down on him. He managed to get up a fair speed, and run about six furlongs before the express collided with his tender. The express driver had reversed and braked and had reduced speed to about 25 mph. There was no derailment or damage, but it is interesting to compare similarities with the Hawes Junction disaster on the Midland 43 years later. Colonel Yolland suggested shifting the junction, moving the box from the middle to the south end of the station, and that the signalman should move the points.

The 9.15 p.m. was again involved in an incident on 16 July. It was a heavy train, 14 vehicles, two only of which were brakes. Due to engine trouble, it was 47 minutes late leaving Grantham. Although the Retford pilot was attached, it was an hour late at Milford Junction. Both drivers saw Bolton Percy distant against them, whistled for brakes, applied tender brakes and reversed their engines. They had probably been trying to regain the lost time. The rails were greasy. The express was still travelling fast enough, when it hit a shunting goods train, to throw the leading engine on its side and derail some train engine wheels. Eight passengers and the rear guard were hurt. While it had no bearing on the accident, one of the rules was infringed at Retford, for the pilot should have been attached behind the train engine instead of in front.

Fog has always been the railwayman's greatest hazard. There were several minor mishaps due to it during this period, but only two serious accidents. By coincidence, both occurred at Knottingley and involved the morning 'Parliamentary' from Leeds. The first happened on 22 November 1853 in dense fog. The 7.40 a.m. from Leeds was directed by a pointsman to proceed into the platform, but while it was on the crossing, a L & Y goods train appeared out of the gloom. Both trains were moving slowly, but impact of the collision was sufficient to derail the G N engine, 166, and turn over the first carriage which was crowded, and almost every occupant was injured. The second occurred on 8 January 1863 in thick swirls of fog when the 7.30 a.m. from Leeds ran into the 7.30 a.m. 'Parliamentary' from York. The first carriage was wrecked, one passenger was killed and there were many claims for injuries.

Torrential rain caused sudden flooding near Carlton on 14 August 1857 and both roads were washed away. Within a few minutes of each other an up fish train and the 8.45 p.m. down train were thrown off the rails. A number of passengers received injuries. Although the company at first denied liability, it eventually paid out substantial sums as cases were taken to court.

Accidents on GN trains on the MS&L line were expensive. On 6 August 1851 a train, delayed near Woodhouse Junction by a MS&L coal train, was run into by a MS&L goods train. Damage to rolling stock was not extensive, but settlement for injuries totalled over £2,000. It transpired at the inquiry that relations between the two companies had so deteriorated that they ceased to advise each other of running of excursion, or other special trains.

Although in 1851 Sturrock had informed his directors that Clarborough tunnel on the MS&L was not signalled, no action was taken. When a collision occurred in it on 11 April 1854, the GN was held responsible. The tunnel, 605 yd long, was at the top of a long gradient of 1 in 120. A GN coal train toiled up this from Retford so slowly that it attracted the attention of people by the lineside, who came forward at the inquiry to give evidence. One, a gamekeeper, stated that he walked over the tunnel quicker than the train had passed through it. Meanwhile a MS&L goods train which had left Retford, a mere three miles away, a quarter of an hour behind the coal train, was steadily reducing the interval, and caught up with it in the tunnel. The engine and tender were thrown on their sides, and both driver and fireman lost their lives. According to the rules, the GN guard should have protected his train since it was losing time in a section, and as he failed to do so, it was GN responsibility. Over £1,000 was awarded in compensation to the footplatemen's widows and dependents.

One wonders at what sort of speeds the MS&L ran goods trains. On 25 February 1857 the GN train which left Retford at 8.30 a.m. for Sheffield, after passing Checker House at about 20–25 mph, was run into by a following goods. The passenger train had only a goods truck, a compo carriage and a brake van behind the engine and no harm was done, other than that the rear van became disconnected.

On 8 September 1852 the 9.10 p.m. GN train from Sheffield came to grief on the Dory House embankment, nearly 35 ft high, on the Sheffield side of Woodhouse Junction. The engine left the rails and went down the bank on the inside of a slight curve to the right. The train fell down the opposite side of the embankment (on a down gradient of 1 in 137). The engine was 29, only recently converted to a tank, and behind it were two loose-coupled vehicles followed by a 'first', a 'second' and a van. The guard was killed and the driver fatally injured. The Inspecting Officer, who arranged a test run with a similar train on 17 September, thought that the goods wagons, not fitted with screw couplings, had set up excessive oscillation. He criticised the short wheelbase of the rebuilt engine, inferring that there was too much overhang at the leading end. The engine was running chimney first. Sturrock explained that the short wheelbase of some of these rebuilt engines allowed them to be turned on a 16 ft carriage turntable.

A broken crank axle on engine 203 caused a nasty accident to the 5.0 p.m. from Manchester on 23 January 1859. The train was running at about 50 mph down 1 in 115 at Pigeon Bridge, 7¼ miles east of Sheffield, when the crank axle snapped. The road burst under the train, the driver and fireman were severely hurt and a number of passengers injured. At the inquiry, by Captain Ross, statistics about broken axles were supplied by the locomotive department. From the figures, it did not seem that a critical mileage in the life of a crank axle could be determined. The axle which failed in this instance had been fitted in October 1855 to 203, which had afterwards run 62,704 miles. Every one of the 12 engines of her class had broken their crank axles at least once while running trains.

Returning to GN metals, the new Manchesters had not long been in service before an accident befell an up express. On 24 September 1857 the 9.30 a.m. from Manchester, engine, four carriages and brake van, had just passed Tuxford and was approaching the bridge over the Newark road when the last two carriages and the van left the rails. The remaining carriages ran 40 yd south of the bridge before somersaulting down the bank. Four people were killed and many injured. No explanation of the accident could be determined. The pro L&NW *Herapath's Railway Journal* was convinced that it was due to high speed, estimating (almost hopefully) that the disaster would cost the GN over £30,000, inferring that such would be just retribution for filching some L&NW Manchester traffic and emphasising its opinion by going into gruesome detail of mutilations suffered by victims.

1853 was an unfortunate year. Captain Galton, in compiling the Board of Trade report, attributed ten out of 76 principal accidents to the GN. Five, he said, were caused by the engine leaving the rails and three others by breakage of engine tyres. On 21 January, a broken tyre caused the derailment of a GN train at Womersley on the L&Y. The train was on a 13 ft embankment at the time. The engine ran 680 yd before falling down the embankment, followed by its tender, a horse box and a guards van. The horse box was smashed across the tender and the horse killed. The van fell on the tender and was not much damaged. The rest of the train remained on the embankment with the leading carriage off the rails. This accident was closely followed by two more due to the breakage of engine tyres (supplied by the Bowling Company, and butt-welded, contrary to Sturrock's written instructions) to the 2.0 p.m. down express. In the first instance, 98 shed a tyre near Carlton on 10 February, with no more damage, or injury. On 17 March a tyre came off 72 near Tallington, causing single line working, until the engine was removed during the night.

Wagon failures caused a number of accidents. On 7 May the 10.30 p.m. down goods, 45 wagons and two brake vans, was hauled by two engines. The drivers became aware that part of the train had broken away, leaving only two wagons attached to them. Being on a down gradient, they ran forward to keep clear of the loose vehicles. A wagon spring became detached causing the wagon to jump the road, which derailed the wagons, blocking both roads near Holme. A broken axle on 8 October caused a pile-up which blocked both roads at Bawtry. On 15 November another axle breakage resulted in an accident near Rossington. Five NB wagons had been marshalled in the rear of an up goods, on one of which the failure occurred. Several wagons were thrown into the path of the 9.15 p.m. down express. The engine, 67, was derailed, but neither she nor her train were much damaged.

Failure of NB goods vehicles were becoming too frequent to be tolerated. So after that derailment Clarke stopped them running over the GN. In January he extended the embargo to include passenger carriages, for on New Years Day 1854 a plucky passenger crawled along the carriage roofs to give the alarm to the driver of the overnight express from Edinburgh. The train was safely brought to a stand, and it was discovered that an axle had broken under a NB 'third'. The passenger was rewarded with a present of £5.

The 5.0 p.m. express was in the news again on 11 December 1855. While it was passing Ranskill, the guard heard the ballast being thrown up, and sounded the cord alarm, causing the driver to stop the train. The tyre of a 'second' had broken. Some fragments had torn through the carriage floor, bringing it off the rails, yet none of the occupants came to any harm.

Both roads at Tuxford were blocked on consecutive evenings in April 1857. Both accidents were caused by broken axles. The first, on the 14th, derailed an up coal train, and the second wrecked the up Scotch goods. Traffic had to be diverted via the Loop. Reporting on these, Sturrock explained that in order to clear the wreckage he had to slew the road to get his cranes to work, and requested provision of three larger cranes to be stationed at Doncaster, Peterborough and London, which were ordered from the Kirkstall Forge Co. The older and smaller cranes were then kept at Leeds, Hitchin and York or Bradford. The up night mail broke away near Barnet tunnel in the early hours of the following 8 May. The tyre of a NE fish wagon broke and the vehicles behind it were derailed, no casualties being reported.

Only one serious accident occurred in 1858, near Carlton on 29 June. The 5.0 p.m. down express was again the victim, the whole thrown off the road through breakage of an engine tyre. The engine remained upright, but the tender was turned upside down and the leading van turned on its side. Only one passenger received serious injuries. There were no casualties on 30 July 1859, when the engine (225) of the same train cast a tyre while passing St Neots, derailing the engine and two carriages.

On 5 June 1860 the overnight train from Edinburgh due at 9.15 a.m., had as penultimate vehicle, a convict carriage belonging to the Directors of Scotch Prisons, kept for them by the NB. A badly welded tyre broke under it about ½ mile north of Southgate station. The guard sounded the alarm, and all means of stopping the train applied. The rear van was derailed on the crossover and a composite carriage turned over, but again there were no casualties.

A few weeks later came what may have been the luckiest escape from a major disaster in GN history. The day was Saturday 27 July. The 10.0 a.m. from Edinburgh, due at King's Cross at 9.30 p.m., comprised two brake vans, seven carriages and another brake in the rear. As the express, nearing London, entered 'Tottenham' tunnel at about a mile a minute, the driver saw fire flying from the right hand driving wheel. As he shut off steam, the engine plunged over on to the down line. The left hand leading wheel was torn off and the engine returned to the up rails and travelled against the wall of the tunnel, coming to rest leaning against the tunnel wall after running 400 yd. The up line was torn up for 150 yd, rails and chairs being wrenched off the sleepers. One rail was forced through the tender and another through the leading van's floor. There were about 50 passengers in the train and all escaped harm, but there were some injuries among servants, including the fireman whose hand was crushed against the tunnel wall. The Wood Green signalman, alarmed by the non-appearance of the train, and hearing whistling from the tunnel, tested his telegraph instruments and, being unable to contact Southgate, promptly turned his signals to danger in the face of the 8.50 p.m. down express, which was pulling up when it met the fireman and a guard. These trains normally passed near the tunnel but, luckily, the down express had been five minutes late starting. The down line was not cleared until 5.30 a.m. for single line working. The accident was caused by fracture of the driving axle. The engine, 206, (Hawthorn 2-2-2) had run 10,000 miles since last repair on 1 April. In his report, Sturrock wrote that he had 'stopped that class of engine from running trains'. Coming so soon after the Pigeon Bridge accident, this was not surprising. Some time afterwards he obtained authority to purchase 12 new crank axles. It could well be that these were fitted to the 'Hawthorns' for it was to be more than another decade before the first of the class was replaced. The Wood Green signalman, J. Baker, was presented with £5 for his prompt action in averting a collision in the tunnel. But a year or two later the poor fellow died from cancer.

225 was again the cause of an accident for, while running the 3.0 p.m. from Manchester at high speed on 4 April 1863, the left hand leading tyre broke. The driver was thrown down twice before he could close the regulator and the fireman was unable to apply the tender brake. The train was approaching Little Bytham, and the engine ran through the ballast before being deflected by a crossing to the coal drops on the up side of the north of the station, coming to rest when its wheels fell between the girders of the last coal drop. The leading van was across the coal sidings, the first carriage leaned against the telegraph wires before falling 10 ft to the ground, the second was pitched down the first coal drop, a composite was on its side, while the rear van remained upright with only one pair of wheels off the road. Many passengers were injured, four seriously, but no lives were lost.

Scanty precautions were taken in early years to protect gaps in the rails while platelayers were making repairs. If a driver failed to observe a green flag beside the line, he had little chance on a down gradient of stopping his train in time to prevent a derailment, yet responsibility was on him. Placing warning detonators was an additional precaution taken later. From about 1854 signals were kept at danger until the rail had been replaced. By this time there had been several such derailments, but none had serious results.

The E L line curved sharply as it joined the Loop at Boston (later East Lincolnshire) junction. On 1 March 1857 the road spread under the night mail from Grimsby. The train, hauled by two tank engines, had consisted of six fish wagons and three carriages, but when it pulled up in Boston station only two fish wagons were still with the engines. The remainder had derailed on the curve. In 1862 the permanent way on the Loop line was still largely that laid 14 years earlier. On 2 April the 2.5 a.m. mail from Peterborough was derailed while travelling at about 40 mph just after passing Algarkirk station. The wooden trenails had given way, allowing the road to spread under the train. The engine fell over, the brake van was smashed, and the two carriages fell on their sides. The driver and the guard were both thrown to the side of the line but not severely hurt, and there were no passengers in the train that morning. The engine was 216. The Inspecting Officer recommended that chairs should be secured to sleepers by an iron spike in addition to the trenails. As has been seen, these officers were already insisting on iron spikes before they sanctioned opening of new railways. It became the practice to cast the chairs with three holes, and insert one spike, and two trenails.

1860 was a bad year. The first accident was on 23 April to the 10.0 a.m. down express, wrecked at Hatfield. It consisted of ten vehicles, York brake van, Newcastle compo, Leeds compo, Halifax compo, Bradford compo, Huddersfield compo, Liverpool compo, Manchester 'second', Manchester 'first' and Manchester van. A rail broke under the engine as it passed over it. The engine, and first five vehicles ran through the station, the last (the Bradford compo) off the rails. The wheels were torn from under this which fell on its side and was dragged along the 'six foot' for 145 yd. A passenger, Leonard Pym, was thrown out and was found dying in the 'six foot'. The engine and tender broke away from the vehicles. The after part was also derailed, some carriages colliding with wagons of a coal train on the up line. A 4 ft length of check rail flew up and killed a platelayer standing at the line side. Captain Tyler was informed that the broken rail had been turned several times. He strongly recommended the directors to provide continuous brakes on passenger trains. Only one passenger, Mr Pym, died from his injuries. He, son of Francis Pym the late director, a wealthy young man, had ten children, but neglected to make a will. All his property was entailed to his eldest son, leaving no provision for his widow and nine children. The GN had to pay over £11,000. At the trial, the GN's counsel suggested that had he kept his seat, instead of standing at the window, he would probably have escaped with his life!

Unusual circumstances attending some accidents now to be related read more like fiction than fact, but the descriptions come from official records. On 3 August 1851 a down goods was passing Stevenage when the driver, Bradley, observed that he was short of water. He whistled to the guards for brakes, uncoupled his engine from the train while it was still moving, and ran forward to Hitchin, to take water. While at the water crane he heard his train bearing down on him, for the guards were unable to stop it. Quickly he decided to run into a siding, and re-set the points to enable the runaway to run by him, down the main line. Luck was not with him, for his engine stood on a dead-centre and would not budge. He jumped from the footplate leaving the regulator open. A heavy collision took place. The engine, 117, moved smartly down the siding, through the stops, and over the embankment, damage being estimated at £135, with further expense of £75 for getting her back on the rails. Wagons were also damaged. Sturrock, in his report, estimated the entire damage at nearly £500. Bradley was let off lightly, merely reduced to firing.

A complete blockage at Werrington junction on 19 April 1853 was the work of a pointsman, who by mistake, turned a down main line goods on to the Loop and then, realising his error, reversed the points under it, which became largely wreckage. The bill for damaged merchandise and killed and injured cattle was heavy.

On 9 April 1855, Driver Poulton lost his life under peculiar circumstances, knocked off the roof of a carriage by a bridge near Claypole. He, a 30 year old senior driver, was an inveterate gambler, and had been in the habit of leaving the footplate, climbing on to the carriages and down on to the footboards, to find an acquaintance with whom he could place bets! Another sporting individual backed his last loser on the GN some four years later, when the widow of James Davis claimed compensation for the death of her husband, who was described as an 'inebriated trotter-vendor', and was alleged to have lost his life trying to board a train in 'Tottenham' tunnel while returning from Barnet races.

The down distant at the level crossing south of Peterborough station was normally kept at danger until it was 'whistled off'. Drivers were so used to the road being cleared in response to whistles that they were in the habit of running harder than they should if they were to have their trains under control by the time they reached Crescent level crossing. Inevitably this led to a collision. On 7 November 1855 Peterborough station was so congested with traffic that an up goods had to be shunted to the down line and the 5.0 p.m. down express struck it. Some damage was caused and there were several claims for injuries. Sacré, then in charge at New England, was aware of this dangerous practice, and reprimanded for turning a blind eye.

The stupid error by a signalman at Hitchin on 8 September 1859 resulted in injuries to 35 passengers in the 9.15 p.m. down Scotch express. He had set his junction and signals for the Midland train, due at 9.35 p.m., running 35 minutes late. Learning that the 9.15 was ready to leave Hitchin station, he belatedly put signals against the Midland train, and gave the express a clear road. The engines met practically head-on at the junction. There was only slight damage to the Midland train, but two GN carriages mounted the ends of those preceding them.

Colonel Yolland inquired into the death of a gate-keeper at Spalding on 30 August 1860 and severely censured the management for 'allowing fly-shunting which, although against the regulations, was constantly performed'. The driver of a goods train, induced to shunt some coal wagons, drew nine out of an up siding and then 'kicked' them through a crossover into a down siding, but the impetus was such that they ran through the siding on to the down line, and then knocked down the gate-keeper.

The 10.0 a.m. from Edinburgh met trouble again on Wednesday 10 October 1860. As it was leaving Peterborough, a pointsman mistakenly altered some points and switched it into a siding where it collided with some grain wagons. The GN then installed a disc signal to work with the points.

On 7 December 1864 the 2.20 p.m. 'pick'-up' from Peterborough was to be shunted at Welwyn for an up Manchester express to pass. There was some confusion between the head and rear guards. In the darkness the latter turned the points for the down siding instead of the up. In consequence the train backed across the down line. The down main signals were flung to danger, but too late to prevent the 7.0 p.m. Midland train from colliding with the wagons. Fourteen passengers were injured, some severely. Both lines were blocked for 2½ hours until single line working was possible.

A mechanical failure to engine 326 led to a serious accident on 1 June 1865. While working an up goods train, she stopped at Sutton gatehouse. The driver found that a bolt had come out of an eccentric strap. Retford pilot came, and assisted the train to Retford, where the foreman rashly decided to send the crippled engine back, tender-first, to Doncaster, working on one cylinder. The motion was disconnected but the rod was left loose, until the driver borrowed a piece of rope from the signalman at Ranskill and tied it up. The cripple got under way again and travelled all right until after it passed Rossington, but failed to reach Balby box, where the signalman queried its whereabouts. His colleague at Rossington displayed a green caution signal, and waved a green hand lamp to the 9.15 p.m. express which was even then approaching. Two miles beyond Rossington, the express crashed into 326, threw it off the rails and pushed it 120 yd. Two carriages were derailed and fouled the up line. Sixteen passengers were hurt, and the driver of 326 (who had been underneath it) was found dead under the train. That section was worked on the time interval with the electric telegraph as auxiliary, trains being forwarded to the next two stations. After a train passed, the signals were kept at danger for five minutes and then at caution for a further eight minutes. Captain Tyler recommended installation of the block system.

The layout at New England included a triangle, used for turning engines. The two western angles ran into blind sidings, but there were points at New England North and South boxes which enabled traffic to be turned on to the main line. View of the line from the shed was obscured from the South box by a hedge. On 15 July 1865 an inspector was waiting there for an engine he had ordered. When an engine appeared, he realised at the last moment that it was a runaway and called 'For God's sake, there is something wrong here, where shall we turn it?' The signalman, in a flurry, set the points for the main line instead of the dead end. The engine (352) went steaming off towards the station, passed it at 25 mph and ran into the tail of an up goods which, being market day, had two passenger carriages at the rear. Over 20 passengers were injured. The shed staff had left the engine in gear, with the regulator open. Two cleaners were held responsible, and dismissed.

An up goods train arrived at Welwyn junction just before 5.0 p.m. on 5 November 1867 and began to shunt. Part was detached, and set back on the Hertford branch and through some points into an up siding. The engine and some wagons then returned to the main line ready to set back on the remainder. The guard accidentally set the points for the down main line and called his train back. A down passenger train was approaching, which hit the wagons at 40 mph. Some passengers received injuries and several vehicles were damaged. The signalman had endeavoured, too late, to divert the passenger train on to the Luton branch. This accident again clearly demonstrated the urgent necessity for interlocking points and signals and concentrating operation of points on running lines under signalmen's control.

Welwyn junction had figured in an accident three years earlier, a minor incident involving derailment of a carriage when, on 4 May 1864, the 1.30 p.m. from King's Cross was turning on to the Hertford branch, the points were moved before the third (last) carriage was clear. A rather similar accident took place at Seven Sisters Road (where the new Edgware Branch junction box had Edwards patent locking apparatus) on 16 November 1867, when part of the train due at King's Cross at 4.0 p.m. was derailed. The last two vehicles were left on the north side of the station and the third last was off the rails. The train was stopped after the driver's bell was sounded by the cord alarm. Colonel Rich condemned the GN practice of signalmen returning signals to danger as soon as the engine had passed. He was of opinion that the signalman at the junction touched the points after putting the levers back prematurely, and recommended that signals should not be put back to danger, until the complete train had passed. Nevertheless some years elapsed before the rules were altered to comply with this.

There were several reports of trains running into King's Cross buffer stops. The return excursion from Liverpool, Manchester, Sheffield and Huddersfield, due at 6.40 p.m. on Wednesday 30 May 1860, crashed through the stops. The engine ran across the circulating area and into Old St Pancras Road, where it came to rest against mounds of earth thrown up by Metropolitan construction works. The fireman jumped from the footplate, but Driver Annis stuck to his engine and was uninjured. He said that he applied tender brakes when passing Holloway signal hut, and put his engine into reverse in Copenhagen tunnel. Witness alleged that he reversed his engine inside station limits, but he explained that the gear slipped, and he was again reversing after emerging from Maiden Lane tunnel. The real offender was the MS&L guard in the rear van, who was drunk, and failed to apply his brakes. The Government Officer criticised the lack of brake power, for the train consisted of 33 vehicles with only one brake van at each end. He strongly advocated provision of continuous brakes. There were about 800 passengers, but only 15 complained of injury.

On one or two occasions goods trains had been wrongly diverted into the passenger station, but there was comedy on 2 November 1865. A driver who stopped to take water, spragged the wheels of some wagons, and on returning to his train unspragged them, but omitted to couple up. At Copenhagen tunnel south end, the engine was turned into the goods yard and the points reversed before the loose train appeared. It ran into the station, tearing out the buffer stops, and four wagons went over the top.

The first boiler explosion on the GN was on 1 November 1860. The engine, the *Albion*, belonged to Jay, who was then building the Met, and working on construction of the East Branch at King's Cross. He had purchased the engine nine years earlier (from the EC), which had then been fitted with a new firebox. The engine came into King's Cross to take water, and was at rest when the crown of the firebox failed. Two men were killed in the explosion.

When four years later a GN boiler exploded the incident occurred on another company's rails, while 138 was on hire to the Met. She was about to leave Bishops Road station, Paddington, with the 9.50 a.m. for Farringdon Street when the boiler exploded. The roof of the station was blown off (also the driver's cap), and a train drawing into the station was badly damaged.

The roof of New England repair shop was blown off on Saturday 14 January 1865. The boiler and firebox of 98 were repoted leaking by her driver, so she ceased working on 16 December. The boiler was patched and, still stripped, was resting on two lorries over a pit ready to be tested to 130 lb pressure. It was filled with cold water, and the fire was lit at 1.52 p.m. At 4.20 the pressure was 41 lb, and the man who had ordered the test was in a train on his way home. At 4.25 it was 49 lb, at 5.0 125 lb. Immediately afterwards the boiler exploded. Part of the roof of the adjoining engine shed was also blown off. Three workmen were killed, including a boy blown clean through a wall, what was left of his poor body being thrown on to a tender 50 ft away. Five other men were injured and a number of engines damaged. Total damage was put at £2,500. Captain Tyler was appalled at the foolhardiness of those in authority, who ordered the boiler to be tested with live steam, instead of hydraulically.

Only two other engine boilers failed on the GN, 147 at Ardsley on 7 April 1865 and 116 at Nottingham on 1 January 1866. Neither explosion resulted in casualties. With regard to 116, Sturrock reported that at her last overhaul the safety valves had blown off at 110 lb and had been screwed down to 120 lb, and the boilder had been tested at 140 lb. He added the comment that 'the hydraulic test was a delusion after all'.

The steep gradients in the West Riding caused wagon runaways. On 26 January 1861 some breakaway L&Y wagons crashed 40 ft into the GN Leeds goods yard. A few weeks later, on 11 April, 26 wagons broke away from a GN goods train when passing Holbeck, and ran back into the low level station where they struck a rake of 14 L&Y carriages. Damage was about £2,000. At Laister Dyke on 7 December 1864 some fly-shunted wagons ran over the summit and collided with a L&Y coal train. Then at Howden Clough on 18 June 1866 the guards of a shunting train left their vans on the line without screwing down the brakes. Six wagons were backed into them. They ran down the 1 in 40 bank with the wagons following. The engine was sent after them. In attempting to couple them up, the driver was thrown off and killed. On two occasions passenger trains were involved. On 4 July 1860 a L&Y coal train ran into a long GN excursion standing at Holbeck while tickets were collected. No casualties were reported. In December 1863 a broken coupling was the cause of some wagons running back into a passenger train at Holbeck, and some passengers complained of injuries.

There was an accident at Wortley Junction on 18 August 1862, caused by officials being overzealous. The 10.15 a.m. excursion from Leeds to King's Cross had been delayed 20 minutes at Holbeck waiting for a connection off the NE. It consisted of 14 vehicles and on leaving Holbeck made slow progress up the 1 in 50. A Leeds–Bradford train was behind it, in charge of a young hand, only made a driver three days earlier. The district agent, Symonds, called to him to assist the train in front and then, thinking that he had not been heard, clambered on to the footplate, followed by Rouse, the Leeds locomotive foreman. Rouse took over the driving and contrived to collide so heavily with the rear of the excursion that it broke into three parts, and 25 passengers were injured. It transpired that assistance was not necessary for the excursion engine was equal to its task and working well.

There was a minor incident at Leeds on 3 April 1866, when the regulator stuck on an engine backing a train into Central, and two people were injured. A derailment on the Cambridge branch on 3 July has already been mentioned in chapter IX, due as stated to the poor state of the permanent way when the GE handed back the line. It occurred about two miles west of Royston. The train, the 10.20 a.m. from Hitchin to Cambridge, consisted of a tank engine (a rebuilt Little Sharp, probably No. 1 itself, see chapter XIV), a brake second, two firsts, and a brake second. The engine, in good condition, having run only a small mileage since its last general overhaul, left the rails and ran along the ballast for over 60 yd before rolling over into a field. The carriages were derailed, and becoming detached, ran another 30 yd before the leading vehicle toppled over, the others remaining upright. The driver and fireman were killed, and nine people injured. Two were company's servants, and the others were installing the electric telegraph along the branch.

The final accident to be described in this volume occurred in 1866. It was a highly destructive one, for three trains were in collision in Welwyn North tunnel, and a fire which subsequently broke out destroyed many wagons and their contents, and blocked the line for more than two days. The facts are of much interest and are given in some detail. They differ from the usual version given which contains inaccuracies. It happened just before midnight on Saturday 9 June. A northbound train of 35 empty coal wagons and a brake passed Welwyn at 11.20 but failed to reach the next signal box at Knebworth. The engine was one of the latest Kitson-built 0-6-0's, new in March 1865. The train had got about 400 yd into the tunnel, when one of the tubes in the engine burst so that escaping steam and water all but put the fire out, and after another 200 yd the train came to a stand. The driver sent his fireman back to inform the guard. Without getting out of his van, the guard proposed that the train should be shoved back down the incline to Welwyn. Without even reminding the guard of his duty to protect the train, the fireman went back with his message to the driver. He, who had already uncoupled his engine, refused to set back, for he knew that such procedure was against he regulations, and soon afterwards heard the sound of a train crashing into the rear of his own. Before long a train entered the tunnel from the north end at a fair speed. He heard this hit an obstruction. He got his own engine on the move, and ran as fast as he could to Knebworth. He had sufficient steam to reach the box, but had to be pushed into a siding by a Midland engine which had arrived there with an up goods.

The signalmen at Welwyn and Knebworth had become confused in their conversation over the speaking telegraph as to the whereabout of the first train, consequently when another 'down' approached Welwyn at 11.36 the signalman cleared the signals for it to proceed. This, the 9.55 Midland goods to Leeds, consisted of 26 loaded wagons and a van. The driver estimated that he had attained 20 to 25 mph when he entered the north tunnel which was full of steam and smoke. He did not see the train in front until he was right on top of it. His engine was derailed, and he was trapped by falling coal for a few minutes. He had no sooner freed himself and helped his fireman than they heard the sound of the train entering the north end of the tunnel, and made the best of their way out over some wreckage to the south end. They informed the Welwyn signalman. Next the driver took his fireman to the inn because he had a badly cut head. He then returned to his engine with a GN fireman, and with the assistance of other men put out his fire with water and put his coat over the chimney to stop the draught. After the first collision, the Midland guard immediately went back with detonators to protect his train, and then returned to the tunnel to look for the GN guard. A man was found lying insensible against the tunnel wall, but when got out, proved to be a 'stranger', afterwards identified as John Rawlings, a Metropolitan cleaner. The guard, Joseph Wray, was later discovered lying dead in the 'six foot'.

The third train involved was the 7.50 p.m. GN goods from Peterborough, a pick-up as far as Hitchin and then fast to London. It originated principally as a meat train from the north, but the meat was supposed to be transferred to the 5.40 p.m. from Peterborough. However, on this night there was some Scotch meat on it. Some was salvaged, some condemned but a lot was burnt. Fifty-five lambs from Meldreth were rescued just in time with only one or two casualties, but the consignments were a mixed lot, one might almost say a mixed grill! In the fog of smoke and steam the driver had no chance of seeing the brake van and other wreckage thrown across his path. His engine was derailed and he immediately did his best to put his fire out. The fire-irons were lost in the collision and as he could not rake the fire out, he damped it down with water from the tender, passed to him in a bucket by his fireman and then placed the coke-board and his coat over the chimney. When the water gave out, he had succeeded in putting out the fire except in the corners of the firebox. After 50 minutes, he came out of the tunnel with the injured head guard who had been riding in the front brake, and struggled over the pile of wreckage. The rear guard, considerably shaken up, managed to get his tail lamps lit again.

Hatfield breakdown train arrived about 1.30 a.m. and, after the body of Wray was found, the work of salvaging the wagons began. Some derailed Midland wagons were jacked back on to the rails and 13 wagons and the brake had been drawn out of the tunnel by about 3.45 a.m., when a small fire started under the GN engine amongst some wood shavings, strewn about from a wrecked wagon of furniture. If a bucket could have been found the fire could have been promptly extinguished, but with a strong draught through the tunnel, and from a ventilation shaft immediately overhead, it soon got out of control and assumed such proportions that the breakdown gangs were driven out of the tunnel. The Hitchin gang had arrived about 3.0 a.m. and had removed 31 empty coal wagons and all but 12 of the loaded wagons and a brake from the up train before they were forced out.

The fire burned all day Sunday with smoke and flames belching out from the top of the shaft. It was not until evening that men could re-enter the tunnel and tackle the conflagration with fire engines. By 9.30 p.m. on Monday the tunnel was cleared of the engines, and the debris (all that remained of the wagons) and both roads repaired. The tunnel was inspected, and was not much damaged. There were some cracks in the ventilation shaft and bricks burned to a depth of 1½ in where the fire had been fiercest. Ordinary traffic was resumed at 3.45 a.m. on Tuesday. The GE offered every facility, so Seymour Clarke soon arranged for traffic to be diverted over it, stopping trains and Midland traffic routed via Hertford, Cambridge, Royston and Hitchin, and expresses and through goods via Hertford, Cambridge, March and Peterborough. The GE provided pilotmen and improvised a special code of headlamps. Coal traffic was suspended, and Welwyn and Stevenage were served by pilot engines.

Cockshott compiled a very full report. He was of the opinion that the fire had been started by drips from naphtha flares carried by breakdown men rather than from the GN engine's ashpan. Rawlings, whose parents lived at Peterborough, had been smuggled into the brake by his friend the guard for a free illicit ride. He remained insensible until Tuesday morning when he died. The dead guard was the real culprit, for he had made no attempt to protect his train, indeed it seemed that he had never left his van until he was thrown out. But the signalmen were also culpable and were suspended. They both had poor records, although they had each received bonuses for good conduct. Bradford, the man at Welwyn, was subsequently dismissed for not obeying the regulations. The crew of the down empties put up a poor show. Neither had a good record. The fireman had been demoted from driving six months earlier. They made no immediate efforts to warn other traffic and when they got to Knebworth, did not attempt to return to the tunnel to see what had happened to the men on the other trains, the fireman eventually going back with the Hitchin breakdown gang.

LOCOMOTIVES AND ROLLING STOCK

As mentioned in chapter 1, the first orders for locomotives and rolling stock were placed on 11 December 1846, shortly after the appointment of Benjamin Cubitt as Locomotive Engineer. Six 2-2-2 passenger engines were ordered from Sharp Bros of Manchester, similar in design to those supplied by the makers to other railways. They had 5 ft 6 in driving wheels and 15 in × 20 in inside cylinders and were provided with six wheel tenders. The price was £1,860 for each engine and £460 for each tender. On 28 January 1847 the firm offered to build up to 20 similar engines in 1848 and 20 or 30 in 1849 if the GN would advance £5,000 at 5% interest. The GN agreed, and, on 5 February, increased the order to 50 engines, allotted numbers 1 to 50 in the company's books. Delivery dates, agreed by Sharps, extended from June 1847 to December 1849, six in 1847, 14 in 1848, and the remainder in 1849. Only two were delivered in 1847 and, at GN request, construction of some later engines was slowed down, so the last two did not come to hand until September 1850. Individual delivery dates of all early engines will be found in Appendix 1. Sharps were requested to deliver the first six to Grimsby by water. However 1 and 2 were conveyed from Sheffield to Lincoln, and 3 and 4 from Derby to Lincoln, by the Midland. 5 and 6 were conveyed by Chaplin & Horne (who had extended their omnibus business to road haulage) by road to points on the EL. One got sunk on the road at Wragby. W. Wilson was paid £322 to convey engines from Lincoln to Louth and £30 for one to Firsby, but these would have probably included some of the goods engines lent to Petos. Later new engines were handed over at Peterborough by the Midland and the L&NW. 32 had evidently undergone some rough treatment for she arrived with her buffer plank broken.

Also on 11 December 1846 twelve 0-4-0 goods engines with four-wheel tenders were put on order. Bury, Curtis & Kennedy contracted to build six Nos 121–6 at £1,800 for the engines and £300 for the tenders. Leading dimensions were 5 ft wheels and 15 × 24 in cylinders. 121 was delivered to the company in March 1848, but the other five were handed to Petos, who returned them in December. Apparently Petos bought the engines, for in January 1849 Burys recommended that they should be paid £10,465 for six, originally costing £12,800. It is difficult to identify the sixth, which according to Bury's reckoning would have cost £2,300, but no doubt it was the one he reported as on loan to Petos when referring to the stock of engines at Peterborough on 29 August 1848.

The remaining six were ordered from Fairbairns of Manchester, generally similar to those by Burys. The wheels, however, were 5 ft 1 in, while the cost of the engines was £20 more and the tenders £20 less. Subsequently the price was reduced to £2,000 for each engine and tender. They were 127 to 132. Fairbairns and Burys had agreed to deliver a few engines in 1847, but none arrived until the following year.

Benjamin Cubitt's next order went to R. & W. Hawthorn of Newcastle on 13 January 1847, who agreed to build 35 engines at £1,876 and a similar number of tenders at £380. The types were twenty 2-2-2 passenger engines and fifteen 0-4-2 goods engines. The singles numbered 51–70, and had 6 ft driving wheels and 15 in × 21 in inside cylinders and were known as the small Hawthorns. The goods engines had 5 ft coupled wheels and 15 × 24 in inside cylinders, numbers 101–115. Hawthorns enquired how the GN proposed to distinguish their engines—by name or number? After consideration, it was resolved that engines should be numbered only. Before the order was completed, Bury recommended that the final 20 should be altered to light four wheeled coupled engines with 5 ft 6 in wheels and 13 × 20 in cylinders at an estimated expense of £1,500, but the board did not agree. Some, if not all, early engines were fitted with four brass number plates at Boston works, 9, 20 and 66 being so treated in August, and 10, 21, 121 and 125 in September 1849. Lamp irons had to be fitted, and head and tender lamps issued to many engines.

The pattern carriages from Walter Williams were delivered as under:

First class	7 February 1848	Cost £524
Second class	15 September 1847	Cost £430
Third class	17 September 1847	Cost £346
Luggage van	24 February 1848	Cost £297
Carriage truck	14 April 1848	Cost £225
Horse box (double)	14 April 1848	Cost £336

Williams was given an order on 31 March 1847 for 20 carriages intended for the EL, six first class, six second and eight third, to be charged for at the same rate as would be decided for the pattern carriages.

When the EL first opened, the company had taken delivery of four 'first', two 'second' and six 'third', one luggage van, and not a single goods vehicle. Williams received a further order for the EL on 11 October, for four composite carriages, to be charged at average price. They cost £524 apiece and were taken into stock as two composite saloons and two coupés. Two engines and some rolling stock were sold to the EL and subsequently re-purchased by the GN. This appears to be only a book transaction.

As soon as Bury arrived, he objected to the carriages from Williams, as too expensive and too heavy. He was authorised to have another set built to his own designs. He instructed Williams, and Joseph Wright of Birmingham to build six vehicles each to his specifications. The prices of the first, second and third class carriages were identical at £390, £270 and £245 respectively. Williams charged £215 for his luggage van (with brake), £130 for the carriage truck and £160 for the horse box against the £210, £152 and £130 of his competitor. Both firms, and Brown Marshall & Co, were given substantial orders. The cost of the three classes of carriages settled down to about £330, £214 and £160, with luggage vans also at £160. Some, if not all, of these carriages were finished in varnished teak. Williams specialised in this livery, and Bury approved of it. There is a strong possibility that GN passenger stock was never anything else but of varnished teak. It was certainly standard by February 1852, when the company agreed to purchase, for £315, a 'first' which Williams had put on show in the Exhibition, and declined to buy a companion vehicle, because it was painted in colours. There is no indication when green was adopted as the standard colour for the locomotive. A mail van was built by Williams for the New Holland route, delivered only on the day before it went into service. Two saloons were temporarily converted into mail vans by Williams.

The only goods vehicles ordered during Benjamin Cubitt's short regime were 60 ballast wagons from Neale & Wilson of Grantham at £75 each, and 20 cattle trucks and 20 sheep trucks from Ransomes & May of Ipswich. Four of the former, with fall down doors, were priced at £150, and the remainder at £142, while the sheep trucks cost £147 each.

From July 1848 the company began to contract for supplies of springs, wheels, axles, etc., which were forwarded to builders of goods and passenger vehicles, who in some cases constructed little more than frames and bodies.

Sixty open goods wagons were ordered from Ransomes & May on 13 April 1848, increased to 120 on 25 July. The price quoted was £98 each, delivered at Ipswich. The GN accepted the terms, provided the wagons were handed over at Peterborough, and it was left to Bury to negotiate with the makers. The GN paid £114 each for the first 20 and £98 each for the remainder. The first two of these were taken into stock on 23 October, and on the 31st, six covered wagons arrived from Joseph Wright who, on 10 August, had undertaken construction of 120 at £86 each.

The company was without goods brake vans until 28 November when two arrived from Joseph Wright. By an oversight this class of vehicle had been omitted when the contracts were placed. In consequence, Bury had urgently to order six at £143 each and seek authority for purchase in retrospect. In the early years the end panels of all brake vehicles, goods and passenger, were painted red.

Bury was instructed to have two or three coal wagons and cattle trucks built as patterns. The coal wagons were exhibited for manufacturers at Boston, and at Bishopsgate on the EC, in September 1849. Soon afterwards 350 were ordered from Smith & Willey and 300 from Ashburys. An offer of 300 second-hand L&NW coal wagons by Huish was declined. During 1849 many more open and covered wagons were put out to contract. Bury was authorised to obtain ten pairs of timber trucks.

The company had now provided for a supply of most classes of carrying stock. The system of distinguishing the rolling stock was curious, for every single type of carriage and wagon was numbered in its own series commencing at No. 1, a chaotic mess which Stirling cleared up.

With nearly 100 engines delivered or on order, Bury had little opportunity to exercise his talents as designer. There was the isolated instance of the engine he had personally ordered from Bury, a 2-4-0 passenger engine No. 100. She was taken into stock on 24 April 1849 with no price set against her, but the GN ultimately paid £2,200. The coupled wheels were 5 ft 9 in and the inside cylinders were 15 × 22 in.

Five six-coupled goods engines built by Hawthorns were taken into stock between 2 October and 27 November 1850, apparently ordered during Bury's superintendence. They had 5 ft wheels and 16 × 22 in cylinders (all GN 0-6-0's had inside cylinders), and were 116 to 120.

An engine was bought from Petos on 14 June 1849, built by C. Tayleur of Vulcan Works, and given the number 133. There was no indication of the details of her construction and one can only imagine that she was similar to the other Tayleur engines acquired in July 1850. There is some confusion as to how many engines were bought from Petos. Five were shown as taken into stock on 31 July 1850, and allotted the numbers 133 and 159–162. However, as has just been stated, a No. 133 had already been taken on the books. On the previous 18 April four of these had been valued to the company by J. V. Gooch, of the EC, as under:

(Petos Nos)		
1 delivered August 1847	Worked 237 days	Present value £1,921 0s 0d
2 delivered August 1847	Worked 298½ days	Present value £1,851 10s 0d
4 delivered November 1847	Worked 403 days	Present value £1,740 0s 0d
6 delivered November 1847	Worked 395½ days	Present value £1,749 10s 0d

These were 0-4-2 tender engines with 5 ft coupled wheels and 15 × 22 in inside cylinders. 159 and 160 were later in the year sent to be repaired at £200 to £250 each, while two others were lent to Brassey. Then in February 1852 it was discovered that with regard to No. 162, 'no such engine existed'. Thus the number remained a blank until 1 July 1863, when it was allotted to one of the engines taken over from the LB&HJ. From Sturrock's reports it is learned that an ex-Peto engine was used for some time as a stationary boiler at Boston and later moved to Doncaster for a similar duty. Now the question arises, was she the original No. 133? Had she been deleted from the running stock, and her number been re-allocated to the second Peto engine? Since the first engine had cost a mere £1,100, it is a matter of conjecture as to what her condition was. It is known that she was fitted with two new tyres at Boston in February.

Bury must have drawn up the specifications for the next two classes of new engines, but he was leaving, replaced by Sturrock (see chapter II), before tenders for their construction were opened on 26 March 1850. E. B. Wilson undertook to build ten passenger engines and tenders at £1,775 each, and ten goods engines and tenders at £1,825 each, to be delivered in 16 weeks from date of order. They offered to supply another five of each class with delivery in 20 weeks. Hawthorn's representative was then called in, undertook to supply the remaining five passenger and ten goods engines required on the same terms as Wilsons with delivery in 20 weeks. The passenger engines were 2-4-0's with 6 ft coupled wheels and 16 × 22 in inside cylinders, the Hawthorns numbered 71–75 and the Wilsons 76–90. The goods engines were 0-6-0's with 5 ft wheels and 16 × 24 in cylinders. The Hawthorns received numbers 134–143 and the Wilsons followed, 144–158. Sturrock, soon after his appointment, ordered modifications to the goods engines then building. Both firms agreed that the price should be increased by £100 to £1,925. The Haigh Foundry was paid 5s on each of about 20 engines, including 91–97 and 143, for the patent right on the mode of fastening on the wheels. It was arranged that builders should be paid half in cash and half in mortgage deeds for three years bearing 4½% interest. Similar arrangements were made from time to time with other contractors for locomotives and carriage stock.

About the time these engines were ordered, offers were received from the LB&SC, and EC, which had surplus engines to sell. Timothy Hackworth also wrote from Shildon, offering to dispose of an engine he had on hand. These offers were declined, but nevertheless the GN was feeling the pinch for goods engines. A little later in the year, when the traffic department wanted more power, Sturrock was authorised to buy a few odd engines which one or two builders had almost ready for delivery. He paid £2,000 each for one engine from Hawthorns and two from E. B. Wilson. Soon afterwards he was instructed to pay up to £1,900 for one engine offered by Shepherd & Todd. They were all 0-6-0 tender engines, with 5 ft wheels and 16 × 24 in cylinders, numbered 163–166 in the order described, and taken into stock in the autumn. A fifth, 167, was purchased from Wilsons soon afterwards and entered in stock in February 1851.

Baxter, with Thomas Wetherel the director, put Sturrock on the track of two passenger engines which Wilsons had for disposal, of the firm's well known 'Jenny Lind' type. Arrangements were made for them to be sent for trial. They were 2-2-2's with 6 ft driving wheels and 16 × 22 in inside cylinders. Given GN numbers 201 and 202, they arrived in November 1850 and February 1851 respectively. Wilsons agreed to accept £2,000 for each of them in the following July, but they were not on the stock book until February 1852. On several occasions Sturrock reported favourably on their performance, and it is surprising that he did not add to their number.

The GN main line offered something of a challenge to the moderately powered engines then owned. Yet on 4 December 1850 ten passenger engines, totally unsuited to the line, were ordered. Would-be makers were informed that drawings might be seen at Boston. Sixteen firms put in tenders. The order went to Longridges, Bedlington, who tendered £1,600 for each engine and tender. T. R. Crampton's patents were incorporated in their design. They were 4-2-0's, with 6 ft 6 in driving wheels behind the firebox, 16 × 21 in cylinders which drove a dummy crankshaft, numbers 91–99 and 200. In March 1851 Sturrock went to France to investigate the performance of some similar Cramptons on the Nord, and returned with enthusiastic reports. However, when the GN engines began work, these ungainly machines lacked sufficient adhesion, and were speedily converted to conventional 2-2-2's, although 200 underwent a transitional transformation as a 2-4-0 for a short time. A royalty of £50 was paid on each engine to Crampton on account of his patents. As a result of his visit to France, Sturrock had some hot water foot warmers made and tried. The directors approved, and foot warmers were in general use for first class passengers from January 1852.

In 1850 two Hawthorn coupled engines were sent to Wilsons for repairs and alterations. Sturrock received authority for this unusual procedure, when he pointed out that there was a turntable connection at Leeds with Wilson's works, and cost of haulage over foreign lines to and from Hawthorns would be saved. Engines from various makers continued to be sent to Wilsons for major repairs, until the GN provided accommodation for repair work.

Early in 1851, the necessity for more goods engines was becoming pressing. On 25 February Brown Neilson of Leeds agreed to build twenty 0-6-0's with 5 ft wheels and 16 × 24 in cylinders at £1,790 for each engine and tender, numbered 168–187. Twenty similar engines were ordered from Fairbairns at the higher price of £2,000, to be numbered 188–199 and 300–307. Fairbairns were affected by a prolonged strike of their workmen, which eventually forced them temporarily to close their works as from 10 January 1852. The GN cancelled half the order, and looked around for a builder free from the prevailing strikes, and did not give Fairbairns the opportunity to tender for future engine contracts. The ten engines ultimately completed received numbers 198, 199 and 300–307.

Thirty more 0-6-0's were ordered on 14 May 1851, with 5 ft 3 in wheels and 16½ × 24 in cylinders. Wilsons contracted to build ten, but failed for some reason not apparent. R. Stephenson & Co built ten at £2,320 for each engine and tender, numbered 308–317, while J. Nasmyth & Co of Patricroft, constructed ten at £2,220, 318–327.

In the autumn of 1851 Sturrock felt the need for more passenger engines, and recommended purchase of 20 single, and 10 coupled, engines. He explained that he had been running 80,000 miles a week, and 91,000 miles when the excursion traffic was at its peak and now with this additional traffic almost ceased, was still running over 83,000 miles per week. He considered that 64 engines should be in steam daily requiring a stock of 125, whereas the present stock was only 101. He reported 11 instances of the Sharps breaking their crank axles in the last four months, which he attributed to the high speeds they had to run with their small driving wheels, rather than fault in design or construction. He reminded the board that the imminent opening of the Towns line would call for more engine power. He proposed to alter one goods engine to a tank engine for shunting at Lincoln and Doncaster and, if successful, to alter two more. Actually he rebuilt all 12 four-coupled goods engines 121–132 as 0-4-2 tanks, the first six being supplied with saddle tanks, while 127–132 received side tanks.

There was no response to his appeals for more power. At the end of November he was back again, requesting 12 new passenger engines without tenders. He proposed to alter 12 little Sharps to tanks for about £400 each, so 12 tenders would be released for the new engines. He was authorised to spend £4,800 on these conversions. On 13 January 1852, the 12 engines, for which he had drawn up specifications, were ordered from Hawthorns at the price of £1,675. They were 2-2-2's with the 6 ft 6 in driving wheels and 16 × 22 in inside cylinders, numbered 203–214. They were known as the Large Hawthorns.

In March Sturrock was authorised to convert another 12 Sharps. An order was given to Wilsons for ten 0-6-0 goods engines to take the place of those cancelled out of the Fairbairn order. Numbered 188–197, they cost £1,945 each, and were given the tenders released by the latest Sharp conversions.

At the Board of Trade Inquiry into the Dorey House accident of 8 September 1852, in which one of these conversions ran off the road, Sturrock provided a list of rebuilt Sharps with the date on which they left the shops:

No. 19	24 January	No. 18	25 June
No. 46	11 March	No. 35	25 June
No. 40	19 March	No. 42	30 June
No. 45	19 April	No. 39	3 July
No. 10	28 April	No. 29	19 July
No. 1	10 May	No. 28	26 July
No. 6	19 May	No. 11	27 July
No. 9	22 May	No. 31	3 August
No. 2	26 May	No. 37	4 August
No. 50	21 June	No. 33	7 August

No. 32 was turned out a few days later and worked a test train at Dorey House.

In July 1852 Sturrock reported that he understood that the L & N W was building an engine which would be capable of running 100 miles at speeds of up to 60 and 65 mph. They were the 'patent' 2-2-2's built at Wolverton, but they never attained such speeds, and only had a short life. He thought that the GN should reply to this threatened competition, and on the 27th, was authorised to design such an express engine and have it built. Hawthorns undertook construction at an estimated cost of from £2,200 to £2,400. The engine, delivered on 6

August 1853, cost half as much again, and Sturrock was called upon to explain the bill for £3,500. He stated that he had modified the engine while building, and increased the tender capacity, now on 4 ft 5 in wheels instead of the intended 4 ft. He explained that the cost of building an individual engine was larger than the cost of one of a batch. He continued that the price of materials had risen, and considered that Hawthorns had under-estimated in the first place. He concluded with the opinion that they had built his engine without gaining profit. 215 was a 4-2-2 with a domeless boiler, 7 ft 6 in driving wheels and 17 × 24 in inside cylinders. Save for her bogie and smaller drivers, she was well described as a standard gauge edition of Gooch's 'Great Western.' The pressure was 150 lb and the heating surface 1,719 sq ft. Towards the end of the year Sturrock reported that the engine had been working between London and Peterborough, and her performance was successful. At the same time he would not advocate construction of further engines of her class for ordinary services on the line. Many years later, at an interview with Mr G. A. Sekon, editor of the *Railway Magazine*, Sturrock stated that he had undertaken to the board, if permitted to use engines of the type at least on the GN section, if not throughout, to run from King's Cross to Edinburgh in eight hours, stopping only at Grantham, York, Newcastle and Berwick. But he added that there was no demand for such high speeds at that time. This claim of Sturrock's has been accepted by such responsible writers as Bird, W. J. Gordon, and R. A. H. Weight, but it is not supported by contemporary records. It is probable that some such service was discussed. Sturrock further claimed that the engine had attained 75 mph, and was used continuously for 100 miles stretches—presumably from King's Cross to Grantham. A further claim by Sturrock about the engine is however to be found in Joy's diaries of the late 1850s. Sturrock told Joy that some directors had chaffed him, saying the engine had not done anything wonderful, but one day, he and the directors found the engine at Hitchin with a load of 14 coaches. They spoke to the driver, and the train ran 31 miles to Holloway ticket platform in 28 minutes, frightening the guard.

Like many engines built ahead of their times, 215 did not prove really safe or successful. There were blast pipe troubles, and even one or two derailments. The bogie had not sufficient side play. It has even been suggested that at first the engine had fixed leading wheels like its broad gauge prototype. In the circumstances, it is not surprising that the engine did not have a long life, being withdrawn in 1870. The drivers, however, had a much longer career, which will be described in volume II.

Sturrock further claimed that the design was a contributing cause for

Stirling's famous 8 footers. It is interesting to note that with these engines on the GN section, Edinburgh was reached in 8 hours, in the race of 1888, only 35 years later (see vol. II).

More goods engines were still required. On 17 May 1853 five were ordered from Kitson, Thompson & Hewitson at £2,750 for each engine and tender, and five from Hawthorns at £3,025. The Kitsons were 333–337 and the Hawthorns 328–332. Fourteen days later Wilsons were successful with their tender of £2,575 for ten similar engines, 338–347. All were 0-6-0's with 5 ft 3 in wheels and 16 × 24 in cylinders, as were 25 ordered on 3 January 1854. Sharp Stewart & Co (formerly Sharp Bros) of Atlas Works, Manchester, contracted to build 15 at £2,980, numbered 348–362. Vulcan Foundary, Warrington, supplied five at £2,925, numbers 363–367. The remaining five were to have been built by Wilsons but again, for no apparent reason, the order was not fulfilled.

Within a few weeks Sturrock was asking for another 25 goods engines. He proposed that tenders should be obtained for 21, and that the other four should be purchased from Charles Williams. He stated that these four, which he had designed, were built by Wilsons for Williams in connection with his contract with the Oxford, Worcester & Wolverhampton. Two were 2-4-0's, bought for £3,100 each and given numbers 216 and 217. They were stated to have 5 ft 9 in coupled wheels and 16 × 24 in inside cylinders, but after No. 216 came to grief at Algarkirk on 2 April 1862, the particulars supplied at the inquiry showed that the drivers were then 5 ft 6 in and the cylinders 16½ × 22 in. The other two were 0-6-0's with 5 ft 3 in and 16 × 22 in cylinders, costing £3,000 each and numbered 368 and 369. The remaining 21 were all 0-6-0's with similar dimensions. Orders were given on 28 February 1854 to Wilsons for 11, 370–380; Kitsons for five, 381–385, and Sharps for the remaining five, 386–390. The Wilsons and Sharps cost £3,100 each, and the Kitsons £3,150.

The hilly L B & H J line called for engines specially designed for heavy gradients. Soon after it opened Sturrock approached the board for authority to obtain six such engines. Hawthorns secured the order with their price of £3,100, 2-4-0's with 6 ft 6 in coupled wheels and 16½ × 22 in cylinders, 223–228.

The GN took over the Ambergate's stock on 30 June 1855. Records give few details about these nine engines apart from their numbers. The following are the particulars quoted by G. F. Bird in his excellent *Locomotives of the Great Northern Railway*:

AN & B

No.	Type	D.W.	Cyls.	Makers	Year	GN No.
1	0-4-0T	5′0″	11″ × 17″	Wilsons		218
2	0-4-0T	5′0″	11″ × 17″	Wilsons		219
3	0-4-0T	5′0″	11″ × 17″	Wilsons		220
4	2-2-2	6′6″	16″ × 22″	Hawthorns	1855	221
5	2-2-2	6′3″	15″ × 20″	Wilsons	1855	222
6	0-6-0	5′0″	16″ × 24″	Wilsons	1850	391
7	2-4-0	5′0″	16″ × 24″	Wilsons	1855	392
8	0-6-0	5′0″	16″ × 24″	Wilsons	1855	393
9	0-6-0	5′0″	16″ × 24″	Wilsons	1854	394

Opening of two more West Riding lines in 1857, Wakefield–Leeds, and Gildersome–Ardsley (chapter V), presented fresh problems. Sturrock wrote that the operation would mean discontinuing use of the small Sharps, and using coupled engines, due to the steep gradients. He continued that for the present he had arranged to work the lines with powerful coupled engines with one of the side rods taken off. No doubt he implied that he was using 0-6-0's as 2-4-0's or 0-4-2's. He proposed to alter eight Sharps into front coupled at an estimated cost of £300 each, which was authorised.

In 1859, Sturrock designed his best express passenger engine. These graceful locomotives were 2-2-2's with 7 ft driving wheels and 17 × 22 in inside cylinders. The order for 12 engines was split between three firms apparently to expedite deliveries. Nos 229–232 were built by Kitsons at £2,630, 233–236 by Sharps at £2,900, and 237–240 by Stephensons at £2,800.

Six 0-6-0 goods engines were taken over from the LB & HJ on 1 July 1863, given GN numbers 162 and 395–399. Bird gives some details. He was unaware that 162 was from the LB & HJ, but stated that it was by Kitsons. Of the others he listed 395 and 396 as being by Kitsons with 5 ft wheels and 16 × 24 in cylinders, 397 by Kitsons with 5 ft 3 in wheels and 16 × 24 in cylinders, and 398 and 399 by Hudswell Clark in 1863 with 5 ft wheels and 15 × 23 in cylinders. Bird depicted No. 399 as a tender engine, yet in 1863 Fraser reported on the success of the new tank engines acquired, which gives rise to a suspicion that 398 and 399 were tank engines.

Two years later, when the GN absorbed the WY, it took over another five engines which received GN numbers 261–263 and 470 and 471. Bird believed that 261, a 2-2-2, was built by Sharps for the EL, with 5 ft 6 in driving wheels. 262 and 263 were 5 ft 6 in 2-4-0's by Wilsons and 470 and 471 were six-coupled tanks by Manning Wardle with 4 ft 2 in wheels and

15 × 22 in cylinders. 470 rejoiced in the name of 'Marquis'. Bird's list gives the year of construction of these two as 1867, which is difficult to reconcile with the GN book which shows them as taken into stock in 1865, and remembering that the WY was absorbed in that year. Sturrock reported that all these needed repairs, and that one cost £240 to put it in order. From inference this would have been 261, apparently acquired by the WY for working excursion trains. The engines, fitted with condensing apparatus officially to work the Metropolitan in the emergency of August 1863, described in chapter X, were 110, Hawthorn 0-4-2, 161 (ex-Petos 0-4-2), several Hawthorn 0-6-0's including 138, some Wilson 0-6-0's including 155, and a few Sharp singles rebuilt as tanks.

Since 1863 Sturrock had been experimenting with a device which he had patented (No. 1135 of 6 May 1863). This was a steam tender which allowed him to utilise dead tender weight, to procure more adhesive and tractive force. He first took a spare Sharp tender and fitted it with two 12 × 17 in cylinders. These drove a crank axle fitted to the middle pair of wheels, the three pairs of wheels being connected by coupling rods. Steam was passed by pipes from the boiler. Exhaust steam was conducted into a condensing contrivance in the tender tank. In June 1864 the directors arranged with Sturrock that the company should be charged one half (not exceeding £50) for patent rights, as compared with other railways. Several of these tenders were constructed at Doncaster, some with 4 ft 6 in wheels and others 4 ft. In August Sturrock reported that the cost of making a new steam tender with 4 ft 6 in wheels was £816, and with 4 ft, £800. The cost of altering a GN tender was £787, and for a MS&L £750. In December he was authorised to expend £15,000 on these conversions.

Contracts were let for construction of engines complete with steam tenders. Hawthorns received an order for ten, Kitsons the other ten. The Kitsons were 400–409 and the Hawthorns 410–419. These 20 were the only engines taken into stock with the indication that they were fitted with steam tenders.

Further engines of the class, but without tenders, were ordered on 6 December 1864. Neilson supplied ten at £2,295, 420–429; and Kitsons ten more for £2,250, 403–439. Bird listed these latter as Hawthorns, and quoted the relevant maker's numbers. However, the contract was let to Kitsons and the stock book took them in as such. Kitsons were paid for them and there was no mention of the contract being sub-let.

Sturrock next designed some 0-4-2 tanks, especially for working over the underground lines. A contract for ten was awarded to the Avonside

Engine Co of Bristol on 6 December 1864. They had 5 ft 6 in coupled wheels and 16½ × 22 in cylinders, and were fitted with condensing apparatus. They cost £2,350 each and were 241–250. Sturrock referred to them as 'Metropolitan' engines. The term stuck. Throughout the life of the GN, any passenger locomotive working over the Widened Lines was known as a Metropolitan or Met engine. The *Railway Times* commented on the improvement of the working of the local services from Hatfield once these engines were in use.

Deliveries of new engines were seriously delayed by strikes throughout the iron industry in general, and engine building works in particular. With business expanding, and engines and wagons tied up at Holloway, the GN was desperately short of power and wagons. For several half-years the expense of hiring engines amounted to over £3,000 and wagons were often hired. In January 1865 the traffic people lamented that 25% more coal could have been carried if the company had sufficient engine power and siding accommodation. Much of the blame could be laid on the board, for the directors rarely acted upon the recommendations of Seymour Clark and Sturrock fast enough.

The Met was now in a position to return favour, and in December 1864 lent three engines (4-4-0 tanks), put to work on the local trains at an expense of about £190 a month. The MS&L also came to the rescue. Some engine diagrams which were in force from 19 December 1864 show:

	Ardwick	dep. 7.30 p.m.	Two MSL engines
arr. 5.30 a.m.	King's Cross	dep. 9.35 p.m.	
arr. 7.30 a.m.	Ardwick.		
	Peterborough	dep. 2.18 a.m.	One MSL engine One GN engine
arr. 7.50 a.m.	Leeds	dep. 9.30 p.m.	
arr. 3.00 a.m.	Peterborough.		
	Peterborough	dep. 2.10 p.m.	One MSL single passenger engine
arr. 5.25 p.m.	Doncaster	dep. 6.19 p.m.	
arr. 8.25 p.m.	Peterborough	dep. 6.00 a.m.	
arr. 7.07 a.m.	Grantham	dep. 11.23 a.m.	One MSL coupled passenger engine
arr. 1.00 p.m.	Retford	dep. 4.25 p.m.	
arr. 6.25 p.m.	Peterborough		

The MSL engines were manned by their own men, accompanied by GN pilotmen.

The GN lent some engines to the LC&D. On 11 September 1860 the directors agreed that engines should be lent, and six were on terms to be fixed by Sturrock, but the board declined to lend carriages and brake vans. According to Bird, the engines were 52–57. He, and other writers, suggest that they were lent two years earlier while the LC&D was still the East Kent, but this does not appear to have been the case.

Thirty more 0-6-0 goods engines with ordinary tenders were ordered on 7 February 1865. These again had 5 ft wheels and 16 × 24 in cylinders. Neilsons built ten costing £2,900 each, 440–449, the Vulcan Foundry six at £2,975, 450–455; Avonsides five at £3,000 456–460, and Hawthorns the remaining nine at £3,250, 461–469.

On the same day ten 2-4-0 engines were ordered from Sharp Stewart at £3,160 for each engine and tender, with 6 ft coupled wheels and 16½ × 22 in inside cylinders, 251–260.

With strikes continuing, the directors considered having engines built on the continent. Cail et Cie of Paris were willing to supply goods engines at £3,500 each, and Chas Everard of Brussels 12 engines at £3,000. Both offers were declined.

Sturrock was authorised on 21 March 1865 to obtain two 0-8-0 tanks from Avonsides, intended for goods traffic over the Widened Lines. They were generally similar to a pair of engines which Avonsides had supplied to the Vale of Neath. They cost £3,608 each, were adapted to the Met tunnels and platforms and fitted with condensing apparatus. They had 4 ft 6 in wheels and 18½ × 24 in outside cylinders, numbers 472 and 473.

Six 2-2-2's were ordered on 9 January 1866 from the Yorkshire Engine Co and John Fowler & Co. The price for each engine and tender from both builders was £2,890. Two months later it was decided that they should be 2-4-0's, at an additional cost of £175 each. Dimensions were 7 ft coupled wheels and 17 × 24 in inside cylinders. Fowlers were 264–266 and the Yorkshires 267–269.

The system of entering the precise date of delivery of each new engine ceased after 1 July 1863. From 1866 it became the practice to denote merely the half-year in which they were added to stock.

Sturrock reported on 16 January 1866 that the 50 steam tenders ordered were all at work, and giving satisfaction. Since only 20 steam tenders were purchased from outside builders, 30 must have been converted, or constructed in the Plant. No direct reference has been discovered which would lead to the belief that this figure of 50 was exceeded. Bird's story that orders were given for steam gear to be stripped from tenders of later engines prior to delivery must be incorrect, as the gear was never ordered. It seems probable that the number was confined to 50.

Three days later Sturrock wrote that the ten 'Met' engines had taken the place of four small GN Sharps (rebuilt as tanks, which were being repaired to work the St Albans and Dunstable branches), and the hired Met engines. The 0-4-2 tanks were successful. Ten more were ordered on 20 March 1866, five from Neilsons costing £2,380 each, 270–274, and five from Avonsides at £2,480, 275–279. This series was Sturrock's swan-song.

In 1862 he had commenced to use Bessemer steel tyres, and to fit carriages with wood-centred Mansell wheels. With two exceptions to be mentioned, all vehicles continued to run on four wheels only. As a result of the report on a minor accident at St Neots, Clarke wished for a trial of Fay's brake and recommended that it should be tried on new 40 ft carriages, to be ordered 'outside'. Doncaster Works was unable to undertake building these carriages, for it already had orders for passenger brake vans and composite carriages with which it was unable to cope 'owing to difficulties in obtaining materials from stores and inadequate facilities'. These had to be built by contractors too. Williams received the contract on 9 March 1858 for two 40 ft 'firsts' and two 40 ft 'seconds' at £450 and £380 each respectively, still on four wheels, with a wheelbase of 27. Williams was subsequently allowed another £35 per carriage for fitting the brake. No report on the success or otherwise of the brake is available. In April 1863 it was resolved that these long carriages should be converted to eight carriages of ordinary length for use over the Met.

A first class carriage was built at Doncaster for the L&SW in the spring of 1863, for £352 19s 11d. New carriages for local services, ordered on 13 January 1865, were constructed in pairs close coupled together. Twenty-two pairs of firsts were built by the Metropolitan Railway Carriage Co at £281 per carriage, and a similar number of seconds at £210 by Ashburys who also built 22 second brake composites with gas compartments at £245. Until 1863 all carriages had oil lamps. Then a few trains to Hitchin were altered to use gas, a supply of which was carried in a compartment in the brake vans. A new royal saloon was built in 1866 (to take the place of the three old saloons), which ran on six wheels. Doncaster commenced to turn out some six wheel brake vans, about this time, the extra pair of wheels being intended to provide additional braking power on heavy passenger trains.

The provision of more East Coast Joint Stock vehicles in 1866 has been described in chapter IX. The new brake vans then built had six wheels. As older joint stock vehicles were replaced, they were taken over, pro rata, by the parent companies.

Wagons, for the carriage of coke, delivered by John Ashburys from the end of 1850 were constructed of iron. Towards the end of Sturrock's tenure, the capacity of new coal wagons was increased from six to nine tons. Some old ones were re-constructed to carry a similar quantity. Side chains on wagons were dispensed with in 1857.

In June 1859 Sturrock was instructed to visit foreign countries to investigate use of oil as a lubricant. He found that some railways were successfully using it in preference to grease for axleboxes and introduced it on the GN. He was informed in April 1865 that the prohibition of the use of coal for passenger trains was rescinded. Seymour Clarke wrote to John Ramsbottom, locomotive superintendent of the L&NW, about the use of coal on its passenger trains, and after a favourable reply, persuaded his directors to sanction its use on the GN. A little over 7s a ton was paid for the quality which Sturrock considered best. From that time onwards, the Executive Committee received many claims for compensation in respect of line-side fires.

Much has been written about the shortcomings of Sturrock's steam tenders, but little can be found in official records. Two failings can be substantiated. First, the bill for repairs was uncomfortably high as the engines had long fireboxes, so that the boilers would make steam rapidly enough to provide for two sets of motion, and the strain imposed called for almost daily repairs to leaky tubes. Secondly footplatemen, already agitating for better conditions, had a natural objection to working what amounted to two engines for the price of one. While these engines could and did haul about 45 wagons against the 30 or so, the normal load for a conventional six-coupled engine, sidings so far provided were not long enough to accommodate the extra wagons. Soon after Stirling took control, he made his first report, dated 22 November 1866, analysing the steam tenders' performance. The figures proved that their abnormally high cost of repairs by far outweighed any advantage they possessed in capability for hauling greater loads. This was the death knell to Sturrock's expensive experiment. By 30 June 1867, nine tenders had been dismantled. Stirling received authority to build new tenders for the 20 engines ordered without tenders, and by then, eight had been completed. Stirling's report on the condition of the rolling stock (particularly on the locomotives) was not flattering to Sturrock's management.

Very soon Stirling persuaded the directors of the need for 40 new engines. Orders for these were placed on 12 March 1867, 20 0-6-0 goods engines with 5 ft 1 in wheels and 17 × 24 in cylinders, ten by John Fowlers, 474–483, and the others by Neilsons, 484–493. Each engine and tender cost £2,350. The second 20 were 2-4-0's with 6 ft 7 in coupled wheels and 17 × 24 in cylinders, ten from Avonsides, 280–289, and ten from Yorkshire Engine Co, 290–299, price £2,370 each.

Stirling soon got the Plant organised, and before the close of the year built three engines there. On 29 April he reported on the 50 original Sharps engines, stating that 21 had been renewed and he now proposed to renew the other 29 out of revenue at the rate of six each half-year. (This report infers that Sturrock had not converted eight Sharps into front-coupled engines as per the authority of November 1857.) For a start Stirling proposed to replace three for use on the Leeds and Bradford traffic. The directors approved. In this manner, Stirling practically obtained a mandate to replace worn out engines by new ones without further authority from the board, and seven years elapsed before any more locomotives were built out of capital. The new engines took the numbers of those they replaced.

His initial design was for an 0-4-2 mixed traffic engine with 5 ft 7 in coupled wheels and 17 × 24 in cylinders. The cost of these engines was as under:

No. 18, £1,673 12s 3d less value of scrap £178 8s 10d = £1,495 3s 5d net
No. 23, £1,703 10s 6d less value of scrap £161 7s 11d = £1,542 2s 7d net
No. 40, £1,633 0s 8d less value of scrap £142 1s 8d = £1,490 19s 0d net

The average cost of engines and tenders was £1,922 15s 4d. These engines received the Doncaster Works numbers 1, 2 and 3 respectively.

The position of shed foreman-cum-district locomotive superintendent at Peterborough was one of the most important once the Towns line was opened. Thomas Owen had been in charge from the first, and when he was overtaken by a mental illness in 1854 he was succeeded by C. R. Sacré. In 1859 Sacré resigned to become locomotive superintendent of the M S & L. But the next four men resigned to take positions elsewhere. Francis Cortazzi (assistant at Doncaster) went in 1860, followed by W. S. Brown who resigned in the next year. James Johnson (who left Louth to take charge at Doncaster), moved to Peterborough and stayed only two years. Alfred Sacré was next but in 1865 he resigned to join the Yorkshire Engine Co. All the promotions and resignations resulted in a frequent 'General Post' among the men at the minor sheds. At this stage, R. C. Hornby was at Peterborough and C. Troward at Doncaster.

There was no obvious reason why Sturrock should have retired so early in life. It has been said that he married a wealthy widow, or inherited a small fortune on her death. There is no doubt that he was in a position to live very comfortably for the next 40 odd years. He hunted and shot, and, in his own words 'sat as a J P until he was too deaf to hear the witnesses'. He died on 1 January 1909 at the age of 92. He is probably remembered best for increasing the steam pressure of his boilers from 80 lb to 150 lb, and for his invention of the steam tender. Even if No. 215 failed to come up to expectations, Sturrock did design some splendid engines, as witness the GN's predominance in speed. The 7 ft singles, 229–240, made a name for themselves. Despite a propensity for fracturing crank axles, the large Hawthorns, 203–214, were allocated to working the best trains in the 1860s. The converted Cramptons and 'Jenny Linds' ran well on the lighter trains, especially the Manchester expresses of 1857.

Appendix I

DELIVERY DATES OF LOCOMOTIVES 1847–STURROCK'S RESIGNATION, 1867

No.	Date	No.	Date	No.	Date	No.	Date
1	29 Oct 1847	**38**	18 Dec 1849	**75**	10 Jul 1851	**112**	16 Jan 1849
2	29 Oct 1847	**39**	28 Dec 1848	**76**	28 Apr 1851	**113**	31 Mar 1849
3	– Feb 1848	**40**	28 Dec 1849	**77**	29 Apr 1851	**114**	25 Apr 1849
4	– Feb 1848	**41**	4 Mar 1850	**78**	3 May 1851	**115**	15 May 1849
5	30 Mar 1848	**42**	4 Mar 1850	**79**	18 May 1851	**116**	19 Oct 1850
6	30 Mar 1848	**43**	29 Mar 1850	**80**	24 May 1851	**117**	26 Oct 1850
7	13 May 1848	**44**	29 Mar 1850	**81**	7 Jun 1851	**118**	6 Nov 1850
8	13 May 1848	**45**	20 Jun 1850	**82**	13 Jun 1851	**119**	6 Nov 1850
9	10 Jun 1848	**46**	20 Jun 1850	**83**	21 Jun 1851	**120**	27 Nov 1850
10	10 Jun 1848	**47**	29 Jun 1850	**84**	30 Jun 1851	**121**	30 Mar 1848
11	1 Jul 1848	**48**	29 Jun 1850	**85**	30 Jun 1851	**122**	– Dec 1848
12	1 Jul 1848	**49**	4 Sep 1850	**86**	18 Jul 1851	**123**	– Dec 1848
13	25 Aug 1848	**50**	4 Sep 1850	**87**	27 Jul 1851	**124**	– Dec 1848
14	25 Aug 1848	**51**	28 Oct 1848	**88**	9 Aug 1851	**125**	– Dec 1848
15	21 Sep 1848	**52**	10 Nov 1848	**89**	25 Aug 1851	**126**	– Dec 1848
16	21 Sep 1848	**53**	25 Jan 1849	**90**	21 Sep 1851	**127**	24 Oct 1848
17	7 Oct 1848	**54**	8 Mar 1849	**91**	21 Apr 1851	**128**	11 Nov 1848
18	7 Oct 1848	**55**	31 Mar 1849	**92**	11 May 1851	**129**	19 Dec 1848
19	24 Dec 1848	**56**	5 May 1849	**93**	31 May 1851	**130**	1 Jan 1849
20	24 Dec 1848	**57**	19 Jun 1849	**94**	21 Jun 1851	**131**	8 Oct 1849
21	– Dec 1848	**58**	16 Aug 1849	**95**	17 Jul 1851	**132**	19 Oct 1849
22	– Dec 1848	**59**	30 Aug 1849	**96**	29 Jul 1851	**133**	14 Jun 1849
23	17 Apr 1849	**60**	14 Sep 1849	**97**	17 Aug 1851	**133**	31 Jul 1850
24	17 Apr 1849	**61**	4 Oct 1849	**98**	22 Nov 1851	**134**	27 Nov 1850
25	9 May 1849	**62**	5 Nov 1849	**99**	21 Feb 1852	**135**	4 Dec 1850
26	9 May 1849	**63**	15 Aug 1850	**100**	24 Apr 1849	**136**	14 Dec 1850
27	11 Jul 1849	**64**	17 Aug 1850	**101**	8 Apr 1848	**137**	19 Dec 1850
28	11 Jul 1849	**65**	28 Aug 1850	**102**	8 Apr 1848	**138**	27 Dec 1850
29	1 Oct 1849	**66**	4 Sep 1850	**103**	8 Apr 1848	**139**	9 Jan 1851
30	1 Oct 1849	**67**	7 Sep 1850	**104**	27 Apr 1848	**140**	18 Jan 1851
31	20 Oct 1849	**68**	23 Sep 1850	**105**	23 Aug 1848	**141**	27 Jan 1851
32	20 Oct 1849	**69**	2 Oct 1850	**106**	30 Sep 1848	**142**	4 Feb 1851
33	21 Nov 1849	**70**	10 Oct 1850	**107**	28 Oct 1848	**143**	11 Mar 1851
34	21 Nov 1849	**71**	17 May 1851	**108**	19 Nov 1848	**144**	25 Oct 1850
35	6 Dec 1849	**72**	25 May 1851	**109**	29 Nov 1848	**145**	24 Oct 1850
36	6 Dec 1849	**73**	21 Jun 1851	**110**	19 Dec 1848	**146**	28 Oct 1850
37	18 Dec 1849	**74**	21 Jun 1851	**111**	16 Jan 1849	**147**	18 Nov 1850

No.	Date
148	22 Nov 1850
149	25 Nov 1850
150	2 Dec 1850
151	12 Dec 1850
152	18 Dec 1850
153	28 Dec 1850
154	17 Jan 1851
155	20 Jan 1851
156	20 Jan 1851
157	31 Jan 1851
158	31 Jan 1851
159	31 Jul 1850
160	31 Jul 1850
161	31 Jul 1850
162	1 Jul 1863
163	8 Nov 1850
164	28 Oct 1850
165	2 Dec 1850
166	27 Oct 1850
167	10 Feb 1851
168	24 Oct 1851
169	1 Nov 1851
170	8 Nov 1851
171	22 Nov 1851
172	29 Nov 1851
173	6 Dec 1851
174	15 Dec 1851
175	19 Dec 1851
176	24 Dec 1851
177	3 Jan 1852
178	17 Jan 1852
179	31 Jan 1852
180	31 Jan 1852
181	7 Feb 1852
182	16 Feb 1852
183	21 Feb 1852
184	13 Mar 1852
185	20 Mar 1852
186	1 Apr 1852
187	7 Apr 1852
188	28 Aug 1852
189	7 Sep 1852
190	16 Sep 1852
191	5 Oct 1852
192	29 Oct 1852
193	11 Nov 1852
194	29 Nov 1852
195	7 Dec 1852
196	2 Jul 1853
197	15 Jul 1853
198	22 May 1852
199	16 Aug 1852
200	29 Mar 1852
201	– Jul 1851
202	– Jul 1851
203	19 May 1852
204	27 May 1852
205	16 Aug 1852
206	28 Aug 1852
207	7 Sep 1852
208	2 Oct 1852
209	23 Oct 1852
210	30 Oct 1852
211	28 Dec 1852
212	1 Feb 1853
213	16 Mar 1853
214	1 Sep 1853
215	6 Aug 1853
216	30 Mar 1854
217	30 Mar 1854
218	30 Jun 1855
219	30 Jun 1855
220	30 Jun 1855
221	30 Jun 1855
222	30 Jun 1855
223	29 Jun 1855
224	23 Jul 1855
225	31 Jul 1855
226	9 Aug 1855
227	17 Aug 1855
228	8 Sep 1855
229	12 May 1860
230	22 Jun 1860
231	28 Jun 1860
232	1 Aug 1860
233	9 Jun 1860
234	27 Jun 1860
235	3 Jul 1860
236	28 Feb 1861
237	8 Aug 1860
238	8 Aug 1860
239	7 Sep 1860
240	6 Oct 1860
241	1865
242	1865
243	1865
244	1865
245	1865
246	1865
247	1865
248	1865
249	1865
250	1866
251	1866
252	1866
253	1866
254	1866
255	1866
256	1866
257	1866
258	1866
259	1866
260	1866
261	1865
262	1865
263	1865
264	1866
265	1866
266	1866
267	1867
268	1867
269	1867
270	1866
271	1866
272	1866
273	1866
274	1866
275	1866
276	1866
277	1866
278	1866
279	1866
300	16 Sep 1852
301	23 Oct 1852
302	30 Nov 1852
303	29 Dec 1852
304	5 Aug 1853
305	24 Sep 1853
306	17 Oct 1853
307	23 Dec 1853
308	15 Dec 1851
309	1 Jan 1852
310	1 Jan 1852
311	17 Jan 1852
312	31 Jan 1852
313	10 Feb 1853
314	21 Feb 1852
315	13 Mar 1852
316	20 Mar 1852
317	2 Apr 1852
318	27 Jul 1852
319	5 Oct 1852
320	11 Nov 1852
321	19 Nov 1852
322	18 Dec 1852
323	31 Dec 1852
324	19 Jan 1853
325	20 May 1853
326	10 May 1853
327	30 Jun 1853
328	21 Nov 1853
329	30 Nov 1853
330	21 Dec 1853
331	21 Jan 1854
332	11 Feb 1854
333	25 Oct 1853
334	9 Nov 1853
335	30 Nov 1853
336	16 Dec 1853
337	30 Dec 1853
338	8 Feb 1854
339	17 Feb 1854
340	28 Feb 1854
341	11 Mar 1854
342	30 Jun 1854
343	12 Jul 1854
344	22 Jul 1854
345	3 Aug 1854
346	12 Sep 1854
347	27 Sep 1854
348	22 Jul 1854
349	29 Jul 1854
350	2 Aug 1854
351	9 Aug 1854
352	14 Aug 1854
353	25 Aug 1854
354	19 Sep 1854
355	29 Sep 1854
356	2 Oct 1854
357	14 Oct 1854
358	23 Oct 1854
359	26 Oct 1854
360	31 Oct 1854
361	14 Nov 1854
362	18 Nov 1854
363	28 Nov 1854

No.	Date	No.	Date	No.	Date	No.	Date
364	9 Dec 1854	**392**	30 Jun 1855	**420**	1866	**448**	1866
365	15 Dec 1854	**393**	30 Jun 1855	**421**	1866	**449**	1866
366	21 Dec 1854	**394**	30 Jun 1855	**422**	1866	**450**	1866
367	29 Dec 1854	**395**	1 Jul 1863	**423**	1866	**451**	1866
368	30 Mar 1854	**396**	1 Jul 1863	**424**	1866	**452**	1866
369	30 Mar 1854	**397**	1 Jul 1863	**425**	1866	**453**	1866
370	17 Oct 1854	**398**	1 Jul 1863	**426**	1866	**454**	1866
371	13 Jan 1855	**399**	1 Jul 1863	**427**	1866	**455**	1866
372	30 Jan 1855	**400**	1865	**428**	1866	**456**	1866
373	12 Apr 1855	**401**	1865	**429**	1866	**457**	1866
374	22 Jun 1855	**402**	1865	**430**	1865	**458**	1866
375	30 Jun 1855	**403**	1865	**431**	1866	**459**	1866
376	31 Jul 1855	**404**	1865	**432**	1866	**460**	1866
377	14 Aug 1855	**405**	1866	**433**	1866	**461**	1866
378	29 Aug 1855	**406**	1866	**434**	1866	**462**	1866
379	18 Oct 1855	**407**	1866	**435**	1866	**463**	1866
380	7 Nov 1855	**408**	1866	**436**	1866	**464**	1866
381	13 Jan 1855	**409**	1866	**437**	1866	**465**	1866
382	25 Jan 1855	**410**	1865	**438**	1866	**466**	1866
383	9 Feb 1855	**411**	1865	**439**	1866	**467**	1866
384	24 Feb 1855	**412**	1865	**440**	1866	**468**	1866
385	18 Feb 1855	**413**	1865	**441**	1866	**469**	1866
386	19 Dec 1855	**414**	1865	**442**	1866	**470**	1865
387	28 Dec 1855	**415**	1865	**443**	1866	**471**	1865
388	1 Jan 1856	**416**	1865	**444**	1866	**472**	1866
389	3 Jan 1856	**417**	1865	**445**	1866	**473**	1866
390	3 Jan 1856	**418**	1865	**446**	1866		
391	30 Jun 1855	**419**	1865	**447**	1866		

Appendix II

EXECUTIVES AND OFFICERS 1846–1867

Chairmen

William Astell[1]	1846–1847
Edmund Beckett Denison	1847–1864
George Hussey Packe	1864–1867

Deputy Chairmen

Edmund Beckett Denison[6]	1846–1847
Samuel James Capper[1]	1846–1847
George Hussey Packe	1847–1864
Hon. Octavius Duncombe	1864–1867

Directors

William Amsinck[8]	1846–1867
James Arbouin[1]	1846–1861
Hon. William Ashley[3]	1846–1847
Frederick Pratt Barlow[2]	1846
John Barff[1]	1846–1864
William Sprott Boyd[3]	1846–1847
John Brightman[3]	1846–1847
Robert Walter Carden[3]	1846–1847
Duncan Macdonnel Chisholm[3]	1846–1847
James Nesbit Colquhoun[1]	1846–1854
Hon. Octavius Duncombe[4]	1846–1850 1858–1864
John Carles Dundas[2]	1846
Richard Ellison[1]	1846–1850
Henry John Enthoven[2]	1846
John Nathaniel Foster[3]	1846–1847
Robert Gill[1]	1846–1849
Joseph James Hegan[2]	1846
John Peirse Kennard[2]	1846
John Milligan Laws[1]	1846–1849
John Learmouth[3]	1846–1847
William Skinner Marshall[1]	1846–1848
James Meek[1]	1846–1862
Samuel Mills[2]	1846
William Morley[3]	1846–1847
William Mountford Nurse[1]	1846–1850
George Hussey Packe[5]	1846–1847
Francis Parker[1]	1846–1862
Archibald Frederick Paull[1]	1846–1848 1857–1861
John Pickersgill[1]	1846–1849
Francis Pym[1]	1846–1860
Frederick Ricketts[3]	1846–1847
Rev. Humphrey Waldo Sibthorp[2]	1846
Thomas Wetherel[1]	1846–1858
Charles Chaplin	1846–1860
John Harvey Astell[9]	1847–1867
Isaac Burkill	1850–1860
George Humphrys	1850–1852
Graham Hutchinson	1850–1858
Charles Atticus Monck	1850–1857
George Walker[9]	1852–1857
Charles Wilson Faber[9]	1854–1867
Charles Turner[9]	1859–1867
Edward Christopher Egerton[9]	1862–1867
Samuel Waterhouse[9]	1863–1867
Lord Colville[9]	1863–1867
Robert Tennant[9]	1863–1867
Christopher B. Denison[9]	1865–1867
William Firth[9]	1866–1867

Managing Director

James Milligan Laws	1846–1848

Superintendent & Locomotive Engineer

Edward Bury	1849–1850

General Manager

Seymour Clarke[9]	1850–1867

Secretaries

James Ryder Mowatt	1846–1858
Henry Oakley[9]	1858–1867

Accountants

Andrew Mylne	1846–1847
Thomas Reynolds	1847–1857
Henry Oakley	1857–1858
James Church Grinling	1858–1865
William Grinling[9]	1865–1867

Locomotive Engineers

Benjamin Cubitt	1846–1848
Edward Bury	1848–1850
Archibald Sturrock	1850–1866
Patrick Stirling[9]	1866–1867

Engineers

John Miller	1846–1847
Joseph Cubitt	1846–1855
Walter Marr Brydone	1856–1861
Richard Johnson[9]	1861–1867

Superintendents of the Line

John Denniston	1849–1853
Walter Leith	1853–1863
John Currey	1863–1865
Francis Pickersgill Cockshott[9]	1865–1867

Goods Managers

George Thompson	1849–1862
John Ashley[9]	1863–1867

Mineral Managers

P. M. Middlemiss	1850–1861
John Ashley	1862
William Newton[9]	1863–1867

Storekeepers

William Pulford	1848–1866
W. Nicholls[9]	1866–1867

Solicitors

Robert Baxter	1846–1853
Joseph Leech[9]	1846–1867

Notes

1. Directors named in the Act.
2. Directors named in the Act and ballotted off the board 25 July 1846.
3. Directors named in the Act and ballotted off the board 27 February 1847.
4. Director named in the Act and elected Deputy Chairman December 1864.
5. Director named in the Act, elected Deputy Chairman March 1847, Chairman December 1864 and continued in office after 1867.
6. Director named in the Act and elected Chairman March 1847.
7. Elected 25 July 1846.
8. Director named in the Act and continued in office after 1867.
9. Continued in office after 1867.

BIBLIOGRAPHY

General Works

Acworth, Sir William, *The Railways of England*, John Murray, 1889

Allen, Cecil J., *Railways of To-day*, F. Warne, 1929

Allen, Cecil J., *The Great Eastern Railway*, Ian Allan, 1955

Ahrons, E. L., *Locomotive and Train Working in the Latter Part of the Nineteenth Century*, Heffer, 1927

Ahrons, E. L., *Development of British Locomotive Design*, Locomotive Publishing Co., 1925

Anderson, P. Howard, *Forgotten Railways of the East Midlands*, David & Charles, 1973

Bird, G. F., *Locomotives of the Great Northern Railway*, Locomotive Publishing Co., 1st ed. 1902; 2nd ed. 1910

Bucknall, Lt. Col. R., *Our Railway History*, (published by the author) 1945

Cassell's Railways of the World, Cassell, 1924

Cassell's Railway Wonders of the World, Cassell, 1935

Casserley, H. C., *Britain's Joint Lines*, Ian Allan, 1968

Christianson, R. and Miller R. W., *History of the North Staffordshire Railway*, David & Charles, 1971

Dow, G., *History of the Great Central Railway*, Locomotive Publishing Co., Volume I 1959, Volume II 1962, Volume III 1965

Dow, G., *The Alford and Sutton Tramway*, Oakwood Press, 1968

Ellis, C. Hamilton, *The Trains We Loved*, Allen & Unwin, 1948

Ellis, C. Hamilton, *The North British Railway*, Ian Allan, 1959

Ellis, C. Hamilton, *The Royal Trains*, Routledge & Kegan Paul, 1975

Fellows, Canon R. B., *Railways to Cambridge*, Oakwood Press, 1948

Ferriday, P., *Lord Grimthorpe*, John Murray, 1957

Foxwell, E., *English Express Trains*, E. Stanford, 1884

Foxwell, E. with Farrar, J. C., *Express Trains, English and Foreign*, E. Stanford, 1889

Franks, D. L., *The Great Northern and London and North Western Joint Railway*, Timetable Enterprises, 1974

Gairns, J. F., *Railways for All*, Ward Lock, 1923
Gordon, D. J., *Regional History of Railways of Great Britain*, Volume 5 *The Eastern Counties*, David & Charles, 1968
Gordon, W. J., *Our Home Railways*, F. Warne, 1910
Griffiths, R. P., *The Cheshire Lines Railway*, Oakwood Press, 1947
Grinling, C. H., *History of the Great Northern Railway*, Methuen, 1st ed. 1898, 2nd ed. 1903, 3rd ed. (by Borley H. V. and Ellis, C. Hamilton) 1967
Grinling, C. H., *The Ways of Our Railways*, Ward Lock 2nd ed. 1910
Hodge, P., *The Hertford Loop*, Southgate Line Trust, 1976
Howden, J. R., *Book of Railways*, Grant Richards, 1910
Hoole, K., *The Hull and Barnsley Railway*, David & Charles, 1970
Joy, H., *Railways of West Riding*, Ian Allan, 1970
Lambert, R. S., *The Railway King 1800–71*, Allen & Unwin, 1934
Leech, R. H. and Body, M. G., *The Stirling Singles*, David & Charles and Macdonald, 1965
Leleux, R., *Regional History of the Railways of Great Britain*, Volume 9 *The East Midlands*, David & Charles, 1970
Lewin, H. G., *The Railway Mania and its Aftermath*, Railway Gazette, 1937
LNER publication, *The Flying Scotsman*, 1925
'Manifold', *The North Staffordshire Railway*, Henstock of Ashbourne, 1950
Marshall, H., *History of the Lancashire and Yorkshire Railway*, Volumes I and II, David & Charles, 1960
Nock, O. S., *The Railways of Britain*, B. T. Batsford, 1948
Nock, O. S., *The Great Northern Railway*, Ian Allan, 1958
Nock, O. S., *The Railway Race to the North*, Ian Allan, 1958
Nock, O. S., *The Caledonian Railway*, Ian Allan, 1961
Normington, T., *The Lancashire and Yorkshire Railway*, Heywood of Manchester, 1895
Pattinson, J. Pearson, *British Railways*, Cassell, 1893
Pendleton, J., *Our Railways*, Cassell, 1896
Robbins, M., *The North London Railway*, Oakwood Press, 1934
Ruddock, J. G., and Pearson, R. E., *Railway History of Lincoln*, J. G. Ruddock & Ferbners, 1974
Scott, Rev. W. J., *Great Northern Speeds*, Kegan Paul, 1889
Scott, Rev. W. J., *Kinnaber*, Kegan Paul, 1895
Stretton, Clement C., *The Midland Railway*, Methuen, 1895
Steel, W. L., *The London and North Western Railway*, Railway and Travel Monthly, 1914

Tatford, B., *Story of British Railways*, Sampson, 1946
Tomlinson, W. W., *The North Eastern Railway*, Andrew Reid & Co., 1915
Thomas, J., *Obstruction Danger*, Blackwood & Sons, 1937
Tuplin, W. A., *Great Northern Steam*, Ian Allan, 1971
Vallance, H. A., *History of the Highland Railway*, Stockwell, 1938
Weight, R. A. H., *Great Northern Locomotives 1847–1947*, (published by the author) 1947
Weight, R. A. H., *Railways before the Grouping: the Great Northern*, Ian Allan, 1950
Wilmot, G., *The Railway in Finchley*, Barnet Libraries, 2nd ed. 1974
Wright, N. R., *The Railways of Boston*, Richard Kay, 1971
Young, G. L., *Great Northern Suburban*, David & Charles, 1977

Periodicals
Bradshaw's Railway Guide
Bradshaw's Railway Manual
Directory of Railway Officials
Illustrated London News
Locomotive Carriage and Wagon Review
Luton Recorder and Bedford News
Modern Railways
Railways (later Transport) and Travel Monthly
Railway Gazette
Railway Magazine
Railway News
Railway Pictorial
Railway Times
Railway Year Book
Railways
Trains Illustrated

Reports
Board of Trade reports on accidents and on opening of new railways
Directors' meetings
Directors' reports
Engineers' reports
Shareholders' meetings reports
Law Reports, Hare's 1851, Exchequer 1854, Law Times, 1861
Railway and Canal Cases, 1850–5
Reports of the Railway and Canal Commission

Halsbury, *Laws of England (Hailsham edition) 1932–7*, Butterworths
Articles:
'Carriers' by Bruce Thomas KC and E. Maxwell (Butterworths)
'Railways' by Lord Wright and R. E. Manningham Buller (now Lord Dilhorne)
Statutes, Public and Private

INDEX

Index

A creative textile journey

STICKS AND STONES

by Annette Morgan

TEAMWORK
CRAFTBOOKS

Sticks and Stones
First published in 2013 by Teamwork Craftbooks

Photographs by Annette Morgan, Kevin Mead at Art Van Go, Louise Batten and Jono Batten.

I would like to thank Chris and Gail Lawther for their superb design and editing skills in making this book possible. Thanks also to my wonderful family for their love and support – the Morgans, the Peaurts and the Battens!

ISBN: 978 0 9553499 8 0

British Library Cataloguing in Publication Data
A catalogue record for this book is available from the British Library

Designed by Teamwork, Christopher and Gail Lawther
100 Wiston Avenue, Worthing, West Sussex, BN14 7PS
e-mail: thelawthers@ntlworld.com website: www.gaillawther.co.uk

Printed by Foundry Press, Unit A, Foundry Lane, Horsham, RH13 5PX
www.foundry-press.co.uk

Contents

Introduction

Since I became involved in textiles in the early 1990s, my inspiration has always been the world around me. I take lots of photos and I may use them for inspiration, transfer the images directly to fabric or manipulate the images on my computer using design programmes.

The focus of this book is to show you how you can use a topic for inspiration, how to get started with design ideas, and then how you can transfer your ideas to fabric. I am primarily an 'art quilter,' so many of my techniques may seem to be quilt-related, but these are all ideas which can be used for embroidery – I've included some samples of embroidery in this book too. This is not a book of projects, but one which I hope will inspire you to create your own works of art.

I have included some of Daniel Morgan's work in this book as I feel it complements my own. Dan is my husband; he trained as a painter and taught art for many years, both in high schools and in adult education. We often work in the same space and comment on each other's art – but only when asked! Dan's work (see *Terrace,* right) is more pictorial than mine, whereas much of my work has developed into an abstract way of thinking, looking at elements of shape, colour and line.

Annette

Inspiration

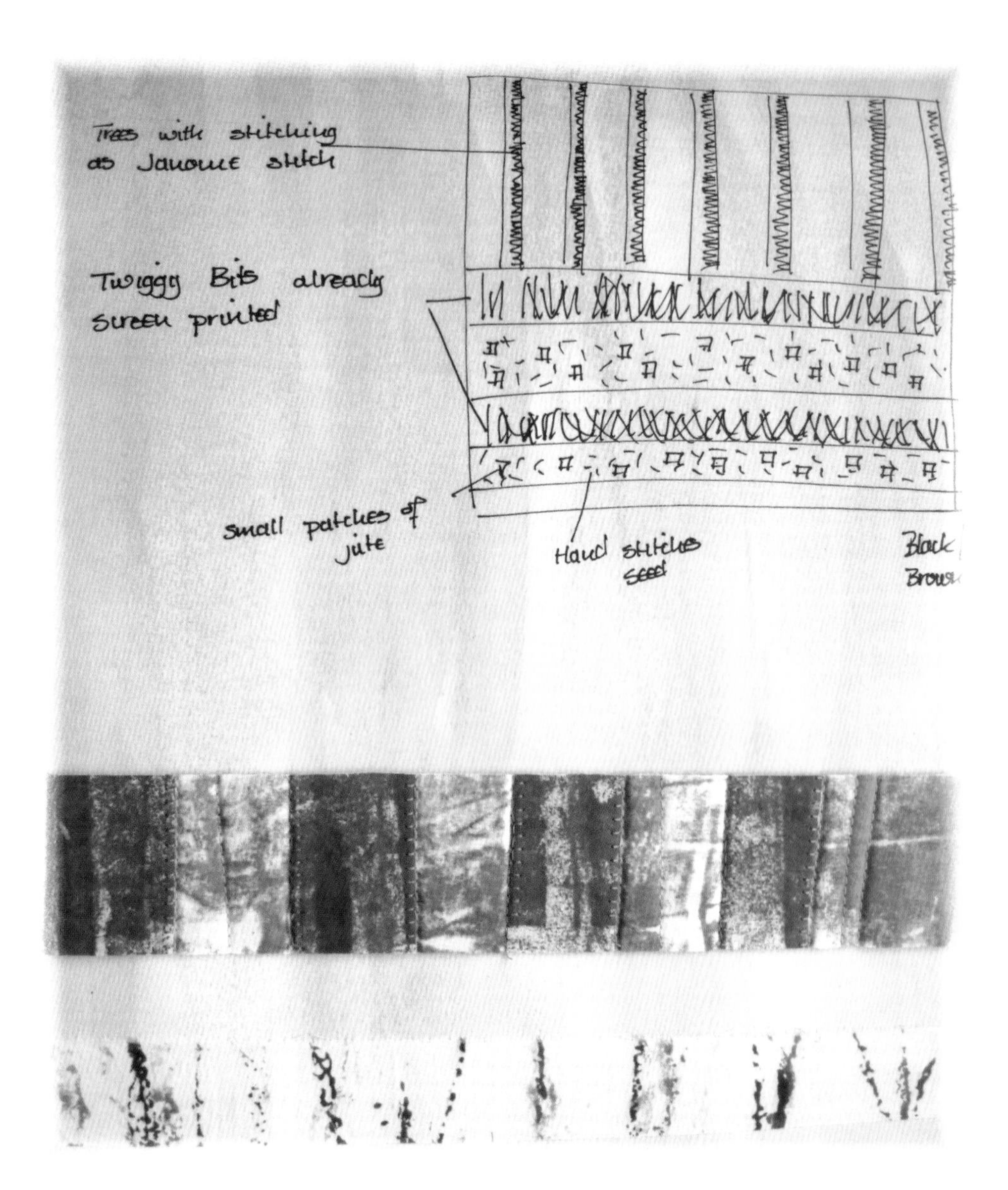

My inspiration comes from what I see around me – hence the title ***Sticks and Stones***. I now live in Thetford, having lived in other parts of East Anglia for most of my life. Thetford is surrounded by the Brecks and Thetford Forest. The Brecks is an area lying on the borders of Norfolk and Suffolk; it has a unique landscape with sandy soils, glowing with purple heather and marked by wind-twisted Scots pines. The local buildings are made using flint which was mined locally, and many cottages – including our own – have pantiled terracotta roofs.

I confess that I'm not very good at drawing, but I do make quick sketches to focus my mind; often I work in an intuitive way. Some teachers insist that you should draw every day, and build up wonderful detailed sketchbooks, but I find this too restrictive for me – and I know that stitchers can find the thought of these beautiful sketchbooks rather intimidating.

You need to work in a way that suits you and your style of working. Some people like to have several projects on the go at once, but others just like to work on one thing at a time and see it through. I often work in a series, and this allows me to develop new skills, and play around with different techniques I may not have tried before; it also provides a body of work which could be exhibited. I have to say here that I like the *process of making*, and if my work gets exhibited, sold or selected for shows then that's a bonus for me.

My preferred method is to take photos of what I see around me (and indeed actual photos have now found their way into my work). If I only drew or held images in my head, I know I would miss the finer details which are captured by film/pixels. I also take photos of smaller pieces of work and transfer these images to fabric, and in turn include these in my work – look closely and you will see them! They have become part of the whole, and some viewers have missed them ...

I play around with images, screen-print what has inspired me from those images using silk screens or thermofaxes, make small embroideries or just use scissors on paper or fabric – with these I *can* draw!

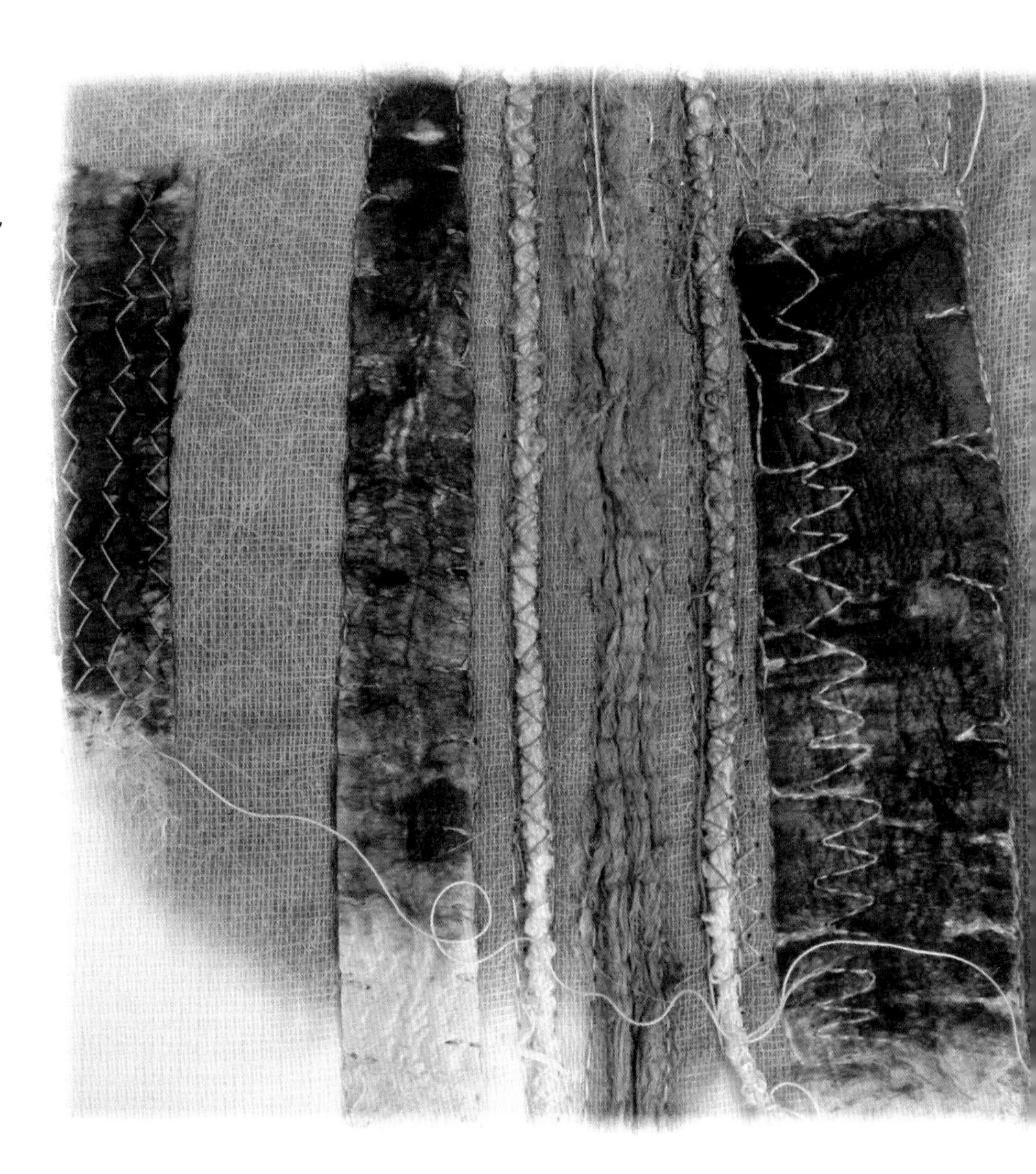

Opposite: notes from my sketchbook for the Sticks and Stones *hanging on page 29*

Right: sample of applied silk rods painted with textile ink

STICKS AND STONES INSPIRATION

Thetford forest is planted with Corsican pines; the planting of these is rotated to produce wood for – among other things – telegraph poles. Areas are cut down when the pines are mature, and then left fallow before being planted again. In some areas wild flowers grow in profusion, including foxgloves, thistles (below) and lupins.

Lines of Scots pines can be seen crossing the Brecks, and they have become a distinctive feature of the landscape. They were planted many years ago as windbreak hedges to stop the precious topsoil blowing away, and to create large areas for sheep farming. The twisted pines are a key feature of the Brecks area logo, and my husband has painted many pictures of these trees, including *Scots Pines* (left).

Many of the older buildings in Thetford were built using flint, and the church in the centre of Thetford, St Peter's, is known as the Black Church as it's faced with dark-coloured flint. Flint has been used in this area since prehistoric times and several mines have been found near Munford, in an area known as Grimes Graves. The mined flint would have been made into sharp implements such as arrowheads and axes. In Brandon flint was knapped to make flints for guns. Looking around the town, flint for building has been used in many ways and the photos on this page demonstrate this.

Chalk is also a local building material, and often the thick walls of cottages (including ours) were made from chalk then faced with flint, with chalk incorporated into the walls. Clunch is the East Anglian word for chalk, and clunch pits are often found in flint areas, as the two are used together.

Words of Inspiration

I often find it helpful when I'm thinking of a subject to brainstorm ideas. I do this as a spider diagram (mind-map) or I make lists of words – this help to focus the mind! Shown here are some of the words and ideas I came up with for the local area when I was doing the initial research for the ***Sticks and Stones*** collection – see page 34 for more ideas along these lines.

Glossary

clunch: chalk which was cut into building blocks and forms the inner part of walls in old houses

rabbit warrens: areas where rabbits were farmed for the their meat and pelts

meres: small lakes

electric forest: an event during winter when the forest is lit up at night; a bonfire is lit and stories told

forests glades wood bark wood piles

avenues of deciduous trees birch trees

pine trees wild flowers muntjac deer

deer walkers dog-walkers sandy soils

rabbits rabbit warrens Ministry of Defence land

firing range meres open spaces

skies sunsets birds bracken

electric forest total darkness flint

chalk clunch brick pantiles

colours greys and black of the flint

white of the chalk,

greens and browns of the forest,

pinks of the wild flowers

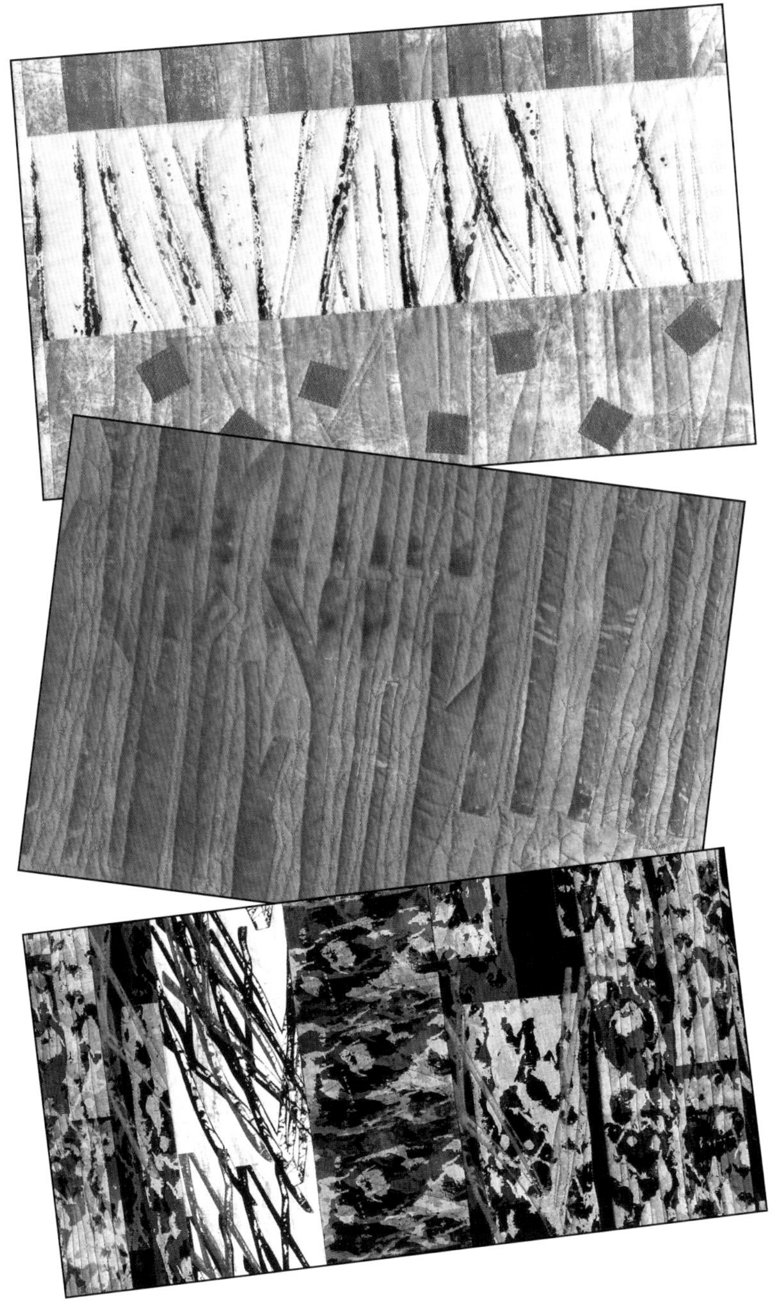

Sticks and Stones GALLERY

The collection of quilts on the following pages is from my exhibition called ***Sticks and Stones***, first exhibited at the Festival of Quilts in Birmingham 2013 and then travelling to other venues. The collection is based mostly on photographs and thoughts about the building materials used in my locality (flint and chalk) and the forest, which is right on the boundaries of Thetford.

I wanted to use my inspirations of Thetford along with my favourite fabric colouring and stitch techniques, which I have developed to suit my own style. I like nothing more than decorating my own fabrics, and I can spend several days screen printing fabrics with simple freezer paper stencils and thermofax screens – I then have a large stash of fabrics ready to hand whenever the creative urge to make a quilt arises! I find great satisfaction in this process of making and designing my own printed fabrics, so that everything I incorporate into my work demonstrates my own personality.

Thetford Forest 1

Inspiration: photographs of trees in Thetford Forest

Techniques: *left-hand section,* images of trees manipulated on the computer, transferred onto fabric using T-shirt transfer paper, then cut and pieced. *Middle section,* screen-printed fabric with procion dye paste. *Right-hand section,* dyed fabric, screen-printed with discharge paste using a thermofax screen with my own design. Machine quilted.

Size: 30 x 130cm (11.5 x 51in)

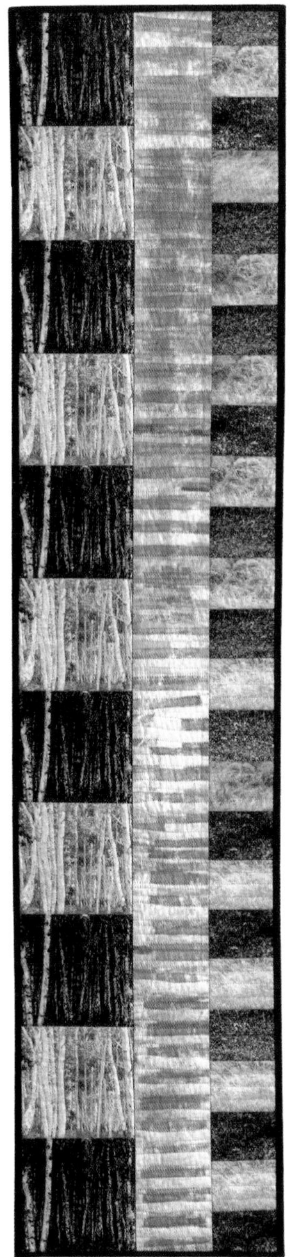

Thetford Forest 2

Inspiration: photographs of trees in Thetford Forest

Techniques: *left-hand and right-hand sections*, image manipulated on the computer, transferred onto fabric using T-shirt transfer paper, then cut and pieced. *Middle section*, fabric screen-printed with procion dye paste. Machine quilted.

Size: 30 x 130cm (11.5 x 51in)

Pink Birch Bark 1

Inspiration: a photograph of birch bark

Techniques: I made a thermofax screen based on photographs, then screen-printed the fabrics using textile screen inks and discharge paste. Machine quilted.

Size: 80 x 96 cm (23.5 x 37.5in)

Pink Birch Bark 2

Inspiration: a photograph of birch bark

Techniques: I made a thermofax screen based on photographs, then screen-printed the fabrics using textile screen inks and discharge paste. Machine quilted.

Size: 31 x 104 cm (12 x 41in)

Silver and Pink Birch and Bark

Inspiration: a photograph of birch bark and young birch trees

Techniques: I used a thermofax screen which I'd created based on photographs, then screen-printed fabrics using textile screen inks and discharge paste. Machine quilted.

Size: 99 x 110 cm (39 x 43in)

Brown Birch and Bark

Inspiration: inspired by birch trees and their bark, and playing around with the screen-printing designs

Techniques: I made a thermofax screen based on photographs, then screen-printed fabrics using textile screen inks and discharge paste. The brown fabric was hand-dyed. Machine quilted.

Size: 87 x 132cm (34 x 52in)

Breckland Pines

Image of Scots pine trees; created with polystyrene block prints, using acrylic paints.

North Stowe

Polystyrene block-printing using acrylic inks

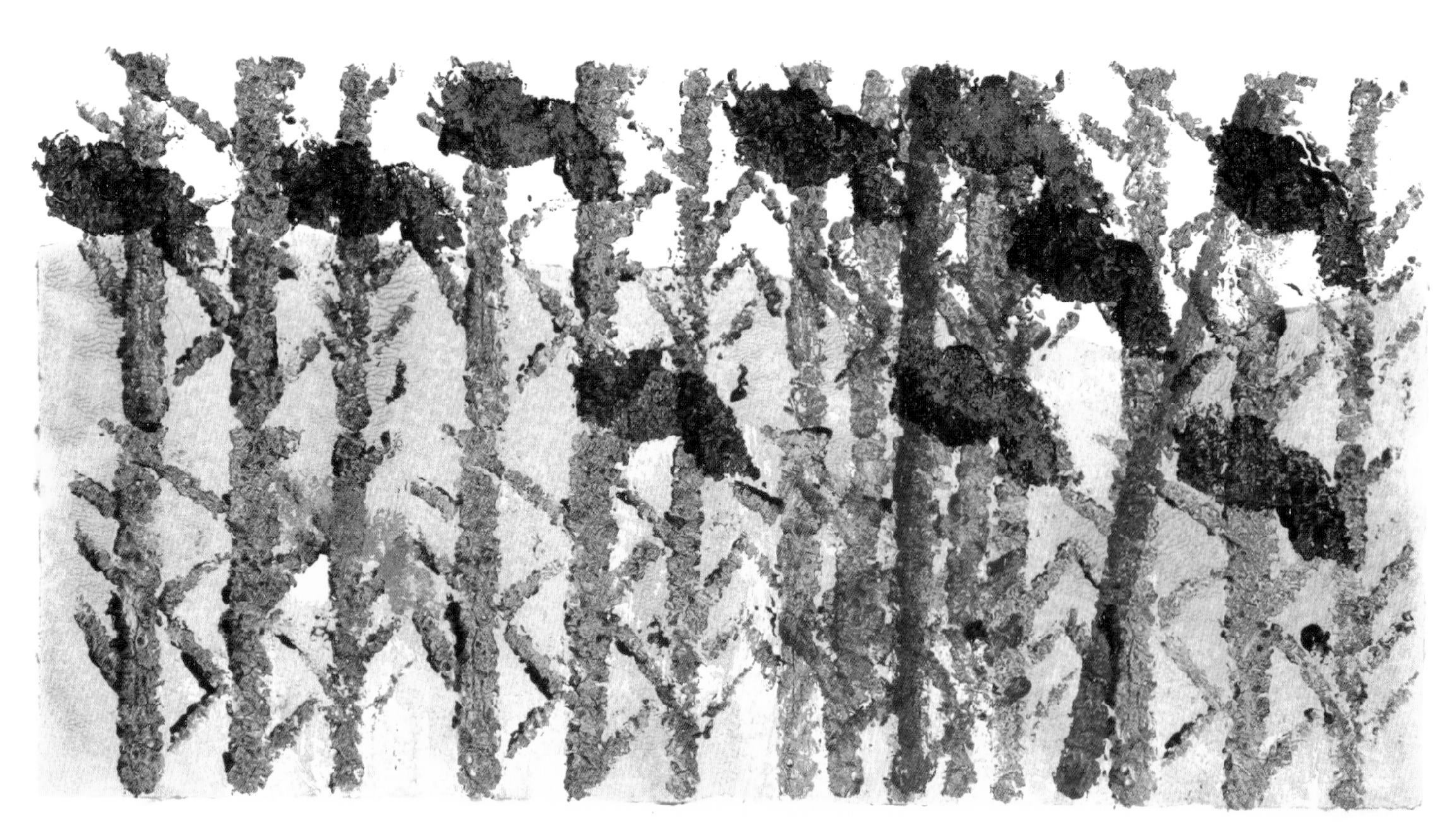

Pine Cones

Polystyrene block-printing using acrylic inks

Thetford Priory 1

Inspiration: photos taken of Thetford Priory ruins

Techniques: I printed the photos onto paper and T-shirt transfer paper, then printed them onto white fabric. Machine quilted, with scrim applied and brushed with paint to highlight the texture.

Size: 31 x 107cm (12 x 42in)

Thetford Priory 2

Inspiration: photos taken of Thetford Priory ruins

Techniques: I printed the photos onto paper and T-shirt transfer paper, then printed them onto white fabric. Machine quilted, with scrim applied and brushed with paint to highlight the texture.

Size: 31 x 107cms (12 x 42ins)

Red Trees

Inspiration: based on artwork in my sketchbook

Techniques: wholecloth white fabric screen-printed using a freezer paper mask. Machine quilted.

Size: 76 x 102cm (30 x40in)

Sketchbook inspiration

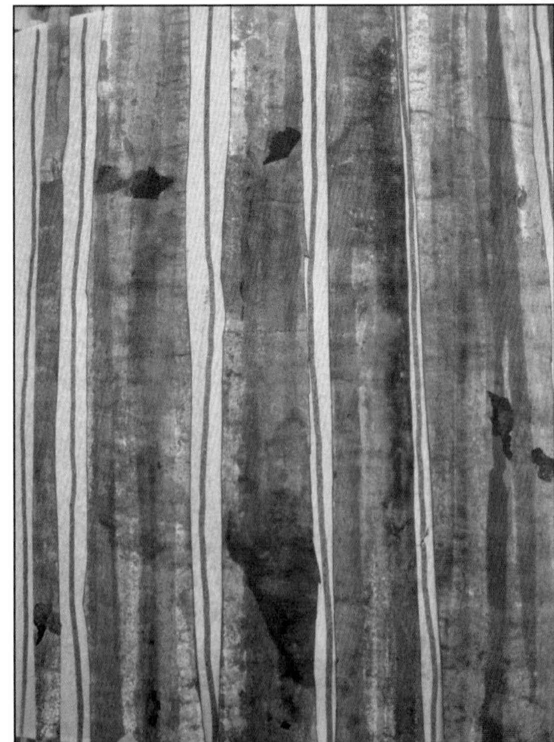

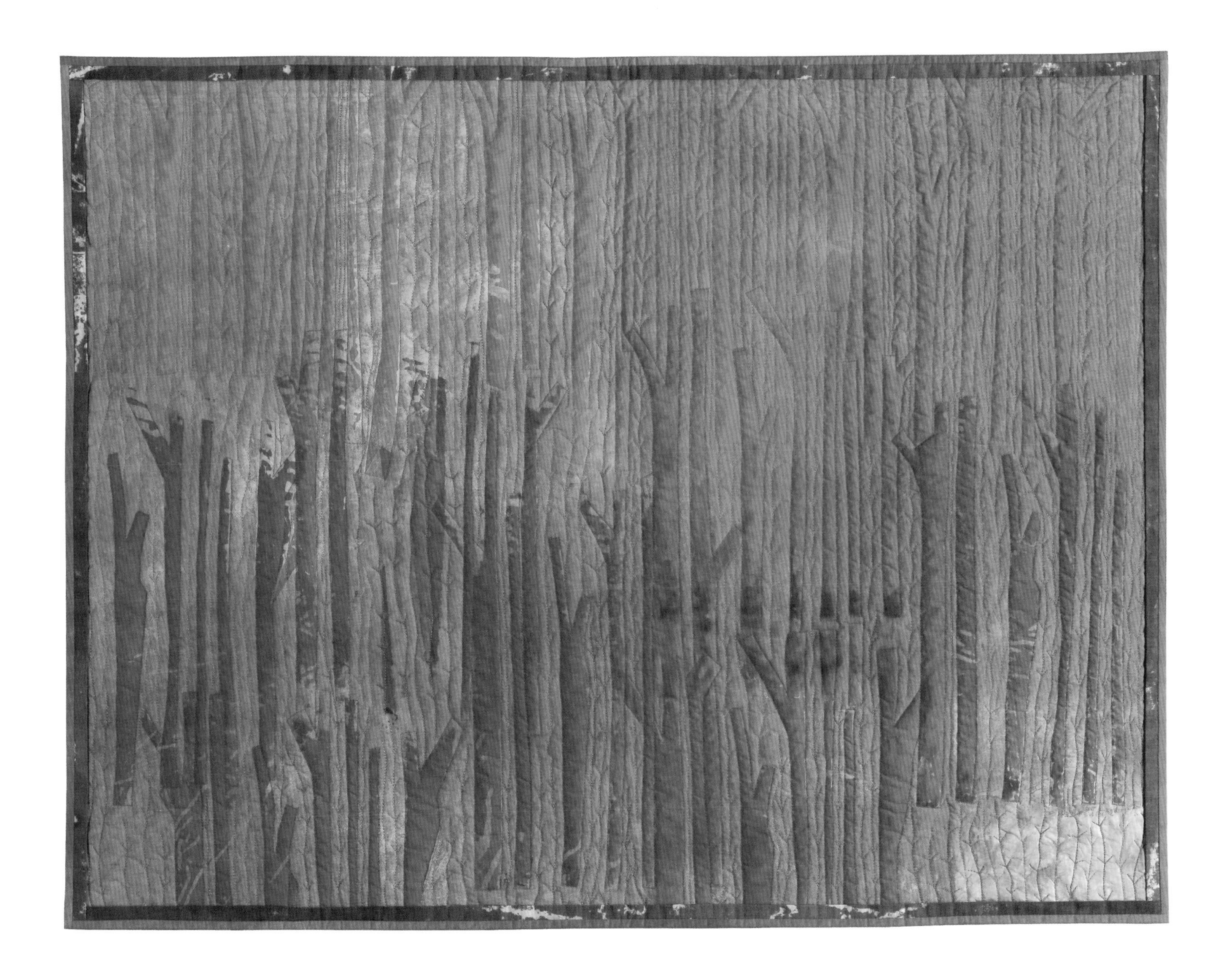

Sunset Rhythm
Polystyrene block-printed with acrylic paints

Winter Rhythm
Polystyrene block-printed with acrylic paints

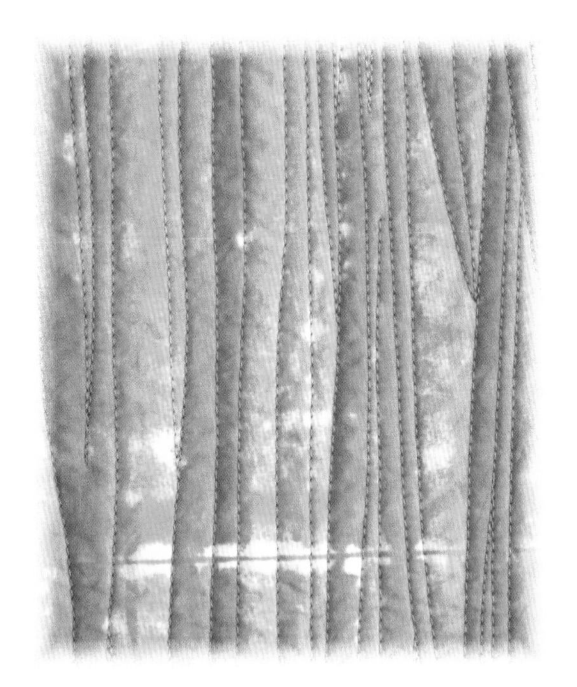

Grey Trees

Inspiration: shapes of trees cut into a paper mask for silk-screening

Techniques: screen printed, machine quilted.

Size: 56 x 79 cm (22 x 31in)

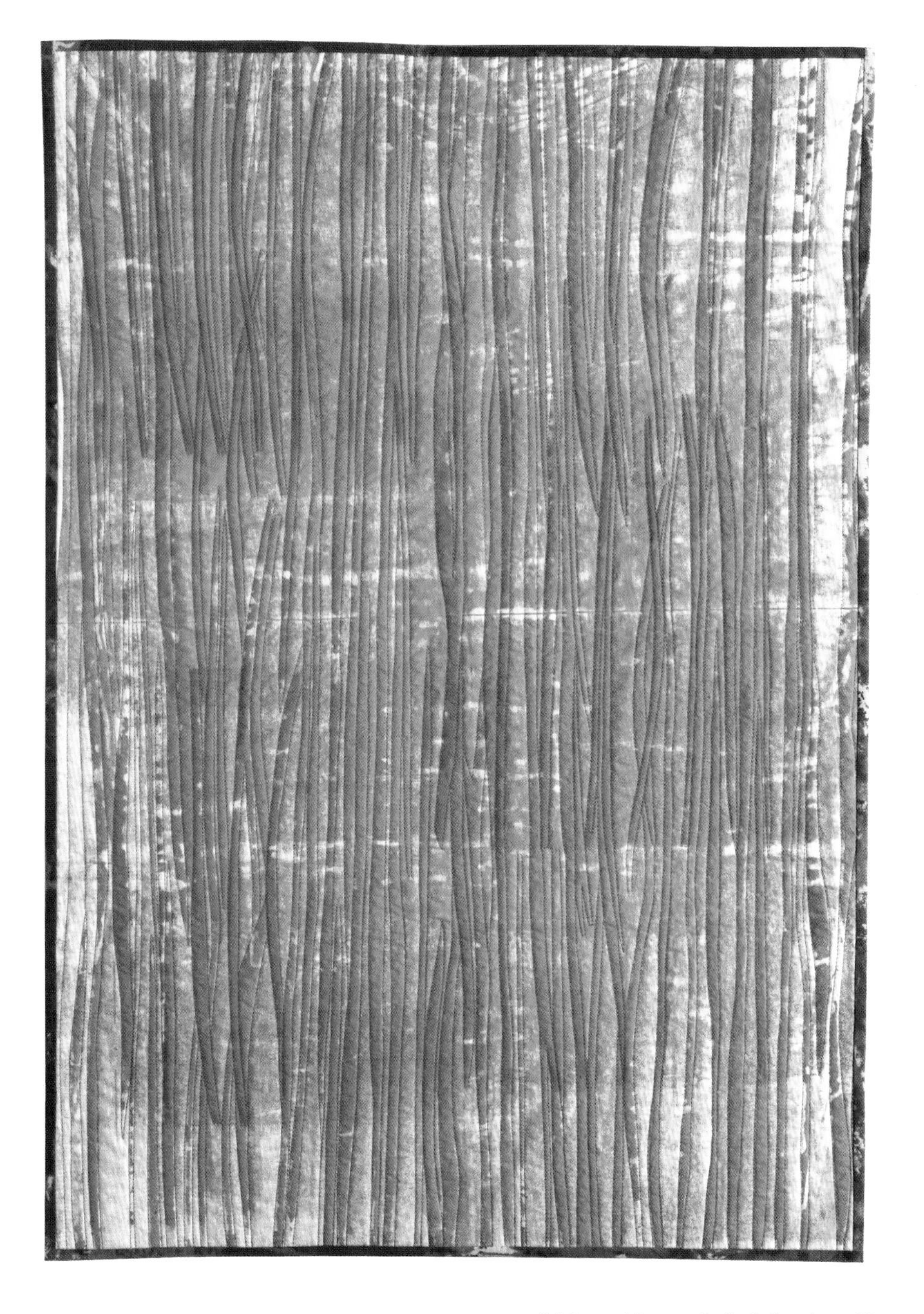

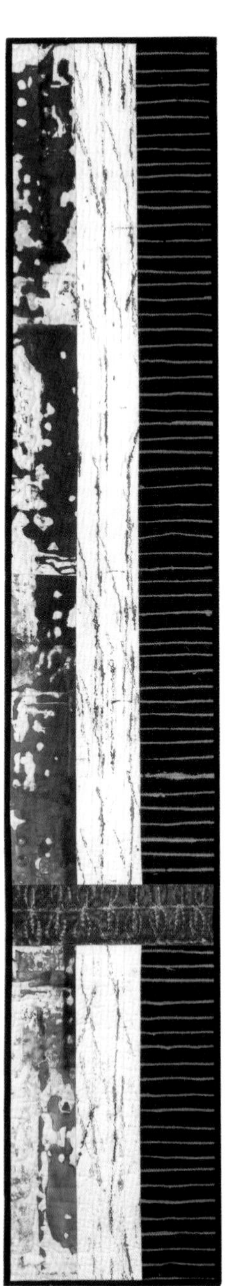

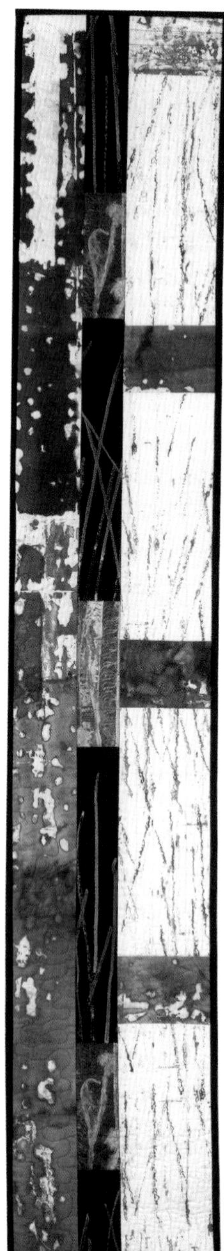

Sticks and Stones Triptych

Inspiration: flint walls and sticks

Techniques: screen-printed and discharged fabrics, machine-embroidered fabrics photographed and printed onto fabric; machine pieced and machine quilted.

Size: each panel is 26 x 138 cm (10 x 54in)

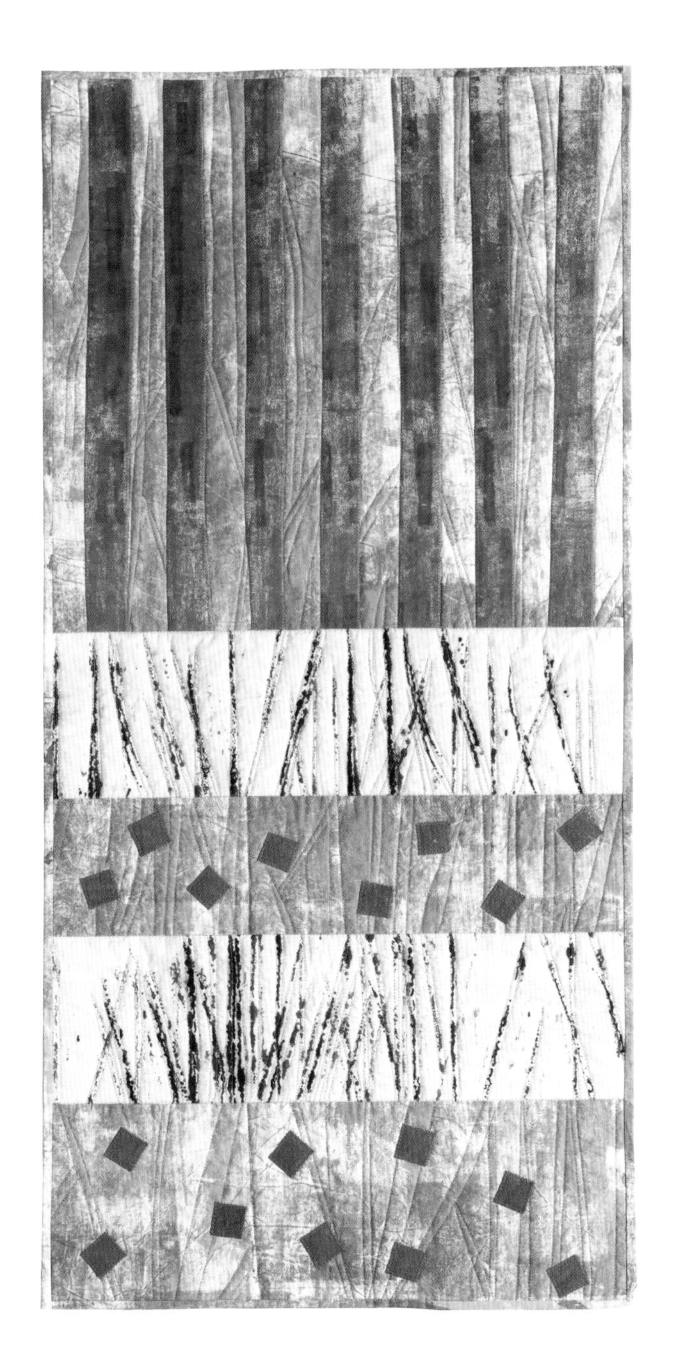

Sticks and Stones ...

Inspiration: experimental marks made on fabric following the tree theme

Techniques: screen-printed fabrics created using paper masks; I machine quilted the piece, and applied small squares of bark cloth.

Size: 49 x 102cm (19 x 40in)

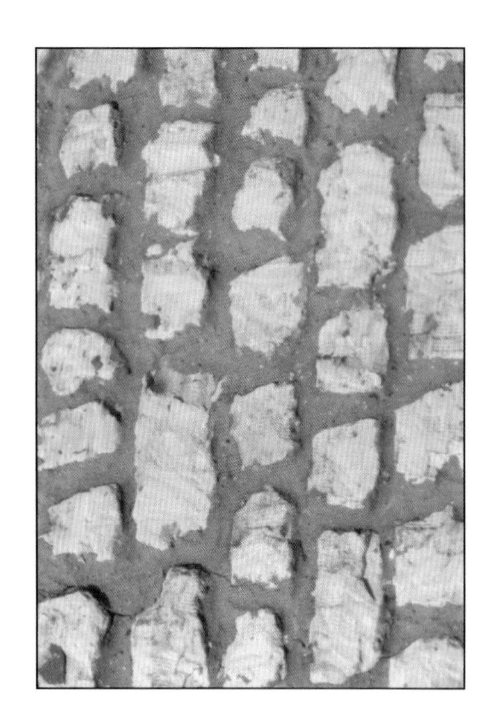

Chalk, Flint and Jags 1

Inspiration: based on flint walls

Techniques: screen-printed fabrics, and photos of flint walls transferred onto fabric; I used a rollerball pen to paint dye paste and discharge paste onto fabric to create the stick design. Collaged, machine quilted.

Size: 60 x 80 cm (23.5 x 31.5in)

Chalk, Flint and Jags 2

Inspiration: based on flint walls

Techniques: screen-printed fabrics, and photos of flint walls transferred onto fabric; I used a rollerball pen to paint dye paste and discharge paste onto fabric to create the stick design. Collaged, machine quilted.

Size: size 69 x 104cm (27 x 41in)

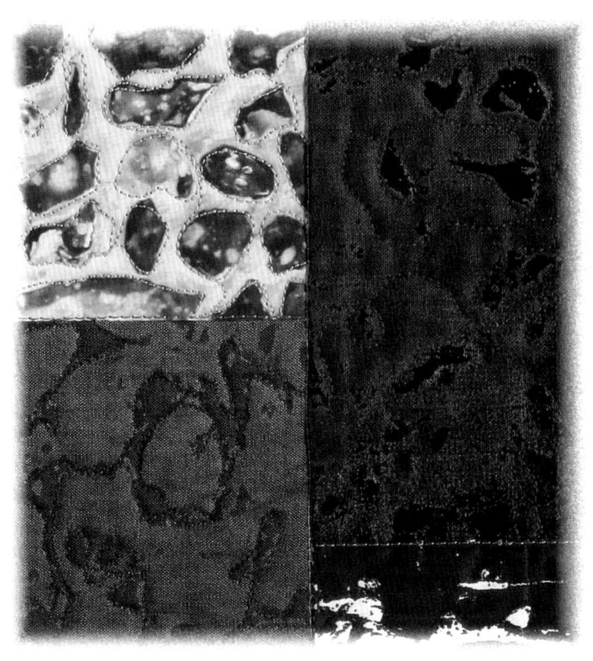

Chalk, Flint and Jags 3

Inspiration: based on flint walls

Techniques: screen-printed fabrics, and photos of flint walls transferred onto fabric; I used a rollerball pen to paint dye paste and discharge paste onto fabric to create the stick design. Collaged, machine quilted.

Size: 57 x 97 cm (21.5 x 38in)

Chalk, Flint and Jags 4

Inspiration: based on flint walls

Techniques: screen-printed fabrics, and photos of flint walls transferred onto fabric; I used a rollerball pen to paint dye paste and discharge paste onto fabric to create the stick design. Collaged, machine quilted.

Size: 30 x 97 cm (11.5 x 38in)

Graveyard

Polystyrene block-printed

Getting started

INSPIRATION

Why not try your own spider diagram/ mind-map (see pages 8-10) using one of these ideas as inspiration?

- your locality: is there something special about the local buildings and architecture, or landscape?
- the sea: consider the cliffs, flora, fauna, shells, seaweed, beach-huts, fairgrounds, harbours, boats, boatyards ...
- insects: some insects such as butterflies, moths etc have wonderful patterns and designs on their wings.
- architecture: think about specifics – doorways, arches, modern buildings, old ruins.
- holiday visits: maybe you've been to the arctic or somewhere such as Iceland, with the wonderful colours and textures of the volcanic landscape and the different colours of ice, snow, rocks and animals. Or perhaps you've had a holiday in an exotic location such as India or China, with all their rich colours, smells and spices. And other holiday destinations around the UK and on the continent all have their own distinctive textures, colour-schemes and local features.
- a city location such as London, Glasgow, Paris, Rome etc. Consider the architecture, parks, underground signs, porticoes, bridges, churches.
- a countryside location, for instance a ruined abbey, a stately home, rivers, trees, flora and fauna.
- museums can be wonderful sources of inspiration; there may be a particular exhibition which interest you such as a costume display, jewellery, ceramics or ancient history.

Once you have decided on your topic, gather your thoughts together and make yourself a list or spider diagram/mind-map; this helps you to focus on ideas.

Above: Fisherman's hut, Felixstowe ferry
Below: South Coast beach

Scarborough Fair

I took my inspiration for these pieces from photos of a seaside funfair at Scarborough. I printed the images onto paper and cloth, then collaged and machine-stitched them.

You may be drawn to particular colours, shapes, textures, and these in turn may lend themselves to techniques you like to use such as painting and dyeing fabrics, appliqué or piecing.

Write down whatever comes to mind – you may like to think about it over a cup of tea, or over several days before you put your thoughts down on paper!

Church Tower
Polystyrene block-printed

DESIGN

For me colour, shape and line are the key elements in my work, and we'll look at each of these individually.

Line and shape are mostly interchangeable; you can't have one without the other, and colour is important for the impact it can make.

In the following pages I've made some suggestions for getting started on the actual design process.

Colour Studies

This is something that I teach my City and Guilds students during the design module. Studies like this help to focus your mind on the colours in the pictures you have, and also help you decide and work out the coloured fabrics and threads you might want to use – and anything that you might want to dye or colour before you start making anything.

- Take photos of your desired subject.
- Analyse the colours that make up these images and paint small squares of the colours you can see in acrylic paint, watercolours or crayons. If you don't have paint around, tear swatches out of magazines and stick them onto paper.

Even in something that appears monochrome, such as a flint wall, you will find that there are varying shades/tints and tones of grey/black and white

Here are definitions of three terms which are often used to describe different colours.

Tint = colour plus white

Tone = colour plus grey

Shade = colour plus black

Try working in varied colours, other than the ones you see in your photos – this will add a different dimension to your work!

In the example below most of the fabrics I used were black, white, green and some discharged fabrics. Over-printing in pink (to create the colour of foxgloves and other wild flowers) added real interest to the printed fabric, and gave it a zing!

Line

As I said previously I'm not very good at drawing, but if I have a pair of scissors in my hand then I can usually cut a shape of a tree or flower, and this comes in handy when I need to cut a template for screen printing for example.

If you're not very good at drawing you can blow up your photos by using a photocopier – or you may have an A3 printer. Then trace off the shapes using tracing paper or an acetate sheet. Acetate sheets work well for design work, as you can cut out your design and use it as a template to draw round or to make a stencil.

You can create further designs by overlapping certain elements using the acetate sheet and/or tracing paper (see the images of overlaid trees, below); you can leave some lines out and add other lines if needed, to help balance a design.

Designs can also be transferred to a thermofax screen (see page 54) and then transferred to fabric, or made into prints (see below).

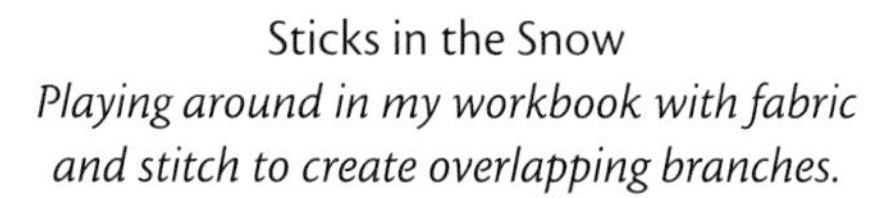

Sticks in the Snow
Playing around in my workbook with fabric and stitch to create overlapping branches.

Shape

A good starting point for beginning to explore shape is by working with coloured papers (and black paper in particular) on a white paper background; you can produce abstract designs in this way (right).

As you play with these ideas consider how you could use them: for instance, these design ideas could lend themselves to making templates and stencils to use in screen printing. You could make simple printing blocks from potatoes, polystyrene and pizza bases! It can be quite helpful to experiment with printing designs on paper, as I describe in the next section, before printing onto fabric.

Simple printing

- Potato prints are very easy. Cut a potato in half, cut out the design and leave the potato to dry, cut side down, on kitchen paper for 10 mins. Using a brush dipped in acrylic paint, paint onto the cut surface of the potato and print onto fabric or paper.
- Pizza bases make simple line-printing blocks; all you do is to cut the pizza base into sections and draw into the sections using a ballpoint pen. Then paint the surface with acrylic paint as above, and print; the line you have drawn will appear as a white line on the coloured background.

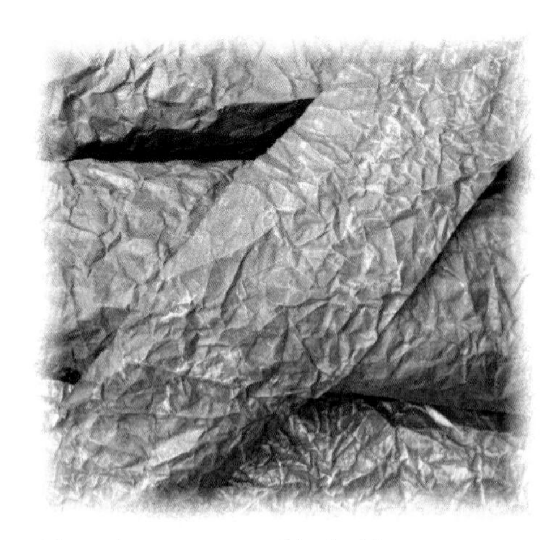

Above: brown paper rubbed with wax crayons, sprayed with coloured inks and brushed with gold paint

Below: stitched collage using decorated papers, scrim, polyester fabric cut with a soldering iron and sari ribbon

- Another idea is to take a piece of board and cut it into manageable shapes; glue string onto the surface with PVA, arranging the string in interesting shapes, and allow the glue to dry. If you want to make the blocks waterproof, paint the surface with Marvin Medium™ and allow it to dry – you can then wash the blocks without them disintegrating! Print as before.

Decorated papers

These are ideal for using in design work; collage is very effective for textile designs, and I use collage a lot. You could also use these decorated papers for book covers, book marks, wrapping paper – the list is endless.

- Make a monoprint by applying paint to the surface of a plastic sheet, then drawing into it with sticks, combs etc; lay paper on top and rub with your hand to ensure a good contact. Add water and more paint to the surface and repeat.
- Draw marks onto paper with wax crayons, then paint a wash of inks/ dyes/paints over the top.
- Grate wax crayons onto paper, cover with baking parchment and iron. Cover with a wash as above. This technique works well with the scrapings of oil paint sticks too!
- Place paper onto a textured surface such as a wall, fence or path, rub with crayons or oil paint sticks, then apply a wash.
- Paint Quink ink onto paper. Let it dry and paint marks with bleach – nb, some brushes disintegrate in bleach, so use old ones.
- Lay paper over printing blocks and rub with wax crayons, then cover with a wash. Repeat using different colours.
- Spatter coloured paints onto paper, then cover with a wash.
- Spray paint onto papers using a spray bottle; cover with a wash.
- Wet a sheet of paper, lay crumpled, strongly-coloured tissue paper on top, press these onto the paper and leave to dry. This will produce a soft-coloured effect on the background paper.
- Apply paint/inks/dye to newspapers and allow to dry.
- Scrumple up brown paper, flatten it out again, and then apply paint and/or rub with crayons or Markal™ oil-paint sticks to bring out the texture.
- Iron black FuseFX™ to papers to create a web-like effect.

All the above papers, once they're dry, can then have different things applied to them; try drawing, printing or stamping images on top of the surface you have created. Make marks with paints, brushes or thick

Pages from my workbook, showing line exercises using decorated papers

pens. Write words, messages, quotations which might apply to your chosen theme.

GOOD TIP

Ruth Issett paints some of her papers with a clear varnish, which highlights the colour and texture.

Ideas for using papers in design work

- Cut papers into strips and weave them.
- Try cutting the papers into curves and then weaving.
- Use paper strips to form grids over other papers.
- Overlay papers with acetate designs.
- Use decorated papers for creating collages.
- Work with positive and negative images.
- Cut out motifs or shapes and apply them to another paper

I keep interesting printed papers too, such as paper carrier bags, wrapping papers and newspapers (especially foreign ones), and use them for collage work.

Making a design/sample book

Now you have experimented with line, shape and colour, how about making yourself a design-cum-sample book? Get a spiral-bound notebook in whatever size you'd like to work with, and colour the pages. For my book I used walnut ink crystals dissolved in water to paint the pages. You could do this technique with watercolour paints, watered-down acrylics etc. Don't wait until each page is dry – I go through the whole book, and where the pages are touching each other you get interesting textural effects. Every so often, turn a few extra pages over to enable the preceding pages to dry.

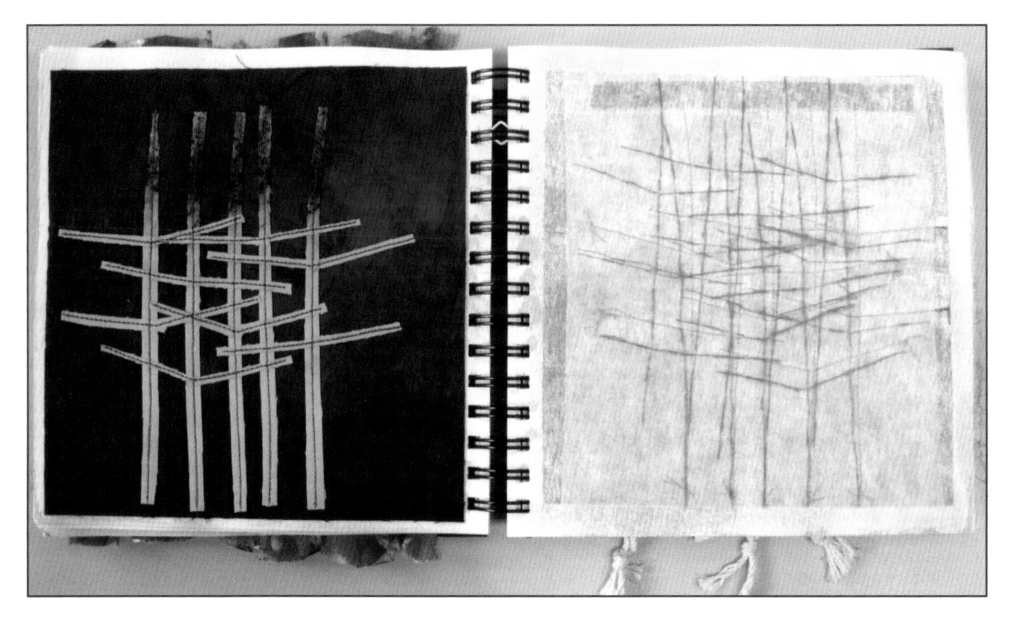

With my theme of trees, I looked at the linear aspect and played around initially with line. I then thought about texture, using stitches on my sewing machine, FuseFX, newspaper, brown paper, carrier bags, plain and coloured papers, felting and embellishing, stamping and stitching.

You could order your sketchbook in the following way:

- at the front you could put some photos of your source ideas and a mind-map or list of words.
- then start playing around with your design ideas and try some of the following ideas.

Pages from my workbook, showing the use of different media from simple line tracings to using newspaper and FuseFX

Collages
These can be made using fabric, decorated paper, cord, string, plastic etc. Some carrier bags have nice fabric handles and decorated sections which are great for cutting up.

Stitched samples
There may be pre-programmed embroidery stitches on your sewing machine that you haven't used before – I found some stitches which looked like bark on the side of a tree and experimented with them. Stitches can be elongated by changing the stitch length, producing interesting results; also, the stitched fabrics can be cut up and rearranged.

Try stitching on paper and/or plastic, as well as on unusual fabrics such as metal or velvet (below).

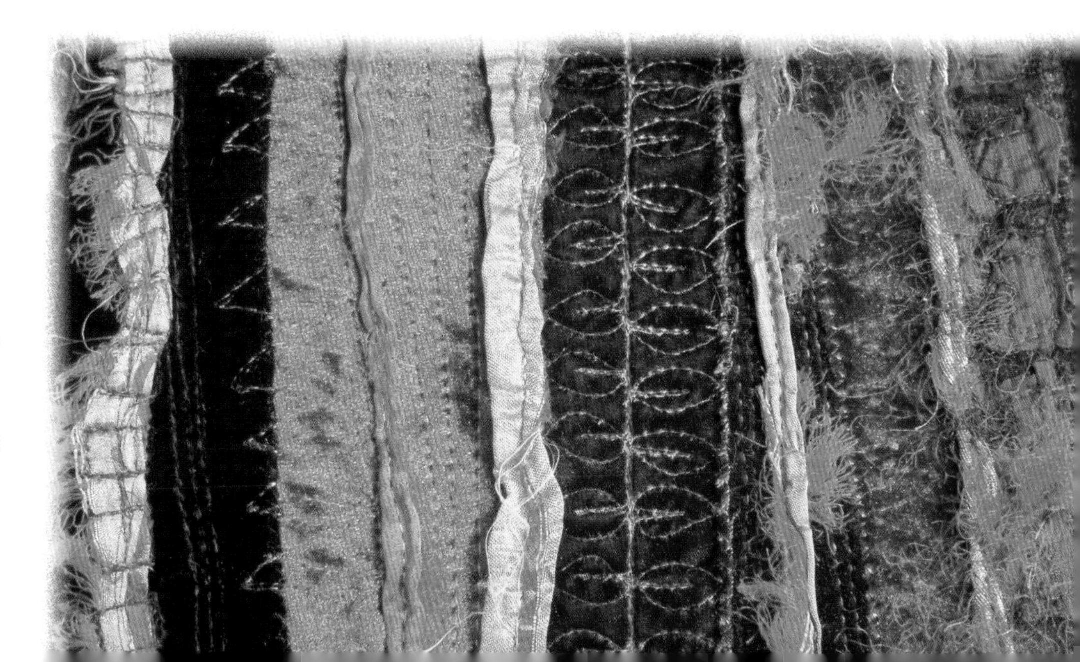

Try turning your stitched sample over, too; often I find that the stitch lines on the back of a sample give me a new design – or perhaps several new ideas.

Couching

Couching involves catching down cords, threads etc with hand or machine stitches. A machine zigzag works well, as do various hand stitches.

Weaving

Woven strips of fabric, knitting yarns and machine-made cords create exciting new fabrics. You could pin strips going in one direction on a base of iron-on Vilene™; weave more strips in the opposite direction, and once they are all in place iron them down onto the Vilene.

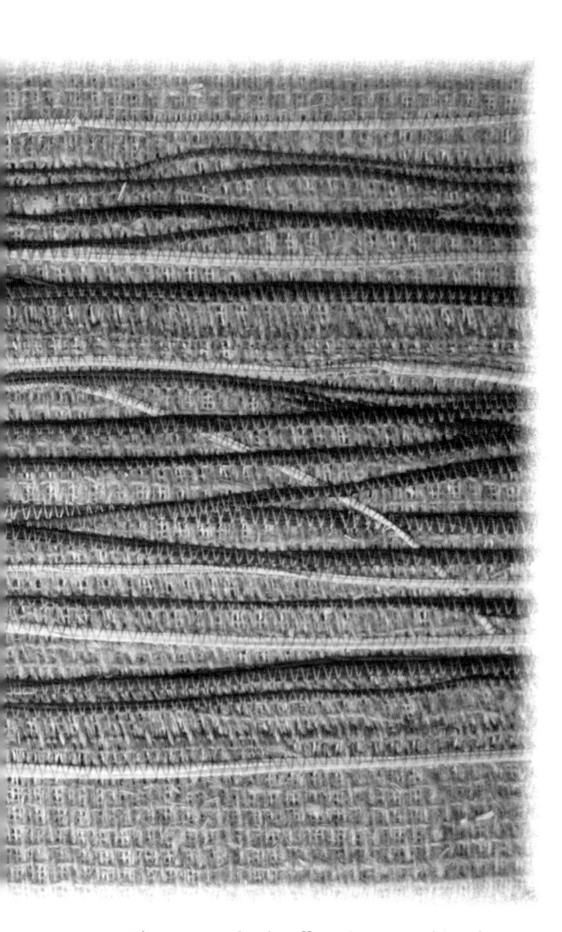

Above: couched raffia, zig-zagged in place; right: different coloured raffia; far right: woven yarn sample

Techniques

FUSEFX™

I am a great fan of FuseFX, a very fine bonding web; it can be used in so many ways:

- sandwich black FuseFX between layers of sheer fabric or plastic to create a new fabric, which can then be cut up and appliquéd; try cutting shapes out with a soldering iron as well as using scissors.
- layers made as above can be stitched into (you may want to use a frame or a hoop to prevent puckering – or you may want the puckering!), then again you can cut up this composite fabric and apply the shapes to a background.
- iron large or small pieces of black FuseFX over areas where you need shadows.
- iron FuseFX onto a background; dry-brush it with paint to create texture.
- experiment with other media such as papers, plastics, cloth etc, placed on top of the bonding layer and ironed in place. This can then be stitched into, and other layers applied on top.

I use the layering principle: if you don't like it, add another layer of various media or paint until you achieve the desired effect.

Misty Fuse™ is another bonding agent and is a cross between Bondaweb™ and FuseFX; it's rather like a solid layer of FuseFX.

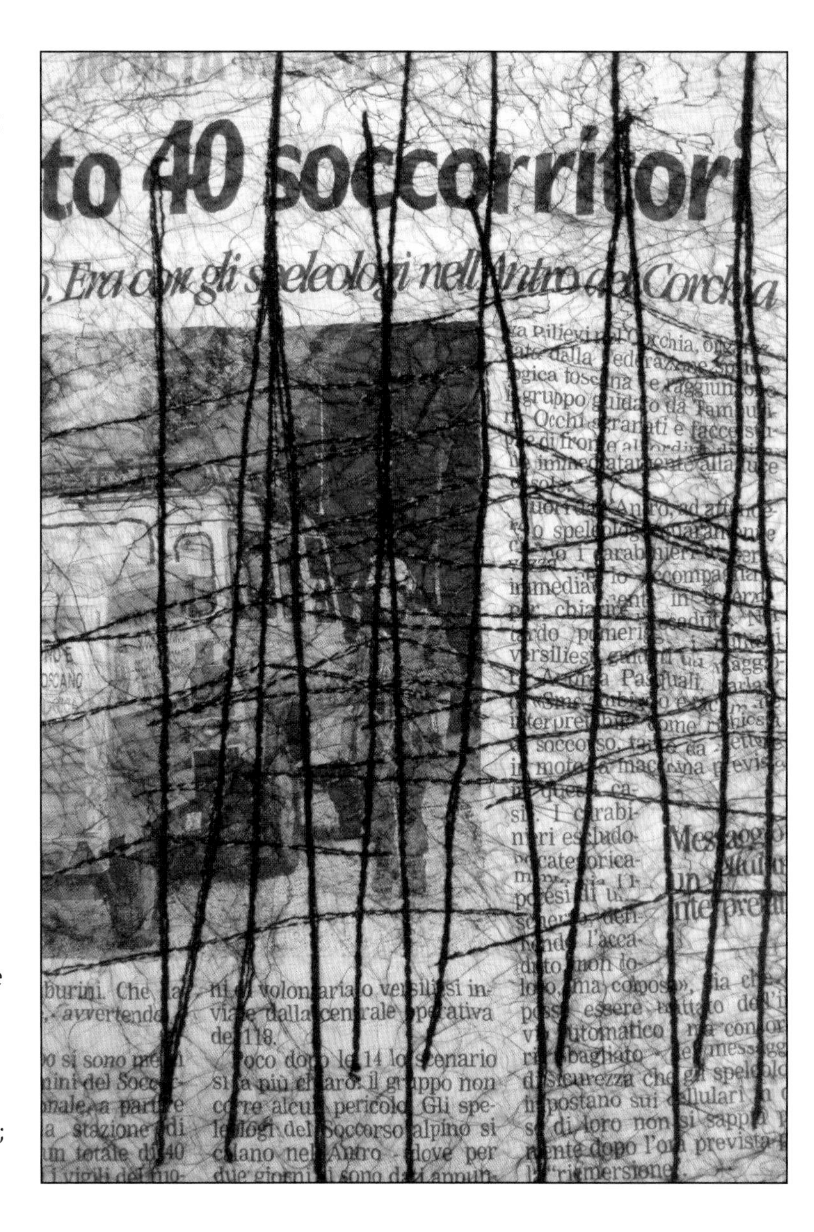

Design using newspaper, stitch and thread

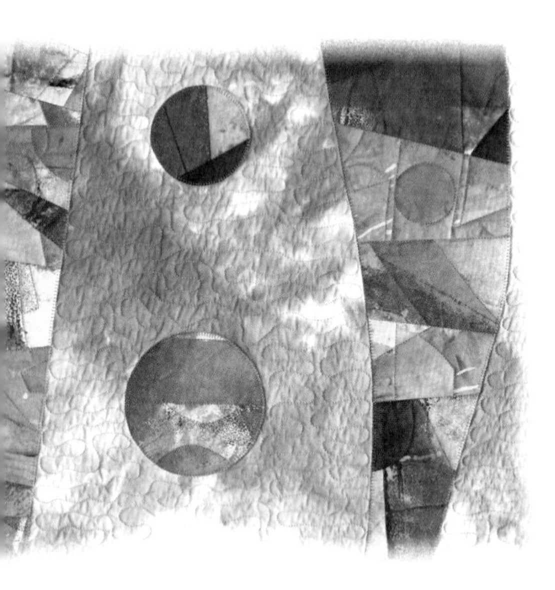

Above: detail of Bristol Tiles

Opposite: screen printing using freezer paper as a stencil

SCREEN PRINTING

I was introduced to screen printing in 1998 by Judith Trager in the USA. She used freezer paper as a mask, with very good results. I have since learnt other methods and developed my own way of doing things!

Silk screens can be bought from various suppliers; you can make your own, but the results may not be as good – it can be difficult to get the mesh of the screen taut enough to screen through. You can treat the wood of the screen with varnish to protect the wood, or use duct tape to cover the edges of the screen and provide a 'well' that the paint can sit in.

When it comes to the 'paint' for creating your prints, you have various options. Textile screen inks are readily available, and come in various colours which can be mixed – follow the manufacturer's instructions. Acrylic paints work well, but the paints may dry on the screen unless you clean it promptly. Acrylic paint also needs to be ironed once it's dry, to fix the colour to the fabric. Dye paste works very well, but may lose its effectiveness if you store it for a while.

Requirements for screen printing

- silk screen
- squeegee – I use small grouting tools from DIY stores
- freezer paper
- pencil
- masking tape
- textile screen inks or alternative (see above)
- fabric

Preparing to print

Cover your work surface with an old blanket and then a plastic covering. Tape your ironed fabric in place.

I have a big board covered with an old blanket; when I want to screen print I cover it with a drop cloth and pin my fabric to it. It doubles as a design board when it's propped up against a wall.

Basic method of screen printing

1. Cut a piece of freezer paper to the size of the whole screen, with an overlap at the top and bottom.
2. Draw your design on the freezer paper, remembering that the design will only work in the actual mesh part of the wooden screen. The shiny side of the freezer paper will be against the screen, so remember to cut the design according to how it will appear – ie, you may have to reverse the image.
3. Place the screen on the freezer paper, and smooth the overlap over the top and bottom of the screen; fix the paper in place with the masking tape.

Above: Pay the Ferryman *(with detail opposite)*

4 Put your colouring medium at one end of the screen and, using the squeegee, 'pull' the paint across the screen. You will need to do this several times to get a good image.

TIPS

- If you want single images spread across the fabric, cover the image you have just printed with a piece of newspaper or kitchen towel; this will avoid any 'ghosting' or marks from the screen.
- You can re-use the freezer paper stencils many times; just leave them to dry and store them with your screens.
- Rest the screen on top of a bucket when it is still in use between pulls.

Mono-printing with the freezer paper stencil

It occurred to me one day that the inks/paints I was using adhere to the shiny side of the freezer paper stencil which is against the screen, and consequently are covered in paint. Try printing through the screen and then peel the freezer paper from the screen; place it face down on the fabric – this produces a mono-print, making a negative print of the design.

Try working randomly over a large piece of fabric; it creates wonderful designs.

Other ways to create masks for screen printing designs

- Torn papers: place some torn paper shapes onto the fabric in a pleasing arrangement. Put some paint into a screen, then place the screen on top of the papers. As you spread the paint through the screen, the paper shapes will stick to the underside of the screen; they will then stay in place, and you can use the screen repeatedly.
- Torn masking tape: place torn strips of masking tape onto the underside of the screen, and make sure that they are stuck as firmly as possible.
- Iron-on Vilene can be placed on a screen and fixed in place with masking tape. This method works well with dye paste; the paste comes through the Vilene slightly, producing interesting effects. I don't recommended this method if you're printing with inks or acrylic paint, though.
- You can apply flour and water paste to a screen, leave it to dry, then scrape designs into it – or you can scrape into the paste when it's wet and then leave it to dry. NB be wary of using sharp implements when you're scraping into the paste: they can make holes in the screen.
- You can also apply a semi-permanent mask using a blocking/filling agent (see page 51).

Working with dye paste

When you print with ordinary textile inks or paints they are solid colours, and when you print over the top of a first layer of colour, you obscure the layer beneath. In contrast, using dye paste creates a translucent effect; underneath layers of colour are partially visible through the dye paste design. When using dye paste (which is made up of water, procion dye and a thickener known as Manutex™), the fabric will take on some of the colour of the first print, and the colour of a second print will merge with the first. For example if you print an area in yellow dye paste and then overprint with blue dye paste, you can get shades of green.

In case you don't know what Manutex is: ***Manutex*** is the trade name of the thickener, and ***sodium alginate*** is the chemical name.

Manutex RS is a 'jack of all trades' thickener which can be used for any type of screen printing, but you may not get the fine definition that you can achieve with the two types mentioned below.

Manutex S700 (the one supplied by Kemtex, see page 72) is stable on an alkaline surface (soda ash) and with procion dyes. It gives clear line definition.

Manutex F has a high solid content and low viscosity. It's used for overprinting, and to achieve good line definition on fine fabrics.

Recipe

This is my recipe for making dye paste.

1 First of all, in a large jar/container, mix together the following ingredients and stir until dissolved:

- 1 litre warm water
- 20g urea
- 1tsp Calgon™ (in hard water areas)
- 20g soda ash

2 To turn this liquid into a paste, sprinkle on 50g of Manutex, stirring constantly with a whisk (keep a whisk to be used only for this purpose). Leave to stand for a few hours or overnight. Add more Manutex if the paste is too thin, and water down the solution if it's too stiff; it needs to be of a thickish consistency, not too runny.

3 To colour the paste, mix 1-2tsp dye powder with just a little warm water. Don't add too much water, otherwise you will dilute the colour, and don't stint on the amount of dye powder you use, otherwise the colour will be very weak. Add this mixture to 250-500ml of the prepared paste, according to the strength of colour you require.

NB ***with all chemicals take care, wear a dust mask, and use only utensils kept for dyeing. Once the dye powder is in solution you can dispense with the mask. Wear old clothes and shoes, and rubber gloves; cover all your working surfaces to protect them, and any nearby surfaces where the colours or chemicals might splash.***

4 Use the dye paste as mentioned in the screen printing section, printing your selected design onto the fabric. Once you have decorated your fabric you need to cover it with plastic (dustbin liners work well for this) and leave it to cure for 48 hours; I cover it with plastic while it is still wet, and then roll it up.

5 Once the design is dry and cured, wash the fabrics in warm soapy water and rinse in the usual way. If you wish you can add Synthrapol™ or Metapex™ to the final rinse, which helps to set the colour in the fabric.

Left: detail of Bristol Tiles

Screen printing with drawing fluid and screen filler

My daughter, Louise Batten, likes to use this technique for some types of printing. You can use this technique to create your own custom printing screen, which is semi-permanent and can be used multiple times. The technique is sometimes known as 'negative method' or 'direct block-out.'

The drawing fluid is applied first, temporarily masking out the area to be printed (right, above). The screen block is then applied, and the drawing fluid removed (right, below). You can achieve quite a lot of detail with this method by tracing a design onto the screen.

Drawing fluid and screen block are manufactured by several different companies, so ensure that you always follow the instructions on the product packaging; the instructions given below are for general guidance. Do a test run in the corner of an old screen before committing yourself!

You need:

- blank silk screen
- bottle of drawing fluid
- tub of screen filler (sometimes known as screen block)
- squeegee the appropriate size for your screen
- paint brushes
- soft pencil

Applying the drawing fluid

1 Tape the edges of your screen with masking tape as you would for printing.

2 Place your screen on a covered table face down (flat side down). Draw your chosen design onto the screen with a soft pencil.

3 Prop the screen up so that it is not touching the table surface. Using a paint brush, apply the drawing fluid over the drawn design.

4 Allow the drawing fluid to dry completely (this process can be speeded up with the careful use of a hair dryer).

Applying the screen filler

5 Mix the screen filler thoroughly. With the screen face down (flat side down) on the table, pour a good amount of screen filler into the well as you would when printing.

6 In a single pull, drag the squeegee across the screen, covering the whole surface of the screen with a thin layer of the screen filler.

7 Carefully scoop any remaining filler back into the container, then leave the screen to dry thoroughly. Do not use a hairdryer at this stage, as the heat may damage the screen filler. Drying times vary between brands, and may take up to 24 hours.

Fabric printed using the drawing fluid and screen filler technique

8 If you hold the screen up to the light you'll be able to see if the filler has missed any areas. If so, you can carefully fill these gaps in using a paint brush dipped in screen filler.

Removing the drawing fluid

9 This process varies from brand to brand, but most are removed by gently rinsing or sponging with cold water.

10 Allow the screen to dry thoroughly again before using it for printing.

Removing the filler

To remove the filler so you can use the screen again you will need to follow the manufacturer's instructions; some you soak in hot soapy water and wash out gently, and some brands may need to be removed with bleach and hot water.

Discharge techniques

'Discharging' is the process of removing the colour from cloth by using a bleach-type product. There are lots of discharge products on the market which do the job, but the one I like to use is discharge paste.

I mostly use my own dyed fabrics to discharge, and I generally screen the paste through a silk screen onto the fabric. The product is left to dry, and then you iron over the paste: hey presto, the colour disappears! Sometimes bought fabrics don't discharge at all, so it's worth testing the technique on a corner first.

You can't guarantee the colour that you'll obtain once the paste has been applied, which is part of the appeal of the technique; the final colours may range from yellows, through to grey and pinks. Some black fabrics are made specifically for discharging, including speciality fabric available from Whaleys (see page 72).

I often use discharge paste on fabric first, and then over-print with two different colours; this adds a depth and texture to the overall design. These pieces of fabric (right) were dyed, discharged, and then over-printed.

Thermofaxes

Thermofax screens are a brilliant addition to the screen printer's portfolio; they enable artists to create designs through drawing or photography, then these designs are made into screens. As thermofax screens are light and portable, they are a delight to use and clean.

The actual thermofax is a machine which transfers the design onto a mesh, which is then made into a screen; the machines are very expensive, but there are several suppliers in the UK now. The screens are very portable and easy to use. They wash and clean well, and can last for an average of 200 pulls. The size of the screen can be varied according to your needs, and can range from as small as A5 to as large as A3.

To have a screen made you need to photocopy your design onto paper and send it to the supplier – an ink-jet design printed out from your computer will not work.

I often print my photographs onto paper, and play around with cut-outs until I am happy with the result; then I have it photocopied and send it to the supplier.

Use the thermoxfax screens with the colouring products of your choice – inks, paints or dye paste. You can use them with discharge paste, too, and create layers of interest.

Right: thermofax using discharge paste; left: Silver birch tree trunk used as a design for thermofax; middle: printed photo of tree bark cut ready for thermofax design; below: cut out print of birch trees

IMAGE TRANSFER

There are many techniques for transferring images to fabric from your camera; I have covered these in a previous book called ***Creative Fabric Techniques*** (see page 72).

The method I like to use is T-shirt transfer paper. This is readily available from all major stationers; it's made for domestic use with an inkjet printer, and is very easy to use. The paper has a plastic surface onto which the image is printed, and this is then ironed onto fabric.

There are two types of T-shirt transfer paper: one is for use with white fabric, and the other for dark fabrics. I used to use the one intended for white fabric, but you have to create a mirror image of your design first of all, using a computer or a suitable photocopier, before you print it onto the paper. The paper printed with your design is placed face down on the fabric and ironed in place, then the backing paper is removed. You need to use white fabric, as parts of the picture will be translucent and the white fabric needs to show through.

I now prefer to use the transfer paper manufactured for dark fabrics, as it's much easier to use. You don't have to create a mirror image of your design before you print it, and once it's printed you just peel off the backing paper; you can also use it on any colour of fabric.

How to transfer an image

1 First, select the photograph that you want to use. Remember that your photos can be manipulated in various ways on your computer: I use either Paintshop Pro, or Classic Photo Art Master which is a very easy programme to use.

2 Print your chosen picture onto the transfer paper, remembering to insert it into your printer so that the ink comes into contact with the correct side of the paper.

3 Peel the image off the backing paper and iron it onto the fabric – you will need to use baking parchment to cover the image when you are ironing it on, as otherwise you will melt the image. You will find it best to use plain white fabric at first, then once you see what the technique can achieve you can experiment with other fabrics and colours.

4 The fabric you've created can now be cut up and used in patchwork, or stitched into with machine embroidery.

During the making of work for the exhibition that inspired the book I have taken photos of already stitched pieces, and then included them in my work as part of the patchwork – many people haven't noticed this!

Opposite top: photographic image transferred to fabric
Opposite below: photograph altered on computer
Above: samples showing image transfer, dry-brushed with acrylic paint

QUILT COLLAGES

I have always liked working with collage, not just when I'm designing but working with fabrics too. I mostly work intuitively, and audition fabrics and ideas as I go along: this is where a design board is useful. The board I currently use doubles as my printing table! It's made from a large piece of MDF covered with an old wool blanket from a charity shop, stapled to the back; this in turn is covered in a white sheet, also stapled to the back.

A design board is very helpful when you're structuring your quilts, as you are looking at the design face on (rather than downwards onto a table or the floor), so the perspective is at the right level.

How to get started

1 Select your fabrics – these might not necessarily go together; you could use bold prints and small prints in the same piece, or very busy fabrics together. Contrasting fabrics look good.

2 Set up a design board, then start cutting your selected fabrics into sections, squares and oblongs, and place them on the design board.

3 Overlap the fabric patches if necessary until you are happy with the placement and the design.

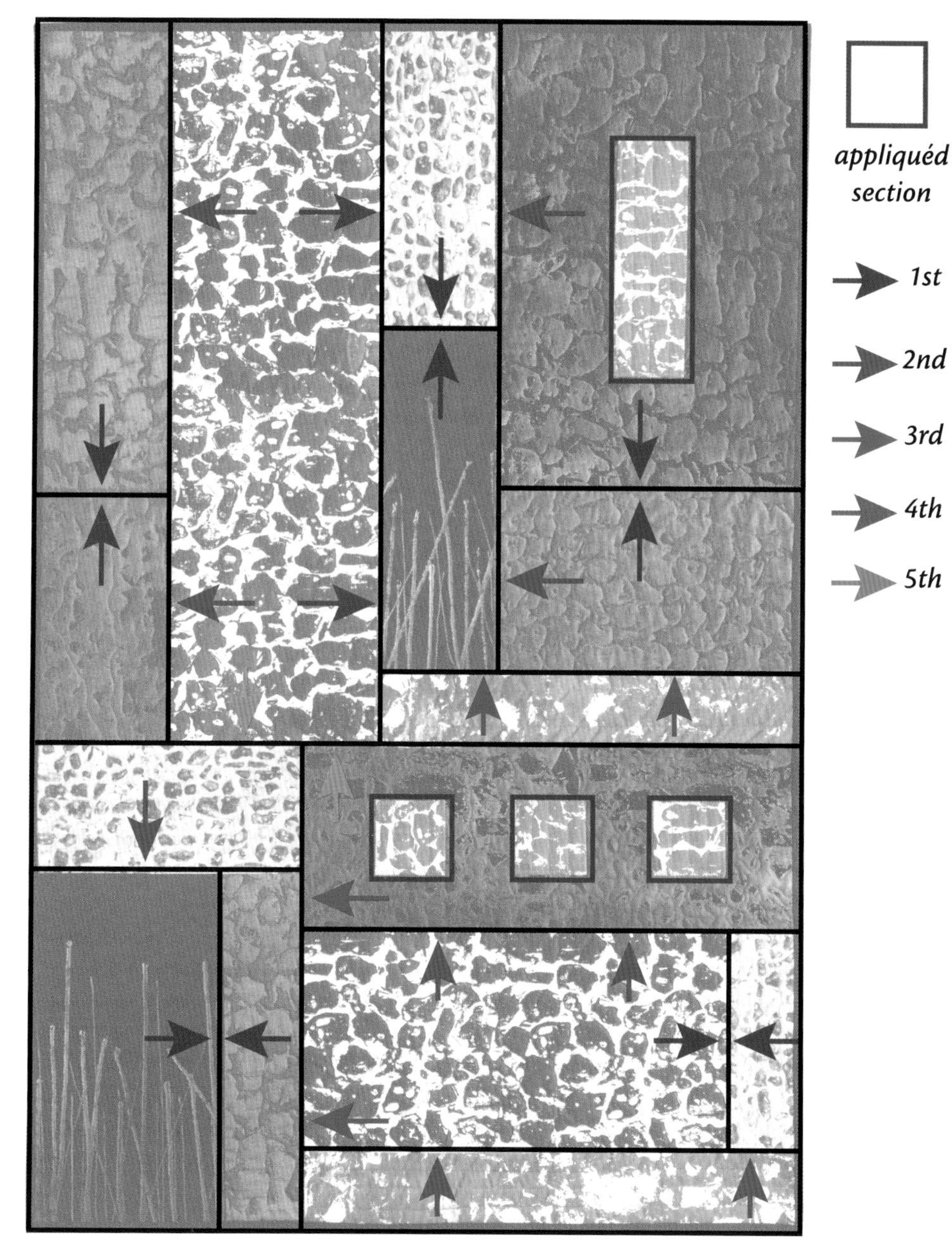

4 Now it's time to stitch the pieces together. This is where you will often have to make adjustments in the design to fit the pieces together comfortably – a bit like doing a jigsaw! The diagram on the right shows the order in which I joined the patches to build up the design on *Chalk, Flint and Jags 2* (above). I use quarter-inch seams and press the sections as I go.

5 Complete the quilt by layering the quilt top with wadding and a backing and stitching through all the layers.

SEEDHEAD THEME

This group of quilts was made for an exhibition of work by Anglia Textile Works, an art quilt group, at The Knitting and Stitching shows in the autumn of 2012. They were based on drawings and sketches made of poppy and cow parsley seedheads.

After I made the initial drawings of the seedheads, I used a technique by Jane Dunnewold called India ink resist. It's a very simple process and this is my method:

1. Draw your design onto watercolour paper.
2. Using white acrylic paint, paint the background of the subject to cover the negative space, and allow the paint to dry.
3. Once the paint is dry, paint the whole surface with India ink, and leave for 2-3 minutes.
4. Wash the excess ink away by holding the paper under gently running water, and allow to dry again.

What I like about this process is that you end up with very strong images (left), but also you have texture on the background which adds further interest. I then transfer these images into thermofax screens.

The quilts on pages 61-63 were made using this method:

Strippy Seedheads *(right)*

Strippy quilts, which originated in the north-west, have always been a special love of mine, particularly as I have ancestors and a maiden name (Peaurt) coming from Allendale.

This fabric was dyed with pink and green dye, then discharged using a thermofax screen. Once I had pieced it in strips I felt it needed a bit 'more,' so I made a template of the cow parsley shape and drew it onto the fabric. The quilt was quilted, and then the shapes were painted in with emulsion paint!

Seedhead Triptych *(left)*
Here I was playing around with the poppy thermofax screen on white, black and brown fabrics. I felt the fabrics lent themselves to quite dramatic placements, and so decided to make a triptych. Each piece measures 50 x 30cm.

Silver Seedheads *(right)*
This quilt was made using a method that involves transferring paper onto a sheer fabric, using a silk screen and matt medium. My daughter used to work for a well-known confectioner during college and university; a roll of silver paper was being thrown out which she rescued – it worked perfectly for this method! In most transfer techniques, the paper sits on the underside of the sheer fabric, which may then be laid on another fabric. With this piece the silver paper looked wonderful on the top of the fabric. It was laid on a pre-screen-printed fabric and quilted; once quilted, it was screen printed with a poppy seedhead motif.

EMBROIDERY

This section is all about the inspiration for embroidery that I have taken from my theme of flint and trees. There is such a cross-over between patchwork and quilting and embroidery these days; in the past they were like two separate entities, but happily that's no longer true.

I like playing around with all sorts of techniques, and I hope that one or two ideas here will spark off your imagination too! There are also lots of ideas in the sketchbook section (see pages 42-44). I often gather together items which may fit into my theme (left). I rarely buy threads or fabric specifically for a project, but I was tempted by some gorgeous threads here and started hand couching different colours of raffia.

These 'ingredients' may inspire you to try some different techniques. Photograph **a** shows dyed threads, wadding and silk fibres; **b** features African bark cloth, silk ribbon and African fibres. Think about how you could use particular materials in: appliqué (including raw-edge); working in strips; couching by hand or machine; hand stitching; free machine embroidery. Try working on different base fabrics; my samples show furnishing fabric (**c**); knitted fabric strips applied to hessian (**d**), a base fabric covered with fabric threads (**e**), and one with a woven design (**f**).

a
b
c
d
e
f

These samples were made by gathering together bits and pieces, including turquoise metal shim (a very thin, lightweight metallic sheet), and laying them on a base; I then applied and stitched the pieces in place.

Here I was playing around with pieces of velvet and sari ribbon – this was then photographed and I used the image in the ***Sticks and Stones Triptych*** on page 28.

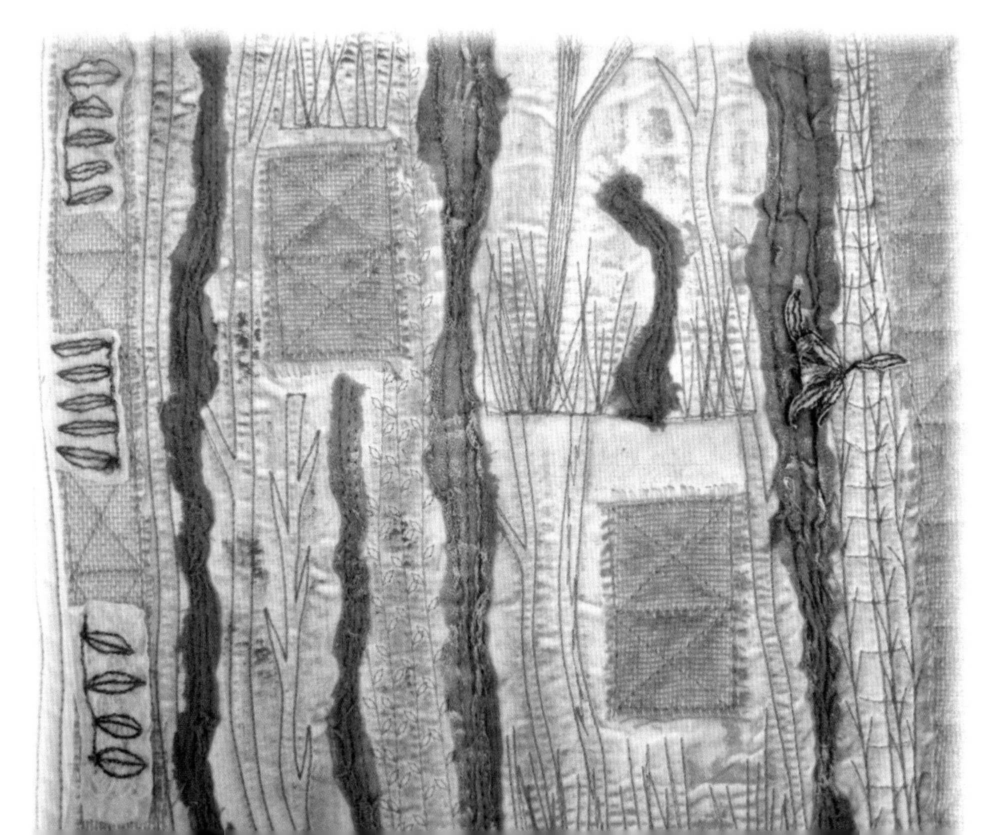

In this piece I was playing around with hessian on a cotton background, experimenting with stitch designs for a commission piece.

These stitched pictures were made by drawing the design onto fabric first (calico or cotton fabric works best) and then putting it into a hoop. I densely stitched all over the background fabric until I had filled in all sections, released the fabric from the hoop, turned the edges in and mounted the pictures.

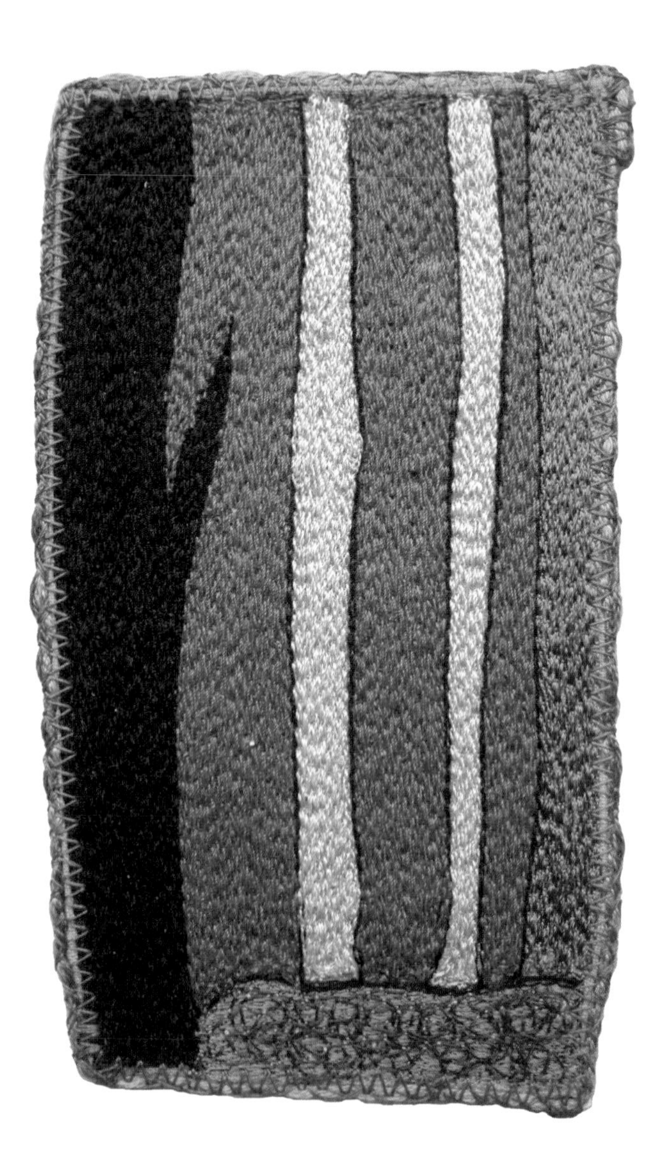

Someone gave me some upholstery fabric (see page 65, top), which I laid on a piece of Vilene to stabilise it. I then stitched by machine over the design woven into the fabric, before couching down threads and sari ribbon to look like ferns (below).

This little stitched sample (right) grew out of the line design in my sketch book, using a potato print and machine stitching on an open-weave white fabric. And, to close this section, a little bit of fun – they could be trees or fungi!!

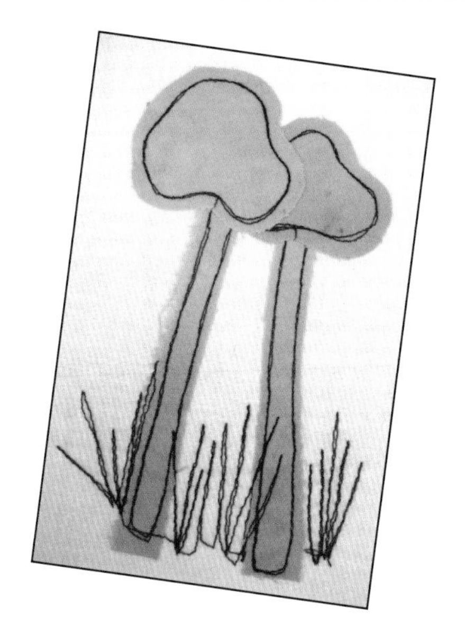

About us

Annette Morgan is an award-winning textile artist, author, teacher and Qualified Quilt Judge. Her work has been selected for exhibitions world-wide, and has featured in many books and magazines. She is an ex-President of the Quilters' Guild of the British Isles, and founder of *Contemporary Quilt*, a specialist interest group of the QGBI. She is co-founder of *Anglia Textile Works*, an art quilt group based in East Anglia, a member of *Tin Hut Textiles*, and also an Honorary Member of the QGBI.

Annette has stitched from a young age, and it was her father who taught her to knit and sew. Having grown up in a forces family she attended 13 different schools; she went on to train as a nurse in the Royal Air Force, and trained as a Theatre Sister at Charing Cross Hospital in London. During her late thirties and forties she became seriously interested in textiles and completed her City and Guilds qualifications in Norwich. Since then her feet have hardly touched the ground with exhibitions and teaching worldwide, as well as teaching City & Guilds courses in Cambridge and Ipswich. When she is at home she enjoys spending time with her family, and cooking!

Dan Morgan grew up on a small farm in the Severn Vale of Gloucestershire and has loved exploring the countryside since his childhood. From 1967-1971 he studied Fine Art at the Gloucestershire College of Art in Cheltenham. Art teaching in secondary schools followed, in Cambridgeshire and later in Norfolk, interspersed with times of being involved in church leadership.

In recent years he has aimed to explore his interest in the patterns of the landscape around him, particularly the Brecklands and the forest that are close to his home in Norfolk. He is fascinated by the traces of ancient landscape that have not quite succumbed to the order of mechanised farming and forestry; in his work he draws on elements both from these, and from the remembered landscape of his childhood.

Annette and Dan have two children: Joel, who is an emerging scriptwriter, and Louise – married to Jono from New Zealand – who works for the NHS and also enjoys sewing and cooking!

Contact details:

12 Melford Bridge Road, Thetford, Norfolk IP24 2HH

annette@annettemorgan.co.uk

www.annettemorgan.co.uk

Suppliers and sources

George Weil
Fabrics, dyestuffs
George Weil & Sons Ltd, Old Portsmouth Road, Peasmarsh, Guildford, Surrey GU3 1LZ
01483 565800
www.georgeweil.com

Art Van Go
Synthrapol, Metapex, FuseFX, sketchbooks
1 Stevenage Road, Knebworth, Hertfordshire SG6 3AN
01438 814964
www.artvango.co.uk

Kemtex
Very good advice on all types of dyes and dyeing supplies
Chorley Business and Technology Centre, Euxton Lane, Chorley, Lancs PR7 6TE
01257 230220
www.kemtex.co.uk

Thermofax Screens
custom-made screens, inks and advice
Foxley Farm, Foxley, Towcester, Northamptonshire NN12 8HP
www.thermofaxscreens.co.uk

Glitzy Quilts and ***Creative Fabric Techniques*** can be bought from www.vivebooks.com (formerly www.rainbowdisks.com)